THE MARGINAL
REVOLUTIONARIES

THE MARGINAL
REVOLUTIONARIES

How Austrian
Economists Fought
the War of Ideas

Janek Wasserman

Yale UNIVERSITY PRESS
New Haven & London

Published with assistance from the foundation established in memory
of Henry Weldon Barnes of the Class of 1882, Yale College.

Yale University Press books may be purchased in quantity for educational, business, or promotional use. For information, please e-mail
sales.press@yale.edu (U.S. office) or sales@yaleup.co.uk (U.K. office).

Set in Galliard type by IDS Infotech Ltd., Chandigarh, India.
Printed in the United States of America.

Library of Congress Control Number: 2019934601

ISBN 978-0-300-22822-9 (hardcover : alk. paper)

A catalogue record for this book is available from the British Library.

This paper meets the requirements of ANSI/NISO Z39.48-1992
(Permanence of Paper).

10 9 8 7 6 5 4 3 2 1

TO MEGAN

CONTENTS

ACKNOWLEDGMENTS

Like all intellectual work, this book is the product of collective effort. Many individuals, groups, and institutions made the project possible, and I owe many debts of gratitude. The Botstiber Institute for Austrian-American Studies provided a fellowship that permitted me to conduct the formative archival research for the project. A fellowship from Duke University's Center for the History of Political Economy allowed me the time and resources to complete the manuscript. The University of Alabama Research Grants Committee and the Rockefeller Archive Center provided grants that sustained this research in its earliest stages. Yale University Press offered support for research and writing. Seth Ditchik, my editor, believed in this project before I had written a single word. Andrew Katz offered invaluable assistance with his copyedits.

I wish to thank the many libraries and archives that allowed me to use their collections. Knowledgeable librarians and archivists at every stop facilitated this work. The staffs at the Austrian National Library, Austrian State Archives, Columbia University Rare Book and Manuscript Library, David Rubenstein Rare Book and Manuscript Library at Duke University, Grove City College Library, Harvard University Archives, Hoover Institution Archives, League of Nations Archives, London School of Economics Library, Wilfrid Laurier University Archives, M. E. Grenander Department of Special Collections & Archives at SUNY-Albany, New York Public Library Manuscript and Archives Division, Rockefeller Archive Center, University College London Library, and Wienbibliothek im Rathaus offered me assistance as I worked through a wide array of materials. I would like to acknowledge the Grove City College Library for permission to cite from the Ludwig von Mises Collection. I thank the estate of F. A. Hayek for granting permission to quote from his correspondence and other materials. I am especially appreciative of the help from the Duke University and University of Alabama librarians, who tracked down any and all resources that I requested.

Over the years, I have presented portions of this research in a number of forums; the feedback I received has made this a better work. Conferences for the Austrian Studies Association, German Studies Association, History of Economics Society, Organization of American Historians, and the Society for U.S. Intellectual History proved stimulating and constructive. Invited talks at the Austrian National Bank, CenterAustria at the University of New Orleans, and Southern Methodist University alerted me to the potentially broader appeal of this subject, especially in Austria (where, to my surprise, the soon-to-be president Alexander van der Bellen was in the audience). Individual chapters and the entire manuscript went through workshops that sharpened the final product into a more cohesive whole. Duke's Center for the History of Political Economy (three times!), Southern Methodist University's Department of History, the Triangle Intellectual History Seminar, and the University of Alabama History Department all showed great hospitality, and they offered feedback that I have tried to incorporate. I wish to thank anonymous reviewers at *Research in the History of Economic Thought and Methodology* and for the *Quiet Invaders* edited volume for their comments.

Of course, my greatest debts are to colleagues, friends, and loved ones. One's work is only as good as one's surrounding social circles and networks, and I am indeed fortunate to have so many exceptional people around me. Bruce Caldwell and Guenter Bischof have helped this project since its inception. Bruce invited me to Duke several times and read the entire manuscript, offering his unparalleled knowledge on Friedrich Hayek and the Austrians. Even though we disagree on some points, he has always treated my views with respect. Meanwhile, Guenter invited me to the CenterAustria, where he showed me true New Orleans hospitality. He also convened a wonderful workshop on Austrian emigration in Vienna, where I presented some of my initial findings. At the University of Alabama,

Teresa Cribelli, Daniel Levine, James McNaughton, Margaret Peacock, Erik Peterson, and Alexa Tullett helped create a *Geistkreis* of remarkable fertility. Erik and Margaret read the entire manuscript and shaped it for the better. James offered an unmatched reading of the introduction. In Vienna, Klaus Taschwer and Hansjörg Klausinger have offered their time and expertise. Klaus has shared his knowledge of interwar German nationalism and academic antisemitism with me. He also published a kind article on my work in *Der Standard*. Hansjörg's amazing knowledge of interwar Austrian economics has helped me avoid factual and interpretive errors. He has commented on conference papers, articles, and book chapters over the years, always exhibiting forbearance toward my work. My own "non-Austrian Austrians" are Alys George, Erin Hochman, and Heather Morrison. Three better companions in the Austrian capital I cannot imagine. Erin deserves a special thanks for organizing a series of events in Dallas. Along the way, I have met a number of scholars who have become intellectual companions and fellow travelers. Venus Bivar has been a great interlocutor since we met in Sleepy Hollow. Daniel Bessner shared his ideas on modern libertarianism on many occasions. Noah Strote, a frequent café denizen, helped keep the final drafting stages from bogging down. I am greatly obliged to Quinn Slobodian, who has shared his pathbreaking scholarship on globalism and the contemporary Right with me. He also included me in an informative GSA panel on populism that improved my own analysis immensely. Robert Leonard read the penultimate version of the manuscript, offering constructive criticism and suggestions based on his unsurpassed knowledge of interwar Viennese intellectual life and Austrian economic traditions. I hope the revisions meet with his approval. At various stages, Jennifer Burns, James Chappel, Malachi Hacohen, Kevin Hoover, Lloyd Kramer, Anthony LaVopa, Emily Levine, Steven Vincent, and Roy Weintraub offered their trained expertise, for which I am thankful. Finally, my doctoral advisers, Hillel Kieval and Gerald Izenberg, have continued to provide sage wisdom and career counsel.

I have also enjoyed positive support from numerous individuals associated with the contemporary Austrian School and its legacies. Peter Boettke, Erwin Dekker, Stefan Kolev, and Scott Scheall each read most or all of the manuscript, sharing their considerable knowledge with an outsider. Despite our differences of opinion on the Austrian tradition, they have been outstanding intellectual foils. I am particularly indebted to Pete, who was willing to invite a critic and skeptic of Austrianism to an Austrian Economics workshop in 2018.

Much of *Marginal Revolutionaries* was completed in that quintessentially Viennese cultural site, the coffeehouse. O. Henry's, Red Cat, and Seeds in Birmingham, Mad Hatter's and Joe Van Gogh in Durham, Café Bräunerhof and Café Möbel in Vienna were my homes away from home. I thank the staffs for their service and endless supplies of caffeine and pastries. To the people whom I met there, I thank you for your sociability and conviviality. Regular gatherings with friends at the Alcove, Good People, and Loosa Brews also engendered an esprit de corps, even if we never created our own drinking songs. Instead of Alpine hikes, I also benefited from a lively Birmingham running community that kept body and mind in harmony. Chelsey and Sammy Palmer, Doug and Meg Smith, and Connor and Taylor Wann contributed more to this project than they know.

Finally, my family has been there every step of the way, hearing more about Austrian economics than any person should have to. My in-laws, Bobbie and Will Williams, and brother-in-law Connor have welcomed me into their family with open arms. My sister, Rachel, and brother-in-law James are constant sources of pride and academic inspiration. My parents have displayed a limitless love and kindness, even in my most solipsistic periods. Megan, my partner, deserves the greatest credit of all. This project would have been impossible without her patience and magnanimity. Thank you for everything—this book is for you.

INTRODUCTION

Americans searching Amazon's best-seller list in June 2010 would have encountered a surprising title at the top, above the likes of books by Stieg Larsson, George W. Bush, Malcolm Gladwell, and Michael Lewis: Friedrich Hayek's *Road to Serfdom*. The "Definitive Edition" had appeared in 2007, yet it sold only six hundred copies a month for a year and a half. Then the combined effects of the Great Recession and the election of Barack Obama quadrupled its sales. The book sold seven thousand copies in 2008, twenty-seven thousand in 2009. Talk of stimulus packages and "socialized medicine" and the rise of the Tea Party movement spurred further sales. These factors alone did not account for the one hundred thousand copies sold in June 2010, however. The person who made Hayek a household name was the conservative media personality Glenn Beck, who devoted an hour-long Fox News episode to *Road*. Beck discussed how Hayek had fought against central-government planning and collectivization after World War II, trying to save the West from bondage and unfreedom. Beck maintained that "we are in a similar war today, but if you don't know history, you probably aren't even aware of it." Joined by two scholars affiliated with the libertarian think tank the Ludwig von Mises Institute, Thomas Woods and Yuri Maltsev, Beck implored his millions-strong audience to take the first step in the struggle and read the anticollectivist playbook: "Why don't we teach this everywhere? Find out for yourself. Go online now and order it."[1]

Beck demonstrated little knowledge of the actual contents of the book and revealed a faulty understanding of the historical context in which it appeared. While the scrolling text on Fox News referred to the "Austrian Economist" Hayek, Beck himself made no reference to Hayek's background or his economic ideas. He repeatedly compared *Road to Serfdom* to Ayn Rand's work, even though Hayek accepted progressive income taxes, public education, national health insurance, and minimum welfare provisions in *Road*. Beck also showed no awareness of who Ludwig von Mises was, stumbling badly over the Austrian's name, while failing to acknowledge that Mises was also an Austrian School economist with similar political and economic views to Hayek's.

Nonetheless, Beck's promotion of *Road* was a milestone in an unexpected renaissance of popular interest in the Austrian School. Earlier that same year, the economist Russ Roberts and the director John Papola created a "rap battle" video pitting Hayek and John Maynard Keynes against each other. The two economists-turned-pugilists went toe-to-toe over macroeconomic policy advice and business cycle theory—with Hayek portrayed as getting the better of the argument. The video went viral, recording more than a million YouTube hits in its first few months. (It has now been viewed over six million times.) In October 2011, Nicholas Wapshott published a best-seller, *Keynes Hayek: The Clash That Defined Modern Economics*, which assigned world historical significance to the ideas of Hayek, even a quarter century after his death.[2]

This interest crested with the 2012 presidential campaign. After the Iowa caucus, Ron Paul declared, "We are all Austrians now," while the eventual vice presidential nominee, Paul Ryan, admitted to distributing *Road to Serfdom* to staffers. A wave of new media coverage directed its gaze on Hayek and the little-known "Austrian School." "What is Austrian Economics? And why is Ron Paul obsessed with it?" asked then *Slate* columnist Matthew Yglesias, and he was far from alone. Articles on Austrianism appeared in *Bloomberg*, the *Guardian*, the *New York Times*, *Politico*, *Slate*, and the *Washington Post*. Reactions and rebuttals from the libertarian community ensued in such forums as *Reason* and *Cato Unbound*, the latter of which devoted an issue to "Theory and Practice in the Austrian School." Many supporters of contemporary Austrian thought fielded interview requests and wrote thought pieces, weighing in on the school's new relevance. The arrival of the Tea Party as a legitimate wing of the

Republican Party, embodied by the "Paul Revolution," signaled the need for a closer examination of the ideas of Hayek, Mises, and the "radical libertarianism" of the Austrian School.[3]

What these overheated conversations revealed more than anything else was a lack of clarity about what exactly the Austrian School was. The historical and social origins of the movement were particularly opaque in these discussions. How did it emerge and evolve over the years? Who were its members? What did they believe? And why do we still care about the school, and should we? In this book, I will illuminate these historical, cultural, and sociological questions, offering a critical history of the school from its nineteenth-century emergence to the present.

The Austrian School has been at the center of many of the most significant intellectual, economic, and political debates in Europe and the United States since its nineteenth-century inception. A quick look at the school's lasting impacts reveals the range of ideas and the breadth of activities of the collective. Its members participated in the marginal revolution in economics, which shifted our understanding of value from an emphasis on labor and production to the subjective utility preferences of individual consumers. The Austrians were at the forefront of the discipline's professionalization as economists became the most respected—and most controversial—social scientists. They served as Austrian government ministers, advisers to Habsburg royalty and heads of state, and policy experts, in addition to their roles as professors and journalists. They established themselves as the world's most formidable opponents of Marxism and socialism and leading exponents of liberal ideology.

In the interwar era, a new generation emerged to advance earlier intellectual and ideological efforts. First Mises, Joseph Schumpeter, and Hans Mayer, then Friedrich Hayek, Gottfried Haberler, and Oskar Morgenstern made their reputations by the end of the 1920s. They developed innovative understandings of business cycles and monetary theory, which gained a wide hearing in the post–World War I and Great Depression periods. They cultivated relationships with financial and political elites in chambers of commerce, national banks, and conservative political parties. They found transnational support at the League of Nations and the Rockefeller Foundation. The younger Austrians of the Hayek generation cemented the school's reputation in debates with socialists, Keynesians, and New Deal liberals. They advanced a new defense of liberalism, often called neoliberalism, which still informs contemporary political discussions.

After the emigration of many of the school's members from fascist-wracked Europe in the 1930s, the Austrians became best-selling authors, respected political theorists, and economic policy experts in their adoptive homelands. They shaped post–World War II life through such institutions as the Mont Pèlerin Society (MPS), the RAND Corporation, the General Agreement on Tariffs and Trade (GATT), and the Group of Thirty. They spearheaded the successful conservative counterattack against Keynesian economics in the 1970s and ushered in our current age's faith in globalization, free markets, rule of law, entrepreneurship, and neoliberalism. They helped inspire the "Washington Consensus" at the World Bank and International Monetary Fund, which has played a significant and troubling role in the Latin American debt crises in the 1980s, the East Asian crisis of the late 1990s, and the 2008 global economic crisis.

Hayek and especially Mises also motivated a generation of American libertarian and free-market activists who took Austrianism in a radical, political, and ideological direction. Since the 1970s, a small group of scholars has identified as Austrian economists, and they have kept alive some of the core methodological positions of the original school. The much-greater impact of Austrianism has been as an ideological basis for a growing number of conservative think tanks and foundations, like the American Enterprise Institute, Atlas Network, Cato Institute, Heritage Foundation, Hoover Institution, and Institute for Economic Affairs. The Austrians have served as the intellectual muses and totems of free-market business and political leaders like the Koch brothers, Ron and Rand Paul, Paul Ryan, and many others. Most troublingly, radical populist, neo-Confederate, and white supremacist groups associated with the US Alt-Right, the Alternative for Germany, and the Austrian Freedom Party have employed Austrian ideas to defend their extremist positions. Not only have these new directions shocked contemporary observers; they probably would have amazed and aggrieved the school's original members.

How a small collective of haut bourgeois central European scholars and their sophisticated ideas have survived and continued to exert such symbolic power in today's imagination—eighty years after emigration and a quarter century after the last Austrian-born scholars in the group passed away—is the subject of this book. *Marginal Revolutionaries* is the first critical intellectual history of the Austrian School from its emergence to the present. It is also a biography of a group of individuals who were much more closely bound together than simply sharing a set of doctrines would suggest. The group included a diverse membership, and its story involves the intellectual output of the school, its rich correspondence and interaction rituals, and the myriad organizations and institutions fostered by its contributors. Its history and influence extend from fin-de-siècle Vienna and its vibrant coffeehouse culture to contemporary rallies of the populist radical Right. A picture emerges of a collective that lived by Hayek's motto "Nobody can be a great economist who is only an economist." Typically interpreted as a statement of Hayek's commitment to interdisciplinary research and broad humanistic values, the quotation also tells us about the ways that the Austrians blended philosophical and ideological values, scientific work, and policy intervention, creating a radical mélange. As Marxism's mirror image, the Austrian School not only interpreted the world but also sought to change it.[4]

A living and evolving social grouping grounded in particular historical contexts, the school and its members must be considered well beyond their scholarly output, in conversation with an array of other intellectual and political currents across time and place. The Austrian School story is simultaneously a family biography; a history of economic thought; a sociology of knowledge; a transnational, political history; and a history of political ideologies. Like the Austrians themselves, their story must be ecumenical and interdisciplinary if we wish to understand them, especially in their unexpected historical roles in organization and institution building. This history must also operate on different scales at different points in the story. It is equally a tale of bourgeois European culture, fin-de-siècle Vienna, interwar Austria and central Europe, the World War II and Cold War eras, a neoliberal age, and our divided present. It is a story of the Austrian "world of yesterday," of Atlantic crossings, of modern capitalism, and of conservative revolution. Only by fanning out from interpersonal social interactions to the local, national, and, finally, global levels can we appreciate the school in its kaleidoscopic variety.[5]

The Austrian School of Economics: Not Austrian nor a School nor Economics?

If anything, it is the profusion of materials on the Austrian School that makes understanding the school such a challenge. To cover as broad a canvas as possible, we must sift through a vast array of sources and scholarships to understand the school. With a few notable exceptions, this scholarship has focused on individuals and ideas rather than the group and its social characteristics. While acknowledging the centrality of economic theory and the works of its leading exemplars, this account is first and foremost a family story of a *school*.[6]

This begs the question, What is a school? This seemingly benign query is tougher to answer than it appears, especially given the protean quality of the Austrian School across its long history. The tradition has endured for 125 years and survived transatlantic processes of emigration, assimilation, and translation. It has seen at least six—perhaps as many as seven or eight—generations of scholars bear the Austrian mantle. At each historical stage, it has had myriad participants with changing intellectual and ideological priorities. To comprehend our shape-shifting subject, we have to explore the school's evolving composition, intellectual interests, and institutional formations across time.[7]

A number of problems crop up when trying to reassemble the Austrian School in its multiplicity and multifariousness. First there is a membership question. Present-day US "Austrians" like Ron Paul identify Austrianism with Mises, Murray Rothbard, and, to a lesser extent, Hayek. This definition offers little in the way of explaining what made the Austrians a school, especially in Austria. The historian Tony Judt does little better, associating the tradition with four figures: Hayek, Popper, Mises, and Schumpeter. This is also a curious assemblage. No one would object to the inclusion of Hayek and Mises. The same is not true of Schumpeter, whom Hayek excluded from the tradition in a 1968 article. Even more problematic is Popper, who did not participate in any of the school's activities and was not even an economist. Even the most attentive scholars steeped in the tradition only mention a few additional names in standard presentations. These include Carl Menger, the founder of the school, his students Friedrich von Wieser and Eugen von Böhm-Bawerk, and occasionally some current scholars. If an October 2018 Austrian economics workshop I attended is any indication, figures before Mises and Hayek are known but primarily serve a symbolic rather than substantive purpose in current research. The list of exclusions is almost always more interesting than the inclusions. If we return to Hayek's article, he mentioned twenty-four scholars across four generations who contributed to the pre–World War II school. A recent study identified over forty members in the school's European phase. For example, Hayek's cohort contained many significant social scientists who rarely appear in narratives of the school, including Martha Steffy Browne, Herbert Furth, Gottfried Haberler, Fritz Machlup, Ilse Mintz, Oskar Morgenstern, Paul Rosenstein-Rodan, Alfred Schütz, Gerhard Tintner, and Erich Voegelin. These names do not even the fecundity of that peer group. Mises's and Schumpeter's generation also included dozens of scholars. In short, if we cannot identify members, we can hardly assess the school's ecumenical positions and its diverse influence.[8]

If deciding on members is challenging, so is dividing the school's existence into coherent, historical phases. While the school traces back to the 1870s and 1880s, it is the school's postemigration work that receives the lion's share of attention. This is ironic, because Hayek himself argued that the Austrian School ceased to exist in the wilderness of emigration. Moreover, the émigré Austrians were better known for their social theory and political philosophy than their economics. The focus on post–World War II developments occludes the role of early Austrian thinkers during the Habsburg and interwar Austrian periods. It also misses the school's role in the emergence of professional economics. The experiences of late-imperial Austria—including the rise and fall of the Austrian haute bourgeoisie, the emergence of mass politics "in a new key" (German nationalism, social democracy, Zionism), the efflorescence of modernist culture—informed Austrian ideas and the school's combative interactional style. There is a tendency to romanticize this earlier period without engaging it closely. Even Hayek wistfully called the pre–World War I period a "golden age," which its members at the time would surely have contested. Contemporary scholars still debate whether the 1930s and 1940s represented a rupture within the tradition. The connection between the European school and its US reincarnation, especially after its 1974 "rebirth," has been the subject of repeated disputes.[9]

There are also intellectual difficulties to unravel. Does a school require a coherent body of ideas, a core set of principles, or dogma? Those who have worked within the tradition have long grappled with this question, going back to the 1880s. Ironically from the right and left, respectively, Glenn Beck and Tony Judt identify the Austrian School primarily with Hayek's thesis in *Road* that central planning necessarily leads to "authoritarian repression and ultimately fascism." Consequently free-market society is the antidote to this perilous road. Ron Paul, following Murray Rothbard, reduced the Austrian tradition down to a few principles: a subjective theory of value; marginal utility; time preference (humans value present goods more highly than future goods); anti-interventionism and antistatism; laissez-faire. In Hayek's more sophisticated conceptualization, he identified two major strains of the school, one following Menger and Böhm and another trailing Wieser. Fritz Machlup, another member of the school, identified eight—later six—core propositions. A popular definition today enumerates ten. The relationship between methodological questions about individualism and subjectivism and political ones about liberalism, libertarianism, and market capitalism has been contentious since the school's founding. Failure to accept certain precepts can be grounds for exclusion or expulsion from the school. Schismatics have come to define the school today.[10]

Finally, there are questions about the school's broader economic, political, and intellectual impacts. Scholars of free-market conservatism, neoliberalism, and libertarianism have placed the Austrians at the center of their accounts. They see Vienna as the seedbed of capitalist internationalism and globalism. Hayek's MPS has become the locus classicus of neoliberalism. Popular commentators have positively linked the Austrians to the fall of Communism, the triumph of the West, and "the end of history," on the one hand, and negatively to Pinochet's Chile, the Koch empire, the Tea Party, and the Alt-Right, on the other. How these diverse impacts developed—and what precise role the Austrians played in them—requires further elaboration.[11]

These problems illustrate why there is still such confusion surrounding the Austrian School tradition. Many Austrian-born economists were not "Austrian economists," and most contemporary Austrians are in fact Americans. There were often several Austrian branches at any time, and it is unclear how today's dogmatic varieties connect to the earlier ecumenical central European collective. Given the low esteem that mainstream economics has for Austrian economics today and the undeniable affinity between libertarianism and Austrian economics, it is also fair to wonder whether Austrian economics is really about economics (and not ideology) anymore. I would not blame readers who are tempted to throw up their hands at this point and, channeling Voltaire, declare that the Austrian School of economics is not Austrian nor a school nor economics. In spite of these challenges, however, it is indisputable that an Austrian School *existed*, and it has transformed our world. We must therefore press on and grapple with these paradoxes and problems in search of our elusive school.[12]

Reconstructing the School

So how does one go about surmounting the difficulties of integrating such a welter of individuals, contexts, theories, and institutions? One of the first of many ironies associated with the school, then, is that a school dedicated to individualism and subjectivism is better investigated by studying the group, not individuals. Tracing interpersonal interactions and changing group configurations can give us a better sense of the school. Controversies typified the Austrian group as it strived to become a worldwide center of attention. Institution building, processes of identification, and factional conflict are integral. We are therefore less interested in saying what the Austrian School *is* or what it *believed* than in what it *did*. Considering the Austrians as nodes in a larger field of forces, we will see how they shaped economics, politics, and thought and how they were reflexively shaped by their social and political environment.[13]

Using this sociological approach, we can discern several phases in the Austrian School story. These are rough categorizations, yet they assist us in tracking the school's remarkable evolution. Additionally, we will see the very notion of a school transform. Prior to the late 1880s, no real school existed, yet a fascinating prehistory established the parameters for a thriving group to emerge. The "first" school flourished in Vienna until the Great War, establishing distinctive ideas and a wide array of interactional spaces in which members could develop their views and ply their influence. This version was the fullest articulation of a distinctive tradition: they advised royalty and served as senior bureaucrats; they led policy commissions and directed scientific associations; they became internationally recognized scholars. The next phase covered the interwar years. Much of the organizational structure of the school had collapsed along with the Habsburg Empire after the Great War. The school's reemergence coincided with the appearance of a new cohort sustained by new associations (Mises's famous seminar), patronage (chambers of commerce, the Rockefeller Foundation), and controversies. This is the "second" school. After the dislocations caused by the Great Depression, fascism, emigration, and World War II, a subset of its members reinvented the tradition in dialogue (and tension) with the US academy and a transnational network of conservative and free-market elites. While some members continued to respond to professional economics discussions, most moved toward more engagement with social theory and policy work. The Austrians therefore found themselves at the heart of a large neoliberal thought collective. They successfully brought their Austrian experiences to bear on the intellectual, ideological, and institutional landscape of the Cold War United States and Europe. The last phase, which continues to the present, represents another important transformation. Prior to emigration, the Austrian descriptor referred to a geographic site and implied that Viennese interactional rituals, not a dogma, constituted the school. More recent expressions of the school and its tradition, exemplified by Mises's New York City salon of acolytes, have been doctrinal ones. "Austria" became a metaphorical idea, rooted in dogma. The story of this reimagined, ideological school explains some of the enduring appeal of Austrian ideas—and why most members of the original school expressed ambivalence about the 1970s Austrian "revival" and probably would recoil at what Austrianism has become.[14]

Outline

We begin our quest for the Austrian School in the fragrant climes of coffeehouse Vienna. Chapter 1 opens in the Habsburg Empire in the middle of the nineteenth century—a period called the "founder's era," or *Gründerzeit*—with the class out of which the school emerged, the *Großbürgertum*, or haute bourgeoisie. Early members of the school— Menger, Wieser, and Böhm, to name the most prominent—came of age in the post-1848 Habsburg Empire, a period of liberal reform in higher education, a self-confident bureaucracy, rapid industrial growth, and triumphant liberalism. Nothing embodied these developments more than Vienna's Ringstrasse, the newly constructed boulevard that circled the historic city center on which the parvenu liberal class built emblems to its greatness: the opera house, national theater, city hall, and parliament. The parents and grandparents of school members gained noble titles for their contributions to Austrian modernization. The Mengers, Böhms, and Wiesers all carried a "von" in their names, designating aristocratic privileges. So would Mises, Hayek, Haberler, and others. The Austrian School was from its inception at the same time a "most successful scientific school" and a "highly influential 'old boy' network."[15]

It was within this liberal world of cultural, political, and business elites that the Austrians developed their theories. It was also where they fought for relevance. As Menger and his allies introduced the marginal utility revolution, they faced multiple adversaries—in the Habsburg state and bureaucracy and in German-speaking universities and professional associations. Their marginal revolution was a transnational event. Economists across the Atlantic world called into question earlier theories about economic value and reconsidered concepts of production and consumption. The revolution sparked conflict within economics as the field underwent professionalization and specialization, and the Austrians were on the front lines. The Austrian revolutionaries argued for an economic approach that emphasized the role of individuals and their subjective demands rather than the state and the national economy. They preferred deductive theoretical models to empirical and statistical approaches, yet they valued both sides of the economic project. They crossed swords with Marxists, classical economists, and the hegemonic German Historical School. To wage their battle, the Austrians established economics seminars, a professional society, and a journal for theoretical and policy debates. They became adept organizers, fiery polemicists, and vocal ideologues, key characteristics of the group's thought style going forward.[16]

In the years leading up to World War I, the school became a formidable force. Chapter 2 recounts this story. Led by the consummate insider Böhm, the school's members served as ministers of state, senior bureaucrats, and bank presidents, and they advised on the most pressing matters within the

Austro-Hungarian Empire. They attained university professorships and attracted students from across the empire and the globe. Austria transformed into a hub of modern economic thought. The pre–World War I intellectuals Schumpeter, Mises, and Hans Mayer established themselves as scholars of economic methodology, economic history, money and credit theory, and business cycle research. They defined themselves against the German Historical School and their new bête noire, the Austro-Marxists.

Fin-de-siècle Vienna, the setting of this "golden age," is famous for the number and density of its intellectual circles, from which the school members drew inspiration. Gathering in Art Nouveau coffeehouses, elegant Ringstrasse salons, and the offices of the Habsburg *Großbürgertum*, dozens of modernist groups assembled every week to lecture, debate, and gossip. These avant-garde circles included luminaries such as Karl Kraus, Sigmund Freud, Arnold Schönberg, Adolf Loos, Gustav Mahler, and Gustav Klimt. Dozens of additional circles existed in the sciences and politics, including the seminars of the Austrian School. In these spaces, school members delighted in intellectual jousting. In spite of intense theoretical differences, Böhm, Wieser, Schumpeter, Mises, and dozens of others sustained a school. The Austrians distinguished themselves with their methodological rigor and devotion to "value-free" science. These engagements brought friends and foes to Vienna, whether the German social theorist Max Weber or the Russian Bolshevik Nikolai Bukharin. This was the most dynamic and catholic period of the school's history.[17]

The Great War shattered the "world of yesterday" of the Austrian School. The collapse of the Habsburg Empire, the eclipse of the Austrian bourgeoisie, and the inception of an uncertain Austrian republic loomed over the school and are the subject of chapter 3. School members lamented the empire's end, the crisis of the postwar Austrian state, and the threat of socialism. They set aside strictly economic work for new forms of engagement. Not only did the war shake their intellectual beliefs and worldview, but it threw their very existences into flux too. Academic and bureaucratic jobs disappeared. The politics of interwar Austria, which pitted a social democratic left against a Catholic conservative right, left little room for the "excluded middle" of patrician, German liberals. While the leaders of the Austrian School—now Schumpeter, Mises, and Mayer—kept alive the seminars and circles, tensions mounted. The Austrians turned increasingly to conservatives and elites to shore up their social position.

The next generation, which coalesced in this context, consequently had to seek opportunities outside the academy and even outside the country, a situation that chapter 4 illumines. Its members drew on the robust intellectual culture of "Red Vienna," but they also relied on a process of transatlantic enrichment that introduced US social scientific ideas to Europe, and European scholars to US universities. Over a dozen school members traveled to the English-speaking world during the 1920s and 1930s. They brought new theoretical ideas with them to the United States and carried back cutting-edge empirical approaches. Their connections to business elites in the International Chamber of Commerce and the Rockefeller Foundation helped them attract global allies. They also took on roles as public intellectuals, writing for popular audiences and creating institutions to disseminate their work. They extended their influence into policy and business affairs, playing roles in the Ministry of Finance, the Vienna Chamber of Commerce, and the Austrian National Bank. Yet the Austrians were more than economists: they conducted freewheeling salons, wrote drinking songs, debated Goethe and Shakespeare, and took ski trips and Alpine summer vacations together.[18]

As European politics took an authoritarian turn and the worldwide depression deepened in the early 1930s, the Austrians took center stage with their defenses of free-market capitalism and liberal democracy. With the rise of fascism in Austria and Germany, they relied on their international network of friends and patrons to sustain and protect them. Their forced emigration raised the specter of the school's disappearance. The members of the school did disperse, yet they remained committed to their beloved tradition in various ways. They rallied together against emerging trends in economic theory and policy, especially against Keynesianism and state economic planning. Additionally, as witnesses to the collapse of their civilization, they envisaged ways of restoring the Austrian tradition on European shores. This took the Austrians in new directions, and economics took a back seat to social and political theory, as well as ideological activism.[19]

It was in emigration that school members broke out of technical economics and into social theory and political philosophy, recasting the ideas associated with the school. Chapter 5 details how school members retreated from economics and took a political turn. With such publications as Hayek's *Road to Serfdom*, Schumpeter's *Capitalism, Socialism, and Democracy*, and Mises's *Omnipotent Government*, Austrians brought their political values and worldviews to new audiences.

The Austrians used their organizational acumen and networking savvy to create institutions to propagate their liberal, elitist thought style, on which chapter 6 expounds. In the MPS, the Alpbach Forum, and the Vienna Institute for Advanced Studies, the Austrians sought allies in the fight for Western liberalism and Austrian social science. They strove to restore European civilization—exemplified by Habsburg cultural and scientific traditions. The Austrians moved beyond intellectual work and into movement building. They courted journalists, (European) liberal politicians, and antistate, pro-business financial backers. Through these endeavors, the Austrians were pivotal to the reconstruction of US conservatism, European liberalism, and transnational neoliberalism. Moving beyond the idea of limiting an already-existing state, neoliberals like the Austrians imagined how to create a state that protected economic freedom from government planners, international governing institutions, and democratic polities alike.[20] The Austrians thus helped build postwar neoliberalism, which, in the name of freedom, prioritized the creation of a market-based society sustained by a strong state, the rule of law, and limited democratic involvement. They also contributed to the formation of a number of transnational epistemic communities that advocated trade liberalization, floating exchange rates, state deregulation, and privatization. Austrians played instrumental roles in these communities by persuading institutional actors, state and nonstate, to follow their prescriptions in times of uncertainty and crisis. Through GATT, the Bellagio Group, the RAND Corporation, and others, Haberler, Machlup, and Morgenstern proved adept at behind-the-scenes policy interventions that shaped economic liberalization and Cold War reasoning in the 1960s and 1970s. Perhaps unsurprisingly, the 1980s "Washington Consensus," which coalesced in the halls of the International Monetary Fund, World Bank, and US Treasury, was articulated by a Machlup student, John Williamson. Austrian ideas appeared in myriad, unexpected locations, even as the Austrians themselves approached retirement.[21]

As the last members of the original school aged, they and their followers worked to solidify the school's legacy or legacies. How later generations would imagine Austrianism loomed large for the Austrians, actual and adoptive. This story of memory work occupies chapter 7. US students of Mises established and fought for a distinctive, libertarian definition of "Austrian economics." With the help of conservative libertarian donors like the Koch brothers, a more dogmatic and ideologically inclined version of the school emerged in the 1960s. The conferral of a Nobel Prize on Hayek in 1974 and the initiation of conferences and graduate programs for Austrian economics produced a "revival" of the school. However, US Austrianism lost most of the diversity that had defined the best of the earlier tradition. The last "Austrian Austrians" took part in preserving their tradition, trying to save their nonsectarian "family" from radical libertarians who "have inherited Mises's dogmatism without his genius, and are continuously quoting Hayek without . . . understanding a word of what he actually means."[22]

The conclusion explores the continuing evolution of the school in the quarter century since the last Austrian-born Austrians passed away. US Austrians have built a sustainable "Austrian economics," carving out a distinct place in contemporary heterodox economics. At places like New York and George Mason Universities, "Austrian"-trained scholars have kept alive parts of the original intellectual patrimony. Yet the more enduring legacy today has not been Austrian School ideas but an idea—or, better put, an *ideology*—of the Austrian School. Austrian economists have had a larger impact as champions of free enterprise, market society, and libertarianism than as scholars of entrepreneurship or market processes. In fact, scholarship on the latter, funded by a narrow set of ideological actors, often only serves to reinforce the former. Austrians have become the darlings of radicals who have gravely influenced our world. After the collapse of Communism and accelerating since the Great Recession, it has become de rigueur for self-respecting conservative politicians to pledge fealty to Hayek or Mises. This ideological affiliation has riven the contemporary Austrian movement, raising questions about the imbrication of Austrian economics—and "classical liberalism" more generally—with reactionary politics. Periodic disputes between the major centers of Austrian thinking—George Mason University (GMU) and the Cato Institute on one side and the Ludwig von Mises Institute (LvMI) on the other—have flared up, most recently between the radical but (now more) *salonfähig* libertarianism of Cato, GMU, and the

Kochs and the reactionary variety connected to the Alt-Right in the United States and the xenophobic, populist New Right in Europe. What the current crisis of Austrianism demonstrates is that there is urgent need for a better understanding of the intellectual traditions that inform these contemporary debates and for a firmer disavowal of the ideological machinations of the Alt-Right and the Kochtopus.

Ultimately, this book confirms the historian Tony Judt's surmise that we must think the twentieth century through the Austrian School. Its revolution began with a new method of economic thinking and evolved into a grand strategy for the defense of market society, the rule of law, individual liberty, and private property, and it continues today. Contra Judt (and Glenn Beck), however, we may live in an Austrian era but not because of any one individual or idea. The Austrians created a style of thought that offered a new and appealing defense of free-market economics and po-litical liberalism that enlivened intellectual and political developments around the globe. They built ideological and institutional support through their interactions with various elites. The lessons the Austrians carried in their suitcases from Vienna were therefore richer and more variegated than we typically acknowledge. Their love of freedom, their celebration of capitalism, and their ambivalence about democracy resonate today. These sophisticated ideas have carried a seductive power—especially in simplified and attenuated forms—and they have proven hard to dislodge, even when linked to authoritarian governments, reactionary political movements, or vapid thought leaders.[23]

As Hayek observed, the spontaneous interactions of individuals in a free society often produce consequences well beyond the designs of the par-ticipants. The Austrian School's history confirms this aperçu. *Marginal Revolutionaries* argues that a renewed, critical engagement with this tradi-tion can be used to clarify how economics, politics, and power interact and how ideas, institutions, and influence intermingle to produce the orders in which we live. Understanding these interactions may permit us to change our world for the better.

1

THE PREHISTORY AND EARLY YEARS OF
THE AUSTRIAN SCHOOL

In the orthodox telling of the Austrian School story, in the beginning was Carl Menger: "In 1871 Carl Menger founded the Austrian School in Vienna with his pathbreaking *Principles of Economics*."[1] His *Principles* offered a significant reformulation of core economic concepts like value, price, and production, contributing to an incipient transformation in economics called the marginal revolution. Alongside French, English, and American scholars, the Viennese thinker overturned a century of received wisdom from "classical" political economists such as Adam Smith and David Ricardo. In Vienna, Menger spawned a movement with his words.

Historians of economic thought have noted, however, that an Austrian School of economics did not spring fully formed from Menger's mind or from the pages of *Principles*. In fact, *Principles* was poorly distributed, found a limited readership, received middling reviews, and played a minor role in the vibrant economic discussions of the 1870s. An anonymous review captured the ambivalent response: "Yes, we would greet the book with joy as a smart approach to the recurrent investigations of fundamental principles, if it did not appear with the pretension of a textbook of general economics, since it is really only a mechanical sequence of studies on the concepts of goods, value, exchange, price, and money."[2] Commentators recognized Menger's theoretical acumen, yet they worried about the helpfulness and practicality of his concepts. Consequently, *Principles* did not inspire immediate change. The book, published by a small Viennese press, quickly went out of print. For the rest of his life, Menger refused to allow the book to be reprinted or translated. Consequently, it was nearly impossible to get one's hands on it for over fifty years. His long-planned overhaul, which he worked on until the end of his life, never appeared. At the end of his life, even Menger questioned the book's lasting significance.[3]

Menger's *Principles* was conceptually difficult and ponderously written, and it failed to attract many allies. Menger retreated from academic work, publishing little and taking on few students. By the late 1880s, however, European scholars spoke of an "Austrian School." A growing number of scholars adopted the initially pejorative sobriquet for themselves. The eventual diffusion of Menger's ideas and the emergence of a school owed to three major factors: the efflorescence of a new mode of economic thinking associated with marginal utility theory; the prominent role of the educated middle class—including the Menger family—in Habsburg politics and society; an epochal controversy with the hegemonic German Historical School over economic method and the role of individuals and the state in the economy.

As Menger's case shows, neither an individual nor a text a school makes. In the Austrian case, it took nearly two decades of concerted effort by an array of individuals in the Habsburg academic, political, and business worlds. The rise of an Austrian school of economics owed to the surrounding cultural and political conditions of late imperial Austria more than it did to the ingenuity of Menger. To understand the "birth" of the Austrian School, we will meet the young Carl and return to his Austria, which the author Stefan Zweig has called "the world of yesterday." Menger's fin-de-siècle Vienna centered on the neo-Renaissance halls of the University of Vienna, glittering Art Nouveau and Jugendstil coffeehouses, and the rustic cottages of the Austrian countryside, where well-to-do middle-class families spent their summers.[4]

Young Carl Menger and Ringstrasse Vienna

Given Menger's prominence in the history of economics, the paucity of information about his personal life surprises. We know little about his childhood or adolescence and scarcely more about the final quarter century of his life. Born in 1840 in the Galician town of Neu-Sandez (now Nowy Sacz) to Caroline and Anton Menger, Carl was one of six children. He claimed that his father, a lawyer with liberal political leanings, was the sole intellectual influence of his childhood, instilling an appreciation of Montesquieu, Jean-Baptiste Say, Smith, and Ricardo. This account seems of dubious reliability, since his father fell ill when he was only seven, dying the following year. Prior to his death, Anton was ennobled with the title "von Wolfensgrünen," a significant status marker for any member of the ascendant Habsburg bourgeoisie. The Mengers moved to Silesia shortly after Anton's passing. After finishing high school in Krakow, Carl followed his older brother, Max, to the University of Vienna, where he studied law. His younger brother, Anton, matriculated a year later, but Carl transferred to Charles University in Prague. There he ran afoul of a conservative professor, flirted with German nationalism, and acquired the quintessential mark of a nineteenth-century German university student, a dueling scar.[5]

After Menger had completed his legal studies in 1862, he spent most of the next decade working as a journalist for liberal newspapers across the Habsburg monarchy. He attained great success, drawing political and institutional support from the Austrian state. After stints in Prague and Lemberg (Lviv), Menger arrived in Vienna in 1864. He founded his own newspaper, the *Wiener Tagblatt*, in November 1865; it reached a circulation of thirty-five thousand by February 1866. Part of its popularity owed to its low cost and populist message. It paid close attention to social problems in the empire and examined issues of interest to the middle and working classes. Seeing its success, the liberal imperial government coopted the paper, taking over its financing and distribution. Government authorities then convinced Menger to edit the regime's official organ, *Die Wiener Zeitung*. He worked as a full-time journalist until the end of 1866, when he abruptly resigned. He rented an apartment with his brother Anton and threw himself into theoretical economic work for the first time. Menger spent much of the next four years filling notebook after notebook with economic ideas, which became the basis of his *Principles*.[6]

For aspiring young men like Menger, achieving recognition in the imperial capital meant that one had arrived, for Vienna was the center of the Habsburg world and a beacon of civilization. "There is hardly a city in Europe where the drive towards cultural ideals was as passionate as it was in Vienna," recounted Stefan Zweig in his autobiography *The World of*

Yesterday. "Hospitable and endowed with a particular talent for receptivity," he continued, "the city drew the most diverse forces to it, loosened, propitiated, and pacified them. It was sweet to live here, in this atmosphere of spiritual conciliation, and subconsciously every citizen became supranational, cosmopolitan, a citizen of the world." While Zweig himself was born in 1881, the picture of Vienna he painted invoked the Austria of his father, a member of the liberal generation of the 1860s. His father, Moritz, was a wealthy textile manufacturer, and his mother, Ida née Brettauer, came from a prominent banking family. Often called the *Gründerzeit*, the "founder's era," the period 1859–79 was one of prosperity in the Habsburg Empire, driven by the educated middle classes and industrialists (the *Bildungs-* and *Großbürgertum*), many of whom were assimilated Jews, like the Zweigs. With an unflinching faith in progress and optimism about the empire's prospects, the bourgeoisie reshaped the Austrian capital in its image. The greatest demonstration of this assertiveness came with the construction of the Ringstrasse, the major artery girding the historic city center.[7]

As industrial growth accelerated at midcentury, Vienna and its suburbs underwent profound changes. In 1850, the city incorporated its surrounding districts; however, the medieval city wall still separated the two areas. In 1857, Kaiser Franz Josef announced that the walls would be razed. In 1858, the government initiated a competition for a new urban plan. Many of Vienna's most famous edifices were erected as part of this plan: the neo-Romantic State Opera House, the Natural History and Fine Arts Museums, the neoclassical Parliament building, the Burgtheater, the neo-Gothic City Hall, the neo-Renaissance University of Vienna. When the imperial and municipal governments bickered over finances, private investors and banking institutions took over construction. In addition to the splendid cultural and political landmarks, the *Großbürgertum* constructed lavish residences, turning the Ringstrasse into the empire's hottest real estate destination. On May 1, 1865, with the Kaiser and his wife, Sisi, in attendance, the boulevard opened. It attested to ascendant Austrian liberalism and the splendor of the Habsburg regime.[8]

The liberal *Großbürgertum* not only transformed the geography of the capital but also encouraged new forms of cultural interaction and sociability. Most characteristically, the number of coffeehouses exploded. Cafés

Griensteidl (1847), Ritter (1867), Landtmann (1873), Sacher (1876), Central (1876), and Ronacher (1880) all date from the era. The cafés were open from the early hours of the morning into the wee hours of the night, and educated professionals congregated in these locales to read international news, gossip about business and politics, and carry on intellectual exchanges. The coffeehouse was a key to Vienna's appeal but not just for culinary or aesthetic reasons. As the author Arthur Schnitzler put it, "[It] has something 'old Viennese' about it, which I find congenial. The billiards are much too long, the cashiers much too ugly, the tablecloths much too gray, the lighting much too bad—loud things, which I find very pretty. One can sit very comfortably there." Viennese became habitués of specific coffeehouses: the authors Hugo Hoffmannsthal and Arthur Schnitzler were regulars at Griensteidl, as was Leon Trotsky; Mahler and Freud preferred Landtmann; Peter Altenberg and Vladimir Lenin haunted Central. Carl Menger, too, had a favorite—he and his brothers, Max and Anton, held court at Ronacher. Coffeehouses represented more than just a meeting place; they were a way of life. When authorities decided to demolish Griensteidl in 1897, the satirist Karl Kraus penned a eulogy. The coffeehouses and the interactions they engendered made Viennese life, turning the capital into one of Europe's most vibrant centers.[9]

The Ringstrasse and the coffeehouses of the revitalized inner city inspired a younger generation of intellectuals—from Hoffmannsthal and Schnitzler to the artists Gustav Klimt and Egon Schiele to the architects Otto Wagner and Adolf Loos to the composers Gustav Mahler and Arnold Schönberg and finally to Sigmund Freud, Ludwig Wittgenstein, and Theodor Herzl—to create the first examples of Viennese modernism. Viennese artists questioned the certainties of their parents' generation, delving into uncertainty in the sciences, the dissolution of language and the self in literature, philosophy and psychology, and the reimagining of form and composition in art, architecture, and music. The Vienna of popular imagination is the one these individuals wrought over their *kleiner Brauner* and *Apfelstrudel.*[10]

The intimacy of the coffeehouse universe reinforced an even more substantial network of interpersonal relations among Austria's elites. Dense social and familial connections defined Habsburg cultural life. Everyone within the *Bildungsbürgertum* seemed to know everyone else. They hosted one another for parties and summered and traveled together. The salon and the summer villa were quintessential features of Austrian sociability, like the *Kaffeehäuser*. Families established intellectual dynasties, with several generations serving as leaders in Habsburg universities and government offices. The Mengers became a minidynasty; Friedrich Hayek descended from another. The Exner family was probably the most famous. It produced ten professors across three generations in areas as disparate as physics, meteorology, neurology, biology, and law. The paterfamilias, Franz Exner, inspired the liberal 1848 reforms of the University of Vienna from his position in the first postrevolutionary government. The Exners counted Ernst Mach, Ludwig Boltzmann, and Sigmund Freud as close friends. At their Viennese home and their summer retreat in the picturesque Salzkammergut, the Exners cultivated a remarkable community built on the virtues of skepticism, well-roundedness, and self-fashioning.[11]

Meanwhile Karl Wittgenstein created an iron and steel empire and subsequently transformed his Vienna *palais* into a cultural center. The Wittgensteins sustained Klimt and the avant-garde Secession movement. They counted Brahms, Mahler, Schönberg, and Richard Strauss as personal friends. Although Karl's son Ludwig became the most famous as one of the twentieth century's greatest philosophers, the other Wittgenstein children were celebrated as prodigies and geniuses in their own right. Ludwig's brother Paul, a virtuoso pianist, lost his arm fighting in the Great War. He commissioned the composers Benjamin Britten, Sergei Prokofiev, Richard Strauss, and most famously Maurice Ravel to create works for the left hand only. The Wittgensteins often played with their cousins the Jurascheks, including Felicitas, Friedrich Hayek's mother. Hayek himself was the scion of an academic family. His grandfathers were economists; Franz von Juraschek was a close friend of Eugen von Böhm-Bawerk, one of Menger's most illustrious students. Böhm's sister married Friedrich Wieser, another famous Menger pupil, making the key figures of the Austrian School's founding generation kin as well as colleagues. We can extend these connections ad infinitum. The various "Vienna Circles" that developed in this era—in music, psychology, economics, philosophy, jurisprudence, social reform—owed to this cultivation of intellectual, spiritual, and moral authority in the public and private spheres.[12]

Carl Menger entered this milieu as a young man on the make, and his *Principles* emerged from this heady mélange of collegiality, conviviality, and caffeine. Menger took advantage of family connections and imbibed the bourgeois Vienna scene. His book emboldened a younger generation to build a new thought style that reflected the creativity of Austrian intellectual life.

The Principles of Economics

When *Principles* saw the light of day after half a decade of percolation in Europe's finest incubator of ideas, it signaled the arrival of a precocious talent and sophisticated thinker. Menger's attention to detail and his search for conceptual precision resonated on every page. The book consists of painstaking investigations of several core economic concepts: goods, use and exchange value, exchange, price, commodities, money. The book garnered early praise for its innovative articulation of the theory of goods and the role of production. Later commentators applauded its focus on marginal utility, the role of economizing behavior in the formation of institutions, and the importance of knowledge, time, and error in decision-making. Most importantly, by placing individuals and their subjective preferences at the center of economic analysis, it challenged state-centered models of economics (*Volkswirtschaft* or *Nationalökonomie*) that predominated in the German academy. That said, as we saw, the book met with a mixed response and limited appeal beyond Habsburg universities.[13]

From the outset, Menger emphasized the potentially revolutionary implications of his work. *Principles* was a rallying cry for a new kind of economics: "Never was there an age that placed economic interests higher than does our own. Never was the need of a scientific foundation for economic affairs felt more generally or more acutely." To rectify the deficient state of economics and make it relevant to the greater public, he proposed to "reduce the complex phenomena of human economic activity to the simplest elements that can still be subjected to accurate observation." He said this method was "common to all fields of empirical knowledge." Although he used the word "empirical" throughout the book, Menger did not mean statistical or quantitative methods of data collection. Instead, he called on economists to observe the world of human interaction and identify the essential elements of experience. From there, they could build out deductive systems that applied to complex empirical situations.[14]

For Menger, the starting point was goods. He identified four prerequisites in order for an object to become a good:

1. A human need.
2. Such properties as render the thing capable of being brought into a causal connection with the satisfaction of this need.
3. Human knowledge of this causal connection.
4. Command of the thing sufficient to direct it to the satisfaction of the need.[15]

Here we see both the precision of Menger's thought and the unwieldiness of his prose. This definition placed Menger within the new trends in economic thought that stressed utility and the satisfaction of the subjective needs of individual actors.[16]

Menger then limned the production process, starting from consumption goods and running back to the raw materials that constitute those items. For Menger, long, capitalist production processes were a thing of beauty, since they increased the number of goods and the overall prosperity of human civilization. Like Adam Smith before him, who started *The Wealth of Nations* with a meditation on the division of labor and its role in the prosperity of nations, Menger also marveled over production, though from the vantage of individual producers and their subjective choices. His subjectivist interpretation therefore set apart *Principles* from classical economic theory. For Menger, as human knowledge increased and the uncertainty and errors of past methods were corrected, longer and more efficient production chains emerged that contributed to the advance of human societies "from barbarism and misery to civilization and wealth." Human beings could calculate their needs in advance and the best means for fulfilling them. Like Menger's friends the Exners, who grappled with the concept of uncertainty in their scientific work, he saw the struggle with the uncertain as central to human advancement. Menger's vision of capitalist exchange and its beneficial, civilizational impacts became a staple of the Austrian approach.[17]

After focusing on goods and production, Menger introduced the notion of scarcity and the need for economizing. After one hundred pages of ponderous theorizing, he arrived at the core of his argument: a subjective theory of value and a law of diminishing utility. *Economic* activity requires a careful marshaling of goods, the prioritization of needs, and the maximization of available resources. It is from these calculations that the value of goods arises. Although economic goods possess value, it is not inherent in the things themselves. Menger's description paralleled Stanley Jevons's 1862 work, which is often cited as the first articulation of marginal utility. However, Menger went further, demonstrating how the value of a good derived from the value of the final unit consumed. This finding was so significant that Menger placed it in italics: "*Hence the value to this person of any portion of the whole available quantity of the good is equal to the importance to him of the satisfactions of least importance among those assured by the whole quantity and achieved with an equal portion.*" This understanding served as the basis for later definitions of marginal utility, especially that of his student Friedrich Wieser.[18]

Principles includes novel insights that made their way into economics in later decades. With its focus on production, the role of time, and the importance of the final, marginal unit of a good, Menger's book offered a robust value theory. Menger also ventured a tentative theory of interest. He demonstrated how discrepancies between the value of first-order goods (consumer products like cell phones or cars) and higher-order goods (steel, glass, silicon, etc.) proved the value of entrepreneurial behavior and capital, which identified and produced the profit and growth opportunities inherent in capitalist economies. These themes of entrepreneurialism and capital loomed large in future Austrian work. While less innovative, Menger's history of money also attracted readers, since it pointed to the natural emergence of economic institutions like metal currencies and banking, as well as the subjective and nonneutral qualities of the medium.

As we saw at the beginning of the chapter, however, *Principles* did not launch an *immediate* revolution, for it faced a number of intellectual, institutional, and political obstacles. It received mixed reviews, with some commentators judging it little more than a summary of economic terms. Stylistically *Principles* itself militates against widespread adoption, for its concepts were challenging and the explanations lengthy and abstract. Moreover, Menger's prose is opaque at best, constipated at worst. Menger's first English translator lamented, "Menger's style is unusually cumbersome, even for German. His constructions form complicated patterns of clauses within clauses; they are filled with pronominal referents to these clauses;

and they abound in agglomerations of adverbial fillers. Many of his sentences run half a page or more and expound several independent thoughts." Menger's lack of succinctness and lucidity jeopardized the book's reception.[19]

Personally, Menger also did little to promote the work. In a calculation that would come to characterize the Austrian School more generally, Menger identified the road to prominence with liberal politics and elite (in this case, imperial) influence. From 1871 to 1873, he worked for the Habsburg foreign ministry, and he continued to write for *Die Wiener Zeitung*. He became an adviser to the minister-president Prince von Auersperg. He only resigned from this position in 1873 when he became a professor at the University of Vienna. His lectures usually attracted one or two dozen students, yet only four joined him in his first private seminar. While that seminar grew to sixteen in 1877, Menger's energies were divided between academic intrigues against the economist Lorenz von Stein (with the help of his brother Anton and the Exners) and a two-year engagement as the tutor of the Habsburg heir apparent, Rudolf. Menger instructed Rudolf on economics and politics and squired him around Europe on a grand tour. This appointment reinforced his insider status and permitted him greater political influence, yet it limited his teaching and intellectual influence.

Despite a muted initial reception for *Principles*, intellectual approbation was around the corner. Menger's book was one of the key planks in the "marginal revolution" that transformed the economics discipline. Menger also played a starring role in the field's biggest controversy. The *Methodenstreit*, as the dispute was called, played a crucial role in the self-identification of members of the Austrian School as outsiders, in spite of their evident insider bona fides. In the debate's aftermath, a movement coalesced in the Austrian capital around Menger's supporters, if not the man himself.[20]

The "Marginal Revolution"

Although the rise of marginal utility theory between 1871 and 1874 seems evident today, to contemporaries this was not the case. Menger's *Principles* did not represent a paradigm shift, and it was greeted as a competent yet unexciting work. It appeared almost simultaneously with other seminal works in the new marginal approach from the Briton William Stanley Jevons and the Frenchman Léon Walras, yet for many scholars, the marginal "explosion" reflected longer-term changes. The "marginal revolution" was a slow one, at best. Even if Menger and the other marginalists saw their work as groundbreaking, a gradualist picture better characterizes the social scientific landscape.[21]

At the turn of the nineteenth century, political economy developed rapidly, primarily under the influence of Scottish and English scholars such as Adam Smith, Thomas Malthus, and David Ricardo. Their work introduced a new level of abstraction and theorization to questions of trade, industry, and exchange. These classical economists sought to explain the fundamental principles of human interaction: how human self-interest benefited society, how the division of labor led to greater productivity and wealth, how competition in the marketplace ensured the best prices and outcomes for producers and consumers. They pursued universal laws, emulating the natural sciences. They also looked to mathematics to formalize their work. This process reached its apotheosis with Ricardo, who offered rigorous models of comparative advantage and theories of rent and wages.

While nineteenth-century economists still had much to discover, many areas generated consensus. Scholars agreed on the fundamental significance of labor for the determination of value. The labor theory of value, most associated with Smith and Ricardo, stood as a pillar of classical political economy. In its simplest form, the labor theory argues that the value of a good derives from the labor expended to produce that item. As Smith put it, "What every thing is really worth to the man who has acquired it, and who wants to dispose of it or exchange it for something else, is the toil and trouble which it can save to himself, and which it can impose upon other people." Classical economists focused on factors of production (land, labor, and capital) when assessing the value of commodities, rather than on the utility that goods may have for a consumer. By the time that John Stuart Mill wrote his *Principles of Political Economy* in 1848, he felt confident that the theory of value had achieved perfection: "Happily, there is nothing in the laws of Value which remains for the present or any future writer to clear up; the theory of the subject is complete."[22]

Mill may have believed that classical economics had achieved scientific status, with a focus on confirmation of theories and experimental applications, yet several Continental thinkers dissented. In German-speaking lands, Friedrich List called into question the existence of natural laws that applied in all national contexts. Bruno Hildebrand, Karl Knies, and Wilhelm Roscher extended this critique, attempting to reintegrate historical particularities into economics. Out of these shared concerns, these men formed the core of a German, "historical" school.[23] Meanwhile other scholars doubted the completeness of the labor theory of value. British thinkers steeped in utilitarian philosophy opined that calculations of utility—whether of pleasure and pain or of perceived wants and needs—provided a better means for determining value. Richard Jennings called the labor theory of value "the great fundamental fallacy." In France, Frederic Bastiat and Jean-Baptiste Say advocated utility theory. Jules Dupuit wrote about marginal utility as early as 1844. Auguste Walras, the father of Léon, built his economic edifice on the concept of *rareté*, or scarcity. In German lands, Hermann Gossen produced an early formulation of the law of diminishing returns—that is, that the value of a unit decreases with each additional available unit—in 1855. One could argue that the marginal turn really began in the 1850s, if not earlier.[24]

By the early 1870s, economics reached a tipping point, and it ushered in a revolution in thought, signaling the beginning of the "modern," or "neoclassical," era. Marginalists flipped classical economics on its head. Instead of focusing on the production side of economics, they turned to consumption. It is the satisfaction of the wants of consumers that matters for value, not the labor required for production. What establishes the overall value of a good is the value fetched by the final unit of that item on the market. As more units of a good are produced, the marginal value of the last unit tends to decrease.[25] For example, Apple sells approximately 220 million iPhones each year. The iPhone X costs $1,000. According to the marginalists, it is not the costs incurred in producing the iPhones but the price that consumers are willing to pay that fixes the phones' utility. If Apple chose to produce only one thousand devices, the price would skyrocket because of excessive—near desperate—demand for the latest phone. Conversely, if Apple (foolishly) tried to up production of phones so that there was one for every person on earth (7.6 billion at last count), the price would correspondingly plummet, as Apple frantically sought buyers to clear its inventory. In the final analysis, then, Apple determines price and production levels on the basis of consumer demand. According to marginal utility, the consumer, not the producer, therefore drives the valuation process.

Three men stood at the center of this marginalist turn. William Stanley Jevons worked on utility throughout the 1860s, producing *The Theory of Political Economy* in 1871. Léon Walras, building on his father's work, published *Éléments d'économie politique pure* in 1874. He set to analyzing how organized markets achieved equilibria between buyers and sellers. Carl Menger completed the trinity of the marginal revolution.[26]

The success of this revolution did not simply occur because of the power of the ideas. It owed as much to sociological and institutional changes within economics. At roughly the same time, economists professionalized their discipline, creating new societies, journals, university programs, and research agendas. The national societies the Verein für Socialpolitik (1872), the American Economic Association (1885), and the Royal Economic Society (1890) date from this moment, as do the journals *Zeitschrift für die gesamte Staatswissenschaft* (1844), *Jahrbücher für Nationalökonomie und Statistik* (1862), the *Quarterly Journal of Economics* (1886), and the *Economic Journal* (1890). International conferences also became regular features. By 1890, all major European nations had professional economic associations, peer-reviewed periodicals, annual congresses, and a handful of university economics professors. In the "age of capital," as the historian Eric Hobsbawm has described the period 1848–75, practitioners of the economic sciences became important knowledge producers, policy advisers, and government officials, enjoying a level of influence unique for academics.[27]

In the newly unified German Reich, Berlin was the center of these developments, where economists could contribute to higher education, research, and policy work. The leading figures of the Verein taught there. Adolph Wagner and Gustav Schmoller represented a "younger" German Historical School, which turned increasingly to social policy and statistical analyses in an attempt to gain influence within Otto von Bismarck's German Reich.

Economics did not enjoy the same midcentury success in the Habsburg lands. As late as 1893, an American student could describe Vienna as a backwater, with few courses on the subject: "In all nine courses, occupying just nineteen hours a week. Compared with the nineteen courses occupying forty-eight hours a week offered at Berlin, certainly a rather meagre showing." While the demands of the law degree in Vienna contributed to the lack of enrollment, the student observed, "The demand for a varied economic diet does not exist here as it does in Berlin, and in consequence the supply is also lacking."[28]

How can we account for this state of affairs in the home of the Austrian School, even twenty years after *Principles'* appearance? A lot owed to the peculiar cultural conditions of liberal Vienna. First, a professorship at the University of Vienna, while an elite appointment accessible to only a sliver of the educated classes, was not a prestige position compared to government posts. As the former Austrian minister-president Prince Karl von Auersperg said to Menger upon learning that the latter wished to resign from a government position to be an academic, "You want to become a Professor?!"[29] Political in-fighting, intradepartmental squabbling, and administrative meddling made university life unappealing. Although the University of Vienna attracted notable economists to its faculty, it had a hard time retaining them. Adolph Wagner and Albert Schäffle taught in the Austrian capital in the 1860s and early 1870s, but quarrels with fellow incumbent Lorenz von Stein led to their departure. Moreover, economics did not represent a standalone course of study at the university; it was subsumed in the Law Faculty. Students received only scattershot training in economics as undergraduates, and they had little inclination for such courses. A typical lecture course on economics attracted a couple dozen students. Those who took an interest in the discipline, like Menger's students Eugen von Böhm-Bawerk and Friedrich von Wieser, had to travel abroad to receive formal training. There were no Austrian economics journals and no professional associations either. To an extent, this makes sense, since German Austrians considered themselves part of the broader German intellectual community. However, the interest that Austrians took in German developments was rarely reciprocated. This neglect of Austrian higher education extended beyond Germany. Even as American and British students flocked to German universities to learn the most advanced research and scientific techniques, they rarely looked to Austria-Hungary before the 1890s.[30]

Given the inauspicious conditions within the Austrian academy and a corresponding lack of social scientific institutions, as well as the intellectual marginality of Austria itself, it is clear why Menger's *Principles* could not ignite a revolution in Vienna or German-speaking Europe. These circumstances also made the emergence of an Austrian School less likely. The Austrian-German rivalry allowed Austrian scholars to gain recognition by challenging their German peers, however. The *Methodenstreit* was the most prominent example of these confrontations, and it created a counterpole to the hegemonic German approach in Vienna.

The *Methodenstreit:* "A History of Wasted Energies"

Joseph Schumpeter, a later member of the Austrian School, rendered a negative judgment of the "debate over methods" in his canonical history of economic thought. He explained, "Methodological clashes often are clashes of temperaments and of intellectual bents. This was so in our case. There are such things as historical and theoretical temperaments. . . . We have use for both. But they are not made to appreciate one another."[31] Although the debate concerned significant philosophical issues, it was primarily a dispute between two irascible, vain professors, Menger and Schmoller. Simmering beneath the surface for over a decade, petty resentments erupted into an academic contretemps in 1883. The vitriol bewildered participants and observers. The debate resolved little and cost much. More than any other event, the dispute precipitated the formation of a distinctive Austrian School, yet one must not confuse correlation and causation: the latter-day Austrian approach owed little to this contest of egos. Instead, a new cohort of scholars entered the field simultaneously with the struggle and began to enrich the embryonic Austrian approach.[32]

In the decade after *Principles* appeared, it barely made an impression outside of Vienna. The silence from the German Reich in particular was deafening. Menger did not see himself as a heterodox thinker and wanted to contribute to the improvement of German-language scholarship. He believed that *Principles* advanced recent German work that challenged British political economy. Dedicating his book to Roscher, he sent a friendly greeting to his German allies: "Let this work be regarded, therefore, as a friendly greeting from a collaborator in Austria, and as a faint echo of the scientific suggestions so abundantly lavished on us Austrians by Germany through the many outstanding scholars she has sent us and through her excellent publications."[33] The Germans did not interpret his tract as an overture, however. Schmoller, the emerging leader of the "younger" German Historical School, accused the author of the kind of abstract theorizing associated with the British. Another reviewer accepted Menger's overture with reluctance: "we cannot suppress a certain regret that he has spent his energies . . . in an unbeneficial way."[34]

Menger determined that his next effort would not be brushed off. *Investigations into the Methods of the Social Sciences* arrived to great excitement in 1883. While it shared some common themes with his earlier work in its attention to theory, its tone and content diverged. Menger argued that German economics had ventured onto a false path and now risked complete isolation from the rest of the economics profession if it did not heed his approach. Younger German economists emphasized the historical nature of economic phenomena and statistical and empirical regularities. This concentration resulted in an almost complete denial of the relevance of theory and methodology. Menger called this fixation "misleading," "one-sided," and "unintelligible." Instead of appealing to German scholars in the name of collegiality, Menger attacked them for their shoddy work: "misunderstandings . . . have played a decisive part in the reform of political economy by its German reformers."[35]

Investigations is really two books in one. The first is a work of methodology consistent with *Principles*: it is "concerned with determining the nature of political economy, of its subdivisions, of its truths, in brief, with the goals of research in the field of our science."[36] In the first part of the book, Menger identifies three kinds of science, each with a different epistemological method: individual (empirical), general (theoretical), practical (technical). The first observes concrete phenomena in the world, emphasizing their uniqueness. The second seeks general rules, or types, to organize discrete worldly phenomena. The third develops techniques for applying basic principles to problems. Menger lambasted the German Historical School for failing to distinguish between these approaches. He implored readers to place greater emphasis on theoretical economics, which would help distinguish between approaches and improve economic science.[37]

The obverse side of the Janus-faced *Investigations* is a polemical manifesto. The book alternates subtle methodological meditations with coruscating reviews of German economic work. It concludes with what appears to be Menger's primary goal: the evisceration of the German Historical School. While offering a tour de force exposition of nineteenth-century historical consciousness, Menger asserted that the Germans were not only bad economists but bad historians too. His primary targets were the scholars to whom he had made earlier overtures: Roscher, Hildebrand, Knies. The summary for Roscher, the dedicatee of *Principles*, says it all: "His system of political economy, as every unprejudiced person must admit, is in truth not at all a philosophy of economic history in the sense he himself characterized." Roscher, like the German school, was misguided and confused, incapable of the tasks he set out for himself.[38]

Investigations raises a number of questions about Menger and the inchoate Austrian approach. Why the volte-face regarding German economists? Why such spleen? Unfortunately, the historical record is mum on the subject. While Menger noted in his journals his progress on his "methodology book," he did not elaborate on his antipathy toward the Germans. Likewise, his few surviving letters make no reference to *Investigations* or the *Methodenstreit*. Commentators have postulated that he felt resentment after the ill treatment of *Principles*, especially by Schmoller, yet there is little direct evidence. Others have highlighted lingering Prussian-Austrian tensions after the war of 1866 and the emergence of the Second Reich in 1871 or the increasing German nationalism within the Verein für Socialpolitik. These explanations do not fully explain Menger's mounting frustration, however.[39]

One of the proximate causes of Menger's eruption was the evolution of the German Historical School in the 1870s and 1880s. With the rise of a younger generation, the school's orientation shifted from research to policy. The early school assumed that one could induce economic laws from a close investigation of historical, social, and institutional conditions. Interdisciplinary in nature and modest in its claims, the school offered a broad platform for research. The younger school, associated with Schmoller, turned away from a strictly descriptive program, defining economics as a normative science whose main purpose was policy advising and business counseling. Through the Verein and the bureaucracy of the German state, the younger school championed industrialization policies and the increased role of the state in the German economy.

These policy considerations were a long way from the kind of science that Menger and the Viennese practiced. As we have seen, liberal Vienna was at its zenith in the 1870s, and no place experienced a more exciting renaissance than the University of Vienna. At almost the same time as Menger's appointment in 1873, his brothers, Max and Anton, the philologist Theodor Gomperz, the doctors Carl von Rokitansky and Theodor Meynert, and the philosopher Franz Brentano all received appointments. These men transformed Vienna into a center of positivist science and philosophy. They made theoretical research the primary aim of the university. Brentano published his foundational phenomenological work *Psychologie vom empirischen Standpunkte* in 1874. In it, he argued that the true method of philosophy was scientific and that experience was the only way to knowledge, which required introspection, observation, and experiment. His phenomenological orientation inspired Menger, Freud, and the later Vienna Circle of logical empiricists.[40]

Simultaneously scholars transformed the methodology of the sciences in Vienna from an unreflective objectivism into a critical empiricism. The central emphasis in this turn involved calling into question the primacy of the individual subject. Innovative approaches in a number of disciplines challenged the stability of ontological categories; for example, the physical world, the soul, the state. Instead, they focused on the subjective—the perceptions of observing subjects and their interactions with the surrounding world. Ernst Mach, a Prague professor soon to join the University of Vienna physics faculty, and Georg Jellinek, a prominent jurist, contributed key insights. Mach denied the existence of a real external world outside of perception. He taught physics as a "Kraftlehre ohne Kraft" (mechanics without forces) and psychology without a stable self or ego. The world—and the self—consisted of nothing more than individual perceptions of the world and how we interact with the objects around us. Freud picked up on these insights about the instability of self, conducting psychoanalytic research without a metaphysical concept of the soul (*Seelenlehre ohne Seele*). Hans Kelsen, Jellinek's student and a world-famous jurist, developed a state theory without a fixed concept of the state (*Staatslehre ohne Staat*). Jellinek and Kelsen emphasized the role of norms and positive laws in creating the state. For the Viennese vanguard, science was to be a critical, reflexive project that took nothing for granted.[41]

Carl Menger participated in this avant-garde intellectual sea change. Emboldened by his friends and colleagues, Menger saw his opportunity to transform economics similarly. Economics, known as *Volkswirtschaft* or *Nationalökonomie* in German, traditionally relied on objective categories like *Volk* (people) or *Nation*, and its central object of investigation was the national economy. The German Historical School represented this tradition; Schmoller doubled down by prioritizing state policy. Menger, on the other hand, believed a critical, subjective approach could produce a Viennese countertradition: a "*Volkswirtschaft ohne Volk*" or a "*Nationalökonomie ohne Nation.*" The individual, not the nation, must be the starting point for economic inquiry if one wanted to get to the heart of economic exchange. In 1871, Menger heralded his new science to fellow Germans. After a decade of neglect, the Austrian professor refused to watch economics drift away from science to become a form of state apologetics.

If some people in Vienna were receptive to Menger's philosophical tendencies, the German academic community was not. Two long reviews of *Investigations* appeared: one by Heinrich Dietzel and the other by Schmoller. Schmoller published his own journal, and it was the leading German social scientific publication. In it, Schmoller offered an unenthusiastic verdict. Schmoller applauded Menger for pointing out inconsistencies in the Historical School, and he recognized the benefits of discrepant theoretical positions in economics. Still, he maintained that Menger "had never produced a truly great work" and should thus reserve judgment on others. He ended with a backhanded compliment: "Menger is a sharp dialectician, a logical mind, an uncommon scholar, but he lacks the universal philosophical and historical education [*Bildung*], the natural breadth of horizons, to be capable of appreciating experiences and ideas from all sides." Schmoller defended his own "polemic" on the grounds that Menger's "attacks partially concern [him] personally."[42]

Schmoller's condescending tone probably set Menger off. The German's remark about Menger's accomplishments the Austrian could perhaps forgive. Being called "uneducated" Menger could never forget. For a member of the *Bildungsbürgertum*, the "*ungebildet*" epithet was calumnious. Thus began a two-year war of words. Menger accused Schmoller of bias, superficiality, and vulgarity. He asserted that the German professor used his academic position and journal to intimidate others and to foreclose new research. In exhaustive detail, he catalogued the ways in which Schmoller misread and misunderstood him. The reply to Schmoller—a one-hundred-page pamphlet—evinced Menger's unquenched fury: "The future—and indeed, as I hope a not-too-distant future—will decide whether Schmoller is finished with my methodological investigations, or if I am finished with the theoretician Schmoller." Menger was willing to bet he would have the last laugh: "Only children and fools will henceforth take his methodological views seriously." Menger saw this contretemps as a struggle for the soul of economics, one that he had to win.[43]

The *Methodenstreit* concluded with a passive-aggressive Schmoller open letter. In his *Jahrbuch*, he announced to the German economic community that he had returned Menger's *Streitschrift* directly to the author, unread. He expressed his policy of discarding personal attacks, saying he did not wish "to bore the public by continuing literary feuds in the polemical manner of many German professors." Schmoller felt he did not need to answer Menger to maintain his status. After these salvos, Schmoller and Menger rarely acknowledged each other again in their scholarly work.[44]

It is difficult to declare a winner in the *Methodenstreit*, though if Schmoller won the battle, Menger won the war. On Schmoller's side, several allies such as Adolph Wagner and Heinrich Dietzel distanced themselves from his approach, though Schmoller maintained his prominent academic standing in the German-speaking world. His approach predominated in the academy until the Nazi takeover. On the other side, Menger suffered. He lost support at his own university, where he was outvoted on a measure to reform the law faculty and overruled in the selection of economists to replace Lorenz von Stein and Lujo Brentano. Showing signs of nervous exhaustion, he retreated from academic engagement.[45]

Ironically, the seeds of Menger's vindication were planted while the *Methodenstreit* raged. This redemption, coming in the form of the emergence of an Austrian School, had less to do with the debate than with the consolidation of a group of thinkers who esteemed Menger and studied his ideas. The year of the *Methodenstreit*, 1884, was thus a seminal year for the Austrian School, though not for the reasons one expects. To gain a better sense of how the school actually emerged, we must turn to the group of scholars centered around the brothers-in-arms and brothers-in-law Eugen von Böhm-Bawerk and Friedrich von Wieser.[46]

Böhm and Wieser: Intellectual Entrepreneurs

It is difficult to think of Böhm without Wieser, and vice versa. Born in the same year (1851) to recently ennobled, upper-middle-class families, the two grew up in *Gründerzeit* Vienna. The "von" title that Böhm and Wieser (and Menger) bore was no relic of an earlier age but a symbol of arrival in the late Habsburg Empire. These young men were destined for success. They attended the same elite high school, the Schottengymnasium, where they hobnobbed with future leaders in politics, academics, and business. Government ministers and politicians favored the school, and it provided important connections for these young men. The historian Heinrich Friedjung, later a journalist and prominent German nationalist, was in the same class, as was Alfred III, prince of Windisch-Grätz, future minister-president of Austria, and the longest-tenured president of the House of Lords. Engelbert Pernerstorfer, the leader of an important circle of German nationalists and intellectuals, and Victor Adler, the founder of the Austrian Social Democratic Party, attended a year apart.[47]

After secondary school, Wieser and Böhm (and most of their peers) studied law at the University of Vienna before embarking on civil service careers. They finished their university studies in 1872, the same year that Carl Menger accepted his university appointment, so Böhm and Wieser never studied directly with him. Böhm entered the Lower Austrian Finance Ministry, while Wieser served in the imperial bureaucracy. They came across Menger's *Principles* after graduation. It made an impact, because the young men approached Menger about further study. He encouraged their educational endeavors, supporting their respective applications to the Ministry of Education for leave. In 1875 and 1876, Wieser and Böhm received imperial travel grants to study economics in Germany with Bruno Hildebrand, Wilhelm Roscher, and Karl Knies. The work with Knies proved particularly stimulating. He mentored an impressive group of students in

Heidelberg, including the American John Bates Clark, whose work moved along similar lines as the Austrians'.[48]

Despite a burgeoning intellectual affinity between Menger, Böhm, and Wieser, there is no further evidence of interaction in the 1870s. Menger was busy with the crown prince and his writings on methodology. When he was promoted to a tenured professorship in 1879, he expanded his network of students, but there is no evidence of exchange with Böhm or Wieser until 1884. Meanwhile in 1876, Wieser and Böhm returned to their bureaucratic jobs and wrote little on economics for years. The most significant development within the group was personal: Böhm married Wieser's sister Paula.

When the younger Austrians began to publish in the 1880s, Menger's subtle influence was present. Böhm's first work, appearing in 1881, illustrated his adoption of Menger's theory of goods, though it was hardly the work of a dogmatic disciple. Böhm wanted to determine whether immaterial things like services, intellectual property, and rights could be treated as economic goods. He hypothesized that the marginalist theory of the good could illuminate these concerns. Nevertheless, Böhm drew his main insights from the field of capital and interest theory, not Menger's value theory. Instead, Böhm used the works of his first economics instructor, Albert Schäffle, as well as Knies and Roscher. Ultimately, Böhm argued that legal rights and other immaterial things could not be viewed as goods, since these "goods" derived their value from underlying physical objects rather than themselves.[49]

Böhm's first book attracted little notice. There was only one review in an academic publication, which consisted of little more than a synopsis. Menger himself paid the work scant attention. While he possessed a copy in his library, he only once referenced the book in later works. In spite of this desultory debut, Böhm's prominent social status and his bureaucratic connections helped him secure a professorship at the University of Innsbruck, where he taught from 1881 to 1890. This period, the only extended stretch during which he was an academic rather than a government official, was the most productive of his lifetime. He and Wieser began the organizational efforts that made possible the emergence of an Austrian School. Meanwhile a coterie of scholars inspired by Menger and imperial Vienna produced works that gave shape to an inchoate, and nebulous, movement.[50]

The "Birth" of a School

In the same year that the *Methodenstreit* reached its climax, a new generation of Austrian scholars barraged German economics with a diverse array of social scientific studies. Ranging from the study of costs and value to the origins of interest and capital to the role of business profits in the economy, Austrian authors in Vienna, Prague, and Innsbruck announced their presence to the academic world. Drawing inspiration from Menger and *Principles*, these thinkers typically appealed to one another rather than the elder Austrian in their search for allies. Böhm and Wieser, in particular, made Austrian ideas more accessible by linking them to international—read: British and US—trends. By the end of the 1880s, their efforts met with acceptance: foreign scholars read their works and commissioned translations, and articles on the "Austrian theory of value" appeared. In addition to making their ideas more available, the Austrians attracted others by turning their feelings of resentment and hostility in a more productive direction—toward the critique of socialism. These forays into political polemic had a lasting impact on the development of the Austrian School, which became closely identified with antisocialism, antileftism, and liberal apologetics.

If Böhm and Wieser were the true fathers of the new school, Menger was the holy spirit. Menger began the process of institution building in his role as academic mentor at the University of Vienna, advising the dissertations of about a dozen scholars. Although they had little success achieving positions in the larger German academic community, they thrived in Habsburg Austria. Böhm became a professor in Innsbruck in 1881. Wieser joined Emil Sax at Charles University in Prague in 1884. Eugen von Philippovich, who studied the Bank of England and wrote a best-selling economics textbook, taught at the University of Freiburg before being called to Vienna. Many other students taught as untenured lecturers (*Privatdozenten*) in Vienna while serving in the government. Robert Meyer, who wrote on progressive taxation, served in the finance ministry. Gustav Gross, who studied business profits and wrote a critical biography of Karl Marx, became a representative of the liberal German Progressive Party. Viktor Mataja also wrote on business profits and became Böhm's successor in Innsbruck. He also founded the government's Department for Trade

Statistics. Each of them published notable works in 1884. Other adherents worked as lawyers for the government, served in the Central Commission for Statistics or Chamber of Commerce, and sat on corporate boards at banks and industrial enterprises.[51]

As we see from the diversity of interests and the range of employments, the Austrian School was neither purely theoretical nor entirely academic. Its members spread out into an array of professional communities, yet it was their continued conversations and meetings that cemented a group identity. Whether in the seminar rooms at the University of Vienna, in the airy confines of Cafés Ronacher and Landtmann, in Carl Menger's capacious home and library, or on excursions into the country, the Austrian School was a social network first and last. Friedrich Hayek highlighted these qualities in a retrospective essay: "He [Menger] frequently invited the seminar to a Sunday excursion into the country or asked individual students to accompany him on his fishing expeditions." It was these cultural features that defined the Viennese school experience through the generations.[52]

Of course, there was the theoretical side to the school too. The most significant texts of the embryonic Austrian School were Böhm's *Capital and Interest* and Wieser's *Über den Ursprung und die Hauptgesetze des wirtschaftlichen Werthes* (On the origin and the general laws of economic value). The first book deployed Menger's ideas on value to comprehend how capital could produce greater value over time and how interest made economic sense. Wieser's work offered a concise account of value theory and introduced the term *Grenznutzen* (marginal utility) to the economic lexicon. Wieser also linked his and other Austrians' work to Jevons's, thereby reinforcing the international character of the marginal revolution.

Conceived as a two-book project, Böhm's book criticized existing theories of interest for failing to explain how capital produces more wealth and how interest yields more money in the future. The book provides critical glosses of the major figures in interest theory—from Turgot and Smith to Say and Roscher, Knies and Menger, Bastiat and Mill, and, finally, Marx. In the end, Böhm found existing models wanting, setting the stage for an eventual "Positive Theory of Capital." The second volume then attempts to provide this theoretical foundation for the existence of capital, as well as a justification for capitalist society.[53]

While no scholar escaped Böhm's deft scalpel, Carl Menger fared best. Dedicating the book to "the path-breaking researcher," Böhm explained his project as a work of methodology and exact science à la Menger.[54] Like his intellectual guide, he girded himself for attacks from people with different methodological values: "Whoever attacks critically must prepare himself to be attacked. I do not fear such attacks, I expect and welcome them." Böhm did not, and would not, shy away from a fight.[55]

Like Böhm, Wieser picked up Menger's theory of goods, though he tried to streamline its definition and extend its application to price theory. He also incorporated a critique of socialism into his considerations. He recognized the looming threat of Marxist socialism, both politically and economically, and attempted to undercut it using marginal utility theory. While Wieser's later work surpassed *Origins* in clarity and comprehensiveness, his first book ignited the economics profession, especially in Vienna. Menger, who had previously paid Wieser little mind, wrote a glowing report for his habilitation committee. Not only did Wieser provide a succinct description of the process of value creation; he extended Menger's concept of value to the most vexing questions of contemporary economics, like the expansion of production and income distribution. He also possessed the style of a good propagandist. His definition of marginal utility was remarkable in its simplicity: "Simply put, the value of an individual unit [of a good] is determined by the least valuable of the economically permitted uses of that unit." He linked his formulation with Jevons's "final utility" or "terminal utility." In doing so, he made a convincing argument that Austrian economists did not operate in isolation as heterodox scholars but were at the forefront of modern social science. Finally, he introduced a fascinating theory of imputation (*Zurechnung*), which tied the prices of factors of production to the value of first-order (consumer) goods. His new theory of costs demonstrated how marginal utility could provide new pathways for understanding production processes. In barely two hundred pages, Wieser offered the most compelling case to date for taking Austrian marginalism seriously.[56]

The efforts of Wieser and Böhm bore immediate dividends, as evinced by references to "Austrian Economists," a "Menger School," and an "Austrian School" in the scholarly literature. Economists worldwide hailed *Capital and Interest* as a landmark work. Böhm's renown produced a retrospective recognition of Menger. A supportive 1886 review highlighted this linkage: "With the logical acuity typical of the Menger School, he [Böhm] placed individual theories . . . under his knife and pared away many outgrowths." The author nevertheless recognized a difference between the two men: "In contrast to the other achievements of the Menger School, it leaves nothing to be desired in clarity or elegance."[57] Economists around the globe recognized the cresting Austrian wave. Léon Walras, the leader of the Lausanne School, exchanged letters with Menger and Böhm. Eugen von Philippovich mediated between the German historical and theoretical camps. He then introduced Austrian ideas into his popular German-language textbooks.[58]

To cap this opening act, the first major article defining the school appeared in England in 1888. The author, James Bonar, argued that the Austrians had successfully introduced marginalism à la Jevons in central Europe. He appreciated Austrian critiques of classical value theories, yet he also expressed concerns about their methodological approach. He worried about the Austrians' abstractness and voiced concerns that the "psychological" or subjective approach undermined economists' search for objective value. Universal laws of exchange and economic behavior would be difficult to deduce if each individual determined his or her own set of valuations. The lasting service of the Austrian approach, Bonar maintained, would only become clear when its applications to public affairs become evident. As we will see, the Austrians shared this anxiety and were already developing their practical techniques when this piece came out.[59]

Another important reason for the more general embrace of Austrianism at this time was that the school's main target of opprobrium was no longer the German Historical School but Marxist socialism. Published in the year after Marx's death, Böhm's *Capital and Interest* invited comparisons to *Das Kapital*, the socialist's great theoretical work, which was slowly trickling out, volume by volume. Socialism appeared to be cresting a wave of popularity at the same time as Austrianism. In the years since the German Reich had passed its Anti-Socialist Laws (1878), the workers' movement experienced massive growth in membership. In both Germany and Austria, trade unions became increasingly vocal, while fears of terroristic acts—as were occurring in Russia—mounted. Böhm and the Austrians joined a chorus of conservative, nationalist, and liberal scholars in the attack on socialism. Böhm's book offered a total repudiation of Marx's exploitation and labor value theories. *Capital and Interest* can thus be seen as the beginning of a three-volume cycle—including *The Positive Theory of Capital* (1889) and *Karl Marx and the Close of His System* (1895)—which claimed to offer the final refutation of scientific socialism from the viewpoint of modern economics.[60]

Wieser's book also advanced anti-Marxist critiques. His objections centered on the problems of price calculation in a centralized socialist state. In this way, Wieser anticipated Ludwig von Mises's famous argument about socialist calculation by thirty-five years. Wieser saw the world divided in two camps: either you were an individualist or a collectivist, both methodologically and ideologically. Wieser and the Austrians could only countenance the former. After acknowledging the possibility of either capitalist or socialist societies, he declared that only the former conformed with economic law: "It is an error to believe that 'atomistic' marginal utility calculation only serves the interests of the ruling classes and only the accidental, merely contingent circumstances under which they exercise their dominance. In truth it is based on external facts and such characteristics of human nature that appear inalterable and eternal." Marginal utility was not a bourgeois, individualist ideological outgrowth but a universally applicable science. Neither a capitalist nor a socialist society could escape its dictates. No other system of calculation could exist, and "any attempt through legislative act, promise of recompense or threat of punishment to introduce another rule of calculation will be in vain." Only when everyone—especially socialists—realized that the gift of marginal utility theory "is not a weapon of one man against another" but rather a tool for "all in the economic struggle against nature" would society enjoy all the benefits of free economic exchange.[61]

With the authors' innovative economic and ideological arguments, Böhm and Wieser found broad resonance. Anton Menger, Carl's brother and a professor of law, even preferred their work to his brother's. In his juridical work, Anton took up their antisocialist arguments, criticizing the feasibility of worker control of the means of production and the distribution of goods, along Wieser's lines. An Austrian School was beginning to coalesce in the mid-1880s not just in economics but in political theory, jurisprudence, and philosophy too.[62]

With the Austrians' intellectual reputation assured, they turned their attentions to practical affairs. None of the early members saw themselves solely as economists, let alone as theoreticians. They saw theory, empirical science, and policy as discrete fields equally worthy of engagement. The early Austrians therefore viewed their contributions not only in intellectual terms but also in social and political ones. They increased their political profile and extended their work to matters of civic concern. The new, "public" phase of the Austrian School was under way.

The first major development in a policy direction came from Emil Sax, Wieser's colleague in Prague. A few years younger than Menger, Sax first vied with Menger for academic recognition. After an abortive attempt to gain a position at the University of Vienna, Sax went to Prague in 1879. In 1884, he rallied to Menger during the *Methodenstreit*. His 1887 *Grundlegung der theoretischen Staatswirtschaft* (Foundation of theoretical state economics) represented an extension of subjective value theory into public policy. Sax asserted that economists had successfully shown the scientific nature of private economics, which focused on subjective valuations, production, and exchange in the market economy—what we would today call microeconomics. On the other hand, economists had treated state and social economics (macroeconomics) as a *Kunstlehre*, or practical theory. Sax instead believed that state economics operated according to the same laws as the private economy. Using marginal concepts at the state level would provide a better foundation for policies on trade, taxation, finance, and public enterprise. Sax advocated for active state intervention in areas where the private economy did not adequately satisfy collective needs (defense, transport, public utilities, and market regulation), proposing that taxes and fees on private goods and incomes cover "complete life ends," those ends that exchange could not cover. Everywhere else the state must remain out of market functions.[63]

Sax's fellow Austrians approvingly referenced him when defending the practical side of their approach. Nevertheless, the place of applied economics remained an open question for the school. Böhm and Wieser tried to address this criticism, albeit in divergent fashions. In 1891, Böhm and Wieser each authored articles in English-language journals, intended to popularize the Austrian School. Böhm, the master polemicist, argued that marginal utility was a critical rejoinder to the methodological lacunae within classical economics and the German historical method. While practical concerns were important, he reasserted that theory was fundamental: "The province of the Austrian economists is *theory* in the strictest sense of the word." Only then did Böhm turn to "questions of distribution," heading off potential objections about the abstractness of Austrianism. He enumerated a growing list of Austrian titles that looked at wages, rent, profit, finance, and policy, showing the Austrians' practical side.[64] Wieser argued along similar lines, yet he placed greater emphasis on applied economics. Recognizing that science seeks "its highest laurels on the field of observation," he maintained that the Austrians viewed themselves as experimentalists first and foremost. Wieser identified three directions in which the Austrians would continue to innovate in the subsequent decades: critique of socialist and communist economics, economic theory and methodology, and public finance and state economics. Like Sax, he supported state regulation of the economy and progressive taxation on economic and ethical grounds. He suggested that the wealthy, who derived more benefits from state services than the poor, must pay more for those advantages.[65]

This explosion of publications and commentaries demonstrates that the late 1880s were a propitious moment for the emergence of a new economic school. The Austrians capitalized on the trend toward professionalization in economics. Significant articles on the school appeared in the *Quarterly Journal of Economics*, the *Annals of the American Academy of Political and Social Sciences*, the *Economic Journal*, and the *Nuova Antologia di Scienze* between 1888 and 1891.[66] In the latter three journals, the articles appeared in the very first editions published, reciprocally helping to establish the credibility of the publication *and* the school. Translations of the most significant Austrian works of the late 1880s appeared in short order, encouraging transnational acceptance. Impressively, the Austrian School was even more dynamic than the reviews, translations, and programmatic statements suggest. A slow but steady stream of new works appeared between 1884 and 1887, yet it was the publication wave of 1888 and 1889 that launched the school to new heights of recognition and influence. Nearly a dozen Austrians propelled the revolution onward. Even Gustav Schmoller, Menger's nemesis, had to acknowledge this, begrudgingly admitting of the emergence of "a younger Austrian school."[67]

At this juncture—four years after the pyrotechnics of the *Methodenstreit* and seventeen years since *Principles*—Carl Menger reentered economic discussions with a long article on capital. Echoing his earlier objections about the state of economic science, Menger singled out capital theory as inadequately developed and poorly expressed. In the efforts of Adam Smith and classical economists to devise new concepts, they "allowed the clear and practically meaningful real-life concept of [capital] to go unobserved." He urged a return to commonsense understandings of capital derived from observations of business and industry. Menger explored the conceptual challenges of defining capital before venturing a tentative definition himself. For the first time, Menger drew on other Austrian scholars. He also entered into the discussions about socialism. Lamenting the helplessness of contemporary economics in the face of the socialist theories on the production of wealth, Menger touted Böhm as a ray of hope for liberal economic theory: "Böhm's efforts with capital and interest reveal their great significance from this vantage." Menger believed that Böhm would put to rest any further discussion of Marx's theory in the scholarly community.[68]

Böhm's *Positive Theory of Capital* did not disappoint. He offered a comprehensive explanation of the interest phenomenon while also leveling a blistering attack on labor theories of value. He became a major international figure, embodying the Austrian School even more than Menger. The book was translated into English, making it one of the few German works afforded such a treatment. It went through four editions and inspired several generations of scholars, including Joseph Schumpeter, Ludwig von Mises, and Friedrich Hayek. It also provoked ardent detractors. Henry Carey Baird, son of the American economist Henry Carey, called the book "the most complex, confusing, narrow, hair-splitting, and arrogant criticism." It played a pivotal role in several controversies in the history of economic thought. Böhm and John Bates Clark engaged in a fifteen-year exchange about capital theory. Even decades later, Böhm's ideas prompted debates between Austrian School members and the Chicago economist Frank Knight.[69]

Böhm's greatest innovation was his prioritization of the role of time in the production process, particularly time's contribution to value creation. The surest way of increasing the output of wealth—and enhancing the return of capital—was by extending "roundabout" methods of production. The more time "sacrificed" to the production process and the greater the deferral of present needs for future ones, the greater the overall return.

This was Böhm's famous "time preference." For him, and for many subsequent Austrians, it was the key to capitalism's success. Böhm recognized that roundaboutness was his keenest innovation: "That roundabout methods lead to greater results than direct methods is one of the most important and fundamental propositions in the whole theory of production."[70] Böhm's work offered vital insights into how capital functions as a "tool of production" and why it "naturally" produces a rate of return, or interest. As he noted, humans discount the value of future goods vis-à-vis present ones, so the sacrifice of present value must therefore yield more value—in the form of interest—in the future.[71]

Böhm also introduced the figure of the entrepreneur into his economic theory. Entrepreneurs and entrepreneurial activity would become major features in modern economics, especially in the Austrian School, largely thanks to him. He defined the entrepreneur sociologically as the class of individuals engaged in speculative ventures. They earned their wealth not through the exploitation of labor or land but through their far-sighted commitment to the production of goods. Their dedication to roundabout production methods for future gain distinguished them from other market participants. In extolling the entrepreneur and the creative power of capital, Böhm offered the most trenchant criticism of the labor theory of value to date. Demonstrating that returns on goods come from the interactions of labor, land, and capital over time, he undermined the contention that capital derived solely from the creative power of labor.

Finally, Böhm advanced the Austrian critique of socialism. He claimed to hoist Marxism on its own petard, arguing that the socialist state would of necessity engage in the same exploitation of labor as the capitalist one: "But much more important than any such sporadic obtaining of interest by private individuals is the fact that, in the Socialist state, the commonwealth itself, as against the citizens, would make use of the principle of interest which to-day it reviles as 'exploitation.'" This interpretation was a misreading of socialist theories of exploitation, which did not object to interest or capital per se but to who owned the means of production and who received the profits. Nonetheless Böhm's *Positive Theory* served as a starting point for subsequent liberal critiques of socialism.[72]

In the midst of Böhm's star turn, he promoted his friend and brother-in-law, Wieser. Böhm admitted that he only dealt with the role of capital in the production of wealth and could not provide a full accounting for the distribution of value across the factors of production. Wieser's theory of imputation, outlined in his 1888 *Natural Value*, provided the elaboration Böhm sought. Wieser showed how prices, the "objective" valuations of goods that emerged from exchange, related to "natural value," the innate relationship between utility and the good itself. Inspired by Anton Menger and contemporary jurisprudence, Wieser devised a method to assign responsibility to individual factors for the creation of value. In painstaking detail, Wieser showed the relative contributions of land, labor, and capital to value. Using marginal utility theory, he produced a new interpretation of the relationship between price and value, otherwise known as the imputation value.[73] He also extended the emergent Austrian critique of socialism. He argued that even in "communistic" society, the natural values of land, labor, and capital still pertained. Communist society was therefore subject to the laws of imputation and marginal utility. The allocation of all productive wealth to labor, as the labor theory demanded, could not do away with the natural value of land and capital, which appeared in the form of rent or interest. Even if socialists managed to smash the capitalist state, Wieser concluded, they could not destroy the laws of marginal utility or the indispensability of market prices for assessing value.[74]

With a clearer mode of expression and evenhanded tone, *Natural Value* met with easier acceptance than either Menger's or Böhm's works. It was rapidly translated, and it received favorable reviews. Wieser presented himself as part of a growing contingent of Austrians who were pushing the marginal revolution forward. Wieser's work was also striking because it highlighted rather than downplayed disagreements within the school. In contradistinction to Böhm, Wieser stressed creativity and novelty over dogmatism. He extolled Sax's work on state policy, and he singled out figures rarely associated with the school as vital contributors—namely, Rudolf Auspitz and Richard Lieben. These mathematically savvy Viennese, poised at the intersection of a number of the most prominent Viennese circles, took marginal utility in directions that few of their contemporaries could fathom. Their *Untersuchungen über die Theorie des Preises* (Investigations on the theory of price) attested to the creative energy simmering within fin-de-siècle Vienna. The Austrian School of Böhm and Wieser and Auspitz and Lieben was no mere economic movement; it was a cultural one too.

Auspitz, Lieben, and Fin-de-Siècle Vienna

After a long day of sightseeing in Vienna's majestic inner city or along the famed Ringstrasse, weary visitors will often find their way into the famed Café Landtmann for a coffee and pastry. Situated next to the neo-Renaissance Burgtheater and opposite the neo-Gothic Rathaus and neoclassical University of Vienna main building, this juxtaposition hardly diminishes the café's own splendor. Located in an ornate, nineteenth-century construction designed in the historicist style of the time, the café's home dazzles the eye, with its five-story, white-and-pastel facade. The building is one of Vienna's choicest addresses. The edifice, built in 1873 during the height of Austrian liberalism, is the Palais Auspitz-Lieben, named after the wealthy families who erected it. Richard Lieben and his siblings, along with his cousin and brother-in-law Rudolf Auspitz, planned and financed its construction. The Palais was more than a family home; it was also a center of Viennese modernism. Café Landtmann was popular with the Mengers, Ludwig von Mises, and Max Weber. Bertha Zuckerkandl-Szeps, heir to a newspaper empire and an early proponent of the Secession movement, hosted her salon there from 1917 to 1938, attracting Johann Strauss, Gustav Klimt, Arthur Schnitzler, Alma and Gustav Mahler, and many others.

The Liebens represented the Austrian *Bildungsbürgertum* in its greatest glory. Ignatz, the patriarch, was an industrialist and banker who left part of his fortune to establish a prize honoring the greatest achievements in the sciences. The Lieben-Preis was a forerunner of the Nobel Prize and is still viewed as the "Austrian Nobel." Ignatz's children achieved great fame too. Adolf became a chemistry professor in Prague before attaining the directorship of the Chemistry Institute at the University of Vienna. Ida, a brilliant thinker and salon leader, married the famed philosopher Franz Brentano. Richard became vice president of the Credit-Anstalt, the largest financial institution in Austria-Hungary. Richard was a precocious scholar and mathematical savant, and the family honored him by introducing a Richard-Lieben-Preis, which was awarded from 1912 to 1928. Helene, an accomplished painter and student of Georg Decker, produced one of the most famous portraits of the Austrian national playwright, Franz Grillparzer. She married Rudolf Auspitz, a sugar magnate and head of the banking house Auspitz, Lieben & Co.[75]

The Lieben clan demonstrated an astounding range of interests across disciplinary boundaries; Richard's work in economics reflected this diversity. Advanced knowledge of mathematics and the physical sciences informed Auspitz and Lieben's *Untersuchungen*. Like Menger, Jevons, and Böhm, the authors recognized the need for greater exactitude in the economic sciences. As opposed to the other Austrians, however, they did not look to empirical or commonsense knowledge for inspiration. Instead, they turned to mathematical models, which they believed could approximate real phenomena. In this way, they hewed closer to Léon Walras, with whom they carried on a productive conversation about partial and general equilibria. They viewed their theoretical contribution as part of the growing conversation within the economics community on marginal utility, especially in the Austrian capital. Their interests echoed Wieser's, and they made explicit reference to Gossen, Walras, Jevons, and Menger. Recent work by Böhm and Wieser received additional recognition. In *Untersuchungen*, Auspitz and Lieben showed their allegiance to international science and Viennese intellectual life.[76]

Despite Auspitz and Lieben's indebtedness to other economists, their work little resembled anything that came before it. Relying on graph, curve, and set theories, Auspitz and Lieben plotted intricate interactions between use and demand, cost and supply, supply and demand, and other core economic concepts. As a result, they are viewed as independent co-originators of indifference curves. They also anticipated several of Vilfredo Pareto's contributions on imperfect competition and monopoly prices. Their work on stocks, banking, and finance inspired scholars like Irving Fisher. Even today their work stands out for its precocity. While most economists were still struggling with algebra and only the most advanced had begun to tackle calculus, Lieben and Auspitz anticipated the formalist turn of post–World War II economics by decades. While their use of mathematics distanced them from other Austrians, members of the prewar Austrian School, from Wieser to Schumpeter, included them proudly in their tradition. Moreover, given the centrality of the Auspitz-Lieben family to Viennese intellectual life, it is easy to see why they were regarded as integral to the burgeoning movement. They were "Austrians" through and through.[77]

The contributions of Auspitz and Lieben and Böhm and Wieser barely scratch the surface of the late-1880s Austrian explosion. The efflorescence of Austrian economics moved in step with similar developments in other disciplines in avant-garde Vienna. Robert Zuckerkandl, brother of the anatomist Emil and brother-in-law of Bertha Zuckerkandl-Szeps, published an investigation of price theory. Emil Sax, Viktor Mataja, Johann Komorzynski, and Hermann Schullern zu Schrattenhofen produced noteworthy texts in 1889. Vienna became a bastion of social scientific theory, burnishing the capital's reputation as a center of European modernist thinking. The Austrians were on the way to creating their *Volkswirtschaft ohne Volk*.[78]

Building Institutions and Influence

For a school to succeed, it takes more than ideas, however. It also requires organizations to transmit ideas, interactions between peers, and transmission across generations. The Austrians, especially Böhm and Wieser, took to the task of school building with gusto. The Austrians organized an economics association to deal with contemporary social, political, and economics affairs. They also created a journal to disseminate findings. These endeavors anchored the economists in Austrian affairs and offered them an institutional foothold in German-speaking central Europe. As opposed to a purely theoretical focus, the Austrians asserted that their mission consisted of addressing practical life through scientific inquiry. In this, the economists resembled the psychoanalyst circle forming around Freud, which established clinics and fought for school reform, and the followers of Ernst Mach, who turned to social democracy, monism, and freethinking to challenge Austrian conservatism. For all of them, theory had to serve life.[79]

The new institutions of the Austrian School exemplified the group's diverse concerns. For Böhm, division of labor was the order of the day: "Our age stands under the sign of the division of labor. We specialize, in order to become master of a limited field." Collective endeavor alone assured scientific and social success: "What no individual knows alone, we all know together, if [we] have proper, animated contact with the intellectual spirit of the time." Institutional endeavors promised a way forward for the sciences and Western society. The Gesellschaft Österreichischer Volkswirthe (Society of Austrian Economists, GÖV) and its journal, *Die*

Zeitschrift für Volkswirtschaft, Socialpolitik und Verwaltung (*Zeitschrift*) represented the school's actualization. In them, the Austrians wedded theoretical and empirical work with liberal policy prescriptions based on an assumption that educated experts could solve the problems of the day—if political elites listened. This kind of institution building and influence peddling came to characterize the school through the generations.[80]

In 1888, Böhm, Gross, Max Menger, Philippovich, Lieben, Meyer, and Lorenz von Stein resuscitated the GÖV, a moribund trade organization, transforming it into an academic society. They viewed it as a counterpart and rival to the German Verein für Socialpolitik. By 1892, the Gesellschaft had 225 members and published a journal to rival Schmoller's *Jahrbuch*. The first issue called all hands on deck—the list of contributors included Sax, Wieser, Zuckerkandl, Mataja, and Gross. A younger generation also contributed. Walter Schiff, Eugen Schwiedland, and Hermann von Schullern took on active roles reviewing books. Economists of international repute like Knut Wicksell and Franz Oppenheimer affiliated with the paper. The GÖV's membership grew to nearly three hundred by 1900.[81]

The GÖV and the *Zeitschrift* cannot be viewed as exclusive organs of the Austrian marginalists, yet they did represent the integral confluence of economics and politics, theory and praxis, and knowledge and power in the late Habsburg Empire. In all of this, Böhm and his allies had starring roles. Theory took a back seat to economic and social policy. The Austrians drove early conversations on tax policy, currency reform, labor relations, worker insurance, and public-housing initiatives. Böhm used the society to encourage the intermingling of politicians, bureaucrats, and academics, who could work together to devise better political solutions. Böhm's primary practical interest was the "social question." He urged political leaders to use smarter economic policy to alleviate poverty and social unrest. Eschewing "panaceas" like laissez-faire or strict protectionism, he advocated for sensible, time-tested state interventions that could achieve narrowly circumscribed aims. Böhm believed that liberal interventions could produce better outcomes at the national and international level. Starting from individualist rather than nationalist assumptions, the Austrians created an alternate model of liberal policy promotion to the heavy-handed modus vivendi of the German Verein.[82]

While these ideals were progressive for the German-speaking *Bürgertum* of central Europe, Böhm and the early Austrians were no radicals. It was up to their class, the *Bildungsbürgertum*, to produce solutions for society. Paternalistic progressivism, a staple of the Austrian liberal tradition, best describes the elitism of the early school. Its organizational efforts and attendant ideological beliefs set a precedent for liberal intervention that characterized the future school too. As one astute observer suggested, "[The Austrian School] was a school for learning and practicing statecraft dominated by extremely influential, if not to say powerful men, the entrance to which was sought by ambitious young men interested in social advancement precisely because it was an avenue to important social positions."[83]

In 1891, Henry Seager, an American scholar trained at Johns Hopkins and the University of Pennsylvania, traveled to Europe at the behest of his advisers, Herbert Baxter Adams and Richard Ely, to study at Berlin and Vienna, the recognized centers of international economic thought. Writing in the first volume of the *Journal of Political Economy*, he linked the work being done in the Austrian capital to the most important developments around the world: Alfred Marshall's at Cambridge and Schmoller's in Berlin. He lauded Menger as a lecturer nonpareil, whose engaging, conversational style attracted a cadre of "talented young men" to his views. He marveled at the comprehensiveness of Menger's library, which contained every major scientific work in five European languages. For Seager, Böhm's weekly seminar was the finest debating society in central Europe. Instead of having a main lecture or presentation, "the presentation of papers is simply secondary; they are designed to introduce, but never to take the place of, the general debate which is to follow." Collective endeavor and debate were the keys. The seminar possessed a high degree of coherence, since the participants had all studied under Menger and Böhm and shared their orientation toward marginal utility theory. Seager's final assessment was an endorsement of the Austrian project: "The value . . . consists in the encouragement it gives to original thinking and in the sharpening effect it has upon the critical faculties of all those who take part in it. It has been to me the most valuable economic course I have had in Germany." Even if Berlin's institutional apparatus was superior, he maintained that the

Viennese were winning the battle of ideas. Vienna was becoming a magnet, "attracting . . . economic students from all countries."[84]

That Austria was a premier destination in 1891 for economics would have been shocking twenty years earlier, when Menger finished his *Principles*. This chapter has traced this surprising story of the Austrian School's emergence. It is replete with heated controversy and ironic consequences. Carl Menger's relative lack of success with *Principles* restricted his orbit to the Viennese intellectual world, just as Vienna itself was coming into its own as an international scientific capital. The domestic network of scholars and professionals connected to the University of Vienna, both within and without economics, emboldened his work. An emergent coterie of Austrians then popularized and extended his insights. The younger generation deserves most of the credit for establishing a school, with its organizations, journals, and private seminars. While Böhm may have claimed that "theory in the strictest sense" was the sine qua non of the school, the Austrians brought practical and political considerations to the fore in their institutions. The Austrians wrote on political and social issues, participated in governmental activities, and sought social, political, and economic influence. In the decades leading up to the Great War, the Austrian School would become a full-fledged intellectual and political force. While ideas were primary, power and influence mattered too.[85]

2

THE GOLDEN AGE: THE AUSTRIAN SCHOOL
IN THE "LAST DAYS OF MANKIND"

After a narrow escape from an Arkhangelsk prison in northern Russia, the twenty-three-year-old Bolshevik revolutionary Nikolai Bukharin stole into Vienna via Germany in August 1911. He took up residence in 1912, remaining there for almost two years. At the outbreak of the Great War in August 1914, the Habsburg government arrested him as an enemy alien and exiled him to Switzerland. He reunited with Vladimir Lenin, another Habsburg expellee, in Zurich, where they hatched plans for a Russian revolution. Before Bukharin's expulsion, the Russian subversive relished his time in the Habsburg capital, having selected Vienna deliberately. Bukharin wished to study "bourgeois economics," and no other city promised a better education: "I had long been occupied with the plan of formulating a systematic criticism of the theoretical economy of the new bourgeoisie. For this purpose, I went to Vienna." For this budding theoretician, the Austrian School embodied the best and most dangerous in the bourgeois tradition: "Our selection of an opponent for our criticism probably does not require discussion, for it is well known that the most powerful opponent of Marxism is the Austrian School." Bukharin knew that the most formidable enemy of socialism lurked in Vienna's splendor.[1]

While the primary reason for his Vienna sojourn was a confrontation with the Austrian School, Bukharin accomplished more than he anticipated. He assisted a young Joseph Stalin, also living in the Habsburg capital, with his work *Marxism and the National Question*. He also wrote an important rebuttal to marginal utility theory in *Economic Theory of the Leisure Class*.

The treatise, which became the definitive account of marginal utility theory in the Soviet Union, evolved beyond a critique of the early Austrian School and its key members Carl Menger, Friedrich von Wieser, and Eugen von Böhm-Bawerk. Bukharin also recognized a rising group, including Ludwig von Mises and Joseph Schumpeter, whom he had met and debated in Böhm's seminar. The Böhm seminar became a significant site of intellectual disputation in a city famous for its circles. Conversations often spilled out of Böhm's office into Viennese coffeehouses, where debate raged into the wee hours of the morning.[2]

Vienna truly was the center of the world for many activists, artists, and intellectuals. Stalin and Bukharin were joined in Viennese coffeehouses by Leon Trotsky. Josip Broz, later known to the world as Marshal Tito, the leader of post–World War II Yugoslavia, worked in a nearby suburb. Most famously, a young Austrian from the provinces, Adolf Hitler, received his early political education while eking out a living as a postcard seller. Vienna was home to some of the most famous movements of the twentieth century associated with Viennese modernism: Freud and psychoanalysis; Gustav Klimt and the Viennese Secession; Arnold Schönberg and the Second Viennese School of classical music; Ludwig Wittgenstein and the "First" Vienna Circle of logical positivism. The women's movement enjoyed broad support, Zionism and pan-German nationalism originated there, and socialism, under Austro-Marxist leadership, flourished. The capital attracted people not only from the Habsburg provinces but from around the world. In particular, exiled radicals selected the city for its dynamic possibilities.[3]

The Austrian School of economics experienced its "golden age" in this environment, nourished by the surrounding intellectual and political ferment. According to Friedrich Hayek, who gave the era its sobriquet, it was "the period of the school's greatest fame."[4] A well-defined school had emerged by 1890, armed with a coherent intellectual, ideological, and institutional identity. In the following decades, its leaders expanded the school's influence in Austria and abroad. This involved increased political involvement and conscious efforts to transmit ideas and values to a new generation. By 1914, the school no longer relied solely on Menger, Böhm, and Wieser for direction; younger thinkers carried the Austrian tradition forward. The contentious debates of the fin-de-siècle era, especially in Böhm's seminar, were harbingers of subsequent European events, which pitted imperialists against republicans, conservatives against liberals, and liberals against socialists. The combative young Turks of the Austrian School, primarily Mises, Schumpeter, and Hans Mayer, ensured the school's continuation. Facing formidable foes like Bukharin, Rudolf Hilferding, Otto Bauer, and Otto Neurath sharpened their thinking and their polemical tone. The give-and-take of these exchanges had a profound effect on the scholarship and the worldviews of all involved and shaped the political and intellectual landscape of the interwar era.

This chapter follows the evolution of the Austrian School in the two decades leading up to the Great War. It traces how the movement built its clout within the Austrian state and academy. It also explores how the Austrians expanded their international reputation by becoming socialism's foremost enemy. Homing in on Böhm's famous *Privatseminar*, we see how the prewar school developed its antileftist and anti-Marxist reputation. By looking at the development of a younger generation of scholars, the school's methods of knowledge transmission and intellectual succession come into focus. Finally the chapter looks at the continued role of Austrian institutions of culture—seminars, salons, coffeehouses—in the school's development. The prewar disputes with German historicists and socialists set the tone for subsequent controversies, and it cemented the school's predilections for virulent antisocialism, liberal interventionism, elite skepticism of democracy, and defense of free markets and capitalism. Even if the "golden age" was not as glorious as Hayek reported, the prewar Austrian School enjoyed a stability and coherence that subsequent iterations never enjoyed.

Knowledge and Power: The Austrians Ply Their Influence

After the successful establishment of an institutional and intellectual basis in the late 1880s, the Austrians began to engage in the policy deliberations of the Habsburg Empire, shaping the economic program of the late imperial regime. Böhm and the others took on bureaucratic roles and rose to high ministerial positions. They recruited one another to advisory commissions. They enacted changes to trade and currency policies that had enduring impacts on Austria well after the collapse of the empire. While declaring themselves to be apolitical, their actions evinced a clear ideological orientation, which supported the interests of the emergent bourgeoisie through liberal economic and political reforms that overturned the protectionist views of conservatives and resisted the democratic and socialist ones of the working classes.

Central to this engagement was Böhm, who reentered the Viennese scene primarily as a politician, not as a scholar. After the abrupt departure of Lujo Brentano from the University of Vienna in 1889, Böhm appeared to be the heir apparent to his chair, but the minister of finance swooped in and offered him a position as the head of the department in charge of tax reform. Böhm spent the 1890s rising through the ranks of the bureaucracy: he was appointed head of the tax department in 1891; he acted as vice president of the currency commission; he served three terms as minister of finance. Most of the key economists from this period likewise served in dual capacities as intellectuals and bureaucrats. Böhm's coeditors at the Austrian economics journal *Zeitschrift* were Theodor Inama von Sternegg, an honorary professor and the head of the state statistical commission, and Ernst von Plener, scion of a prominent liberal political family and a minister of finance in his own right.[5]

Working with fellow school member Robert Meyer, Böhm drafted a white paper and a bill that formed the core of the 1892 currency reform bill. The Austrian bimetallist currency, based on the values of silver and gold, had experienced large fluctuations in the decades since the Austrian Compromise of 1867. The Crash of 1873 hit the Habsburg industrial and financial sectors especially hard. It undermined confidence in the Austrian currency, the *Thaler*. Austrian liberals sought to revive the economy, restore the currency, and stabilize economic conditions. The government tasked a currency commission with devising a policy to make Austria more competitive within the central European and world economies.

Serving as the lead government representative at the hearings in March 1892, Böhm helped assemble a who's-who of Austrian economists, bankers, and liberal power brokers. Of the thirty-six members of the commission, six were members of the Austrian School. They included Richard Lieben, Viktor Mataja, Emil Sax, and Carl Menger himself. Franz von Juraschek, a jurist and economist, Böhm's close friend, and Friedrich Hayek's grandfather, also participated. So did editors of the major liberal newspapers, *Die Neue Freie Presse* and *Die Wiener Allgemeine Zeitung*, and the directors of the largest banks in the empire. Menger took the lead, advancing a gold standard position. He dominated the proceedings, first with an ardent defense of a gold-based currency, then with a passionate rejoinder to Theodor von Taussig, a conservative banker. Using marginal utility theory, he suggested that money itself was not a neutral medium that objectively measured the value of goods. Relying on two different metals only increased the volatility of prices and values, since each one possessed variable subjective valuations. To reduce uncertainty, a more stable currency regime based on a single precious metal was needed. Menger, with the assist of an inspired defense of gold from Sax, carried the discussion. The government adopted a "shadow" gold standard. Menger declared victory a year later.[6]

Menger, Böhm, and their allies also drove through tax reform. The early Austrians argued for a progressive income tax on liberal and marginalist grounds while advocating for targeted state intervention in economic affairs. Since the time of Maria Theresia and Joseph II in the late eighteenth century, the Habsburg state and its powerful bureaucracy underwent significant expansion, yet revenues lagged behind. Property taxes and indirect taxes did not cover state expenditures. After the unsuccessful wars of the 1860s and the economic downturn of the 1870s, these problems became more acute. By the 1880s, resolving the "social question" added to the state's budgetary woes. The emergence of mass immigration and a poor urban industrial class further threatened the stability of the empire. Liberal Austrians, deeply invested in the Habsburg state, recognized the need for reform to stave off revolution. Austrian officials took a page out of Otto von Bismarck's playbook in the German Reich, proposing welfare, housing, and insurance measures. In order to pay for these proposed changes, liberals argued that the state needed to rationalize its tax code and broaden its revenue base. For the reformers, the Austrian School foremost among them, a direct, personal income tax was deemed necessary to maintain order and shore up the hegemony of the *Bürgertum*.[7]

Members of the Austrian School steered the tax discussions. One of the first and most influential pamphlets calling for a progressive income tax came from Emil von Fürth, a jurist at the university, close ally of the Mengers, and the father of Herbert, a participant in the post–World War I school. Wieser, Auspitz, Mataja, Sax, and Richard Reisch all published articles on taxation. The Austrian parliament consequently convened hearings. Böhm again directed the proceedings. The chairman of the hearings was Carl Menger's brother Max. Thirty-six commissioners participated in nearly fifty sessions between February 1892 and October 1896, when the parliament passed a progressive tax based on individual incomes. Robert Meyer, a student of Carl Menger's, wrote the final legislation. Böhm composed the preamble. Böhm argued that since the wealthy benefited considerably more from state expenditures—through educational opportunities, infrastructure usage, and the protection of property rights—progressive taxation made sense on marginal utility grounds. Each *Thaler* of state expenditure had greater value for the wealthy; hence, they should want to contribute more to the state's coffers.[8]

Any gains from the currency and tax reforms were short-lived. After another crash in 1893, the Austrian economy remained stagnant for years, plagued by persistent deflation—which was exacerbated by the gold standard—that disproportionately hurt the lower classes, whose ranks swelled as conditions worsened. The population of Vienna soared to 1.8 million people in 1900—a 200 percent increase in fifty years—as Habsburg subjects fled crushing poverty in the provinces. Inadequate housing, unemployment, and public health crises plagued the city. This spurred new populist movements like Karl Lueger's antisemitic Christian Social Party and Viktor Adler's Social Democratic Party.[9]

Despite these ongoing social and economic challenges, the Austrian School economists demonstrated a newfound confidence in their ability to shape imperial policy and impose liberal solutions. The bureaucratic and political engagement of the Austrian School in the 1890s represented an increasingly significant dimension of the school's program. This kind of behind-the-scenes engagement and influence peddling remained a defining characteristic of the school. While this activism largely derived from members' liberal values and a concern for the Austrian state, it also arose in response to the threat to the status quo they perceived from Marxism.

Contra Marx(ism)

When Marxist socialism came into its own in the 1890s, liberal economists, especially the Austrians, reacted with alarm. After two decades of political suppression, the Austrian and German states removed their proscriptions on socialist activities in 1888 and 1889, respectively. Austrian socialists founded the Social Democratic Workers' Party (SDAP) under the leadership of Viktor Adler. The Germans followed suit, creating the Social Democratic Party of Germany (SDP) in 1890. Within a decade, the SDP commanded over 27 percent of the vote in national elections. The SDAP received close to 20 percent by 1907. Complementing these developments in central Europe, socialists around the world united to form the Second International in Paris on July 14, 1889, the one hundredth anniversary of the storming of the Bastille. Over four hundred delegates and three hundred organizations from twenty countries participated in the event. Freedom of assembly, collective bargaining rights, franchise reform, and labor legislation figured in socialist party programs, all of which seemed to threaten the dominant political and economic interests of the time, whether conservative Prussian Junkers or the liberal Viennese *Großbürgertum.*[10]

If these developments indicated that Marx-inspired socialism had reached political maturity, the publication of the final volume of Marx's masterwork *Das Kapital* provided an intellectual foundation. Marx had conceived of *Kapital* as a four-volume work; only one appeared during his lifetime. The first volume came out in 1867 and received an immediate international readership. It dealt with the production of capital through the exploitation of labor and the contradictions inherent within the capitalist mode of production. The second volume, edited and released by Friedrich Engels in 1885, treated the circulation of capital within the market system. It highlighted the role of "money owners" and "entrepreneurs" as the agents of capitalist activity. It stressed the social nature of capital creation—social labor made capital growth possible. The third volume appeared in 1894 and focused on questions of profit and interest. It argued that rates of profit tended to decrease over time, suggesting that the capitalist mode of production would eventually cease to produce adequate surplus value to sustain economic growth. The fourth volume on surplus value never appeared in a complete edition. Nevertheless, *Kapital* offered a comprehensive challenge to bourgeois economic theory and set the terms for political and economic debates for the next several decades. Vienna—with its entrenched liberal traditions, vibrant socialist movement, and combative intellectual culture—was ground zero for these conflicts.

Vienna was a natural site for a liberal-Marxist standoff, and Böhm led the charge. As we saw, Austrian economists had leveled sustained criticisms against socialism throughout the 1880s. They also attacked the labor theory of value on which socialists, especially Marxists, built their economic theories. When the third volume of *Kapital* appeared, it found a limited readership among rank-and-file socialists, and it met with a general dismissal from bourgeois economists—except in Vienna. Böhm saw the full dangers of the work and responded at length. In the 1896 *Karl Marx and the Close of His System*, he took Marx to task for the shortcomings of his theory of value and his misrepresentations of the capitalist mode of production. Böhm, already the most illustrious Austrian economist and one of Europe's foremost social scientists, gained an audience across the transatlantic world for this blistering attack. Within two years, multiple editions and translations appeared. His critique of the "transformation problem"—how Marx accounted for the transformation of the value of commodities into market prices—became the starting point for many future Marxist economic theorists.[11]

Although the work was a critical economic appraisal first and foremost, Böhm employed his famous polemical skills in belittling the Marxian position. He disparaged Marx as a writer undeserving of popular or scholarly renown. He contended that the scholarly community had already reached a consensus that Marx's theories were plagued with weaknesses and inconsistencies that should have seen *Kapital* relegated to the dustbin of history. Böhm nevertheless took the task of intellectual vivisection seriously, dismantling Marx's edifice plank by theoretical plank. Böhm claimed to have found a fatal flaw in the Marxian system and its account of the emergence of profit: "To speak plainly his solution is obtained at the cost of the assumption from which Marx has hitherto started, *that commodities exchange according to their values*. This assumption Marx now simply drops." According to Böhm, Marx, using his labor theory, could not explain why profits on the same amount of capital remained the same, regardless of the labor contribution to that capital. To salvage his claim about declining rates of profit, Marx cast aside his foundational assumption that commodities exchange for their labor value. Böhm saw this criticism as the coup de grace against the entire Marxian apparatus: "Marx's third volume contradicts the first. . . . This is the impression which must, I believe, be received by every logical thinker."[12]

Böhm saw the Marx rebuttal as more than a scholarly debate but a struggle over worldviews. After laying waste to Marxian economics, he ventured an alternative vision of economics and, by extension, capitalism. For Böhm, it was not enough to point out the logical fallacies of Marx's system; he had to trace the origins of the errors. These all derived from the "objective" labor theory of value. In its place, a "psychological" theory was needed, which corresponded more closely to the reality of commodity exchange and the valuation of goods. Marx's static labor-value theory stripped capitalism of the very mechanism that explained its dynamism: "Marx's theory of surplus value aims at nothing else than the explanation, as he conceives it, of the profits of capital. But the profits of capital lie exactly in those regular deviations of the prices of commodities from the amount of their mere costs in labor." Marx oversimplified concepts of supply, demand, and competition, denuding them of their force. If one took these concepts seriously—as the marginalists did—one came to opposite conclusions about capitalism and its potential for growth and prosperity.[13]

Central European socialists responded to Böhm's broadside with deadly seriousness. The pamphlet occupied a central position in the incipient "revisionist controversy" in German-speaking central Europe. A unique convergence of events sparked this debate. The rise of socialist parties across Europe spurred optimism within the movement's ranks. Socialists began to reassess their theory and praxis. A key figure in these deliberations was Eduard Bernstein, a friend of Marx's and the executor of Engels's will, who published *Evolutionary Socialism* in 1899. Bernstein advocated for a gradualist rather than a revolutionary transition to socialism, achieved through parliamentary action and government reform. He argued that Marx's economic predictions about the demise of capitalism had not come true. Rather than remaining true to Marx the visionary's conclusions, socialists must follow Marx the scientist's methods and revise their theoretical positions. In challenging Marx's assumptions, Bernstein contested the reliability of the labor theory. He approvingly referenced Böhm to explain commodity production and value creation in capitalist economies. Bernstein maintained that socialists had to reckon with the findings of liberal economists if they wished to create a socialist society.[14]

Leading Marxists viewed Bernstein's work as apostasy. They focused their ire on his use of "bourgeois" economics to update socialist theory. Karl

Kautsky and Vladimir Lenin assailed Bernstein for his abandonment of Marxian socialism and historical materialism. Rosa Luxemburg, the Polish-German Jewish socialist thinker, called out Bernstein for his reliance on faulty theory. She believed that Marx's theory reflected lived social experience under capitalism, while Böhm's utility theory was empty and obfuscating, serving the conservative ideology of the bourgeoisie: "Böhm-Jevons abstract utility is merely a thought picture, or really a picture of thoughtlessness, a private nonsense, for which neither the capitalist nor any other human society can be made responsible, only bourgeois vulgar economics." Böhm's subjectivism, and marginal utility theory more generally, was the expression of monied interests and their shallow, consumerist ethos. By supporting Böhm, Luxemburg argued, Bernstein rejected socialism.[15]

The revisionist controversy produced more heat than light. It highlighted the tensions inherent within the socialist movement between gradualists and revolutionaries, but it did not decide the course of international socialist politics. Nor did it resolve who represented the "true Marx." Perhaps the greatest significance of the feud was its introduction of a new generation of theoreticians such as Luxemburg and Lenin who updated and reshaped Marxism for the twentieth century. "Bourgeois vulgar economics," best exemplified by Böhm and the Austrian School, became the greatest challenge to revolutionary Marxism. Böhm's work had a particularly powerful impact in one site of socialist fertility: coffeehouse Vienna. The burgeoning movement of socialist thinkers associated with Austro-Marxism saw the road to intellectual respectability running through the seminars and treatises of the Austrian School.[16]

Austro-Marxism and the Austrian School

From the cozy confines of Café Central, the famous Viennese coffeehouse, a group of young radicals formulated their responses to Böhm and the intellectual currents pulsing through the city. Max Adler, Otto Bauer, Rudolf Hilferding, and Karl Renner launched the Austro-Marxist movement at a time when the revisionist controversy raged, Sigmund Freud's psychoanalysis took the city by storm, Ernst Mach's ideas inspired a new "logical positivist" philosophy, Viennese modernism reached its apogee, and the Austrian School of economics established its hegemony.

Trained in law, economics, and medicine and inspired by Marxist socialism and idealist philosophy, these Austro-Marxists charted a third way between a series of problematic polarities: between political reform and revolution, between Kantian idealism and Marxist materialism, between deductive theory and empirical practice. Victor Adler, the head of the SDAP, claimed that the movement was not just political but also intellectual: "Marxist thought acts as the most powerful thought lever for the further development of scientific insight, composing a fundamental outlook. However [our studies] also develop a clear and hopefully advantageous image of the areas of specialization in economics, jurisprudence and philosophy that they address as the main currents within social science." Like the Austrian marginalists, the Austro-Marxists wedded scientific insight with social and political concerns. Unsurprisingly, they came into conflict on this shared terrain.[17]

In steering a new course for Marxism, the Austro-Marxists engaged the Austrian School within the latter's institutions. They also created their own. Victor Adler established a foothold within the GÖV, where state socialist views were not uncommon, yet the liberalism of Böhm and his supporters was little disturbed by this incursion. The same was true in the *Zeitschrift*, leading the Austro-Marxists to establish *Marx-Studien* for their theoretical work and *Der Kampf* for practical engagement. Hilferding answered Böhm's verdict on Marxism in *Marx-Studien*. It helped launch Hilferding's career: within a decade of its 1904 publication, he was the foremost Marxist theorist of his generation.

Hilferding offered a careful reading of Böhm's account before rendering a negative verdict. He maintained that Böhm misread Marx, especially on the nature of commodities. Marx's system depended not on the labor theory of value alone but on the social relations that undergirded exchange and the valuation of goods. For Hilferding (and Marx), capitalism and its bourgeois defenders lost track of the social labor that produced goods. Only by returning focus to the role of unalienated labor in social exchange could economists understand the evolution and development of the social world. The error of the psychological school was that its theory of value "starts from the individual relationship between a thing and a human being instead of starting from the social relationships of human beings one with another. This involves the error of attempting from the subjective individual relationship . . . to deduce an objective social measure." In other words, the relationship between the consumer and goods—the starting point of Austrian marginal utility theory—failed to account for the relations of production that made commodities possible in the first place. Only Marx's historical materialism avoided these pitfalls and ensured that "economics is established as a social and historical science."[18]

Hilferding asserted that marginalism would be the death knell of bourgeois economic theory owing to its methodological individualism and its disregard of society. In treating the "individual" as the source of value and as the object of economic science, the marginalists mistook a historically contingent category (the bourgeois *homo economicus*) for a universal one. Their deductions could do no more than confirm the mistaken assumptions and closely held beliefs of the liberal status quo. Marginalism did not signal the victory of bourgeois economics over socialism but its own self-immolation and eventual suicide: "This economic theory signifies the repudiation of economics. The last word in the rejoinder of bourgeois economics to scientific socialism is the *suicide of political economy.*"[19]

Böhm never addressed Hilferding's essay in writing, yet their contretemps played a determinative role in Viennese economic discussions. The exchange between liberals and Marxists left the pages of scholarly journals and reentered the private spaces of *Kaffeeklatsch*, salons, and seminars. Partially in response to the Marx skirmish, Böhm initiated a seminar whose initial meetings were dedicated to socialism. His seminar became a battleground for competing scientific ideas and ideological worldviews. Hilferding took active part, honing his craft in struggles with Austrian School acolytes. Younger thinkers—Hilferding and Bauer, Mises and Schumpeter, the philosopher Otto Neurath—gathered to battle for the soul of Austrian social theory. In this way, Vienna became a microcosm of fin-de-siècle European social science and politics. That the most contentious controversy of early twentieth-century social science erupted in the Austrian capital in 1909 should therefore come as no surprise.

Werturteilsstreit

One thing the Austro-Marxists and the Austrian School shared was a feeling of marginalization, politically and intellectually. Socialists like Hilferding lamented the predominance of Austrian School scholars at

Habsburg educational institutions, and the marginalists complained about their lack of influence in German academics and politics. Struggle was therefore at the heart of their respective projects. If they wanted their viewpoints heard, they had to fight. The fireworks at the 1909 Verein für Socialpolitik congress in Vienna exemplified this confrontational approach to intellectual discourse, as Austrians helped reshape central European social science by disputing the proper relationship between values, scientific method, and policy. As we saw, Hilferding accused the Austrian School of the same sin as the German Historical School—the mingling of ideology and theory. The Austrian economists responded with a forceful articulation of their scientific philosophy and a defense of a "value-free" method.

The *Werturteilsstreit*, or value judgment debate, split Europe's most venerable social scientific association and reoriented the scholarly landscape, joining younger German scholars around Max Weber and Werner Sombart with their Austrian peers against the German orthodoxy. That the culmination of this debate came at a Vienna meeting of the Verein für Socialpolitik attested to the central role that Austrian School scholars played in the shift toward more theoretically rigorous scholarship. The consequent reconfiguration of central European social sciences confirmed the Austrian School's arrival. The consideration of the place of values and ideology in science would remain a feature of the Austrian project henceforth.[20]

By the 1890s, residual tensions between the "younger" Historical School and the Austrians had dissipated. Several German scholars, such as Adolf Wagner and Max Weber, accepted Carl Menger's arguments about the indispensability of theory for scientific investigation. Unresolved, however, was another issue of significance for the Verein für Socialpolitik. As the name of the organization—the Social Policy Association—implied, it was not merely an institution for scientific discussion but also for policy formation. Since its inception, the Verein had courted political favor by offering advice to the German Reich. For Gustav Schmoller, the society's head, ethical and political judgments were indissolubly linked with scientific inquiry. Objectivity was attainable, he maintained, provided that policy recommendations followed logically from scientific investigation and produced social harmony and progress.

Weber and Sombart bristled at the notion that Schmoller and the Verein possessed the key to progress and unity. Their works on capitalism, namely,

Sombart's *Der moderne Kapitalismus* (Modern capitalism) and Weber's *Die Protestantische Ethik und der 'Geist' des Kapitalismus* (*The Protestant Ethic and the Spirit of Capitalism*), suggested that there was no primrose path to the harmonization of all interests in modern society. Moreover, cultural values played a constitutive role in social organizations, meaning that different value systems would produce different policy recommendations. In a famous 1904 essay on objectivity, Weber laid out his research program, which promised a decisive shift from the Verein's policy orientation. Weber posed a series of crucial interpretive questions about objectivity and value judgments: "What is the validity of the value-judgments which are uttered by the critic, for instance, or on which a writer recommending a policy founds his arguments for that policy? In what sense, if the criterion of scientific knowledge is to be found in the 'objective' validity of its results, has he remained within the sphere of scientific discussion?"[21] Weber believed that the Schmoller school confused the "is" with the "ought," assuming that the existing world was the best and only guide for what ought to be. Weber proposed a model that separated scientific research from policy action. Scientists offered evaluations of various courses of actions. The selection of a particular course, however, lay outside the scientist's purview qua scientist. Scientists could inform policy makers about the advisability of their choices, and the scientists could judge choices critically. Claiming that one set of policy preferences was more "scientific" or "objective" was *not* permissible, however: "An empirical science cannot tell anyone what he *should* do—but rather what he *can* do—and under certain circumstances—what he wishes to do." Failing to recognize a distinction between policy and science only undermined the latter.[22]

Weber's objectivity essay signaled a countervailing intellectual tendency in German social scientific circles to Schmoller's hegemonic program. In January 1909, Weber and Sombart created their own organization, the German Society for Sociology. While its members did not withdraw from the Verein, they had drawn battle lines. The 1909 Verein meeting, hosted in Austria for the first time, brought together the schismatic factions, with the Austrian School advocates Eugen von Philippovich and Wieser playing starring roles.

The pyrotechnics exploded during Philippovich's panel on the seemingly anodyne subject of economic productivity. Philippovich claimed that the concept of productivity demanded a better conceptual definition. As was his wont, he tried to mediate between factions. He agreed with the younger Historical School that a concept of productivity solely predicated on the methodological individualism of Adam Smith or the Austrian School was insufficient. However, he averred that the mere compilation of statistics, advocated by the historicists, offered no real hope for social betterment either. He tentatively endorsed Weber's approach to "value-free" science, yet he asserted that the true aim of economics was "the people's well-being [*Volkswohlstand*]." In the final analysis, Philippovich defended the Historical School and its state policies, since the state was the only institution capable of overcoming "special interests" or "momentary desires."[23]

Philippovich's equivocations produced rancor rather than reconciliation. Sombart's response set off a riot. He accused Philippovich of reopening the value judgment debate. How could the Austrian claim that *Volkswohlstand* was the indisputable end of economics? Philippovich had elided his own value judgments in his quest for a more policy-oriented science. Sombart seethed about the shabby state of economics: "Who outside our circle would these days still believe that economics is science?" The assembled crowd erupted in spasms of jeers, cheers, hisses, and screams. Several speakers rose to defend Philippovich. Max Weber interceded to defend Sombart. Weber declared that this dispute was not about "productivity" or "well-being" but about science, politics, and the Verein. The Verein's claims of objectivity rang false: "The intermingling of normative thinking [*Seinsollens*] in scientific questions is the devil's handiwork, with which the Verein für Socialpolitik really too often concerns itself." More chaos ensued.[24]

Though Weber and Sombart ignited the conflict, it was Austrians who drove the discussion. Philippovich and Wieser bookended the debate, and Rudolf Goldscheid, Othmar Spann, and Otto Neurath took active part. Philippovich leveled a blistering attack on Weber's separation of policy and science: "[Economic science] assesses the function of the economy in human society in order to arrive at the foundations for influencing the economy. If you [Weber] do not want to speak here any longer of science . . . well, in my opinion I hold these things as the essence of the development of economics."[25] If policy was not a part of economics, Philippovich did not want to be an economist. Meanwhile Wieser, who served as the official host for the congress, reminded his German guests that they had to reckon with Austrian methodological criticisms if they wanted to maintain their predominance in scientific and policy circles. The historicists could no longer hide behind claims of scientific objectivity or apoliticism.[26]

The Vienna conference did not resolve ongoing tensions between factions. In fact, the resentments and animosities lingered on for decades: as late as 1932, German and Austrian scholars continued to relitigate this fight.[27] Despite this anticlimactic ending, the *Werturteilsstreit* showed that the Austrian School had established itself as one of Europe's foremost social scientific movements by the turn of the century. Within the Habsburg Empire, its members served in prominent positions in the university, the bureaucracy, and the government. In the decade from 1900 to 1910, at least a dozen theses, dissertations, and monographs—and even more articles—appeared that dealt with their ideas, namely, marginal utility theory and the theories of capital and imputation. Studies in German, French, English, Italian, Swedish, and Hungarian attested to the diffusion of Austrian theories. Yet change was on the horizon as the first generation of Austrians reached middle age.

Changing of the Guard: The Austrian School after 1904

At the turn of the century, Böhm was unquestionably the most significant figure in Austrian circles. Dozens of articles dealt with his ideas, including essays from leading lights in the economic community: Enrico Barone, John Bates Clark, Francis Edgeworth, Irving Fisher, Alfred Marshall, F. W. Taussig, Thorsten Veblen, and Knut Wicksell. Writing in 1903, William Scott enthused about *Capital and Interest* and its author: "A glance at the files of the *Political Science Quarterly*, the *Quarterly Journal of Economics*, and the *Annals* indicates that a large proportion of the articles treating of economic theory are either directly upon some phase of Böhm-Bawerk's work or theories, or have been clearly influenced, if not directly inspired, by them." By his 1914 death, Böhm rivaled Alfred Marshall and Léon Walras for the title of world's greatest economist.[28]

By 1904, however, there were signs that the Austrian School was entering a transitional phase. Böhm served full-time in the imperial government and had less and less time for academics. Meanwhile the number of students completing their studies with Menger, Wieser, Sax, or Philippovich declined after 1895. Menger had served as a member of at least fifteen habilitation committees between 1884 and 1895. He had only two more students before his 1903 retirement. Wieser and Sax had a couple of students at the University of Prague, yet they did not participate significantly in Viennese discussions. Wieser's succession to Menger's chair in Vienna only slightly reversed these trends: before the outbreak of the Great War, only one more student (Richard Reisch) received his habilitation and two completed their doctorates (Franz Weiss and Richard Strigl). The school hardly lacked for discussion and debate, yet its future direction was in flux.[29]

The Society of Austrian Economists (GÖV) also experienced intellectual stagnation as Austria underwent a conservative shift. While its membership increased—from 225 in 1892 to 278 in 1911—the Austrian School played a less active role. In 1915, Ernst von Plener, one of Böhm's allies, extolled the contributions of the marginalists to Austrian social science—"The Austrian School produced a transformation here"—yet as early as 1903, those contributions dried up. Böhm left the board; Wieser joined it briefly but departed in 1909. That was also the final year of Philippovich's chairmanship. Thereafter the Austrian School seldom presented at the GÖV.[30]

The Austrian School also experienced a declining influence on Habsburg policy after 1900. Nationalist tensions and politics in a populist key characterized Austria-Hungary in the decades before the Great War, placing German liberals at a disadvantage. After 1893, no party claimed a majority in the Austrian parliament. Between 1904 and 1914, six different chancellors attempted to cobble together ruling coalitions, with limited success. Centrifugal forces began to pull apart the empire. Nationalist groups clamored for greater autonomy, populist parties demanded electoral reform, liberals pursued free trade policies, and conservatives sought tariffs and voting restrictions. The biggest beneficiaries of the changing political landscape made the *Großbürgertum* nervous: the working-class Social Democrats, the petit bourgeois, antisemitic Christian Socials, and the Czech and Polish nationalist parties. Böhm, who had served in the highest echelons of the Habsburg bureaucracy for more than a decade, including three stints as finance minister, retired out of frustration. In doing this, Böhm represented a general tendency within the bourgeoisie. As Carl Schorske argued, many members of the *Bildungsbürgertum* chose to retreat from public life after the "failure" of Austrian liberalism, experiencing feelings of anxiety and impotence in the face of mounting social and political tensions.[31]

In this uncertain moment, the Austrian School members turned to intellectual outlets to maintain their standing, especially the *Zeitschrift*. Böhm had served as editor since the journal's 1892 inception. The Austrian School influence expanded as its members retreated from politics. When the *Zeitschrift* expanded its board from three to five in 1904, it added Wieser and Philippovich. Robert Meyer joined in 1911, meaning that four of the six members had close ties to the school. All were also self-proclaimed liberals. The journal was not a mere mouthpiece for a particular worldview, however. As its title indicated, its remit included issues of social policy and administration as well as theoretical economics. It was in the pages of the *Zeitschrift* that the Austrians refined their ideas and sought continued relevance. School members introduced new themes that advanced the Austrian research program beyond earlier work. For example, Wieser offered a Menger-inspired meditation on the nature of money. He advocated for a new theory that analyzed the historical evolution of monetary exchange, moving beyond "neutralist" theories. He challenged assumptions that changes in the money supply did not affect "real" economic variables like production, consumption, and employment. He insisted that money had to be considered a commodity subject to the same laws of marginal utility as other goods. A searching essay, it played a foundational role in later studies by Mises and Hayek.[32]

Following Wieser and Böhm, a new cohort emerged, which blended Austrian themes with ideas emerging in the international scientific community. Increasingly Vienna served as a node in transatlantic discussions. Many new names graced the pages of the *Zeitschrift*, writing on a variety of subjects. A twenty-three-year-old Ludwig von Mises published his first essay in 1904. It was not a theoretical text—it dealt with retirement policies for Austrian workers—yet it displayed his promise. Mises wrote in the *Zeitschrift* every year thereafter, typically on welfare and labor legislation. Joining him were Schumpeter, Alfred Amonn, Ernst Broda, Hans Mayer, Ewald and Karl Pribram, Felix Somary, and Franz Weiss. With interests that ranged into political and social theory, jurisprudence and mathematics, they reinforced the earlier interdisciplinary commitments of the school.[33]

A quick survey of this group's theoretical output shows continuity with earlier Austrian School thought but also important innovations. Franz

Weiss amplified Wieser's work on money. He demanded clearer differentiation between common usage and scientific conceptualizations of the monetary phenomenon. Drawing on Schumpeter's recent work, he brought Jevons, Marshall, Walras, and Wicksell into Austrian discussions. This also put Weiss's work in close conversation with that of Mises, who combined Austrian ideas with Wicksell's concepts.[34] Meanwhile Alfred Amonn demanded even greater theoretical abstraction than his mentors did. Amonn felt that economists had to go back one level of abstraction further: instead of focusing on the concept of goods first, they had to examine the very nature of economic concepts. Amonn demanded a renewed attention to methods of inductive observation, a subject implied but overlooked by his mentors. Like Amonn, the next two generations of Austrians grappled with the interaction of theoretical and empirical research more directly than their mentors had.[35]

The emergence of this new generation relied on two modes of interaction. First, there were vertical connections to mentors. Böhm and Wieser sustained these scholars and their earliest work, and the founders' ideas served as the basis for research. Equally important, however, were the horizontal ties between cohort members. The younger Austrians responded to one another's work, using their exchanges in classes, seminars, and salons to sharpen their ideas. A closer look at the leading lights of this generation—Schumpeter and Mises—illustrates these dynamics. Each man wrestled with conformity and creativity, viewing his relationship to the Austrian School as a source of inspiration and opposition.

Joseph Schumpeter's Early Successes

Johanna Schumpeter always envisioned grand things for her son, Jozsi. A member of a prosperous German Moravian family, she moved to Graz shortly after the death of Joseph's father. There she met and married a three-star general thirty-one years her senior. The family moved to Vienna in 1893, for it was the only city in the Habsburg Empire that could satisfy the ambitions of the young woman and her precocious son. The Schumpeters inhabited a stately residence behind the Parliament and the Ringstrasse. Using the general's connections, Joseph attended the Theresianum, the most prestigious high school in the empire and a school where education took a back seat to networking and politicking. Schumpeter thrived. Upon graduation in 1901, he matriculated at the University of Vienna with the plan of entering the civil service.[36]

Schumpeter laid claim to the mantle of the Austrian School with his first publications while still in school. Schumpeter, who studied under Böhm, Wieser, and Philippovich, wasted no time jumping into the methodological controversies swirling around the Austrian School. In 1906, Schumpeter published his first essay, asserting that economics required greater methodological precision. Finding the earlier divisions of the *Methodenstreit* passé and unproductive, Schumpeter believed that mathematical forms could offer clarity for both "historical" and "exact" economic approaches. Citing work by Jevons, Walras, Pareto, and Fisher, Schumpeter maintained that mathematics, properly deployed, could further economics by offering better tools for analyzing empirical data and more formal definitions of core theoretical concepts. Schumpeter's intervention set the stage for another round of methodological discussions, especially in Viennese circles.[37]

Schumpeter's early work dismayed his mentors because of his apparent preference for Walras's mathematical approach. That said, Böhm and Wieser still admired him greatly. Böhm not only invited his first scholarly publications but also included him in the seminar that would launch his intellectual career: a 1905 colloquium on Marx. There, he sparred with Hilferding, Mises, and Otto Bauer, the future head of the Austrian Social Democratic Party. After graduation in 1906, Schumpeter led a rakish, peripatetic life. He traveled Europe, networking with German, French, and English economists and mingling in high society. He married an older, upper-class Englishwoman and journeyed to Cairo, where he worked in a corporate law firm and handled the finances of an Egyptian princess.

His intellectual interests did not stray far from economics during these years. He began work on his 1908 text, *Das Wesen und der Hauptinhalt der theoretischen Nationalökonomie* (The essence and content of theoretical economics), while gallivanting abroad. Schumpeter intended the book as his major contribution to social science. It also displayed his ambivalence about belonging to any school. He hoped to overcome the lingering divisions within the economics profession by striking a conciliatory tone: "The oppositions within our discipline come to seem unbridgeable. . . . This is not my standpoint. . . . Almost every 'approach' and every individual author is justified in his claims." Like his peers Amonn and Weiss, Schumpeter thought that synthesis rather than dogmatic conflict would advance economics. He wanted to dispense with the notions of "systems" or "schools" entirely: "It is merely on the grounds of expediency that I speak of a 'Ricardo System,' of the 'Austrian School,' etc." In spite of his cautious attitude toward the elder Austrians, he admitted that he owed his greatest debt to Wieser and Léon Walras, "nearest to whom I stand."[38]

After making a case for a more pragmatic and less contentious economics, Schumpeter directed his focus to the concept of equilibrium, an area where he believed theoretical economics could still develop. Since the publication of Walras's 1874 book, economists had taken great interest in general equilibrium theory, which elucidated how the interaction of supply and demand led to sets of prices that cleared markets. Walras created a system of simultaneous equations to solve for those complex market interactions. Schumpeter believed that Walras's model was a good start, but it was inadequate for understanding dynamic, evolving economies— that is, real, existing capitalism. He observed that equilibrium could be either static—which captured an economy at a discrete moment—or dynamic. Pure theory had thus far only really dealt with the former. He would do the same in *Wesen*, hewing closely to Walras. In drawing attention to dynamic economic models, however, he raised a key concern that animated subsequent Austrian critiques of equilibrium economics, especially his own—that models of general equilibrium based on static assumptions tell us little about actual economic systems.[39]

While *Wesen* did not receive the éclat he desired, it was reviewed in every major economics journal, and it helped launch Schumpeter's academic career. It received mostly favorable assessments from Schumpeter's Austrian colleague Hans Mayer and the American John Bates Clark. Most significantly, Walras responded positively to Schumpeter's treatment of equilibrium. Riding this success, Schumpeter rose quickly in the Habsburg academy. In 1909, he received a tenured appointment at the University of Czernowitz in the easternmost province of the empire. He completed much of his early masterpiece, *The Theory of Economic Development*, there. Two years later, the University of Graz came calling, naming him the youngest full professor in the realm. Schumpeter received his promotion over the objections of the Graz Law Faculty, where several members saw him as a sterile theorist. Böhm allegedly intervened with the Ministry of Education to ensure his pupil's success. This move back to Austria permitted him to make regular trips to Vienna and to participate in its economic discussions.[40]

If *Wesen* opened the door for Schumpeter, it was *The Theory of Economic Development* that cemented his reputation. Significantly, the latter work was also more grounded in Austrian School thought. With *Wesen*, Schumpeter had tried to put some distance between himself and his mentors; in *Theory*, he foregrounded the Austrian foundations of his thought. Schumpeter wanted to extend his earlier work from static models into an examination of the dynamic processes of the modern economy. Looking at the flow of goods through production and consumption cycles, Schumpeter betrayed his indebtedness to Wieser, Böhm, and Menger on every page. He deployed Böhm's theory of roundabout means of production to explain economic change, and he referenced approvingly Menger's theory of higher-order goods. Working from a position of methodological individualism—that is, that economic investigation must start by examining the actions of individuals—he showed how marginal utility theory explained economic activity.[41]

As much as Schumpeter liked economic models, he reveled more in uncertainty. Equilibrium was the exception, not the rule, in complex economic systems. Schumpeter demonstrated that complications arise as soon as one introduces change. Natural disasters disrupt markets, wars decimate city and country, technological advances alter the possibilities of production and exchange—all of these affect economic conditions. Discussing the impacts of broader natural and social phenomena, Schumpeter made a deliberate move beyond the static models of Walras. A more realistic image of the actual economy required more than mathematics and models, so Schumpeter turned to sociology and psychology. At the center of his dynamic model was the entrepreneur, a concept with which he would become synonymous. He developed this concept from Böhm's entrepreneur and Wieser's notion of speculative behavior. Like his predecessors, Schumpeter recognized that some individuals take greater risks to acquire more goods. In pressing their advantage, they transform values and disrupt economic stasis. This was how capitalism functioned best, ensuring constant change and future opportunity. Schumpeter called this process "creative destruction," which served as the basis for his theory of innovation and development and for his most famous theoretical contribution.[42]

By the time Schumpeter was thirty, he had established himself as the most important young economist in the Habsburg Empire. His elders, Böhm and Wieser, recommended him for positions and saluted his intellect and ambition. However, each book also elicited vituperative criticisms from them—Wieser on *Wesen* and Böhm on *Theory*. These interactions reveal the anxieties of influence within the early Austrian School. More importantly they illuminate the school's interactional style. To be a true member of the clan, a scientist had to be prepared for intellectual combat, for only ideas worth defending merited serious consideration.

"Whoever Accepts Our Results Must Also Accept Our Methods"

In reviewing *Wesen*, Wieser rendered an ambivalent verdict. Wieser was fulsome in praising Schumpeter's learning and eloquence, saying he "combine[d] scientific acuity with artistic freedom." When it came to clarifying economics' methodological foundations, however, Wieser categorically dismissed Schumpeter's approach. Wieser felt duty bound to reply because of the affinity between his and Schumpeter's work. He feared that Schumpeter's views would be too closely identified with his own: "Schumpeter indeed adheres very closely to the theoretical orientation to which I belong, and he names me as one of the authors with whom he most closely associates, but for my part I must declare that he only agrees with this orientation in its results while he rejects its psychological method. . . . Whoever accepts our results must also accept our methods." Wieser argued that one could not accept marginal utility theory without accepting its subjectivist method. In Schumpeter's synthesis of different methodological approaches, he arrived at an impossible muddle. Moreover, Wieser believed that Schumpeter mistakenly used the techniques of the natural sciences to shackle the humanities.[43]

Based on the harshness of Wieser's accusations, one could read Wieser's review as a repudiation of Schumpeter's project, yet it was more a chastisement than a rejection. Yes, Wieser called into question Schumpeter's "positivist" epistemology. He dismissed Schumpeter's command of capital theory and marginal utility. Nevertheless, Wieser's *real* objection stemmed from the younger scholar's lèse-majesté. He applauded Schumpeter's stated respect for tradition. With no small degree of condescension, however, he accused Schumpeter of failing to honor that obligation, thereby displaying the impetuousness of youth: "Maybe one day he will learn that methodology must not be the first but the last undertaking of a systematizer. . . . One feels that the author has not yet arrived at a balance and must yet learn to limit himself. Such youthful overreach is the most commendable of all errors; it is the symptom of a great strength." In these words, Wieser combined a personal and a professional attack. The German word for balance (*Gleichgewicht*) is also the technical term for equilibrium. Wieser was suggesting that Schumpeter lacked equanimity and adequate economic acumen. Despite this, Wieser's polemic was neither a disavowal nor an excommunication. In his later work, Wieser referred to Schumpeter's scholarship with approval, and he endorsed Schumpeter's career advancement at every turn. Wieser did not wish to blacklist his pupil; he merely wanted to clip his wings.[44]

The dispute between Schumpeter and Böhm over *Theory* evinced similar characteristics although the disagreements were more fundamental. Schumpeter's ideas about capital and interest flew in the face of Böhm's. Böhm rejected Schumpeter's contention that interest would not exist in a "static" economy. Interest was an a priori feature of all economic systems owing to the role of time, Böhm argued, making the very consideration of an interest-less world nonsensical. To deny the premise that humans valued future goods less than present ones meant the rejection of economic reasoning in toto. In a sixty-page takedown essay, Böhm marshaled his considerable polemical gifts to decimate Schumpeter's approach because "heresy demands it. Too bad that a talent with such a mind and a command of language . . . is not paired with a higher degree of patience and self-criticism."[45]

Nevertheless, Böhm extended certain courtesies to Schumpeter that suggested a hope for future reconciliation. Böhm esteemed Schumpeter's talent and believed him a potential ally, so he permitted the younger Austrian to respond in the *Zeitschrift*. Moreover, he deigned to answer Schumpeter's reply, thereby treating Schumpeter with the respect he often denied to opponents. The two men did not reach an understanding—if Schumpeter was conciliatory, Böhm was intransigent; but Schumpeter did not repudiate his connections to Böhm, nor was he excommunicated from the Austrian School.

Schumpeter answered Böhm's assault with characteristic self-deprecation and irony. He emphasized his indebtedness to Böhm and downplayed their differences. He insisted that the discrepancies between his and Böhm's ideas could be attributed to weaknesses in the presentation of his own theory rather than fundamental disagreements. Schumpeter suggested that he differed from Böhm only on a minor point regarding interest—for Böhm, interest owed to a psychological phenomenon of how humans experience time; for Schumpeter, it related to a historical and sociological reality. Schumpeter ultimately resorted to irony to defuse the standoff. Schumpeter paid fealty to his "highly esteemed teacher and critic," making the wry observation, "let it be said that Böhm-Bawerk's judgment seems to me to be far too mild for someone who committed even a fraction of the errors of which he accuses me." If Schumpeter *had* committed the sins of which he was accused, Böhm's condemnation needed to be even harsher.[46] Böhm rejected Schumpeter's defense, for if one rejected the marginalists' subjective theory of value, one rejected their entire theory. Nevertheless, Böhm still held out hope for the young Austrian. In closing his reply, he flipped Schumpeter's modest proposal for reconciliation on its head: "If he [Schumpeter] pleaded the case that one not reject the good and the fruitfulness of his basic premises on the basis of a deficient presentation on his part, I would believe the reverse: not that a good thing has fallen victim to a poor presentation but that a generally dedicated, perceptive and competent author has fallen victim to an idea that does not permit an irreproachable presentation." Schumpeter's positions in *Theory* were wrong, yet the man himself remained a capable economist and theoretician.[47]

The exchange of ironical barbs and clever repartee reflected the mode of the Austrian School specifically and modernist Vienna in general. The famed literary critic and cultural icon Karl Kraus best embodied this spirit. For over forty years, he published the satirical journal *Die Fackel*, which pilloried callow politicians and artistic and intellectual mediocrities, while offering scathing criticisms of sloppy language and fuzzy thinking. According to the Nobel Prize–winning author Elias Canetti, *Die Fackel* was the defining literary magazine of the fin-de-siècle and interwar eras. Discussing intellectual disputes, Kraus wrote, "I have often been asked to be fair and view a matter from all sides. I did so, hoping something might improve if I viewed all sides of it. But the result was the same. So I went back to viewing things only from one side, which saves me a lot of work and disappointment. For it is comforting to regard something as bad and be able to use one's prejudice as an excuse."[48] Good polemics demanded satire and unfairness. It also was not enough to win one's dispute with intellectual foes; one had to best adversaries in style. Schumpeter and Böhm excelled in these arts and used the tools of the *Gymnasium* and coffeehouse to great effect. Although one can discern the beginnings of a rift between the Böhm and Wieser branches of the Austrian School in this interaction—Böhm's sterner deductivism and theoretical orientation differed from Wieser's (and Schumpeter's) more historical and sociological preferences—the Austrian economic project was still a generally unified one, since its members shared so many cultural, intellectual, and institutional ties.[49]

Schumpeter and Böhm moved on quickly from the dustup. Schumpeter wrote a review of recent economic literature that effusively praised marginal utility theory and the Austrian School. Böhm demonstrated his magnanimity in the final essay of his lifetime, approvingly citing the Schumpeter review. That same year Schumpeter wrote the definitive eulogy of Böhm, a seventy-five-page encomium to the man's greatness. Any animus between the two was short-lived.[50]

If Schumpeter's apprenticeship under Wieser and Böhm and his temporary alienation betrayed the anxiety of influence, Ludwig von Mises's later conversion to marginalism permitted somewhat smoother interactions with his elders. That said, his rise to prominence within the Austrian School took longer than it did for the wunderkind Schumpeter, owing partly to Mises's own origins.

Ludwig von Mises

Ludwig von Mises was born in 1881 to an ennobled German Jewish family in Lemberg, Galicia (present-day Lviv, Ukraine). His grandfather served on the board of two Galician railroad ventures and worked for the Austrian National Bank, earning his noble title for financial service to the empire. His father and uncle were railroad engineers, the latter becoming a prominent proindustrialization journalist in Vienna. The family relocated to Vienna circa 1883 just after Ludwig's brother, the mathematician Richard von Mises, was born.[51]

Mises benefited from the typical education of the *Bildungsbürgertum*, attending the prestigious Akademisches Gymnasium, the oldest high school in Vienna and the second oldest in the empire. Located in the city's historic center, its neo-Gothic home was designed during the peak of the *Gründerzeit* by the famed architect Friedrich Schmidt, who also designed the new Rathaus. The school attracted the intellectual and political elite of the realm. The Exner, Lieben, and Benedikt clans sent their scions there. The composer Franz Schubert, playwright Johann Nestroy, architect Otto Wagner, author Arthur Schnitzler, and poet Hugo von Hofmannsthal number among its artist alumni, and Lise Meitner and Erwin Schrödinger count among its scientists. Heads of political parties, ministers, chancellors, and presidents litter the school's alumni list. In other words, Mises received the best education in the Austrian Empire and benefited from the enormous cultural capital that the elite institution imparted. For example, one of his earliest friends was the jurist Hans Kelsen, the author of the constitution of the post–World War I Austrian Republic. Even among this group, Mises was *primus inter pares*; he was the only pupil in his cohort with an aristocratic title. Like Schumpeter, the young Mises prepared "to take an active part in the great issues of his age."[52]

After high school, Mises matriculated at the University of Vienna to pursue a law degree. Among his peers were Kelsen, Bauer, and two future Austrian presidents, Karl Renner and Michael Hanisch. Carl Grünberg, an economic historian, took Mises under his wing and directed Mises's thesis on Galician feudal relations. Empirical and historical tendencies, which Mises later repudiated, characterized his earliest scholarly output. He wrote on Austrian factory legislation, labor law, and welfare legislation in his first articles. Although he read Menger's *Principles* and learned marginal utility theory in Philippovich's seminar, it was not until 1907 that his work displayed telltale signs of a reorientation. Böhm's private seminar must have played a decisive role, though Wieser's inaugural university address on monetary theory may have provided stimulation too. After graduation, Mises worked as a bureaucrat and lawyer, but he published on banking and monetary theory in his spare time. His work attracted the attention of leading bankers and members of the Böhm seminar, like Otto Neurath and Walther

Federn, an editor of the economics journal *Der Österreichischer Volkswirt*. Mises's intellectual maturation culminated in *The Theory of Money and Credit* (1912), which established him within the Austrian School and helped orient the school toward new concerns like monetary theory and business cycles.[53]

Theory elaborates Menger's ideas about money and then presses into new terrain. Using marginal utility theory, Mises hoped to devise a sound model for money and credit:

> Demonstration of the fact that search for the determinants of the objective exchange-value of money always leads us back to a point where the value of money is not determined in any way by its use as a medium of exchange, but solely by its other functions, prepares the way for developing a complete theory of the value of money on the basis of the subjective theory of value and its peculiar doctrine of marginal utility.
>
> Until now the subjective school has not succeeded in doing this.[54]

By "other functions," Mises meant that the item used for monetary exchange had to have a value determined by use-value and not by exchange-value. Depicting money's origins as a commodity that was subject to the laws of exchange, he demonstrated that the theory of subjective value applied equally to monetary theory.[55] This reasoning served as the basis for his defense of commodity-based currencies like gold, since they possessed a known, more stable value. Mises argued that these insights led to a new monetary theory. The theory challenged the dominant Quantity Theory of money, which stated that prices of goods are determined by the money supply, that is, the amount of money in circulation. Finally, by stressing the subjective features of valuation, he distinguished himself from Böhm and Wieser, who still posited a quantifiable relationship between subjective values and goods. According to Mises, the elder Austrians did not fully allow for the instability of those valuations over time in their search for quantifiability.[56]

With the marginalist premises for the origins and functions of money established, Mises built out a comprehensive theory explaining economic booms and busts as the product of expansionist credit policies enacted by the state. With this insight, Mises offered his longest-lasting contribution to economic thought. He pinpointed the impacts of changes in the money supply on the social, economic, and political worlds, a major innovation in the Austrian approach. When the value of money changed, it had serious social consequences. Since inflation and deflation unevenly affect economic participants, discrete classes of individuals are impacted differently. Because of the baleful effects of price instability, modern states turned to monetary interventions to forestall crises. Ironically these actions only exacerbated problems. By manipulating the price of money through the creation of currency, the state did not change the fundamental values of existing commodities; instead, it distorted the relationship between prices and value. Mises therefore rejected deflationary and inflationary fiduciary measures, though the latter for him was the graver problem. Rising wages and prices produced an illusion of economic growth, setting the economy up for a fall.[57]

Mises devoted much of *Theory* to exploring problems created by expanding the money supply and raising interest rates beyond their "natural" rates. In particular, he examined the role of banks and their use of "fiduciary media." As Mises recognized, our modern system of fractional reserve banking is based on fiduciary media. When banks issue loans, they are not typically covered by actual deposits. Their reserves represent only a fraction of their total liabilities. Mises identified this kind of expansionary credit creation with inflation, which produced booms—and then busts: "The moment must eventually come when no further extension of the circulation of fiduciary media is possible. Then the catastrophe occurs, and its consequences are the worse and the reaction against the bull tendency of the market the stronger, the longer the period during which the rate of interest on loans has been below the natural rate of interest and the greater the extent to which roundabout processes of production that are not justified by the state of the capital market have been adopted."[58] In these sections, Mises extended the insights of two theorists: Böhm and the Swedish economist Knut Wicksell. Wicksell argued that the divergence of the "money" interest rate (the rate used in indirect, money-based exchange) from the "natural" rate (direct exchange, or barter) determined whether price levels remained stable or fluctuated. Mises acknowledged the existence of a natural rate, yet he denied that divergences owed to the use of money as a medium of exchange. Deviations stemmed from fiduciary media, not money itself. Using Böhm's theory of roundabout production methods, Mises argued that artificially low interest rates encouraged entrepreneurs to increase their capital investments, since roundabout production processes were more remunerative in low-interest environments. These decisions led to the overextension of credit and a shortage of liquid assets. Collapse occurred if confidence in the solvency of the banking system wavered. By drawing connections between money and money substitutes, interest rates and inflation, and finally business cycles, Mises diagnosed some of the potential problems with modern banking and credit. He also laid the foundations for a sustained critique of intervention in monetary policy, which he took up in earnest during and after the Great War.

Theory met with a mixed reception internationally, yet it helped establish Mises within Austria. Mises's book was reviewed in Austria, England, Italy, Germany, and the United States; the reviewers included Wicksell and a young John Maynard Keynes. The latter's review is superficial and glib, yet it articulated many of the criticisms expressed by others. Keynes found the book " 'enlightened' in the highest degree possible," but its abstractness offered little constructive insight into monetary or banking policy. Mises's predilection for "criticism of imperfect theories" was an inadequate substitute for creative thinking. Keynes, who did not read the book too closely, passed a damning verdict on Mises—and the Austrian School: "Dr. Mises strikes an outside reader as being the very highly educated pupil of a school, once of great eminence, but now losing its vitality." Keynes did not deny Mises's brilliance—he merely wished that *Theory* had been more informative: "One closes the book, therefore, with a feeling of disappointment that an author so intelligent, so candid, and so widely read should, after all, help one so little to a clear and constructive understanding of the fundamentals of his subject." This was the first of several dust-ups between Keynes and the Austrian School.[59]

If Keynes's commentary was perfunctory and polemical, Wicksell's treatment was the opposite. His overall impression was similarly ambivalent, however. Wicksell described the book as "fluent" and "earnest," and Mises deserved credit for "honoring the ideas of his predecessors, which form the foundations of his own work." Nevertheless, Wicksell deemed that Mises had not succeeded in constructing a coherent theoretical edifice: "He is not immune from a general tendency for eclectic, indecisive statements on treated subjects; all-too-vague, insufficiently developed claims and indeed open contradictions arise not infrequently." Wicksell could not figure out how Mises managed to arrive at similar conclusions to his own given the logical steps the Austrian followed. In contrast to Keynes, Wicksell maintained that the strongest aspect of Mises's work was its practical, not its theoretical, side. When Mises descended from "the vertiginous heights of abstract theory to approach the realm of practical monetary matters," his work shone. He struggled to see how Mises's book surpassed Wieser's or his own. While positively disposed to the book on the whole, Wicksell concluded that Mises should have reflected more on his subject so that his theorizing could catch up with his descriptive abilities.[60]

Perhaps most disappointing for Mises was the mixed reaction from his Austrian mentors. In comparison to Schumpeter, Mises did not receive the same engagement or support. While Böhm's seminar devoted two semesters to *Theory*, Böhm did not review the book or even reference it. Neither Philippovich nor Wieser discussed Mises's work in their respective textbooks, the *Grundriß der politischen Ökonomie* or *Social Economics*. Philippovich's best-selling book, first published in 1893 and entering its ninth edition in 1919, only mentioned Mises's earlier, historicist essays. Even more galling was Wieser's omission, given the centrality of *Social Economics* for the Austrian School's self-understanding. Hayek called *Social Economics* "the only systematic treatise on general economic theory produced by the older Austrian school." While Wieser included *Theory* in the bibliographic entry on credit and money alongside fifty-five other sources, that was the extent of his acknowledgment. Professionally, Mises did not enjoy the support Schumpeter received. He was not advanced as a candidate for university jobs despite his qualifications. This might have been because of Mises's Jewish origins or his irascible temperament, but it nevertheless signaled that his stature lagged behind Schumpeter and several others. In brief, *Theory* gained Mises entry into the economics debates of the 1910s and demonstrated Mises's potential, but Mises himself was not yet seen as the central figure in the next generation of the Austrian School.[61]

The Böhm-Bawerk *Privatseminar*

If Mises's mentors were uninterested in his work, as were many international economists, within Viennese cultural circles, *Theory* experienced a resounding reception. Conservatives, liberals and socialists, philosophers, and social scientists responded to the work. The most heated disputes took place in Böhm's seminar. No fewer than four participants— Schumpeter, Hilferding, Otto Neurath, and Nikolai Bukharin—addressed the book in their own writings. Schumpeter commended Mises for the "strength and originality of his critique," while Hilferding dismissed it as the final death rattle of the "false premises [of] the subjective theory of value." These discordant positions reflected the contentiousness of late imperial Austrian intellectual debates. Böhm's *Privatseminar* became a microcosm of the battles between socialism and liberalism, marginal utility and Marxist economics, and deductive and inductive social sciences. It also shows how bourgeois cultural institutions played a determinative role in the development of not just the Austrian School but also central and eastern European politics and science.[62]

Böhm began offering his regular seminar in 1905, shortly after he resigned as minister of finance. It ran until August 1914, when the outbreak of the Great War, followed closely by Böhm's death, put an abrupt end to the proceedings. Unfortunately, we only have spotty recollections of the seminar—there are no minutes, records, or contemporary accounts of the meetings. The periods 1905–6 and 1912–14 appear to have been the most fertile. The first era involved conversations on socialism and Marxism, coming on the heels of the Böhm-Hilferding debate on Marx's *Kapital*. The second period concentrated on money and interest, using Schumpeter's *Theory of Economic Development* and Mises's *Theory of Money* as centerpieces. In the early years, the key participants were Mises, Schumpeter, and Hilferding; Felix Somary, a future professor, banker, and finance expert; Emil Lederer, a future professor of economics and an editor of the prestigious journal *Archiv für Sozialwissenschaft und Sozialpolitik;* Otto Neurath, member of the Vienna Circle of logical positivism and an unorthodox socialist; and Otto Bauer, leader of the younger Austro-Marxists. Ewald and Karl Pribram, the latter an expert on economic statistics, also attended the early meetings. Richard Strigl, a theorist in Böhm's mold and another future economics professor, and Nikolai Bukharin, the Bolshevik radical, entered the debates in the seminar's latter phase.[63]

As with most Vienna *Kreise* (circles), the Böhm seminar intersected many Habsburg intellectual streams. Modernist Vienna was a series of overlapping circles, joined together by family and school ties, institutional affiliations, and shared cultural values. The Pribrams, for example, represent a fascinating case study. Born in Prague to an ethnic German family, Karl and Ewald's father was president of the workers' insurance firm that employed Franz Kafka. Their brother, Franz, was an intimate of the author, and all three Pribram boys attended the same Prague high school. They formed the core of the Prague Circle of literary modernists, alongside Kafka, Max Brod, Felix Weltsch, and Franz Werfel. Related on their mother's side to the philosopher Karl Popper's family, their uncles Alfred and Richard were professors of medicine and chemistry, respectively. Karl and Ewald matriculated at the University of Vienna to study economics; there they entered Böhm's circle. After graduation, they worked at the Central Office for Housing Reform alongside Mises, Robert Meyer, and Emil Fürth. Ewald married Marianne Fürth, Emil's sister. Karl became an eminent statistician, advising the Austrian and German states on war planning during the Great War.[64]

The Böhm seminar brought distinguished figures like the Pribrams into an eclectic assemblage of talents. The 1905–6 discussions established the seminar's stature, igniting debates that carried forward for nearly two decades. Ostensibly about the theory of value, the colloquy evolved into a referendum on marginal utility and scientific socialism. The arguments between Böhm and Bauer, two of Austria's sharpest polemicists, raged night after night throughout the winter of 1905–6. Hilferding also entered the fray. Finally the notoriously contrarian Neurath must have voiced his views, since he made a name for himself at this time as an expert on socialist economics and planning. Mises found the arguments of his opponents, especially Neurath, risible: "babblers sometimes abused the freedom to speak that was allowed participants. Especially disruptive was the nonsense that Otto Neurath asserted with fanatical force."[65] Neurath espoused an unconventional economics inspired by the work of his father, Wilhelm. Neurath *fils* criticized modern economics and capitalist society, including the Fabians and Marxists, for overly materialist assumptions. He argued for a close interaction between economic theory, social science, and practical life. In particular, he objected to the abstraction and deductiveness of the Austrian School. He took the Austrian School and the marginalists to task for their overgeneralizations about free competition, the autonomy of markets, and the concept of *homo economicus*. Showing the influence of

Ernst Mach's philosophy, he argued that ideas like wealth, wants, and value were relationally determined and required a sociological, not economic, explanation grounded in empirical research. He called into question the foundations of the Austrian School despite the "wide dissemination of Austrian value theory." He targeted Böhm and Schumpeter and their methodological individualism. To effect real change in the world, he argued, one had to balance deduction, empiricism, and praxis. In these discussions, Neurath formulated views that characterized his more famous later activities as a ringleader in the Vienna Circle of logical empiricism.[66]

While the lucubrations of Neurath enlivened the proceedings, the seminar centered on the relationship between theory and policy and the evolution of capitalism, topics that divided Schumpeter, Mises, and Hilferding. We have seen how Schumpeter used the idea of the entrepreneur to construct a theory of economic development that explained the logic and vitality of capitalist society. Mises in turn charted the role of money in economic exchange and the outsized role of monetary policy and credit in business cycles. His *Theory* can be read as a defense of conservative, deflationary monetary policy and, to a lesser extent, austerity politics. Hilferding also wished to explore modern financial conditions but from a Marxist perspective. If his 1902 Marx essay was a defensive maneuver against the depredations of Böhm, *Finance Capital* (1910) represented a positive neo-Marxist program. He confronted not only bourgeois critics but also the "revisionists" within the socialist camp, like Neurath and Eduard Bernstein. In the confines of the Böhm seminar, Hilferding fleshed out the core arguments of his magnum opus. The book bears the imprint of repeated exchanges with Schumpeter and particularly Mises. Hilferding introduced *Finance Capital* as an inquiry into money and capital. Only by examining the "processes of concentration" that eliminate free competition in industry and the ever-closer relationship of bank and industrial capital— which he calls "finance capital"—can one grasp the contours of "the current phase of capitalism," with its cycles of boom and bust. He also offered a penetrating observation about the connection between finance capital and imperialism. Because of capitalism's need for continued expansion, and the industrial and financial sectors' desperate quest for profits, capitalists constantly sought new sources of raw materials, new markets for goods, and new sites for capital investment. This tendency led to larger and larger empires, based on economic imperatives but sustained by political and military force. Contrary to liberal apologists, Hilferding rejected the idea that capitalism was inherently pacifistic; capitalist expansion came at the tip of a bayonet.[67]

Seminar participant Otto Bauer enthused that *Finance Capital* was the logical extension of Marx's work. Socialists across the spectrum, from the German democratic socialist Karl Kautsky to Vladimir Lenin, referred to the text favorably. The impacts of Hilferding's monograph also extended to the broader Viennese world. Schumpeter and other Austrian School members found it easy to reject his social theory of money, but his critical observations about monopolies, high finance, and imperialism proved more challenging. Schumpeter and Mises tackled these problems in their own ways. Like Hilferding, Schumpeter devoted considerable attention to the relationship between capitalism and imperialism, and he acknowledged the penetration of Hilferding's insight. He agreed that capitalism had a tendency toward cartelization, monopoly prices, aggressive economic and foreign policy, and war. That said, it was political action and not the logic of competition and capitalism that produced those phenomena. He therefore rejected Hilferding's historical argument about the nexus of finance capital and imperialism: "It is fundamentally false that imperialism is a necessary stage of capitalism. . . . We have seen that imperialistic dispositions are in fact unfavorable for the life form of the capitalist world." Schumpeter maintained that capitalism tended toward peace.[68]

Mises responded in two ways: arguing for a necessary connection between *socialism* and imperialism and downplaying the deleterious effects of monopolies and concentrated capital. Mises took up the first position in his postwar *Nation, State, and Economy* (1919), when he flipped Hilferding's argument on its head. Only a liberal capitalist society, he averred, could safeguard civilization from socialism and its authoritarian, imperialistic tendencies. Since socialism required heavy state intervention in the economy, it also encouraged interstate rivalry and violence. Liberalism, on the other hand, engendered irenic relations between individuals based on noncoercive economic exchange. Meanwhile Mises made his monopoly argument most forcefully in *Socialism* (1922), which attacked socialist arguments about concentration of capital. Mises did not deny the existence of monopolies in capitalist economies, but he argued that their distortive impact on prices and efficiency were greatly exaggerated. Monopolies were often short-lived and were more often the product of state intervention rather than market conditions. It was best to leave the market to deal with monopolies. He repeated these claims for the rest of his life, inculcating them as core principles within the Austrian School tradition.

Schumpeter and Mises continued the battle with Hilferding and Bauer for the next two decades. This was no mere theoretical debate, after all. The Austro-Marxists distinguished themselves in the intellectual world as early theorizers of nationalism and imperialism and as subtle Marxist theorists. Karl Renner's *Staat und Nation* (*State and Nation*) (1899), Bauer's *Die Nationalitätenfrage und die Sozialdemokratie* (*The Question of Nationalities and Social Democracy*) (1907), and Hilferding's *Finance Capital* challenged liberal assumptions that democratic capitalist societies ensured peaceful coexistence. Recognizing the reality of ethnic conflict, which was exacerbated by economic competition between states, they questioned the imperial geopolitical order. While they supported the survival of a reformed, democratized, and decentralized Habsburg Empire, they did not share Schumpeter's or Mises's sanguine attitudes. With the outbreak of the Great War, these debates took on added significance, as the conflict demolished the old order and required a new one. Austro-Marxist critiques of imperialism presaged leftist criticisms of post–World War I liberal internationalism. In the changed environment of the postwar years, the Austro-Marxists (and Schumpeter and Mises) were cast on the political stage for the first time. Their science now had real-life consequences.[69]

The agonistic energy of the Böhm seminar impelled its members to great accomplishments in a range of areas. The participants recognized that their discussions were not just about economics and the social sciences; they carried world-historical import. Debates about value theory, capitalist development, trade cycles, and imperialism adumbrated the tumultuous conditions of fin-de-siècle Europe in its final days before the Great War. Nikolai Bukharin appreciated the centrality of Vienna to this global struggle in choosing to attend Böhm's seminar. Inspired by Hilferding and confronted by marginal utility theory, the Bolshevik knew that only a direct encounter with the Austrian School could clear the field for the socialists. Likewise Bauer and Schumpeter saw their debates as proxy political battles. As their friend Felix Somary noted, "What linked me to both these friends was the deep respect we shared for the importance of the problems themselves: it was our very freedom from all narrow-mindedness that made objective discussions possible—but only to a certain point. Schumpeter and Bauer were both close friends of mine, but never of each other; they showed mutual tolerance and respect, until in 1919 they were both members of the same government, at which point they became deadly enemies."[70] The line between friend and foe was a narrow one, and it was often mediated by friends and shared cultural touchstones. While politics estranged seminar participants, politics and science were never far apart. Combativeness and ideological conflict ultimately characterized the nature of the Viennese thought style, especially the Austrian School's.[71]

As our consideration of the *Werturteilsstreit* and the Böhm seminar has demonstrated, the Habsburg capital became the epicenter of European social science in the years before the Great War. The Austrian School, in its phase of fullest intellectual and institutional development, was partly responsible for this transformation. Even German scholars, long apprehensive of the more theoretical Austrians, sought allegiances. Weber and Sombart, for example, enlisted the younger Austrians for their journal, the *Archiv*. Mises, Amonn, Richard Schüller, and other school members, not to mention Austrian social scientists more generally, became core participants. In time, Schumpeter became an editor. The significance of the Austrian movement was confirmed when Weber personally sought Wieser and Schumpeter to write the accounts of economic theory and the history of economics for his proposed encyclopedia. In return, Wieser got the University of Vienna to hire Weber in 1918 as Philippovich's successor. Thanks in no small part to the Austrian School, Vienna had become a desirable destination for avant-garde German scholars.[72]

This chapter has shown the evolution of the Austrian School in the two decades leading up to the Great War, as it evolved from an intellectual trend to a full-blown social force. Led by Böhm, Menger, Sax, and Wieser, the school built its intellectual and political clout within the Austrian state and academy. In their seminars, conferences, and journals, they cultivated a younger generation of scholars that introduced new ideas, especially on monetary theory and theories of economic development. The innovations of the pre–World War I period set the tone for subsequent Austrian engagements, which were characterized by virulent antisocialism, liberal interventionism, and the defense of capitalism. While the participants in Hayek's "golden age" did not view the school as rosily as Hayek's generation did, the prewar grouping possessed an enviable stability that distinguished it from later iterations. That stability was ephemeral, however. With the outbreak of World War I, the school saw its world thrown into flux and the values of the *Bildungsbürgertum* terminally undermined. In the coming years, members had to adjust to a new order neither of their choosing nor of their making.

AUSTRIA'S END: THE REINVENTION OF
THE AUSTRIAN SCHOOL IN A
NEW WORLD ORDER

Friedrich von Wieser served the Austrian government in several capacities during the Great War. He became a member of the House of Lords in 1917 and acted as trade minister on three separate occasions. When the Habsburg Empire signed an armistice with the Entente in November 1918, Wieser still occupied his government post. An Austrian patriot through and through, the defeat of the Central Powers and the dissolution of the empire traumatized him. His 1919 book *Österreichs Ende* (Austria's end) represented his attempt to come to terms. Wieser lamented the empire's demise, yet his book was no mere nostalgic reminiscence. It argued that the Austrian people needed a "new heroism" built on the past yet oriented toward a vital future. This would be the task of a new generation: "The old generation, which lived through great imperial Austria, places too much stress on the old with its recollections, and cannot with a clear vision carry a new banner to its goal. The duty of leadership falls to the younger, which fought during the world war and saw great imperial Austria once more in its final brilliance." According to Wieser, a new leader, a Führer, would provide a "German answer" to French revanchism in the form of a quiet and powerful commitment to restoring Austrian greatness.[1]

Wieser acknowledged that his time of influence on practical affairs had passed. Sixty-eight years old, he was one of the last representatives of the old guard from the liberal Austrian heyday, which had served the Habsburg Empire as scholars and civil servants. The only state he had known had ceased to be; in its place, the Republic of German-Austria appeared.

He was no longer a government minister. The House of Lords disappeared, and Wieser's "von" title had been stripped. He could not offer concrete solutions to contemporary problems, since he did not see a role for himself in the postwar order. His elegiac tone reflected an awareness that he belonged with his peers to another time.

Wieser's treatise is not merely a history of Austria's dissolution; it speaks volumes about the Austrian School too. The school's members enjoyed favored status in late imperial Austria. They had connections to the highest echelons of government, and their policy prescriptions often became law. During the "golden age," their views were well represented in the imperial universities, with their ideas serving as the fulcrum for major social scientific debates in central Europe. Postwar transformations jeopardized these advancements. Members of the school struggled to respond to such epochal changes. Carl Menger, who had retired fifteen years earlier, did not publish anything, popular or academic, after 1915. The final written piece published in his lifetime was an obituary for Wieser's brother-in-law, Eugen von Böhm-Bawerk, who died in 1914. Eugen von Philippovich, Wieser's longtime colleague and friend at the University of Vienna, also passed away in 1917. Much like the dénouement of Joseph Roth's novel *Radetzky March*, in which the scion of the von Trotha family—whom the emperor had ennobled—expires nearly simultaneously with the passing of Emperor Franz Joseph, the war's end seemed to symbolize the end of influence for Austria's famed *Bildungsbürgertum*.

With the decline of Austrian liberalism and the corresponding rise of the conservative Christian Socials and working-class Social Democrats, beginning around 1900 but accelerating after the war, the route to direct political engagement for the school seemed largely foreclosed. A massive reduction of the postwar civil service impacted its members, since so many had served in the bureaucracy. Academic possibilities also dwindled. Previously, seven universities serviced the Austrian half of the empire. Austrian School members taught at almost every one, from Czernowitz in the east to Prague in the west. After the war, only Vienna, Graz, and Innsbruck remained. Academic chairs were rare and poorly recompensed, making it difficult for young scholars to enter academia. The Austrian School believed it faced academic marginalization, if not extinction.

In these trying circumstances, younger Austrian economists adapted by seeking new means of making their names and assuring their influence. In the final days of the war, Wieser, Joseph Schumpeter, Ludwig von Mises, and others turned from bureaucratic posts to public outlets. They advocated political and economic solutions in newspaper articles, pamphlets, and short books directed at a wider readership. They defended the liberal state against the threats of conservatism and—more significantly and much more vociferously—against socialism and Bolshevism. In doing so, they reprised the conflicts of the previous decade within their private seminars—with elevated political stakes. The Mises-Schumpeter generation waged a battle of ideas in the overheated intellectual culture of "Red Vienna." They cultivated their own "Vienna circles" and developed institutions that supported a new generation of scholars, which reestablished the international reputation of the school. They also sought support from allies in business and finance, reinforcing their ties to Austrian elites.

This chapter narrates the reinvention of the Austrian School in the post–World War I Austrian Republic. Out of the crisis of the war years, a new iteration of the collective emerged—with new members, intellectual interests, ideological strategies, and institutions. The ascendancy of the Mises-Schumpeter generation as public intellectuals, policy insiders, and seminar leaders assured the continued relevance of the tradition. The chapter tracks the changing of the guard at the University of Vienna, where Hans Mayer and Mises replaced Menger, Böhm, and Wieser, training new students, including the future luminaries Gottfried von Haberler, Friedrich von Hayek, Fritz Machlup, Oskar Morgenstern, and others. This younger cohort faced diminished prospects and an embattled liberal tradition, leaving them feeling more marginalized but also more willing to seek new contacts with domestic conservatives, as well as with international supporters. In the school's most significant elaboration of its project, the Institute for Business Cycle Research, it succeeded in integrating into new transatlantic social scientific networks sustained by US philanthropic foundations like the Rockefeller Foundation (RF). These "transatlantic enrichments" opened a new chapter in Austrian School history, helping the school survive and thrive in the troubled decades to follow.[2]

The End of Empire and the Rise of the Public Intellectual

Wieser was not alone among Austrian School economists in decrying the demise of the Habsburg monarchy. After all, they were almost all members of the German-educated middle class, a class that was famously *kaisertreu* (loyal to the emperor). Schumpeter and Mises also appealed to the general public on behalf of liberal economic and political policy in the hope of mitigating the deleterious outcomes of the war, especially the empire's dissolution. Setting aside the jargon of economic theory, they embraced the role of public intellectual, a status that gained in importance in postwar Vienna. Although Austrian School intellectuals continued to play a role in postimperial civil service, their primary influence was in civil society, where they established research and policy institutions, wrote for journals and newspapers, and exchanged ideas with fellow intellectuals in small circles. Austrian School economists adapted to these circumstances well, becoming successful intellectual and ideological entrepreneurs.[3]

The Great War was an unmitigated disaster for the Austrian Empire. Expecting a quick and decisive victory over Serbia, the army suffered humiliating defeats against not just the Serbs but also the Russians and Italians. The botched Serbian campaign and the rout at Lemberg (Lviv) by the Russians in 1914 belied nationalist beliefs in the inherent superiority of German Habsburgs over the Slavs. The attrition of the *twelve* Battles of the Isonzo on the Italian front highlighted the futility of the Austrian war effort. Support for the multinational empire frayed during the years of fighting: Czech volunteers began to join Entente units as early as 1914. Calls for an independent state mounted. The Austrian state suffered through political instability and economic hardships too. Food and resource scarcity led the war government to institute economic planning, rationing, and wage and price controls. Economically, a black market emerged to address the people's basic needs, and inflation accelerated. Prices rose by 1,500 percent after 1914. Thousands starved to death during the brutal winters of 1916–17 and 1917–18. Millions suffered under conditions of malnutrition and misery. Compounding these privations, Vienna experienced tuberculosis and influenza outbreaks, which persisted after the armistice.[4]

Political turmoil engulfed the Austrian regime. The empire lost its ruler, Franz Joseph, in November 1916. He had sat on the throne since the revolutionary year of 1848. For many, his death was a synecdoche for the death of the empire. The year 1916 also saw political discontent erupt in violence. Fritz Adler, son of the social democratic leader Victor Adler, student of Ernst Mach, and friend of Albert Einstein, assassinated the minister-president of Austria, Count Karl von Stürgkh, in the dining room of the five-star hotel Meissl & Schadn in protest over the war. Adler mounted his own defense, making an impassioned antiwar argument. He was sentenced to death, though the punishment was commuted at war's end. Meanwhile various peace overtures to the Entente in 1917 and 1918 came to naught. By autumn 1918, Austrian elites recognized that the war was lost, yet they hoped to salvage the empire. They expressed a willingness to reform the political structure of the country, granting autonomy to the empire's many national groups. They also conceded that greater democratic participation was needed. They made desperate appeals to Germans, Hungarians, Slavs, and Jews about the historic mission of the Habsburg Empire, maintaining that only a unified Austria could ensure peace and prosperity in central Europe. They courted social democratic and working-class support for reform, to little avail. When the Entente rejected the last-ditch proposals of the Austrian foreign minister and Kaiser Karl in October, national leaders across the empire moved to establish independent states—in Czech lands on October 28; in Slovenia, Croatia, and Serbia the next day; and in Slovak territory the day after. On October 31, Hungary dissolved its bond with Austria, effectively ending the Austro-Hungarian Empire. On November 11, Kaiser Karl recognized Austria's right to determine its own state form and renounced participation in government. The provisional national assembly declared a Republic of German-Austria on November 12.[5]

Men like Wieser, Schumpeter, and Mises had much to lose during these heady days of 1918 and 1919, and they engaged in public affairs with urgency. Self-identifying with German culture, hailing from prosperous, well-connected families, and holding coveted jobs within the academic and bureaucratic establishments, these men were deeply invested in the status quo. They spoke out to defend their state and their values, to maintain as much continuity with the liberal *Gründerzeit* as possible.

Schumpeter's transition is perhaps most fascinating, since his ironical attitude toward politics and public affairs is the stuff of legend. In 1919, he tussled with Max Weber over the relationship of values, science, and politics in a coffeehouse debate over Bolshevism. Weber, recently appointed at the University of Vienna, planned to return to Germany and believed Schumpeter would make a good successor. They had not previously met and, according to Felix Somary, had starkly different personalities. Weber "took nothing lightly," while Schumpeter "took nothing hard." Somary and the historian Ludo Hartmann arranged a meeting at Café Landtmann in the Palais Lieben-Auspitz on the Ringstrasse, where the Mengers and the Austrian School sometimes gathered. The conversation turned to the Russian Revolution, which the sardonic Schumpeter asserted would offer a practical test of socialism's theories. This enraged Weber, who felt the "laboratory" would be "heaped with human corpses." Schumpeter responded, "Every anatomy classroom is the same thing." Things only deteriorated from there: "All around us the café customers stopped their card games and listened eagerly, until the point when Weber sprang to his feet and rushed into the Ringstrasse, crying, 'This is intolerable!' Hartmann followed with Weber's hat and vainly tried to calm him down. Schumpeter, who had remained behind with me, only smiled and said 'How can someone carry on like that in a coffee house.' "[6] While Schumpeter was as ardent an opponent of socialism as there was, he did not believe it to be the scientist's job to meddle in political matters—let socialism dig its own grave. In this dustup with Weber, the hero of "objectivity," Schumpeter ribbed the German over his inability to separate value judgments and scientific evaluation. Schumpeter claimed that if one wished to do politics, one should do politics, but one should not dress it up in scientific garb. Moreover, one must remain civilized in debate—especially in the coffeehouse!

As the anecdote suggests, Schumpeter did not take political speculation too seriously, yet he carved out increasing time for practical policy issues as conditions worsened. Shortly before the armistice, Schumpeter published a widely circulated pamphlet, "The Crisis of the Tax State," in which he examined the possibilities for the postwar economy. He doubted whether a return to the prewar amalgam of free competition and state involvement was possible. Schumpeter recognized the need for an overhaul of the previous order: "The failure of the tax state and a transition to another system for covering the needs of the collective would not merely mean that a new financial system would replace the prewar system. It would moreover mean that what we call the 'modern state' would have to change in its very essence."[7]

Schumpeter, true to his Austrian School roots, argued that the state and its tax system arose out of the economic considerations of individuals. Following Menger, he emphasized the role of institutions like the state in helping individuals attain their (economic) ends: "The state can never be an end in itself; it is ever only a machine for social purposes. In its essence, it stands as the agent of the individual's personifications of ends." Ultimately, state, society, and economy relied on each other to function. In practical terms, this meant that taxes on income, land, interest, and monopolies all had a place. If the state encroached on the creative energies of its people, however, it overstepped its duties. The only form of direct taxation he rejected was on the profits of entrepreneurial activity, since it hindered innovation, decreased prosperity, and deincentivized productivity. If the Austrian state—which had turned to a centrally planned war economy—reinvented itself on a more liberal English model, then it could thrive.[8]

Schumpeter offered a cautiously optimistic assessment of Austrian conditions in 1918. Most significantly, he seemed prepared to participate in the postwar restoration. Schumpeter took an increasing interest in Austrian political decisions as the war progressed, first writing letters to his friend the jurist and politician Heinrich Lammasch. By 1918, he hoped to enter the final Habsburg government under Prime Minister Lammasch. "The Crisis of the Tax State" was his public announcement of political intentions, and he made it clear that he had answers for the foundering Austrian Empire: "There is a question whether the tax state and the organizational form of economic freedom can deal with the oppressive harshness of the postwar situation without collapsing. We can only answer this question with a 'Yes!'"[9]

The Habsburg Empire did not survive long enough to enlist Schumpeter. Lammasch himself, a close colleague of Wieser's, passed away in 1920. Schumpeter nevertheless entered the political arena when colleagues from the Böhm seminar recruited him. In February 1919, Rudolf Hilferding and Emil Lederer invited Schumpeter to join the German Socialization Commission, a body of experts exploring the nationalization of the coal industry. He served for a year, during which Otto Bauer, now the Austrian foreign minister, the head of the Austrian Socialization Commission, and the leader of the Social Democratic Workers' Party (SDAP), recommended Schumpeter for the post of finance minister. Schumpeter accepted, despite his conservative social attitudes and liberal economic positions.[10]

Schumpeter brought his ironical eye and sharp tongue to bear on his work. Schumpeter quipped that he offered his scientific expertise to the Socialization Commission and the first Austrian government to prevent the worst excesses of the socialists: "If a man wants to commit suicide, it is a good thing if a doctor is present." Schumpeter believed unswervingly in his ability to impact world affairs, despite mixed results. As minister, he tried to open up Austria to foreign investment and to expand credit, with limited success. Moreover, his proposals for a large capital levy and for selling domestic companies to foreign investors appalled conservatives, socialists, and nationalist liberals. Schumpeter also opposed union with Germany, a majority position in Austria after the war. He ran afoul of his friend Bauer on this count. When he left his ministerial post after seven turbulent months, only one man had any praise for the idiosyncratic economist—Wieser, who applauded his courage and steadfast commitment to principles. Schumpeter became president and chairman of the Biedermann Bank. The bank went bankrupt in the mid-1920s, leaving Schumpeter heavily in debt. Disappointed and shaken, Schumpeter returned to academia, accepting a professorship in Bonn in 1925. His Viennese friend the journalist Gustav Stolper promoted his case, helping him win the post over several candidates, including Mises.[11]

Mises, like his sometime friend Schumpeter, emerged as a public intellectual in the final year of the war by discussing tax, socialization, and financial policy. While one can dispute whether Mises really became "*the* economist of Austria" in 1918, as he claimed, the end of the war offered him the chance to transcend his earlier role as a backroom adviser. Mises served in the imperial army during the war, distinguishing himself on the northern and Romanian fronts. Interspersed with his frontline tours, he worked in the War Ministry, advising on war planning and economic policy. In the Scientific Committee for War Economics, he reunited with fellow Austrian School students Emil Perels, Karl and Ewald Pribram, and Alfred Amonn. Mises's proposals seldom pleased government authorities, since he opposed expansion of the war effort, central planning, and increased taxation. Schumpeter encouraged Mises to speak out on Austrian monetary problems in the Austrian Political Society, where the two made common cause against the inflationary tendencies of the wartime government. Mises began to publish his opinions in the liberal press in 1917.[12]

Mises distilled these positions into a popular book, *Nation, State, and Economy*. Applying his liberal views, he offered the work as both criticism and positive program. Mises argued that Germany's lack of commitment to the values of the Enlightenment and its preference for authoritarianism, nationalism, and militarism had landed the world in its current predicament. He felt that only a democratic state along English or French lines, coupled with a liberal economy free of protectionism, could sustain the postwar order.[13]

Although the work was not primarily polemical, Mises criticized the interventionist and statist tendencies of German economists—heirs of the German Historical School—for their contribution to the retrograde policies of the German Reich. In their valorization of the German state and nation, German social scientists propped up a society not of the people but of the powerful, especially the aristocratic Junker class. Mises demonstrated the faulty assumptions of the scientific handmaidens of German power politics. He countered with a liberal vision of nationality predicated on the free migration of peoples from one state to another, welcoming citizenship laws, and voluntary integration into the national community. He also defended democracy. For him, the liberal principle was synonymous with democratic governance: "The basic idea of liberalism and of democracy is the harmony of interests of all sections of a nation and then the harmony of interests of all nations. Since the rightly understood interest of all strata of the population leads to the same political goals and demands, the decision on political questions can be left to the vote of the entire people." Mises later rejected such a close correspondence between liberalism and democracy, but in 1917 he was a staunch majoritarian, in contradistinction to German aristocrat-scientists.[14]

Mises offered a full-throated defense of a free, competitive world economy, contending that only a liberal postwar system could achieve prosperity. If nations traded openly with one another, allowing goods and people to move freely, everyone would benefit. Wealth would only arise when laissez-faire was extended around the world. The interest-based politics of the socialists, with their class biases, and the nationalists, with their state chauvinism, only produced conflict. German leaders ignored these lessons, erecting protectionist tariffs that led to increasing conflicts between states and antagonistic struggles for territories and resources. These rivalries culminated in the Great War. Mises's insights in *Nation, State, and Economy* sharpened his critique from the imperialism debates in the prewar Böhm seminar. Mises hoped for a new world order based on liberal individualism and the equality of all persons and nations. The Versailles system of self-determination and international comity did not rise to that level, however. The prerogatives of nation-states—especially the Anglo-Saxon and French ones—continued to take precedence over international standards of rights and justice. Mises instead sought a radically liberal vision that exceeded Woodrow Wilson's inconsistent internationalism.[15]

Nation, State, and Economy announced Mises's involvement in postwar political discussions. He emerged as a respected public commentator and policy advocate. This public profile benefited him in the debate that made his reputation. In the 1920s, Mises owed his greatest fame to his economic arguments against socialism, which precipitated a continent-wide debate about the possibility of an efficient socialist system. Following in the footsteps of his predecessors Menger, Wieser, and Böhm, Mises attacked his opponents with vehemence and vitriol, settling intellectual scores and personal rivalries simultaneously. The very acerbity of the so-called socialist calculation debate left an indelible mark on the Austrian School, further linking its economic theory to antisocialist politics and ideology. The controversy also reveals to us a great deal about the energy and disputatiousness of Red Vienna intellectual life.

The Socialist Calculation Debate and Red Vienna

In the decades leading up to the Great War, Vienna served as the focal point of socialism debates. Austrian School economists acted as the primary critics of socialist theory; Austro-Marxists countered as socialism's foremost defenders. In Böhm's seminar, Schumpeter and Mises tussled with Hilferding, Bauer, Nikolai Bukharin, Lederer, and Otto Neurath over imperialism, capitalism, and socialism. The uncertain postwar order lent added urgency to these prewar theoretical discussions. In Russia, the Bolshevik Revolution swept the continent's most radical and violent Marxists into power. The party's leadership, including Bukharin, moved to institute a communist system based on centralized state planning. Across central and eastern Europe, too, socialism was ascendant. The demands of the war led most belligerent states to coordinate production, creating state-led economic initiatives. In Germany and Austria, the regimes established war planning boards, dubbed "war socialism," to allocate resources. For the first time, nationalization and socialization became acceptable policy positions.

In the postwar German and Austrian republics, the social democratic parties (SPD in Germany, SDAP in Austria) won the most seats in the first elections. Friedrich Ebert and Karl Renner, both socialists, were the first chancellors of Germany and Austria, respectively. Meanwhile Communists and radical Marxists vied with moderate social democrats for power. In January 1919, German Communists and independent socialists called a general strike to protest the new state. The Spartacist Uprising erupted into a street conflict pitting radicals against the army and protofascist paramilitary groups in a mini civil war. Nearly two hundred people died in the fighting. The Communist leaders Rosa Luxemburg and Wilhelm Liebknecht were arrested and beaten to death in captivity. In the spring, another wave of Communist agitation swept through Germany, Hungary, and Czechoslovakia. In April, a cadre of Communists established the Bavarian Soviet Republic (Räterepublik) in Munich, which held power for a month. Neurath served as an adviser and established its Central Economic Office. The suppression of the republic by the army and paramilitary forces resulted in approximately two thousand deaths and a similar number of arrests. Neurath was also arrested for treason and sentenced to eighteen months in prison. Through the intervention of Bauer and the Austrian government, Neurath was allowed to return to Austria. In Budapest, Béla Kun and the Hungarian Communists instituted a short-lived Hungarian Soviet Republic between March and August 1919. Despite the fear of liberals and conservatives about Bolshevik-style socialism, outside Russia the threat was never a serious one. Bolshevism was more significant as an ideological cudgel and bogeyman for liberals and conservatives than as a political alternative.[16]

In these turbulent times, European diplomats, politicians, and theorists faced daunting questions. Could the prewar economic system be reestablished? Could planning and centralization work in peacetime? Was socialism the wave of the future? Moderate socialists took the lead exploring these questions. In Germany, the democratic Marxist Karl Kautsky initiated the Socialization Commission, which attracted Lederer, Schumpeter, Hilferding, and more than a dozen liberal politicians like Walther Rathenau, the head of Germany's wartime planning. Otto Bauer, who chaired the equivalent Austrian Commission, was one of the first to comment on the changes wrought by the Great War and the subsequent revolutions. In a best-selling essay titled "The Way to Socialism," he argued for the necessity of a socialist system and outlined the steps to establish it. Bauer insisted that the recent political revolutions had only been "half revolutions"; central Europeans required a social and economic revolution to complete the job. Democracy was great, but it meant nothing if capitalists and rentiers continued to exploit the immiserated masses: "We are too poor to be able to continue to share the products of our labor with capitalists and rentiers. It is bad enough that we have to pay a tribute to foreign capitalists in the form of war reparations; we cannot remain tribute-bound to domestic capitalists too. There is only one way out from our economic emergency: socialism!"[17]

The social revolution, unlike the political, could not unfold in a single day. It required, according to Bauer, a wholesale reorganization of economic and social relations so that goods were more equitably distributed while supply remained at the same level as before. To achieve such ends, Bauer did not advocate immediate socialization of all means of production or the expropriation of all wealth. Socialists had to convince members of the capitalist class and the educated bourgeoisie that the new system would work for them. Bauer envisioned a stepwise process toward socialism that ensured peace and growth first and equity a close second. He advocated nationalization of key sectors of the economy (large industry, large landholdings, and private banks), socialization of agriculture and housing, and democratization of agricultural and industrial decision-making. Bauer had taken to heart criticisms from Schumpeter and Mises about the perils of socialism, such as diminished production and the loss of entrepreneurial spirit. He had also witnessed with horror the rise of Bolshevism and had resisted Communist incursions into Austria. His version of socialism therefore looked less like the command economy of the early Soviet Union than a democratically socialist economic order.[18]

As the head of the SDAP, Bauer's views demanded attention. Schumpeter dealt with Bauer from within the state apparatus; Mises responded with articles and a book. Mises's monograph *Socialism* propelled the discussion by challenging the very foundations of the socialist worldview: the rationality of any socialist system. In typically acidulous fashion, Mises expressed his anger about the current vogue for socialism and his contempt for socialist thinking. Despite its popularity, socialism had nowhere achieved its aims, nor could it. Meanwhile private property, free trade, and capitalism faced universal opprobrium despite their triumphs. According to Mises, even so-called opponents of socialism had embraced its core principles when they advocated for state intervention in the economic system or spoke in the name of special interests. To correct this "one-sided" acceptance, Mises claimed to offer the first economic investigation of socialism. Even if this assessment is exaggerated and self-aggrandizing—Wieser and Böhm among others had offered thorough commentaries—*Socialism* nonetheless served as one of the starting points for interwar discussions.[19]

Mises defined socialism not only as the public ownership of the means of production but also as a system that dispenses with money as a unit of calculation for the values of raw materials, unfinished goods, and finished commodities. Few socialists at the time in fact endorsed a moneyless or marketless socialism, so this choice raised some questions. Yet this was Otto Neurath's position, which begins to explain Mises's engagement on this point. The lack of money calculation was the fatal flaw in socialism, one that guaranteed irrational actions and inefficient outcomes. Mises summed up his argument: "Once society abandons free pricing of production goods rational production becomes impossible. Every step that leads away from private ownership of the means of production and the use of money is a step away from rational economic activity." For Mises, socialism made economic calculation impossible, spelling the end of economic activity and rational production.[20]

The socialist calculation debate was not merely a question of economics or even politics—it was a battle for the soul of civilization. For Mises, socialism was not just an economic or social system; it was "destructionism." The victory of socialism would mean the retrogression of Europe to a barbarous state: "If the intellectual dominance of Socialism remains unshaken, then in a short time the whole co-operative system of culture which Europe has built up during thousands of years will be shattered." With the advance of socialism, Mises predicted the breakdown of the economy and a return to subsistence living. His apocalyptic vision culminated in annihilation, as he noted in a fit of bathos: "Nomad tribes from the Eastern steppes would again raid and pillage Europe, sweeping across it with swift cavalry. Who could resist them in the thinly populated land left defenceless after the weapons inherited from the higher technique of Capitalism had worn out?" Only if the defenders of liberalism and capitalism rose to the challenge against the hordes of socialism could crisis be averted. Mises's almost Spenglerian vision of the decline of the West resonated with liberals and conservatives who hoped to restore the prewar economic and political status quo.[21]

Mises's battle cry elicited responses from around the globe. Supporters in England and the United States applauded Mises as a defender of Western liberalism against "German" socialism. John Van Sickle—an American economist who later became a patron of the Austrian School as a program officer for the Rockefeller Foundation—commended it for its broad learning and its stridency. He saw *Socialism* as a quintessential work of the Austrians: Mises's conclusions on socialist calculation were the only ones possible starting from the subjective theory of value. The response in German-speaking lands was less favorable. Carl Landauer not only accused Mises, "the great hater of socialism," of an unwillingness and inability to understand socialist theory but also alleged that Mises had betrayed his Austrian origins. By denying the theoretical possibility of a socialist economy, he contradicted Wieser, who had presented money calculation as a natural feature of any economy. Mises had also failed to demonstrate the logical impossibility of socialism at all. Landauer's criticisms characterized the German socialist response—scorn, derision, and dismissal.[22]

In Austria, Mises's work sparked a debate across political and intellectual spectra. The response was more nuanced yet still overwhelmingly critical. Schumpeter and his friend Gustav Stolper, editor of the weekly *Der Österreichische Volkswirt*, argued against premature socialization, but they denied Mises's impossibility argument. Austro-Marxists had little sympathy for the socialism that Mises assailed, so they ignored many of Mises's arguments. Otto Leichter, a prominent Austro-Marxist, and Walter Schiff, a professor of political science at the University of Vienna, maintained that socialist calculation could be more precise than capitalist calculation, since future production needs are better known in a state-coordinated system than by individual entrepreneurs. Perhaps the most innovative response came from a young Karl Polanyi, a Hungarian émigré intellectual and Vienna transplant who later became famous for his work *The Great Transformation*. Polanyi argued for a version of market socialism, wherein economic calculations take place not in the market but between corporate bodies of producers of unfinished goods first and then between producer and consumer associations for finished goods. Markets would exist between the corporate "guilds," while the state would play a role in wage and price decisions. As the wide array of responses reveals, Mises's work forced Austrian socialists to rethink their arguments and approaches, a credit to the liberal's intellectual clout.[23]

As all participants in the calculation debate recognized, it was not just an intellectual struggle; economic ideas had far-reaching consequences. This was especially true for Mises. He argued that the conflict between capitalism and socialism was primarily a battle of ideas. In an anti-Marxist spirit, he argued, "It is ideas that make history, not the 'material productive forces,' those nebulous and mystical schemata of the materialist conception of history. If we could overcome the *idea* of Socialism . . . then Socialism would have to leave the stage."[24] Mises believed that his ideas had broad implications for politics, society, and culture. The socialist calculation debate was but a single front in a larger confrontation over ideologies and worldviews—liberal, socialist, conservative, and soon fascist. In Vienna, these conflicts filtered into the city's salons and scientific associations. Adversaries authored sarcastic editorials and penned jibing songs. They sparred over university appointments, teaching assignments, and the leadership of organizations. The Austrian School of the interwar era was forged out of this milieu, which helps to explain its increasingly ideological tone.

Red and Black Vienna

Postwar Austrian intellectuals faced a brave new world. A republic replaced the Habsburg monarchy, yet communism and socialism appeared ascendant across central Europe. Their home country, previously a multinational empire of fifty-three million people, was now an ethnic German "rump" state of six million, with a third of its inhabitants in the capital. Wags called the city "Wasserkopf Wien" (hydrocephalic Vienna), since the metropolis now dwarfed the Austrian state. Starvation and disease plagued the country into 1919. The economy suffered from rampant inflation until 1923, when a series of loans arranged by the League of Nations stabilized the currency. In return, the Austrian government submitted to austerity measures, arranged by the conservative Christian Social government and American investment bankers, which resulted in hundreds of thousands of unemployed workers. This affected the vaunted Austrian civil service particularly harshly. The Austrian state also ceded economic oversight to the League. With conditions precarious, most Austrians yearned for a union with Germany, believing that the new republic was *lebensunfähig*, incapable of survival.[25]

The republic's two largest parties were the Social Democrats and the Christian Socials, with the socialists dominating the municipal governments of Vienna and other urban centers and the conservatives leading a series of bourgeois coalitions at the national level. These factions controlled politics until 1934 (and, in slightly different forms, from 1945 until recently). These two blocs stood for more than just party political positions; they offered complete and irreconcilable worldviews. The socialists designed their program around the creation of a "new man." They created publichousing projects, expanded family planning and child welfare programs, and transformed public education for everyone from pre-kindergarten children to adults. Their control of Vienna led opponents to dub the city "Red Vienna." The red city was a socialist laboratory. As Polanyi described it somewhat hyperbolically, "Vienna achieved one of the most spectacular cultural triumphs of Western history. . . . 1918 initiated an equally unexampled moral and intellectual rise in the condition of a highly industrial working class which, protected by the Vienna system, withstood the degrading effects of grave economic dislocation and achieved a level never reached before by the masses of the people in any industrial society."[26]

Opposing Red Vienna were Catholic conservatives and German nationalists, two blocs whose shared antisemitism, antidemocratic and antisocialist attitudes, and German chauvinism allowed for frequent collaboration. "Black Vienna," whose supporters hoped to create a "new Reich" by reaf firming German Catholic values, restoring the monarchy and Habsburg hegemony in central Europe, and destroying the forces of liberalism, Enlightenment, Judaism, and Freemasonry, was the locus of these endeavors. Caught in the "excluded middle" was the *Bildungsbürgertum*—the group to which the members of the Austrian School belonged. While not fully sympathetic to the conservative program, members of the liberal classes generally supported Black Viennese leaders over social democrats and progressives.[27]

The Austrians born in the years around 1900 came of age in this charged atmosphere. Mises called for a "battle of ideas," the Austro-Marxists demanded a "struggle" from a journal of the same name, and conservatives like Johannes Sauter militated for a *Weltanschauungskampf* (struggle over worldviews). Intellectual life became a battleground for a number of reasons. First, the diminished prospects for academics made the fight for positions more intense. The hope of a university professorship, always a long shot, vanished. Not only had the number of Austrian universities shrunken from seven to three, but the crown jewel of the system, the University of Vienna, also declined in size. Young students relied more than ever on the patronage of their advisers to receive teaching licenses (*venia legendi*) and to secure the few positions available, either as unpaid *Privatdozenten* or as postdocs and research assistants. The likelihood of regular employment in the civil service, long the default career for the educated classes, also decreased with the elimination of over one hundred thousand such positions in the early 1920s.

The University of Vienna became the front line of warring ideological factions. Student fraternities had a long history at the institution, with the nationalist Deutsche Studentenschaft (DS) and the conservative Cartellverband (CV), an umbrella organization of Catholic associations, most prominent. The dueling tradition, which Stefan Zweig and Arthur Schnitzler described in their fin-de-siècle writing, disappeared, but the thousands of young men in fraternal bodies substituted political violence for affairs of personal honor. The DS became increasingly chauvinistic and antisemitic, provoking frequent riots at the main university building. Nationalist students targeted courses by the Jewish anatomy professor and socialist city official Julius Tandler, resulting in several shutdowns of the university. They introduced an Aryan paragraph into their bylaws in 1920, prohibiting the involvement of Jews, and they fought for a quota system (*numerus clausus*) limiting the number of Jewish students. Increasingly influential as time passed, they counted professors, deans, rectors, and government ministers among their alumni. Most notorious was the "Bear's Den," a cabal of university professors and administrators who secretly plotted ways to wrest power from godless freethinkers and Jews. The DS turned to fascism in the early 1920s before becoming a hotbed of National Socialism in the late 1920s.[28]

The DS represented the German nationalist bloc of conservatives and clashed with smaller socialist, democratic, and Zionist associations throughout the interwar era. The CV emerged as its primary foil, since it alone had the numbers and influential supporters to pose a threat. Though the CV opposed the obnoxious antics and noxious rhetoric of the DS, it had its own issues. It, too, fostered antisemitic tendencies—the CV eventually split over the inclusion of an Aryan paragraph in 1933. Most of its powerful alumni supported the Aryan clause; many wrote antisemitic articles. Its members also took a dim view of democracy and the Austrian Republic, preferring authoritarian politics to "Masonic" and "Jewish" parliamentarianism. Their understanding of Catholicism was a conservative, reactionary one, rooted in the antimodernism of the Church's encyclical *Rerum Novarum*. Monarchism, revisionism, and Habsburg restoration stood as political goals. The CV was an important incubator for ambitious conservatives. Almost every chancellor of the republic (and the Austrofascist state that followed in 1934) was a CV member, along with myriad ministers, bureaucrats, and professors. Its leading lights congregated in the Leo-Gesellschaft and wrote in the popular intellectual weeklies *Das Neue Reich* and *Die Schönere Zukunft*. With the DS and CV in control, socialists and liberals, Austrian democrats and foreign students, Jews and Zionists all found the university a threatening place.[29]

With the formal channels of the civil service and academy often blocked, alternative institutions and associations filled the employment gap. Take the Vienna Circle of logical empiricism as an example. This illustrious group consisted of a few dozen scholars who met in coffeehouses and salons and organized conferences. Its members show the diverse paths to intellectual relevance in this era. Ludwig Wittgenstein, the inspiration for the group, worked irregularly during the 1920s, primarily surviving off his family's vast fortune. He never had an official academic position until he immigrated to England in the 1930s. Otto Neurath, the group's indefatigable organizer and driving force, worked for the public-housing commission in Vienna, ran the city's Social and Economic Museum, freelanced for socialist journals, and taught at Red Vienna's famous adult-education universities. Moritz Schlick, the founder and leader of the Circle, was one of the few university professors, alongside Hans Hahn, Karl Menger (Carl's son), and Rudolf Carnap. Schlick got his student Friedrich Waismann an appointment as an unpaid assistant and librarian. Waismann earned money by adjuncting at the University of Vienna and the adult-education centers. Schlick, however, could not protect another student, Edgar Zilsel, from the antisemitic and antisocialist attacks of the philosophy faculty, especially the German nationalist and authoritarian Othmar Spann. Affiliates of the Circle conducted research at the Psychological and Pedagogical Institutes that the municipal government funded.[30]

Other progressive circles followed the Vienna Circle model for intellectual and social engagement, which emerged out of the "late Enlightenment, socioliberal cultural context" of fin-de-siècle Austria. The psychologist Alfred Adler and his students staffed the city's twenty-eight marriage and child counseling clinics. There they encountered Freudian psychoanalysts, who opened free clinics and became involved with the city's sex and reproduction centers. The city's third major psychological school, led by Karl and Charlotte Bühler, directed the Psychological Institute and employed young social scientists like Paul Lazarsfeld and Marie Jahoda. Their pioneering, interdisciplinary techniques gained worldwide attention when they contributed to *The Authoritarian Personality*, the major post–World War II investigation conducted by the Frankfurt School during its US exile.[31]

Within this world of salons and centers, circles, and institutes, members of the post–World War I generation learned to be creative in cultivating opportunities. They sought broad applications of their ideas and looked well beyond the academy for influence. They networked extensively, seeking allies in and beyond the rough-and-tumble work of Austrian politics and academe. These charged conditions fostered an anxious intellectual environment, whose volatility inspired a diverse array of thinkers, including the philosophers of science Karl Popper and Paul Feyerabend; the mathematician Kurt Gödel; the psychoanalysts Anna Freud, Melanie Klein, and Wilhelm Reich; and the authors Robert Musil and Hermann Broch. The stimulation of Red and Black Vienna also shaped and reinvigorated the Austrian School of the interwar generation.

Geist-Kreis: The New Spirit of the Austrian School

The conditions in postwar Vienna impacted the Austrian School of economists as fundamentally as it did other intellectual movements. Economics as a discipline, in fact, faced daunting obstacles in central Europe. Scholarly associations and publications struggled to stay afloat during and after the war. Paper shortages, rising printing costs, shrinking subscriptions, and inadequate pay affected all journals. Even the preeminent journal of German social science, *Schmollers Jahrbuch*, suspended publishing in 1923. Likewise, the Austrian *Zeitschrift* fared poorly. War shortages precipitated a decrease in size and revenue. The journal ceased publication in 1917, not to resume until 1921. Meanwhile, with the deaths of Eugen von Böhm-Bawerk and Eugen von Philippovich, Friedrich Wieser was virtually the only theoretical economist left with a tenured position in the Austrian Republic. Conservative and nationalist scholars like Othmar Spann received appointments to prominent posts at the University of Vienna, representing a major retrogression from the prewar "golden age" of marginalism.[32]

Students who opposed these trends had to chart their own courses. Some scholars, for example, Karl Popper, Paul Lazarsfeld, Marie Jahoda, and Wilhelm Reich, joined socialist student groups. Young liberals like Herbert von Furth and Friedrich von Hayek created societies for the defense of democratic and republican ideals. Upon returning to the university for the winter semester of 1918–19, they helped found the German Democratic Students' Union, organized as a counterbalance to leftist and rightist student organizations. Although their involvement was short-lived, the teenagers developed a lifelong friendship. They carried their activism to new organizations, and they had a formative influence on the reconfiguration of the Austrian School. As vital as the mentorship of Wieser and Mises was, the friend network around Furth and Hayek played an even more significant role.

Born in 1899 into prosperous, ennobled families from the Viennese *Bildungsbürgertum*, Furth and Hayek seemed destined for professional success in the Habsburg Empire. Furth's father, Emil, was a jurist at the University of Vienna, a member of the city council, and a pioneer in school and housing reform. He also appeared on the income tax commission chaired by Böhm and dominated by Menger in the mid-1890s. His sister, Marianne, married Ewald Pribram, a colleague of Mises's. Emil himself married Ernestine Kisch, the founder and leader of the Austrian women's suffrage movement. Herbert graduated high school with honors in 1917 and served in the army. Upon discharge, he matriculated in Vienna to study law.[33]

Friedrich Hayek's grandfather Franz was a jurist and professor at the University of Vienna. He also went on alpine hiking expeditions with his friend Eugen von Böhm-Bawerk when the latter taught at the University of Innsbruck. Friedrich's father, August, was a medical doctor and botanist who published several books and lectured at the university. His mother, Felicitas von Juraschek, came from a distinguished, land-owning family. The Jurascheks owned a stately, ten-room flat on the elegant Kärnterstrasse, Vienna's premier shopping boulevard, around the corner from the Opera House and the Ringstrasse. The Jurascheks were related to the Wittgensteins, and the families summered in the Vienna woods together. Friedrich himself struggled somewhat in school, changing high schools twice. After graduation, he fought on the Italian front, where he decided to pursue economics when he enrolled at the University of Vienna in 1919.[34]

Intellectually curious and academically driven, Furth and Hayek (and later Oskar Morgenstern) gravitated to the most lively and popular circle at the university, the Othmar Spann Kreis. Spann succeeded to Philippovich's chair in 1919 and immediately announced his presence as a scholar and public intellectual. His first lectures became a best-seller, *The True State*, which railed against the scourges of "individualism, atomism, psychologism, and Marxism" in the name of universalism. He rejected parliamentary democracy and republicanism, saw socialism as a pernicious distortion of true collectivism, and assailed Jewish and Enlightenment ideas. Stressing that the whole comes before the parts, he repudiated scientific approaches that started from individualist premises. In the conservative, nationalistic university atmosphere of early postwar Vienna, his ideas spread like wildfire. Spann drew the best and brightest students to his weekly seminar, where he held forth on the application of universalism to contemporary issues. His followers rose to academic and political positions, and they became activists in the nascent, protofascist "conservative revolution" of the interwar era.[35]

If the Spann-Kreis seems an inauspicious starting point for the next generation of the Austrian School, it was. Ironically, Hayek owed his first encounter with Menger's *Principles* to Spann's course on methodology. Everything about the man ran counter to the ideals of the "individualist" and "psychologist" school, yet he offered a well-rounded introduction to economics, including marginalism. In his private seminar, Spann pitted his illiberalism against Wieser, Schumpeter, Mises, and especially Hans Mayer, Wieser's heir apparent. Spann's attempt to establish a cult of personality grated with independent-minded students like Furth, Hayek, and Morgenstern, and they eventually fell out with him by 1923, with the former two "excommunicated" in 1921.[36]

After Spann's rejection, Furth enjoined Hayek to start a circle. Called the Geist-Kreis, this assemblage of bourgeois, often Jewish, students took an ecumenical approach to intellectual life, weaving together literature, philosophy, history, science, and, of course, economics. As Hayek described it, the Geist-Kreis broadened his horizons and pushed him to become a cosmopolitan: "Not the least gain which I owed to these Jewish or partly Jewish friends of that period is that they were much more internationally minded than my own circle." The circle of about twenty-five men (women were not admitted) met fortnightly for the next seventeen years, enduring hyperinflation, the Great Depression, civil war, fascism, and Nazism.[37] This remarkable cohort, "a collection basin for university outsiders," would shape not just the contours of the Austrian School but also Austria's international reputation as an intellectual mecca.[38] In addition to Furth and Hayek, close friends Morgenstern and Gottfried Haberler joined, as did Fritz Machlup. These men constituted the key members of the postwar Austrian School. Alfred Schütz and Felix Kaufmann, two philosophers of the social sciences, attended. So did Karl Menger, the son of the Austrian School's founder. The philosopher Erich Voegelin, historian Friedrich Engel-Janosi, psychoanalyst Robert Wälder, and art historians Otto Benesch and Emmanuel Winternitz also participated. Outcasts in Austria, these men would enjoy great success in the transatlantic world.[39]

While the circle's interests were diverse, the economists dominated proceedings, especially Furth and Hayek. They were already in the thrall of Carl Menger and, more importantly, Wieser. Wieser's courses were the gateway for this generation. His textbook *Social Economics* was their bible, and rightfully so. The American economist Wesley Clair Mitchell argued that it "holds a place in the literature of the Austrian School such as John Stuart Mill's *Political Economy* holds in the literature of classical theory." It provided an introduction to marginal utility theory, but it also ranged well beyond the determination of values and prices. It enjoined economists to rethink the social implications of economic theory.[40]

Starting from the subjective theory of value, Wieser's investigation moved through four levels of economic activity: individual, social, national, and global. Wieser argued that the Austrian School approach best explained individual economic behavior, yet its early theorizers had not dedicated enough time to explaining how their theory worked in larger social configurations. While questions of value and calculation mattered at all levels, Wieser recognized another force at work: power. The powerful had the ability to distort the socially beneficial effects of free exchange: "Powerful persons are merely in the position, in building up the economic organization, to carry through their personal interests rather than the general interest." Wieser used subjective value theory to ascertain when "social consciousness" and power were in harmony (or opposition) at the local, national, and world levels. As he imparted to his students, this was no abstract problem. Classical economists, with their laissez-faire attitudes, had left the door open to socialist critics. The latter observed and theorized the baleful effects of free markets and capitalism, to which liberals offered unconvincing rejoinders. With the rise of the proletariat and Bolshevism, the realization of an alternative social theory was now available, which threatened the "experience of thousands of years." Wieser's project was to close the "loopholes" in bourgeois theory by pinpointing and addressing the destructive force of power relations in liberal society so that a social economy founded on subjectivist principles could resist the "untenable, impractical" theoretical assumptions of socialism. The second edition of *Social Economics*, published in 1927, brought Wieser's work into conversation with general trends in European sociology, exemplified by Pareto, Michels, and Weber, which examined the connections between the individual and the collective, or "consciousness and society."[41]

Even if Wieser's seminar was "not much to get excited about," his *Social Economics* provided a compelling defense of marginalism while asserting its centrality for contemporary debates about economics, politics, and power. Wieser's social concerns inflected much of the work presented by students. Their essays, debated in heated seminar discussions, later appeared in journals, like the new series of the *Zeitschrift*, the Schumpeter-edited *Archiv für Sozialwissenschaft und Sozialpolitik*, and later the *Zeitschrift für Nationalökonomie*. By the mid-1920s, the school was on firmer footing thanks to Wieser's tutelage and the Geist-Kreis. By 1927, Paul Rosenstein-Rodan, a young devotee, could write that a "New Austrian School" had taken up the mantle of the older generation.[42]

Institutions of the New School

To gain broader acceptance within the economics community and the intellectual world, Austrian economists turned to new publications and associations. They wrote in the liberal Viennese newspapers *Neue Freie Presse* and *Neues Wiener Tagblatt* and popular economic journals *Der Deutsche Volkswirt* and *Der Österreichische Volkswirt*. They participated in social scientific organizations such as the Nationalökonomische Gesellschaft (NÖG) and the Society of Austrian Economists (GÖV) and advocacy groups like the Vienna and Lower Austrian Chambers of Commerce, the Central Association of Industry, and the Industrialist Club. They presented lectures at Austrian universities and at adult-education institutions. They offered seminars to businesspeople on statistics and mathematics. The primary outlets for Austrian economists were the economics journals the *Zeitschrift* and *Archiv*.

The Austrian School used these journals for intramural discussion. Often this consisted of attempts to carve out space for new research that went beyond the work of Böhm and Wieser. On the occasion of the appearance of Böhm's collected works, Otto Weinberger, a member of the Schumpeter and Mises generation, dissected the master's capital theory. Alfred Amonn offered a critical reading of Wieser's late works, especially *Social Economics*, offering a gentle criticism of Wieser's sociological turn. Amonn felt that Wieser deviated too far from pure theory into the realm of social life, and he cautioned others from similar divergences. In this way, Amonn articulated an emerging split between Böhm's tradition of pure theory and Wieser's preference for social economics.[43]

Amonn encouraged his fellow Austrians to concentrate less on socio-logical speculation and more on economic theory, yet the postwar generation did not view the approaches as incompatible. While their scholarly articles demonstrated their technical acumen, their popular work showed a keen social awareness. Multiple articles on monetary and bank theory appeared, most notably from Haberler, Marianne Herzfeld, and Helene Lieser. Furth, Hayek, Kaufmann, and Voegelin wrote on theoretical concerns. Kaufmann lauded marginal utility theory, saying that it offered the most fruitful method for economics. According to him, its subjective theory of value dovetailed with the phenomenological philosophy of Franz Brentano and Edmund Husserl, which was in vogue in the central European academy. Voegelin tried to balance the influences of marginalist economics with the holistic teachings of Othmar Spann and the positivist inclinations of the jurist Hans Kelsen. Kaufmann and Voegelin saw great promise in the subjectivist approach for social theory, with Voegelin especially appreciative of the Austrian focus on the dynamism of human communities and the role of time in human affairs.[44]

Austrian School scholars revealed their intellectual breadth, especially in their embrace of international developments in economic thought. After a fifteen-month stint in the United States, Hayek published on US banking policy, as he began to make a name for himself in business cycle theory. In particular, he challenged the advisability of the US Federal Reserve's discretionary banking policy, which was based on maintaining a stable price level to counteract the fluctuations of the business cycle. Hayek thought these policies were often mistimed and disruptive. Martha Stephanie Braun and Fritz Machlup wrote about British banking history and Knut Wicksell's theories of neutral money, following in Mises's footsteps.[45]

The new cohort of Austrians helped reawaken economic discussions in German-speaking lands after a fallow period occasioned by the Great War. From a later vantage, the 1920s seem an unremarkable period in the Austrian School's history. Its scholars introduced no major theoretical innovations; only Wieser's 1926 *Das Gesetz der Macht* (*The Law of Power*) counted as a novel contribution. Mises's *Socialism* still receives attention, yet its significance owes to its political message more than its theoretical newness.

Nevertheless, the post–World War I era was vital for the re-creation of the school, since it provided opportunities for a new generation to learn and to establish its own modes of interaction. These younger scholars reflected the best elements of the earlier Austrian tradition—its methodological rigor, its ecumenism, and its combativeness. Dedicated to the ideas of their forebears, they were no mere acolytes, showing a willingness to dissent and deviate. They also showed a keen awareness of the changed economic and political conditions in Austria, sensing that they were unlikely to gain power in the academy or the bureaucracy. They consequently developed an "Austro-liberalism" or "neoliberalism" responsive to the times, which updated the liberal values of their predecessors for the postimperial world. In particular, the Viennese economists sought support from new benefactors, especially from industry, finance, and international philanthropic foundations. Three figures loomed especially large during this gestation period: Hans Mayer, Ludwig von Mises, and John D. Rockefeller.[46]

Hans Mayer

When Wieser retired in 1922, the university sought a replacement who could teach theoretical economics. In a shock to many members of the academic community, Hans Mayer, a relative unknown who had yet to publish a monograph, received the appointment ahead of Schumpeter, Mises, or Amonn. The selection reflected the state of academic politics in Austria. Going into the search, the faculty was sharply divided on questions of theory and method. A Wieser acolyte identified with the Austrian School, Mayer was skeptical of methodological individualism, even though he espoused marginal utility theory. This middle position made him more acceptable to the university faculty than the individualists Mises or Schumpeter. Mayer's research focused on the role of time for equilibrium theory (which he identified with the concept of "complementarity"), the imputation problem, and the role of mathematics in economics. In the complicated politics of the law faculty, Wieser's and Spann's intervention on Mayer's behalf was decisive.[47]

With his elevation Mayer commanded respect and even fear in Viennese circles. As the anointed heir to the Austrian School tradition, his opinions mattered. He devoted much of his energy to editorial work, particularly a mammoth Festschrift for Wieser. His students, especially Paul Rosenstein-Rodan and Leo Schönfeld, used his "causal-genetic" explanations of economic change over time to level important criticisms of general equilibrium theory. They identified complementarity—the idea that the utilities of goods are not just based on subjective appraisals of discrete goods but on the relationship between different goods—as *the* outstanding issue in modern economic theory. These dependency relationships meant that attempts to calculate general equilibrium using a series of equations, à la Walras and Pareto, would never explicate real, existing economic conditions. They declared the "New Austrian School" to be the only group equipped to address this deficiency.[48]

Mayer's lasting legacy was a negative one, however. Irascible and provocative, Mayer carried on open feuds with Spann and Mises, devoting more time to thwarting their efforts than advancing his own work. All three men deserve their share of blame for the balkanization of economics at the university, yet Mayer was the main driver. He also heightened the tensions at the *Zeitschrift*. In his role as editor, he frequently excluded authors with whom he disagreed. He acquired a reputation as disorganized, opportunistic, and mediocre, yet younger Austrians kept those opinions to themselves in the name of self-preservation. Morgenstern confided his frustrations to his diary: "Yesterday I met with [Ewald] Schams at Café Reichsrat. . . . We should complain about Mayer. Why doesn't Mayer work? He doesn't write, doesn't read, doesn't finish the second volume, he doesn't act on behalf of the journal, but he sits for hours in the café and talks about Spann. We are all of the same opinion of him." Morgenstern, known for his sharp tongue and implacable criticism, represented the views of his friends well. Nevertheless, he maintained cordial relations with Mayer, since the older scholar controlled Morgenstern's hopes for academic advancement. Morgenstern and his cohort increasingly distanced themselves from Mayer by turning to his rival for the title of leader of the Austrian School: Mises.[49]

"Neither School, nor Community, nor Sect": The Mises-Kreis

From the mid-1920s until the mid-1930s, twenty young men and women congregated every other Friday at 7:00 p.m. in the Lower Austrian Chamber of Commerce in the office of Ludwig von Mises to discuss "important problems of economics, social philosophy, logic, and the epistemology of the sciences of human action." The evenings began with a talk on economic theory, policy, or methodology, and the "always lively discussion" flowed for three hours. The group then adjourned to an Italian restaurant (The Green Anchor) for dinner, when conversation turned to "finer points of theory." From 11:30 p.m. until 1:00 a.m. (or later), the men—women were excluded from this ritual—could be found at the Café Künstler, where the friends imbibed drinks over conversation of a "lighter tone." By the end of the evenings, the seminar participants could be heard singing songs adapted by Felix Kaufmann to well-known drinking tunes. Over two dozen songs have survived to this day. Inspired by Karl Kraus's poetic stylings, the *Lieder* celebrated the Mises circle, marginal utility theory, and economics. Even half a century later, members of the Austrian School recalled the tunes verbatim.[50] The seminar's anthem captured the insouciance of this experience:

> If the mind [*Geist*] is full of wisdom at 10,
> The stomach feels sad and empty,
> But soon it will receive its import tax,
> Because we will go to the Ancora Verde.
> There happiness is our motto,
> With spaghetti and risotto.
> How time flies, no one would believe,
> That the clock already struck midnight.
> But then comes the most genial idea,
> One can yet go to the Künstler Café.[51]

Despite the many positive features of the social and intellectual experience, the Mises seminar arose from his attenuated position in the academy. After Hans Mayer's university appointment, the Böhm tradition, represented by Mises, had a harder time vis-à-vis the Wieserian one. It is not clear that Mises exerted much influence on undergraduates in the early 1920s. This was partly because he was untenured and his private seminar was by invitation only. While he had an undergraduate seminar, Mises's seminar was less popular than Mayer's. And owing to Spann's great visibility, it is likely that Mises's seminar was the least visited of the major interwar economics gatherings.[52]

Nevertheless, the Mises private seminar eventually became the best known. This reflected his improving professional prospects. He began to wield influence at the Accounting Office and the Lower Austrian Chamber of Commerce, and he even gained the ear of conservative Christian Social officials during the hyperinflation. His courses at the university attracted economic students disenchanted with Spann and Mayer. For example, Hayek worked with Mises in both offices after an introduction from Wieser. Wieser remained Hayek's primary mentor, yet Mises played a larger role in Hayek's development after Wieser's death in 1926. Hayek spent 1922 and 1923 enrolled at NYU, and he traveled the eastern United States using his own funds. When he returned to Austria in 1924, Hayek joined the Mises-Kreis, which he loyally attended until leaving Vienna for London in 1931.[53]

Like Hayek, Morgenstern started attending the Mises seminar in 1924. Morgenstern had recently parted company with the "unscientific" Spann-Kreis, and his alienation from Mayer grew after 1929. Morgenstern bided his time before the break, since he needed Mayer's support to complete his habilitation, especially since Spann was firmly opposed to the "Jew" Morgenstern. Morgenstern's first monograph, *Wirtschaftsprognose* (1928), reflected the increased engagement with the Menger-Böhm-Mises tradition. In a scathing critique of economic forecasting, he rejected the possibility of prediction in macroeconomics and business cycle theory. He was the first of the younger Austrians to evince the skepticism about forecasting that became one of the school's calling cards.[54]

Likely encouraged by Hayek and Morgenstern, the complete Geist-Kreis began attending Mises's seminar, constituting half of the seminar's number. The lines between the two gatherings blurred. Haberler and Machlup, who both entered Mises's orbit at this time, displayed the elder's influence in their earliest efforts. They also showed their growing knowledge of international economic trends regarding statistics, business cycles, and monetary theory. Haberler's first book cast doubt on the utility of "index numbers," aggregate data used to better model economic developments. Popular with American economists, especially Irving Fischer, and a younger generation of German economic statisticians, Haberler answered the "index number mania" by denying their explanatory power. The shortcomings of modern statistics, Haberler maintained, were especially evident when it came to assessing the value of money, the price level, and inflation. Machlup, who was an intimate of Hayek, became Mises's only doctoral student. His 1925 book on the gold exchange standard was an extension of Mises's 1912 work. As Martha Steffy Browne reminisced, the young Austrians presented their new research to the seminar, where they challenged one another to produce sharper work.[55]

Despite superficial resemblances to the prewar Böhm seminar, Mises's had a narrower focus and a clearer ideological program. This reflected the changed circumstances of postwar Austria, where political and ideological polarization made "value-free" scientific discussions less likely. An Otto Bauer, Rudolf Hilferding, or Otto Neurath would have been persona non grata for Mises, let alone a Nikolai Bukharin. Mises claimed that he cultivated "neither school, nor community, nor sect," but some topics, especially socialism, were verboten: "Mises was so convinced that he had exhaustively dealt with all the essential questions in the area of socialism, and that all participants in the seminar had the same opinions on the subject, that any such conversation [on that topic] had nothing to offer." All participants were expected to embrace marginal utility theory and liberal politics. The Mises-Kreis songs demonstrate these bona fides. They take shots at those who did not share their views. As they sang in "Mises-Mayer Debate," "I call myself a liberal / But not from days of yore. I say all things differently / Than those who came before. A liberal can anyone be / But in Vienna alone the reasons see. I know this 'cause marginal utility / Sheds light on economy." For the Mises-Kreis, if you were not a marginalist, you were not a true liberal.[56]

In return for ideological and intellectual reliability, Mises helped his seminar colleagues find employment. Using his position at the Chamber of Commerce, which put him in regular contact with businesspeople, financiers, and industrialists, he identified opportunities. Many younger school members—Machlup, Morgenstern, Helene Lieser—followed him into the industrial and financial sectors. Lieser, the first woman to receive an economics doctorate in Vienna, worked for the League of Austrian Banks and Bankers. Machlup ran his father's cardboard factory and lectured to business associations. Eventually Mises helped him get a newspaper column with the *Neue Wiener Tagblatt*, where his pro-industry and pro-finance positions endeared him to bankers and industrialists.

The Institut für Konjunkturforschung (Institute for Business Cycle Research), founded by Mises in 1927 and run by Hayek, demonstrated the convergence of liberal ideas and capital. Austrian School members received patronage from wealthy benefactors from Austria and the United States. In return, they provided their economic expertise. The institute also revealed one of the great ironies of the interwar Austrian School: its most famous innovation was an empirical center that provided forecasts on macroeconomic conditions. Despite the school's disparagement of economic forecasting, rejection of macroeconomic data, skepticism about expert opinion, and concerns about uncertainty in the market process, its members created a renowned forecasting center known most of all for its reports on actual economic conditions, not its theory.

The Rockefeller Foundation in Austria

Despite the location of the institute in Red Vienna, it was an association apart. It was sustained by members of the increasingly conservative Austrian *Großbürgertum* and US philanthropic foundations. A look at its board of trustees reveals the important connections Mises and Hayek had cultivated with the conservative establishment. Besides Mises and Hayek, the other key members—the chairman and vice chairman—were Richard Reisch, the president of the Austrian National Bank and a former student of Menger's, and Walter Breisky, a Christian Social politician and the head of the Federal Statistical Office. Of the other forty-five members, there were representatives of the conservative federal government, lobbying groups for industry, bankers, CEOs, and nationalist professors. The Austrian School, Chamber of Commerce, and private industry held the majority of positions and steered the direction of the institute, with Hayek and Mises in primary control.[57]

Unfortunately for Mises and the institute, the Austrian government, while sympathetic to their efforts, had little funding to offer. The economists therefore cast their nets wider for support, becoming poster children of the transatlantic exchange of social scientific ideas and transnational philanthropy. The intervention of the Rockefeller Foundation (RF) in central European affairs was the decisive factor in the institute's success. The Austrian School was one of the primary beneficiaries of the RF's decision to expand its areas of expertise into the social sciences. The younger Austrians' international reputation owed much to this serendipitous liaison, and their successful transatlantic emigration was facilitated by this intervention.

After the 1924 establishment of the Laura Spelman Rockefeller Memorial Fund, which permitted European social scientists to research in the United States, Viennese economists formed a strong relationship with Alfred Pribram, the RF selector in Austria. A close friend of Freud's and a member of several Viennese circles, Pribram favored Wieser's students. Furth, Haberler, Machlup, Morgenstern, Rosenstein-Rodan, Gerhard Tintner, and Voegelin received fellowships in the next decade. Fellowships, which lasted one or two years, introduced the Austrians to new research trends, particularly the business cycle research conducted at the Cambridge (UK) Economic Service, the Harvard Economic Service, and the National Bureau of Economic Research. As a result of these fellowships, the younger Austrians combined empirical and theoretical work in ways unimaginable to their predecessors. Extended absences from Vienna moreover accentuated the intellectual discontinuity between the earlier Austrian School and the post–World War I generation. The transatlantic exchange had a lot to do with the shifting focus of the Austrian School and would contribute to the postwar divergences within the tradition.[58]

In addition to the international connections established by the RF fellowships, the constellation of RF-subsidized European social scientific research centers created a transnational scientific community in which the Austrians starred. Inspired by the ideas of expert-led social reform of the Progressive era, the RF cultivated elite networks that advanced a liberal, internationalist worldview. Austrian scholars embodied these cultural values and enjoyed unparalleled patronage from the RF. In proportion to the country's size, Austria produced more fellows than any other European country. Joseph Schumpeter, now in Germany, noted the success of the Austrian economists while lamenting German deficiencies. Oskar Morgenstern also observed that Austrians outstripped Germans in international reputation thanks to RF participation.[59]

The RF financed social scientific research institutes across Europe, which became hubs of interwar policy-oriented analysis. The London School of Economics (LSE) received substantial grants to sustain its activities. The RF supported the Paris-based Institut de Recherches Économiques et

Sociales, headed by Charles Rist, and William Rappard's Institut Universitaire des Hautes Études Internationales in Geneva. It granted money to
the League of Nations, including the Economic and Financial Sections.
With the US failure to ratify the Treaty of Versailles and its refusal to join
the League, RF institutions became proxy agents of the US government.
Geneva became a seedbed for liberal internationalist and nascent neoliberal
thought.[60] Meanwhile in Vienna, the RF financed two fledgling centers,
Karl and Charlotte Bühler's Psychologisches Institut and the Mises and
Hayek institute. In backing the latter project, Pribram drew an explicit
connection between Hayek's research trip to the United States and the
center. The RF responded positively, providing a five-year grant totaling
$20,000 ($321,000 in 2019 dollars) beginning in 1931. This was $1,000
per annum *more* than Hayek requested, with the extra funds earmarked
for Morgenstern and Hayek, since "these two men are among the ablest
of the younger economists in the German speaking countries, and there
is some danger that they will be drawn away from Vienna unless conditions
can be made for [*sic*] attractive for them." The RF was right to fear a brain
drain, for Hayek left for London in 1931. Likewise, Morgenstern had
regular employment offers, declining positions at Berkeley and Kiel. The
RF showed its satisfaction by renewing its support in 1936 for two years
at $6,000 per annum and again for three years in 1938, though it canceled
payment after the Anschluss. If the RF helped establish the younger Austrians, it also saved them, since the RF played a pivotal role in the emigration of the Austrian School in the 1930s.[61]

    As Wieser foresaw in *Österreichs Ende*, central Europe in the late
1920s looked little like 1918, let alone 1914. The Austrian School, like its
home country, faced a crossroads. Wieser was the last of the titans of the
early Austrian School, and his 1926 death signaled a major loss. The Austrian School had to reinvent itself in trying circumstances. Despite connections in the government and the academy, Joseph Schumpeter, Ludwig
von Mises, and Hans Mayer confronted major obstacles in their pursuit of
influence. With political access and academic opportunities limited, these
men refashioned themselves. They turned to media and new nongovern-
mental institutions to expand their audience. They also sought new patrons
for their endeavors both within Austria and abroad. The 1920s were

therefore a period of re-creation for the school, setting the stage for its next two decades. While important continuities existed with the "golden age" school, new tendencies also emerged, which pointed away from theoretical economic work. School participants found themselves on the front lines of ideological debates with conservatives and socialists—battles of ideas from which the Austrians would never retreat or relent.

The postwar generation that emerged in the 1920s reflected this new order. Its members debated ideas not just in university lecture halls but in private seminars, salons, "Vienna circles," and think tanks. The cultural dynamism of Red and Black Vienna inspired younger Austrians to incorporate new influences. Their increasing engagement with the transatlantic scientific community exposed them to empirical and statistical approaches that forced them to refine earlier marginalist ideas. By the late 1920s, the Austrian School had stabilized, confidently announcing itself to the international community. Ironically, the international achievements of its members did not improve their prospects at home. This contributed to their jaundiced view of Catholic conservatism and (social) democracy. The latter they blamed overwhelmingly for the ongoing struggles of their once-great country.

If the late 1920s offered a slight glimmer of hope for a second golden age, historical events quickly dashed those dreams. The world economic crisis left Austria teetering on the edge of disaster. The lingering effects of deflation, stagnation, and unemployment called into question many of the Austrians' economic assumptions. Moreover, the rise of fascism and National Socialism loomed over Austria and the democracies of central Europe, leading the Austrians to despair for the liberal, capitalist order. These changed conditions shifted the priorities for Austrian School members dramatically. In addition to their concerns with economic, intellectual, and political influence, they had to add a still more pressing one: survival.

4

DEPRESSION, EMIGRATION, AND
FASCISM: THE AUSTRIAN SCHOOL
GOES TRANSATLANTIC

It was Friedrich Hayek's job to watch international economic trends. As director of the Rockefeller Foundation (RF)–sponsored Institute for Business Cycle Research from 1927 to 1931, he compiled and analyzed statistical data from around the globe, publishing his findings in the institute's monthly newsletter. By May 1929, Hayek had serious concerns about the Austrian and global economies. "While the Austrian economy has shown a notable resistance to the depression tendencies . . . the indices nevertheless show that the unfavorable state of the entire European economy has also produced its effects here." Hayek criticized the world's central banks for failing to adjust interest rates in response to decreased production in Europe, increased financial speculation in New York, and the steady flow of gold from Europe across the Atlantic. Barring a change in monetary policy and a course correction in the US markets, the European economy could only anticipate further setbacks. Hayek hammered home these judgments throughout the summer, as central banks refused to adjust their rates, and capital continued to flow to the overheating US financial markets. He complained that economic decisions had taken a back seat to political ones, which prevented the natural adaptation of the business cycle to changing conditions.[1]

Despite these sanguine pronouncements, Hayek did not foresee the Wall Street stock market crash of October 29, 1929, the event most associated with the start of the Great Depression. In the October institute report composed the week prior to the collapse, Hayek thought he saw the tide turning: "The last four weeks have seen important changes in the entire economic landscape, which address the long-feared sharpening of depression tendencies and simultaneously offer a definite clarification of the outlook for the future." This guarded optimism seems misguided in retrospect, yet it would be unfair to criticize Hayek for failing to foresee an event that no one predicted. Economists around the world fared poorly in their prognostications. Famously, the US economist Irving Fisher prognosticated days before the crash that "stock prices have reached what looks like a permanently high plateau." Conditions in Austria, which Hayek observed closely, took a grim turn. That same October, the Bodencreditanstalt (BCA), one of Austria's most storied financial institutions, announced its insolvency. Headed by Rudolf Sieghart, one of Eugen von Böhm-Bawerk's disciples, the bank faced bankruptcy when it could no longer make payments on its foreign loans. The Austrian government hastily orchestrated its takeover by the Rothschild-owned Creditanstalt (CA) by arranging for the state to take on most of BCA's outstanding debts. Hayek felt that the changes in the international economy loomed over this calamitous result. In November, Hayek confirmed his judgment that "an acute depression had arrived," yet a "very significant relaxation of the world monetary market" should moderate the effects and precipitate a turnaround. If politicians stayed out of financial and economic matters, the world economy would recover in the next year, as prices and interest rates stabilized, wages declined, and production rebounded. Order and general equilibrium would return.[2]

Little did Hayek realize that the economic upturn would not come for years, a period punctuated by the worst war the world had ever seen. By 1933, his codirector and eventual successor at the institute, Oskar Morgenstern, had devised the Kindleberger spiral—which rightly should bear Morgenstern's name—to depict the precipitous decline in world trade from January 1929 to June 1933.[3] The crisis that befell the world economy threw Morgenstern's economic and ideological views—and those of the reconfigured Austrian School—into flux. The school's members reinvented the collective in the interwar era with an array of circles, institutes, and journals and had gained prominence with their monetary and business cycle theory and their defenses of the gold standard and fiscal conservatism. The ever-deepening economic depression shook these beliefs, as austerity policies only exacerbated problems. Meanwhile the defenders of the conservative order, with whom the Austrians often made common cause, moved in an increasingly authoritarian direction. Caught between Marxian social democracy, which they reviled as civilization's great enemy, and fascist-inspired conservatism, with its inconsistent relationship to the liberal values of free trade and individualism, the members of the Austrian School had to reconsider their ideas about democracy, liberalism, and the state. The rise of European fascism was not just intellectually destabilizing for the school. It also forced the younger Austrians to consider emigration from their homeland. Just as the school regained its bearings, it was threatened with dissolution.

This chapter follows the members of the younger Austrian School through the intellectual, political, and economic turmoil of the 1930s. It examines how the Austrians confronted real-world economics in their academic and policy activities, leading them into a series of theoretical debates that had far greater stakes than the ostensible subjects suggested. These discussions show how their anxiety about the collapse of European civilization and rise of collectivism—whether from the right (Nazism) or the left (socialism)—led them into alliances with conservatives and to imagine a reformed liberalism, or neoliberalism, suited to the exigencies of the age. Finally it explores how the Austrians once again reinvented themselves in the early years of emigration. There was nothing inevitable about the survival of the Austrian tradition, especially after a transatlantic journey, yet the school quickly regained its bearings. And while clear divisions began to surface even before emigration, especially between Mises and Hayek on one side and Morgenstern on the other, the school's members relied on their rich heritage and dense interpersonal connections to help each other through these trying times.

At the heart of the Austrian School of the crisis years were five men: Gottfried Haberler, Hayek, Fritz Machlup, Mises, and Morgenstern. These men will be our primary guides to the Austrian School for the next six decades—until the school truly ceased to be "Austrian." To understand the school, we must understand their ideas and organizations, their lives and their actions. How they reinvented the school and the Viennese thought style in this time of troubles is a powerful story of personal adaptation, intellectual translation, and institutional entrepreneurialism.

The Great Depression and the Crisis of
Austrian Economic Thought

Hayek's experience at the Institute for Business Cycle Research in 1929 was symptomatic of the intellectual crisis within the Austrian School occasioned by the outbreak of worldwide depression. The Austrians, like their economist peers across Europe, attempted to explain the global downturn of 1929–33 and devise policy responses. And, like their liberal colleagues in Germany, Scandinavia, the United States, and the United Kingdom, they resorted to solutions—stabilization of the gold standard system, balanced budgets, reduced exchange restrictions, and free trade—that deepened deflationary tendencies, exacerbated unemployment, and perpetuated economic contraction. While economists and historians of economic thought have long debated whether any viable policy alternatives existed, the Austrian School represented the most strident defenders of conventional economic policies. Of the core members of the Austrian School, only Gottfried Haberler moderated his position in the 1930s with the publication of his book *Prosperity and Depression*. The remainder—Mises, Hayek, Machlup, Morgenstern, and Richard Strigl—stuck to their guns. This was reflected in their scholarly work and policy advice to the Austrian state, in articles for the liberal media, in their activities with the International Chamber of Commerce, and within the transnational network of business cycle institutes.[4]

As the Austrians established themselves in the late 1920s, they cultivated an impressive network domestically. Their ties extended in a number of directions. They enjoyed ardent support from liberal newspapermen. Moritz Benedikt, the editor of the *Neue Freie Presse* until 1920, was a classmate of Böhm and Wieser and an early popularizer of marginalism. His son Ernst succeeded him and offered his paper as an outlet for liberal economics. Meanwhile Viktor Graetz, a Menger student, the director of one of Austria's largest companies, and a prominent member of the National Economic Society, ran the *Wiener Neues Tagblatt*. Julius Meinl, scion of an Austrian coffee dynasty—whose shops still dot the Viennese cityscape today—attended salons with the younger economists. Morgenstern occasionally visited Julius at the Meinl family's summer estate. Richard Reisch and Viktor Kienböck, the two interwar presidents of the Austrian National

Bank, had close ties to Böhm and Mises, respectively, attending their private seminars and inviting their advice. These men were the original benefactors of the Institute for Business Cycle Research. Lastly, the Austrian School developed good relations with the Christian Social Party through Kienböck, three-time Chancellor Ignaz Seipel, and Walter Breisky, head of the Statistical Office.[5]

The Austrian economists used the intimate world of Viennese bourgeois culture to advance their personal and professional standing. When the Austrian economy collapsed, they were well placed to offer policy proposals. Ludwig von Mises was a central actor in these developments. He had advised conservative politicians, including Chancellor Seipel, during the crisis years of 1922–23. He advocated austerity measures—cutting state expenditures and laying off tens of thousands of civil servants—and a return to the gold exchange standard to stem hyperinflation and stabilize the Austrian schilling. Mises operated behind the scenes throughout the mid-1920s while Austria negotiated with the League of Nations and foreign investors for loans and better terms of trade. He was joined in these negotiations by Richard Schüller, Carl Menger's last and most brilliant doctoral student, who served as the postwar section chief for trade in the Foreign Office and as a member of the Economic Committee of the League of Nations in Geneva. In the name of economic stability, Mises was willing to see Austria sacrifice a large degree of its democratic sovereignty. Since the publication of *Nation, State, and Economy*, Mises had become increasingly leery of mass democracy and conflicts between liberal economics and democratic governance. Economic stability was his primary goal, which he advocated in his governmental advisory role and in his advocacy work through the Chamber of Commerce. Although he was not fully pleased with the final postwar settlement, Mises took credit for the defeat of Bolshevism and Austria's economic stabilization. He did not accept the blame for the deflation and unemployment that hampered the Austrian economy in the late 1920s, however. He also looked askance at Seipel's increasingly authoritarian tendencies, which the chancellor embraced in the face of growing popular disillusionment with the government and economy.[6]

While Mises countenanced extensive intervention by international financiers in Austrian domestic affairs to smooth market functions, he rejected state involvement in economic decision-making. In *Interventionism* (1929), he inveighed against state meddling with the market process. He felt that interventionism, "a system of restricted, regulated, and directed private property," was ubiquitous. From Bolshevik Russia to fascist Italy, from the Catholic Church to "Mohammedan" Angora and India, everyone considered *how* they should intervene rather than *whether*. Mises made it his mission to counteract ad hoc regulation of the market by state authorities. He attributed this sorry state of the world economy to the "defeat of liberalism," that is, laissez-faire economics. Interest groups struggled for their own gain at the expense of the common good, producing corruption, stagnation, and suffering. For Mises, interventionism, like socialism, was destructionism. "The great crisis, under which the world economy has suffered since the end of the war, has been characterized by statists and socialists as a crisis of capitalism. In reality it is a crisis of interventionism." In Mises's view, states must not engage in unemployment schemes or welfare measures because those perpetuate distortions in wage levels. The economy must be allowed to self-adjust. "Prosperity for all" would then follow.[7]

Mises's home institution, the Vienna Chamber of Commerce, as well as its affiliated organization, the International Chamber of Commerce (ICC), provided him a pulpit to espouse his program of capitalist internationalism. The Vienna Chamber, located on the Ringstrasse in a six-story, Jugendstil edifice covered in Habsburg and Egyptian symbols and a shimmering array of marble, glass, and metal, was Mises's employer for over a quarter century. Hayek and Haberler also worked there in the 1920s. Mises led a three-person Economic Commission in 1930 while serving as the chamber's secretary. Meanwhile the ICC was the most important international business organization of the interwar era. US businesspeople in particular used the ICC to engage in international exchange after the United States refused to join the League of Nations. The ICC and its members sought to tear down tariff walls, increase capital and information flows, and encourage world economic activity. They saw states as economically interdependent and were positively disposed to the Austrian School's globalist vision and individualist precepts. Mises attended his first ICC meeting in 1925; Vienna hosted the seventh ICC congress in 1933.[8]

When the Austrian economy tanked in the late 1920s and early 1930s, Mises hardly changed his tune. The Vienna Chamber of Commerce recommended cuts to unemployment benefits and health and accident insurance in February 1930. As part of the Economic Commission, Mises argued that the Austrian state could not and should not change the interest rate or alter price levels in response to worsening conditions. Instead, wages and taxes had to be lowered to spur recovery. The chamber promoted an "antiterror law" to be used by the Austrian state against striking workers in an effort to "depoliticize the economic." Obviously, these solutions were far from depoliticized, as the state's authoritarian interventions targeted the working classes and socialist political parties.[9]

The travails of Austrian society were painfully demonstrated in one of the landmark sociological studies of the early twentieth century, *Die Arbeitslosen von Marienthal* by the Viennese scholars Marie Jahoda, Paul Lazarsfeld, and Hans Zeisel. The work demonstrated the hardships occasioned by the draconian liberal policies supported by Mises. It documented the increasing despair of a small industrial town on the outskirts of Vienna using time series studies, psychological questionnaires, and fieldwork. While the investigations took place in 1931, the authors traced the town's problems back to the economic policies of the 1920s. The authors identified four major responses by working-class Austrians to the collapse of the industrial sector: "unbroken" defiance, resignation, despair, and apathy. Of the 478 families in town, only 23 percent were unbroken. In general, the Austrian population evinced a declining power of resistance to economic misery. *Marienthal* was a microcosm of the Austrian experience. Unemployment and immiseration were largely a consequence of new measures that stabilized the currency and protected creditors yet left the state with little autonomy. For Mises, these short-term corrections and regulations were unavoidable after years of excess and bad state policies.[10]

Mises's uncompromising attitude was confirmed during the Great Depression. He offered his interventionist reading in a 1930 lecture to the German Association of Industry, a major free trade advocacy group. He also took to business journals, industry newsletters, and the *Neue Freie Presse*. In "Die Krise und der Kapitalismus" (The crisis and capitalism) and other articles from the early 1930s, he rejected the popular interpretation that capitalism had caused the Great Depression and that the end of laissez-faire was nigh. Mises did not deny that the world was in crisis, but the problem was still interventionism: "No one can dispute that the dominant system of the day has failed. It is an entirely different question whether this system is capitalist, or instead whether anticapitalist policies, interventionism, state and communal socialism carry the guilt for this catastrophe." More capitalism, not less, was the way out. In particular, adherence to a gold exchange standard would prevent the booms and busts that drove the recent crisis. Removing price and wage controls, stripping power from unions, and reducing state expenditures would restore stability and encourage growth.[11]

Mises's prescriptions were straightforward measures aimed at the restoration of economic liberalism. Mises consistently advocated this position throughout his life. For him, classical liberalism—with its emphasis on the division of labor, free markets, competition, and entrepreneurial spirit—was the foundation of Western democracy and culture. Only a return to the capitalist order could forestall the collapse of parliamentarianism and the rise of dictatorship. While he saw democracy as a means to ensure nonviolent transitions of power and as the best means of governing to achieve liberal ends, democracy and liberalism were no longer synonymous. Given the choice, Mises privileged economic over political liberty, since he saw the former as constitutive of the latter. Mises was even willing to countenance the fascist critique of democracy: "A democratic constitution and individual freedom is meaningless in a state form whose economy is directed by authorities. The supporters of those dictators that one calls 'fascist' have recognized this and expressed it clearly." According to Mises, democratic states undermine liberal freedoms with their top-down planning and their interventions in the market. By catering to interest groups, too, democratic politicians undermined free exchange. A fascist state that restored individual liberties and stayed out of the economy would be preferable. While Mises was no fascist himself, his endorsement gibed with his support of the antidemocratic and authoritarian Seipel. Fascism was a bulwark against the depredations of socialists and communists: "It cannot be denied that Fascism and all similar dictatorial endeavors are full of the best intentions and that their interventions have saved European values for the moment. The service that Fascism has provided will live on forever in history." Mises had no love for the totalitarian aspirations of Mussolini (or later Hitler), but he believed that oftentimes an authoritarian government may be superior to a democratic one with respect to free trade, private property, and individual liberty.[12]

Mises's attitudes were not unique within the Austrian School. Hayek's assessment of the early stages of the Great Depression traced similar positions, which he laid out in his 1929 book *Monetary Theory and the Trade Cycle*. Following in the tradition of Böhm and Mises, Hayek defended theoretical understandings of business cycles over empirical ones. He saw low interest rates and elevated price levels at the heart of speculative bubbles and economic insecurity. He looked at what caused economies to slip out of equilibrium and identified money as a determining factor. Since money was the basis of exchange and credit and an object of speculation in its own right, it could disrupt the operation of supply and demand if its value fluctuated too greatly.[13] Hayek's response to economic downturns reflected his rejection of the ideas of what he called "quantity theory." Many quantity theorists argued that monetary policy should be used to stabilize the aggregate price level by adjusting the quantity of money in circulation. Hayek dismissed the idea that a deflationary episode should be counteracted by monetary policy. Changing the quantity of money was a blunt instrument that would only exacerbate existing economic imbalances. Hayek granted that deflations were bad, but they owed to maladjusted production, which was caused by artificially low credit rates. In Hayek's mind, economists were a long way from being able to offer adequate prescriptions, so they needed to be more circumspect with their policy prescriptions. In the final analysis, Hayek could only advocate for a slow self-readjustment of the economy. His policy advice in the face of a depression was to tighten one's belt and wait it out, even if there was pain involved.[14]

Hayek made his name with *Monetary Theory*. He received favorable reviews in German, Austrian, French, and Italian journals. More significantly, scholars at the RF-subsidized London School of Economics (LSE) took note, inviting Hayek for a series of four lectures in 1931. The RF, with its financial basis in the conservative financial elite of the United States, became an ardent defender of business cycle research. Recognizing a kindred spirit, Hayek became an early recipient of its largesse. The LSE lectures took a segment of the audience by storm. According to Lionel Robbins, an avid reader of Mises and onetime attendee of Mises's seminar, Hayek's invited lectures were "difficult and exciting; and they conveyed such an impression of learning and analytic invention." Robbins saw Hayek as an ally in his debates with John Maynard Keynes and the Cambridge economic community over the UK government's response to the Depression. With the unanimous support of the LSE faculty, Hayek was appointed the Tooke Chair of Economic Science and Statistics. The publication dates of *Monetary Theory*—1929 in German; 1931 in English translation—turned out to be fortunate, because they predated the nasty deflationary spiral of 1931–32 that announced the arrival of a full-blown economic downturn. Hayek's advocacy of self-adjustment seemed insensitive when industrialized countries like the United States, the United Kingdom, Austria, and Germany suffered unemployment rates in the twenties and thirties, and the worldwide economy contracted by 15 percent.[15]

While Mises offered a grand narrative of intervention and depression and Hayek presented theoretical discussions of price levels, Fritz Machlup offered a more policy-oriented analysis, which he disseminated in academic and popular outlets. Like his mentor Mises, Machlup came from a haut bourgeois, Jewish family. He likewise struggled to find a position in the antisemitic Austrian academy. Machlup wrote his dissertation on the gold exchange standard. In spite of enthusiastic support from Mises, he found no steady academic employment. He instead headed his family's cardboard business. He remained active in academic discussions, however, teaching classes at the university, attending the Mises seminar, and serving as secretary of the National Economic Society. He, Hayek, Haberler, and Morgenstern lunched together several days a week. Mises continued to endorse his pupil, connecting him with the *Neues Wiener Tagblatt* and recommending him for a Rockefeller fellowship.[16]

In the 1931 book *Stock Market, Credit, and Capital Formation*, Machlup offered the first Austrian School study that placed the stock market at the center of economic analysis. The rosy picture he painted of these financial activities is striking, given the book's publication two years after the New York Stock Exchange crash. *Stock Market* concerned itself with the distribution of credit between the stock market and industry and the effects of that distribution on the economy. Machlup intended to vindicate the current credit system and defend the principles of free competition. Weaving together credit, monetary, and capital theory allowed him to tackle "crucial problems of business cycle theory."[17]

Machlup advanced a series of arguments that refuted anticapitalist critics of the modern credit and financial systems. Since individuals and firms merely placed their capital into the outlet that yielded the best returns, the distribution of credit between the stock market and industry made little effective difference. State policy should therefore eschew direct involvement in those sectors. Machlup argued that credit systems were rarely just about economics; politics usually intervened. Following Mises, he suggested that credit expansion, inflation, and the obstruction of capital flows proceeded from bank policies and should be avoided. Most state interventions in capital markets led to instability because they distorted investment and production. While politicians and economists had to decide the proper mix of policies and regulations for the smooth functioning of the economy, Machlup generally placed his faith in the stock market as a "compass" and "steering wheel" for the economy. He felt that allowing the freer operation of financial markets provided security-exchange regulators better signals about the credit system and better data for open market policies. He rejected new policies, coming into vogue in the 1930s, that engaged in inflationary financing of the public budget. Only markets, not the state, could pull the world economy out of its doldrums.[18]

Among this group of "Austroliberals," the only figure who tempered his enthusiasm for Austrian business cycle theory and laissez-faire policy was Haberler. Even so, he remained well within the Austrian pale. Haberler was born to a well-to-do Austrian bureaucratic family with connections to the aristocracy in Liechtenstein, and his early work defended the gold standard and cast a jaundiced eye at index numbers, early statistical measures used to quantify the economy. Inspired by the Geist-Kreis, Haberler argued that spirit, or *Geist*, rather than statistical regularities, were at the core of economic activity and social science. He defended free trade using David Ricardo's idea of comparative advantage and insisted that markets be allowed to self-correct after a downturn. This meant lower tariffs and lower wages and more international trade. People, goods, and capital all had to flow as if borders did not exist if worldwide conditions were to improve.[19]

By the mid-1930s, Haberler was probably the best-regarded member of the younger Austrian School, yet he had begun to modify his positions. *International Trade*, published in 1933, established his reputation. It attracted the attention of Arthur Loveday and the Economic and Financial Section of the League of Nations. The League commissioned him to write a work "coordinat[ing] the analytical work then being done on the problem of the recurrence of periods of depression." The final product, *Prosperity and Depression*, was immediately hailed as a seminal contribution. No less an authority than Joseph Schumpeter regarded Haberler's work as a "masterly presentation of the modern material." The *London Times* also acknowledged the work's significance: "in a mere two years he has done what might have taken some men a lifetime." Haberler struck a pose of neutral arbiter between various theoretical undertakings, placing distance between himself and other approaches, including the Austrian. After witnessing the deepening of the Depression in 1931–33, when deflation and unemployment showed no signs of abating, he began to wonder about the correctness of Austrian explanations about overinvestment, credit expansion, and inflation. Haberler criticized the Austrian School for its inattention to the possibility and effects of a secondary deflation. He sided with Germans like Wilhelm Röpke who considered the possibility of "igniting" the economy with state spending. In the final analysis, though, Haberler endorsed the Austrian view and became even more convinced after an investigation into the failures of Keynesian and monetarist theory.[20]

As the examples from Mises, Hayek, Machlup, and Haberler demonstrate, in the early years of the Great Depression, the Austrian School spoke with virtually one voice about business cycles and economic policy. They emphasized problems with the monetary and credit systems, and they maintained that an excess rather than an absence of state intervention was the fundamental problem. The younger Austrians also shared the opinion that they must not solely analyze conditions but also transform them. This usually meant popular interventions in the liberal media and behind-the-scenes advocacy work for government agencies and business groups. In articles written between 1931 and 1934 by a quartet of Austrians (Haberler, Hayek, Machlup, and Morgenstern), they argued against protectionism, exchange controls, and credit injections into the economy. They supported austerity in state expenditures and domestic price stability and deflation. A return to the gold standard and pro-trade policies were frequent suggestions. They believed that price flexibility and deregulated markets in production and employment, too, would spur recovery.[21]

As this brief sampling of activities demonstrates, the early 1930s were a fertile period for members of the Austrian School. They reestablished a distinctive corporate identity and featured prominently in European policy debates. Moreover, the Great Depression shone a spotlight on the uniqueness of their approach, since they were more aggressively pro-capitalist than other economists were. Their views were widely supported among liberal politicians, the international business community, and economic conservatives. Prominent economists like Luigi Einaudi, the future president of Italy, acknowledged the ascendancy of the Austrian School at the time: "Excellent things were coming out of Austria. . . . There was a time when the Palma di Eccellenza was in Italy, and then it passed to Cambridge, England, and then it passed to Cambridge, United States. But now it seemed to be in Vienna." Economists from around the globe—Robbins and John Hicks in England, Jacob Viner and Frank Knight in the United States, Wilhelm Röpke in Germany, William Rappard in Switzerland—developed their ideas in interaction with the new school. The work of the Austrian School also became a lightning rod for controversy given the forcefulness of its positions.[22]

Hayek-Keynes

The intensity of economic discussions in the early 1930s reflected the urgency that the Great Depression lent to economists' research and analysis. The younger Austrians, who combined disparate economic and social scientific trends, recognized that they no longer just spoke to Austrian elites but to an international audience. As their predecessors Menger and Böhm had done, they stimulated debates within the economics community; the practical stakes were even higher now. Having honed their polemical skills within the circles of interwar Vienna, the Austrians girded for combat. The next decade witnessed three conflicts that defined the school: (1) between Hayek and John Maynard Keynes over business cycles and economic policy; (2) between the Austrians and the early Chicago School over capital and production; (3) between Hayek and Oskar Lange over the possibility of socialist calculation. These conflicts reverberate in debates about the viability of capitalism even today. In the Austrians' reimagining of the twentieth-century economic system, they also initiated debates about a "neoliberal" alternative to nineteenth-century liberalism and the "planned" systems associated with socialism, the New Deal, or Keynesianism.

By the time Friedrich Hayek delivered his LSE lectures in 1931, John Maynard Keynes was already one of the preeminent economists in the United Kingdom. Keynes owed much of his popularity to his unvarnished analyses of economic ideas and his coruscating attacks on opponents. Whether eviscerating the Treaty of Versailles in *The Economic Consequences of the Peace* (1919), castigating the deflationary impacts of the gold standard in *The Economic Consequences of Mr. Churchill* (1925), or fulminating on capitalism's fate in *The End of Laissez-Faire* (1926), Keynes found an audience for his bombast. He was more than a churlish wag, however. The son of a Cambridge economist and a student of Alfred Marshall, Keynes excelled as a mathematician and economist at an early age. He was a fellow at Cambridge and served in prominent roles in the Treasury. In the 1920s, he published a notable book on probability and developed a reputation for a keen ability for applying theory to policy.[23]

After six years of work, Keynes finished his *Treatise on Money* in late 1930, yet its reception was muted by the onset of the Depression. Keynes meant the book as his major statement on contemporary economics, but the problems of 1924–29 were not the same ones as 1930. This left his theoretical exposition and policy prescriptions misaligned, as he acknowledged. He had not developed a means for understanding persistent unemployment, nor had he devised a model that emphasized changes in output rather than prices. His terminology was not always consistent or conventional, which also undermined his exposition. Nevertheless, the *Treatise* anticipated a new direction in his economic thinking, which came to fuller fruition in the 1936 *General Theory*. Looking at the depression phenomenon, Keynes argued that if aggregate savings exceeded investment owing to high interest rates, then unemployment would increase. The conventional policy response of governments to economic downturns—raising interest rates to drive down prices and spending—could then have disastrous consequences. These new ideas provoked extensive conversation within the British economic community. In particular, his Cambridge colleagues Richard Kahn, Piero Sraffa, Joan and Austin Robinson, and James Meade convened the "Cambridge Circus" to discuss and dispute the *Treatise*.[24]

Engaging the Cambridge don and Bloomsbury bon vivant Keynes in an economic debate, as Hayek did in 1931, therefore had cultural ramifications that extended beyond economics. Hayek probably felt he had little choice but to answer the *Treatise* since it trod familiar Austrian ground and found the Austrian School's insights wanting. Keynes theorized the concepts of money and credit and developed a set of applications that flew in the face of Austrian beliefs. As he stated in a 1928 précis, "It must be admitted that advocates of price stability, amongst whom I number myself, have erred in the past when their words have seemed to indicate price stability as the sole objective of monetary policy. . . . To speak or write in this way is to unduly simplify the problem." The implications of this statement ran counter to the approach to price stability and self-adjusting monetary policy advocated by Mises, Machlup, and Hayek. It directly counteracted many of the ideas advanced in Hayek's *Monetary Theory*.[25]

As could be expected, when Hayek delivered his LSE lectures and then visited Cambridge, he received a chilly welcome. These talks became the basis for *Prices and Production*, a work that elaborated the business cycle analysis of *Monetary Theory*. Hayek was viewed by the Cambridge cohort as an errand boy of Robbins, and they dismissed his ideas and mocked his exposition and Viennese accent. They did not comprehend his explanations of the relationship between roundabout production and investment or the correlation between relative price levels, production, and inflation. They also had no sympathy for the Austrian account of the Depression. While Keynes was not present for these lectures, his subsequent reactions demonstrated his awareness of Hayek's views and his agreement with his Cambridge colleagues.[26]

With no small degree of relish, Lionel Robbins invited Hayek to review Keynes's *Treatise on Money* in *Economica*. A two-part review running to fifty pages, it was the most detailed critique the *Treatise* received. It also pulled no punches: "the *Treatise* proves to be so obviously—and, I think, admittedly—the expression of a transitory phase in a process of rapid intellectual development that its appearance cannot be said to have that definitive significance which at one time was expected of it." Hayek accused Keynes and the Cambridge school of dilettantism in monetary and business cycle theory. He damned Keynes's "experimental" approach to savings and investment, asserting that Keynes's "innovations" did not appear new to a Continental economist familiar with Wicksell or Mises. Even though he was willing to grant Keynes "courage and practical insight" and the *Treatise* "astonishing qualities of learning, erudition and realistic knowledge," the theoretical foundation did not bear scrutiny: "the exposition is so difficult, unsystematic, and obscure, that it is extremely difficult for the fellow economist who disagrees with the conclusions to demonstrate the exact point of disagreement and to state his objections."[27]

Hayek's riposte, grounded in theoretical and practical disagreements and articulated in a critical yet respectful tone, nevertheless ignited a firestorm. Hayek attempted to offer an olive branch: "My aim has been throughout to contribute to the understanding of this unusually difficult and important book, and I hope that my endeavour in this direction will be the best proof of how important I consider it. It is even possible that in the end it will turn out that there exists less difference between Mr. Keynes' views and my own than I am at present inclined to assume." Keynes did not take the review in a conciliatory spirit. Hayek dismissed Keynes's macroeconomic policy prescriptions by disparaging Keynes's theoretical system and economic acumen. Keynes, who had been working with the Liberal Lloyd George on a massive public employment scheme, could not countenance this perceived assault. Keynes covered his copy of Hayek's review in annotations before firing off an ill-tempered rejoinder to *Economica*.[28]

Keynes saw their disagreement as a product of different worldviews more than one of economic theory. The divergence centered on their respective interpretations of the economic crisis. According to Keynes, Hayek believed that disequilibrium between savings and investment could be avoided if the quantity of money remained neutral. It was best to allow the economy to work through its fluctuations without any interference. There was nothing that guaranteed that savings and investment would balance, Keynes asserted to the contrary. The economy could face production slowdowns, unemployment, and depression even with savings available for investment. Firms may prefer to sit on their money rather than reinvest during a risky period. A new equilibrium with an elevated unemployment rate would then emerge. For Keynes, this explanation captured the agony of the Depression years.[29] Keynes laced into Hayek, calling his views a "frightful muddle . . . with scarcely a sound proposition in it." He concluded that Hayek's model had little to say to economists who knew that a consistent, noninterventionist monetary policy could not prevent or alleviate crises. Hayek's prescription, "leave it to time to effect a permanent cure," was inadequate. One had to respond to business cycle fluctuations with more than a shrug of the shoulders.[30]

The Hayek-Keynes tiff consumed the English-language economics world. There was only one more public exchange between the main combatants, but a proxy war continued for years. This local skirmish developed into a global debate over the proper response to the Great Depression. D. H. Robertson and Alvin Hansen offered pointed critiques of Keynes's position; Arthur Pigou assailed the style of Keynes's rejoinder. Pierro Sraffa rebuked Hayek, while Joan Robinson extended Sraffa's conclusions. Hayek turned to his friends Machlup and Haberler. Hayek also reached out to Americans, especially at the University of Chicago. At stake, he argued, was not just Austrian theory but liberal economics and the free market system.[31]

Much has been made about the Keynes-Hayek "clash that defined modern economics."[32] We must be careful not to read too much into one academic skirmish. It was not truly the defining moment of modern economics when everyone had to choose between Keynes and Hayek, or Keynesianism and Austrianism, but it did reintroduce Austrian ideas to the English-speaking economics community. It also brought a new cohort of Austrian scholars into transnational conversations. Hayek received a post in the United Kingdom; his *Monetary Theory* and *Prices and Production* were the first books published in English by Austrians other than Böhm or Wieser. Many more were soon to follow. The Austrians rode this newfound enthusiasm and attention in Europe and the United States, and they won themselves converts. Emil Kauder broke with his historicist adviser, Werner Sombart, to espouse Austrian ideas in Berlin. In his role as an economics tutor, he then taught a young Ludwig Lachmann marginalist economic theory, thereby introducing one of the significant figures in the 1970s US revival of Austrian economics to the tradition. International scholars once again flocked to Vienna—figures like Robbins, Frank Knight, Jacob Viner, Howard Ellis, and Paul Sweezy. Thus began a stimulating transatlantic cross-fertilization, which reached a climax in the Austrian-Chicago debates.[33]

The Chicago-Vienna Capital(ism) Debate

At the same time as the Hayek-Keynes affair raged in England, the plain-spoken University of Chicago economist Frank Knight reached out to his friend Oskar Morgenstern to discuss the Depression. After his visit to Vienna and the Mises seminar, he saw great value in the ideas of the Austrian School. "I wish I could talk to you + also Hayek especially, + Haberler too (+ Mises I should add but I didn't find it easy to learn from him, he seems so narrow + unsuspecting, as does Haberler—'between us'!) I've gotten interested in this damned crisis business."[34] Knight thought Morgenstern and his colleagues could assist his work on production and capital. The debate that broke out between Knight and the Austrians, while relatively minor in comparison to the Keynes dispute, nevertheless provides a window on early attempts by liberal political economists to revise their positions to address the perceived failure of classical liberalism. These discussions were also incipient attempts at the formulation of "neoliberalism"—five years before the Colloque Walter Lippmann and fifteen prior to the founding of the Mont Pèlerin Society (MPS), the loci classici of neoliberalism.

After Knight's May 1930 stay in Vienna, he began reading Menger, Böhm, Mises, and Morgenstern for a piece he was writing on marginal utility theory. He turned to Morgenstern, whom he had known since the latter's Rockefeller fellowship, because his work seemed "closest to [Knight's] own topic." Knight was also about to wade into the Hayek-Keynes affair with a pointed response to Hayek's *Prices and Production*. Ironically, Knight criticized Hayek for the very thing for which Hayek disparaged Keynes: lack of a sound capital theory. This sparked a four-year exchange of letters and articles among Knight, Hayek, and the Austrians. Even more striking than the Hayek-Knight exchange, however, was the intensity of the correspondence within the Viennese circle about the obtuse Illinoisan. The confrontation came to represent the first standoff between the most famous free-market economics schools of the twentieth century. And in this early debate, it was the Austrians, not the Chicagoans, who seemed the more extreme defenders of free enterprise and liberalism.[35]

At first blush, Knight was an unlikely figure for such a dispute. Friendly with the Austrians, he readily shared articles with and solicited advice from the Viennese. Knight's work on risk and uncertainty also had method-ological affinities to the skeptical works the Austrians produced in the 1920s. Politically, they shared values, advocating free competition, freer markets, and tight monetary policy. In later years, they made common cause at the MPS and at the University of Chicago. Moreover, Knight expressed sympathy for Hayek after his ill treatment at the hands of Keynes and Sraffa: "In general, I'm in a pretty low 'depression' on the state of economics, and the Hayek-Sraffa altercation . . . is a case in point."[36]

In Knight's search for a working concept of capital, however, he stumbled into irresoluble difficulties with the Austrians. The debate between Knight and the Austrians was technical in nature, yet it had resonances in discussions about the future of capitalism. Fundamentally, the two sides disagreed on the nature and composition of capital, which led to divergent theories about production and the business cycle. Knight believed that the starting point of all Austrian School research, Böhm's capital theory, was erroneous. In a letter to Morgenstern, Knight argued that "any theory of cycles or any other phase of economic life based on Bohm Bawerk's [*sic*] theory of capital is necessarily and egregiously wrong."[37] As we saw, Böhm predicated his theory of capital on the roundaboutness of production. The more time allotted for production processes, the greater the output and return on investment. Knight saw this approach as unrealistic and untenable methodologically. One could not measure the period of production with any accuracy and hence could not explain capital growth or the business cycle using it. Hayek defended the Austrian time preference and the period of production in his response. Hayek claimed that Knight's approach oversimplified production processes, since it used a homogeneous concept of capital. Changes in investment or the interest rate had uneven impacts throughout the economy, so his concept was too reductive. Like two ships passing in the night, the men argued past each other in frequent articles and letters.[38]

The capital theory debate helped to distinguish the Austrian School from the early Chicago School. The inferences they drew from their theories led them to quite different policy prescriptions. Hayek, Mises, Machlup, and the Austrians were more sanguine about allowing the downturn to run its course and more confident about the corrective powers of markets. Knight, supported by his colleagues Jacob Viner and Henry Simons, was less certain. To use Knight's terminology from his 1921 *Risk, Uncertainty and Profit*, he believed that the state had a vital role to play in removing uncertainties in capitalist production and converting them into measurable risk, which entrepreneurs could then use to shore up the economic system. Knight and other Chicagoans therefore decried laissez-faire utopianism, recognizing the excesses of the capitalist order. They admitted a larger role for the state in mitigating problems too. These divisions between laissez-faire and neoliberal thinkers animated debates for decades.[39]

In contradistinction to the divisive Hayek-Keynes controversy, the Hayek-Knight exchange had an integrative effect. In spite of growing disagreements among the Austrians themselves, they realized that they possessed a distinctive corporate identity. As Machlup noted, their international travels and scholarly interactions with the broader economics community revealed to the Viennese their national identity. Their shared interest in business cycles, time structures, and production processes distinguished them from their peers. They felt compelled not only to defend one another but also to articulate their views. While visiting Columbia University, Machlup offered a lecture titled "The Older and the Younger Austrian Economists and Their Problems." He summarized how the younger Austrians now viewed themselves. "If I had to state which thoughts are . . . considered characteristical [sic] for the Austrian School, I would list chiefly three: 1) marg[inal] utility theory; 2) opportunity cost theory; 3) capital theory [roundabout process, time]." For the first time since the 1890s—and not for the last time—the Austrians reflected on their approach. Alongside the earlier concepts of marginal utility, opportunity cost and capital theory had been elevated to orthodoxy, reflecting the Austrians' recent debates with the Cambridge and Chicago Schools and their growing concern with global economics and contemporary affairs.[40]

The Austrians and the Birth of Neoliberalism

The Chicago-Vienna contretemps reveals that the Austrians were not alone in their concerns about economics as a discipline or the state of twentieth-century liberalism. Many intellectuals who styled themselves as "classical" or "nineteenth century" liberals feared for their worldview, as it confronted the political extremism of Hitler, Mussolini, and Stalin on the one hand and the interventionism of Keynes and Franklin Delano Roosevelt on the other. Alongside anxious academics were conservative businesspeople, who espied creeping collectivism in the New Deal and European social democracy. Throughout the 1930s, these groups struggled to find their footing and to drum up support. The 1937 publication of

Walter Lippmann's *Inquiry into the Principles of the Good Society* provided an impetus for a more coordinated reaction against the threats that Mises, Hayek, and the Chicagoans had identified. *The Good Society* initiated a transnational conversation about the salvation of liberalism, capitalism, and democracy. The Austrians were at the center of these developments as theorists, organizers, and ideologues.[41]

Lippmann's *The Good Society* inspired many European and American intellectuals in defense of liberty and the capitalist order. Interestingly the book owed a substantial debt to Austrian ideas. In the 1910s and 1920s, Lippmann was one of the faces of progressive politics in the United States, emphasizing the role of expertise and scientific intervention in public affairs in his books and *New Republic* essays. A friend of Keynes and an advocate of Franklin Roosevelt's political program, it was only in the mid-1930s that his economic views underwent a rightward shift. While he was skeptical of unrestrained laissez-faire capitalism, he lost faith in the efficacy of economic planning. He attributed this new attitude to reading Hayek's *Collectivist Economic Planning*. In a letter to Hayek, he confessed, "without the help of you and from Professor von Mises, I could never have developed the argument." In *The Good Society*, he castigated planning, extolled the free market, and admonished his readers to avoid "authoritarian collectivism." Lippmann called out his former liberal and progressive allies as potential totalitarians. *The Good Society* was criticized from the left by figures like John Dewey for its antidemocratic positions and the right by economists Frank Knight and Henry Simons, who felt the book hewed too closely to Mises's radicalism, but it nonetheless opened up a third way for a "reconstruction of liberalism" that centered on markets, freedom, and democracy in an authoritarian age.[42]

If Hayek and Mises shaped Lippmann's ideological transformation, he exercised a reciprocal influence on Austrian and European liberals. *The Good Society* enjoyed a far more positive reception in crisis-wracked Europe than in the United States. In Switzerland, the German émigré economist Wilhelm Röpke could not contain his excitement, writing to Lippmann, Hayek, Robbins, and Alexander Rüstow. He fantasized about an intellectual collective that would gather in the Alps to discuss ideas. In Geneva, William Rappard enthused about the work, urging his friend Louis Rougier, a French philosopher, to have the work translated. Rougier went one step further by organizing a colloquium in the summer of 1938. Rougier called for "an international crusade in favor of a constructive liberalism." Even though Lippmann raised concerns about the propagandistic tone of Rougier's announcement, he cooperated with the preparations. Rougier turned to Hayek to assemble participants. The final list of attendees included an impressive assemblage of liberal theorists, almost all of whom came from the Austrians' network of contacts. In addition to those already named, the French philosopher Raymond Aron, the British-Hungarian philosopher of science Michael Polanyi, the Austrian phenomenologist Alfred Schütz, and two dozen others attended.[43]

As Quinn Slobodian has recently argued, two major intellectual and institutional streams converged at the colloquium. Wilhelm Röpke had introduced an International Disintegration project, with close ties to the RF, the League of Nations, and the network of business cycle centers. The Austrians were at the center of that node. The other was the International Studies Conference (ISC), a pioneer in international relations. The ISC became part of the League's International Committee on Intellectual Cooperation, the forerunner organization for UNESCO. Ideas radiating from Geneva impressed the organizers, who had convened meetings on collective security, peaceful change, and economics and peace. The "Geneva School" of liberals, which included Haberler, Hayek, and Mises, now turned to the restoration of liberalism as a theme.[44]

When the Colloque Walter Lippmann convened, the members first had to establish an agenda and a mission for their project. The group decided on the following themes: the decline and return of liberalism, endogenous and exogenous factors in these processes, potential policies for the restoration of liberalism, and elements of traditional liberalism that required revision. Consensus on solutions eluded the group. First, they could not agree on what their ideological slogan should be. Was it "liberalism" or "laissez-faire"? Was it "neoliberalism" or "neocapitalism"? "Social liberalism," "liberalism of the left," and "positive liberalism" were also bruited. None attracted many adherents, though "neoliberalism" seemed to stick. The scholars advanced divergent proposals, ranging from Alexander Rüstow, who was critical of "Manchester-style," laissez-faire liberalism, to Mises, who rejected any manipulation of market mechanisms. Röpke and Rüstow, two of the more moderate voices, even assailed the liberalism of the day for placing too much faith in economics. "Economism" signaled a crisis in the social sciences: "The real cause of this deficiency of social sciences seems to be found exactly in the narrow *economic* conception and in the lack of courage and ability in really synthetic interpretation which is connecting up the economic phenomena with the wider aspect of society." Values and institutions mattered too, and social scientists had to incorporate them into their work. This meant going beyond technical economics and technocratic policy. Even if the scholars did not agree on tactics, they shared a strategic vision of movement building and ideological activism. All participants agreed that restricting their work to social scientific research offered little hope for changing social attitudes, particularly in the working classes.[45]

The Austrians and their fellow travelers stressed institution building and persuasion of elites over popular outreach, yet the latter facilitated the former. Crossover works of social theory attracted a readership that opened up institutional opportunities. This became a leitmotif for the Austrian School and the neoliberal movement. The first attempt at a permanent institution, Rougier's Centre International d'Études pour la Rénovation du Libéralisme, foundered in the face of the German Blitzkrieg. It would be another seven years before Hayek, Rappard, and Röpke initiated a new transnational organization. It was not only war's end that enabled the success of the neoliberals but also the wide public readership of their wartime writings, especially within the business community. Hayek, Mises, and the others were the beneficiaries of the need for pro-business ideas, becoming pioneering transatlantic "entrepreneurial intellectuals." Their success owed much to the best traditions of their Viennese predecessors: connections to the financial and industrial elite and access to social sources of influence, prestige, and cultural capital.

Socialist Calculation, Redux

Lurking behind the Austrian defense of liberalism and capitalism was the ever-present specter of socialism. Since the 1880s, the Austrians had viewed their approach as the definitive rebuttal to Marxism and socialism. If the Keynesians and Chicagoans challenged the Austrians to reconsider some of their methodological and policy assumptions, socialism posed an existential threat to their entire worldview. In the shadow of the Great

Depression, Austrians faced a resurgent Marxism, which confronted the Austrians on their former battlefield: the issue of socialist calculation.

When we left the socialist calculation debate in the 1920s, Mises's argument about the unfeasibility of a functioning price mechanism in a state-directed economy carried the day. The worldwide depression prompted a reevaluation. As Western economies stagnated and shrank, the Soviet Union, in the midst of its first Five-Year Plan, appeared to be flourishing. In the United Kingdom, France, and Spain, communist, socialist, and social democratic parties gained in popularity at the expense of liberal parties. Elsewhere in central and eastern Europe, the middle of the political spectrum, including most liberal parties, hollowed out, as the authoritarian and fascist Right and socialist Left grew. Political and economic conditions in the early 1930s seemed to encourage nationalist and socialist economic experiments.

In the face of mounting anticapitalist sentiment and resurgent socialist theory, Hayek edited and published *Collectivist Economic Planning* as a defense of capitalism and a critique of socialism. He introduced the Anglophone world to the German-language socialist calculation debate, featuring a translation of Mises's seminal essay. Hayek and Robbins extended Mises's infeasibility argument. While agreeing with Mises that calculation was theoretically impossible without market prices, they also contended that socialist calculation proved impracticable and inefficient given the sheer number of calculations that the state authorities would have to perform to determine production requirements.[46]

The impetus behind *Collectivist Economic Planning* was a new wave of "market socialists" in the mid-1930s. These scholars contended that Mises and his defenders were wrong about the impossibility of rational calculation under socialism. Fred Taylor, H. D. Dickinson, and Oskar Lange pointed the way to a functioning socialism. Dickinson maintained that socialist calculation was theoretically possible, since planning authorities could just as easily "solve" the economy's pricing equations as could market participants. Taylor believed that a rational pricing model could exist, as long as the state, which owned all industries, maintained exchange relations with its population by paying for labor and charging for commodities. Lange extended the socialist vision the furthest, arguing that since state planners have more knowledge about the overall economy than individuals or firms do, they could make more efficient decisions under socialism than entrepreneurs in the competitive marketplace could.[47]

The market socialists offered a powerful rejoinder to Mises's argument and put the antisocialists on the defensive. Although Hayek had addressed some of the market socialist positions, the points about equilibrium and knowledge required further elaboration. In his 1937 article "Economics and Knowledge," perhaps his most important essay, he offered an explanation for the superiority of free-market economies. Hayek contended that the equilibrium concept that the market socialists deployed suffered from a fatal flaw. While equilibrium explained well the *subjective* choices made by individuals, it did not necessarily extend to *societal* equilibrium. If societal equilibrium consisted of the sum total of all individuals' foresight, plans, and valuations, whenever an individual's valuations shift, the entire equilibrium must change too. Knowing all the relevant "objective data" at a moment in time, as Lange and others proposed, was insufficient for planning, since it did not (and cannot) account for changing individual knowledge and values. The market socialists were therefore left chasing their own tail, solving equations for an equilibrium that had ceased to exist. A fundamental coordination problem existed: the market socialists could not prove that their plans would align with the societal equilibrium resulting from individuals' changed knowledge and expectations. The equilibrium that the market socialists presupposed was undermined by shifts in subjective valuations by individuals.[48]

Hayek proposed a new direction for economic analysis to address deficient knowledge about equilibrium. Rather than the division of labor as the guiding principle of economics, he proffered the division of *knowledge*. The concept of dispersed knowledge became synonymous with Hayek and one branch of the Austrian School. In critiquing planning of all kinds, Hayek defended the powers of the free market as an optimal information processor: "the spontaneous interaction of a number of people, each possessing only bits of knowledge, brings about a state of affairs in which prices correspond to costs." Only a spontaneous, free market could bring about societal equilibrium and the harmony of interests that the socialist planners believed they could engineer. "Economics and Knowledge" opened a new front in the battle between liberalism and socialism by placing the concept of knowledge front and center. It placed socialists back on the defensive, since they had to account for ever-shifting individual preferences if their system was to appear viable. In the article's radical defense of subjectivism and methodological individualism too, "Economics and Knowledge" was a logical extension—and important reformulation—of the original Austrian marginalist position. Austrian theory in its new iteration had the potential to transform not only economic thought but also social theory and policy. Hayek was no longer just talking about goods but information, ideas, and orders too. In the ensuing years, Hayek, joined by his Austrian peers, applied these lessons to great effect.[49]

Family Feuds

Overall, the younger Austrians displayed more similarities than differences in the 1930s, especially in their shared emphases on marginal utility theory, theories of production and capital, and free trade. They also espoused complementary ideas about the Depression, inflation, interventionism, and socialism. They coordinated their efforts in correspondence and in seminars, late-night café rendezvous, and excursions in the Viennese countryside. The repeated controversies—with Keynesians, Chicagoans, and, of course, socialists—galvanized their corporate identity.

While the members of the Austrian School engaged on similar topics, operated in the same circles, and presented a unified front to the outside world, fault lines existed and increased in the crisis years. Behind the scenes, they squabbled more than ever. Debate had always provided the school with its vitality and nervous energy—Menger and Böhm argued, and Böhm, Wieser, and Schumpeter famously jousted—yet the younger school was perhaps even more disputatious. Tensions between the so-called Wieser and Böhm branches intensified. The former stressed research on time constructs and equilibrium theory, while the latter emphasized the role of capital, production, and interest in the generation of business cycles. The Böhm branch also doubted the applicability of equilibrium concepts and mathematical models. These differences separated Mayer and his followers (primarily Paul Rosenstein-Rodan, Leo Schönfeld, Gottfried Haberler, and Oskar Morgenstern) from Mises and his allies (Machlup, Richard Strigl, and, to a much lesser extent, Hayek). While school members were united in their belief in liberal government, they voiced increasingly intense displeasure with each other. Even as the international community recognized the rebirth of the school, the years of crisis tested the school's internal coherence. This mounting tension makes the school's survival in emigration that much more intriguing. The dislocations caused by the school's emigration in the 1930s heightened internecine tensions, precipitating the creation of a reoriented school in its US incarnation, with new branches splitting off and taking on lives of their own. The family feuds of the 1930s tell us a lot about the elements that defined the early Austrian tradition— and define the movement today.[50]

As school members' voluminous correspondence attests, gossip, rivalry, and politics fueled their interactions as much as economics discussions. Almost every participant was opinionated and obdurate, and they harbored grand ambitions for themselves. By the late 1920s, they found the Austrian academy suffocating, and they had growing issues with their mentors. Most of the younger generation tired of Hans Mayer's petty grudges and his lack of productivity. Morgenstern held numerous conversations with peers who shared his antipathies. Because of Mayer's shortcomings and the increasing significance of the Mises circle and the institute, allegiances shifted during the 1930s. A typical debate revolved around who was the greater economist, Schumpeter or Mises. Morgenstern recounted one such discussion: "Haberler and I for S[chumpeter]; Hayek for Mises. Certainly much by Schumpeter is false, but he is more talented, he sees more, inspires more." Haberler and Machlup maintained cordial ties with Schumpeter and held high opinions of him despite their closeness to Mises. Yet even the warm, lifelong relationship between Schumpeter and Haberler experienced rocky moments when individual ambitions entered the equation. Schumpeter's appointment at Harvard jeopardized Haberler's temporary position there in 1932. Haberler's eventual appointment smoothed over that rough patch. Meanwhile Machlup marveled at Schumpeter's stature at Harvard just a few years later: "He is an acknowledged central point. Everything revolves around him."[51]

Attitudes toward Mises also showed volatility in these years, with dissatisfaction arising over his political views and his idiosyncratic epistemology. His staunchest defender was Machlup, who expressed the most enthusiasm for Mises's successes; yet even he worried about mounting conflicts between the implacable Mises and his colleagues. Haberler and

Morgenstern turned more decisively against Mises. While Haberler still adduced the same causes for the economic downturn as his fellow Austrian did, he no longer believed that conventional liberal measures could put an end to the vicious cycle of deflation, contraction, and unemployment. He wrote more on the phenomenon of "secondary deflation," wherein governmental deflationary measures failed to correct the previous inflationary episode and instead provoked further contraction. Haberler began to wonder whether banks had to loosen credit and increase spending. Partly owing to these reconsiderations, Haberler wearied of Mises's unswerving advocacy of laissez-faire. He described Mises's positions as "laughable exaggerations" and viewed Mises's economics as simplistic and dogmatic.[52]

Morgenstern had even more visceral reactions to Mises. While he shifted allegiance away from Mayer in the 1920s, his enthusiasm for Mises's ideas remained tepid. In the 1930s, Morgenstern became more mathematically inclined under the influence of Karl Menger, Carl's son, alienating him from Mises, who privileged verbal modes of economic expression and disdained mathematics. Occasionally Morgenstern's animus boiled over, demonstrating not just intellectual differences but also perhaps a latent antisemitism born of his German nationalist background. After one Mises lecture, he declared the talk "impossible." When Menger and Mises sparred over mathematical economics and questions of ethics, Morgenstern lost all patience. He accused Mises of "talk[ing] pure nonsense" and wished he could create his own seminar to supplant Mises's. In his next monograph, *The Limits of Economics*, Morgenstern offered Mises no quarter for his "naïve" attitudes. He accused Mises, who limned an a priori epistemology of economics, of failing to grasp the aspects of "practical life" with which science must grapple: "*A priori* theory would be very easy if it were possible to dispense with the necessity of dealing with reality and the flux of economic events and if it were sufficient to lock oneself in a room and invent the world of facts, adopting the attitude that if theory and reality did not agree, so much the worse for reality." For Morgenstern, it would be great if there were a single "action" that explained all economic behavior, as Mises maintained. While "nothing easier could be wished for," this kind of empty theorizing, Morgenstern intoned, had "nothing to do with the real world."[53] Finally, in his liberal dogmatism, Mises did not practice his ideal of "value-free" science. Instead, like the socialists, his political judgments clouded his science.[54]

Morgenstern increasingly charted his own path that led him away from his earlier economic work. Though his output still possessed a clear Viennese accent, it had little in common with his compatriots'. Interestingly, Morgenstern's attack on Mises did not precipitate a total rupture, however. While never close, they cooperated at a major RF-sponsored conference in Annecy in 1936 and found much common ground on economic policy and the role of experts in decision-making. It was the Hayek-Morgenstern relationship that suffered more under the strain. This is significant, since Morgenstern's and Hayek's research moved on similar lines during these years. They had worked together at the institute before Hayek's departure for London and maintained a cordial relationship. Drawing from Wieser's work, they focused on the role of time in economic considerations. They also singled out perfect foresight and equilibrium concepts as crucial for the development of economic science. Nevertheless, Hayek responded icily to *Limits* and its score settling. In a letter to Morgenstern, he wrote, "If one is supposed to be grateful for being sent a book, and one does not agree with it at all, and one knows the author too well to handle the matter in one phrase, the only way is to make the letter a counter conclusion. . . . That you were rude to some of my friends makes it even more difficult." In response, Morgenstern had harsh remarks for Hayek and his friends, whom he accused of abandoning science for politics.[55]

If Hayek and Morgenstern had the most heated interactions, the other younger Viennese also sparred with one another and gossiped behind each other's backs. But they never lost touch. Morgenstern and Haberler, old high school friends and hiking buddies, tended to side with each other. Haberler endured Morgenstern's rants about Mises and his dismissive attitudes toward fellow economists. Nevertheless, he pushed back too, chastising Morgenstern for the negativity of *Limits*. As Hayek's work became more convoluted and abstract in the late 1930s, Haberler lamented Hayek's growing ignorance of reality. Haberler and Machlup wrote each other frequently as both men traveled, first as Rockefeller fellows and then as professors in the United States. They exchanged their articles and manuscripts before publication, soliciting feedback from each other. But they also ran into difficulties. Haberler's critical stance toward Hayek's theories of production and capital vexed Machlup, who accused his friend of a "Hayek polemic" in one of their exchanges.[56]

The snarkiness of the Austrian correspondence reveals the simmering tensions within the school. While the Austrians presented a relatively unified front to outsiders, they also evinced the petty differences and jealousies, the resentments and rivalries, and the uneasy social dynamics that typify groupings of strong-willed individuals. In spite of the myriad criticisms and grudges they held, the school did not come apart. Even Hayek and Morgenstern continued to correspond after their major spat. They still attended the Mises seminar fortnightly and ate lunch together several days a week. In other words, the school dynamic proved stronger than their personal or doctrinal differences. When emigration, fascism, and war blew apart their world, they were confronted with what would happen to their school in the absence of social rituals that built solidarity. They responded with collective purpose, which ensured the school's survival.

Auf Wiedersehen, Wien

Even though the Austrians were not political refugees and few experienced overt persecution, economic and political conditions drove the school from its homeland. Fortunately for them, their connections to international elites, especially through the RF, eased the school's successful transition to the Anglophone world. By 1933, most of the Austrians realized that they had no future in central Europe. The Depression bottomed out in 1933, when more than a quarter of Germans and Austrians were unemployed. Recovery was nowhere in sight. Several of the largest regional banks went under, and deflation reigned. Fascism was also on the rise. The National Socialists came to power in Germany in early 1933. In Austria, the Christian Social Chancellor Engelbert Dollfuss suspended parliament in March 1933. Cracking down on the socialists and the Nazis, Dollfuss's government curbed civil liberties and operated without the legislature for a year. In February 1934, a brief civil war erupted when socialists took to the barricades against the authoritarian actions of Dollfuss. The rebellion was quickly crushed, socialist leaders were exiled or executed, and the Christian Socials established a one-party, Austrofascist state. The Austrian School members, especially Mises, greeted the destruction of the socialists and the new state with approval. The Austrofascists supported sound money and the gold standard, yet they turned against Austrian

School economic policy, advocating "corporatist" economics inspired by Catholic social theory, Othmar Spann's universalism, and Italian Fascism. This was a blow for the Austrian School, especially Mises and Morgenstern, who had supported the Christian Socials and advised its leaders for more than a decade.[57]

As school members sought better working conditions abroad, Austria as home and inspiration still played an outsized role in their thinking. Hayek is the best example of this loyalty. Although Hayek had resided in London for six years when "Economics and Knowledge" appeared, it was a quintessential Viennese product. He cited Karl Popper as the basis for his philosophy of science. For his concept of "equilibrium analysis," he deployed Hans Mayer's definition. His depiction of a priori logical constructs relied on Mises's epistemological work. On the role of time factors in economic analysis, he drew on Rosenstein-Rodan. He referenced Karl Menger's sociological work. He relied on Morgenstern's insights on perfect foresight and equilibrium for his own argument. References to other Austrians rounded out the reference list. Hayek had a loyal following in London, yet his work remained rooted in his *Heimat*.[58]

Hayek returned to Austria regularly throughout the 1930s to see family and friends. He summered in Salzkammergut, that splendiferous Alpine landscape of lakes, meadows, and mountains, where he put his prodigious hiking skills to use. Mises and Haberler also ventured back in summertime. The Austrians saw no future in their homeland, however. Writing to Machlup, Hayek lamented the brain drain from Vienna: "That you want to become a 'full time economist' is generally pleasing but that you intend to emigrate from Vienna makes me really sad. I absolutely understand—even though I am struck ever more and more strongly with the passage of years by my own expatriation—but that the emigration of intellectuals from Vienna has become a mass phenomenon, especially in our economic school, hurts me deeply."[59] This resignation became a recurrent theme. On a Vienna trip in April 1936, Hayek ran into Mises and Alfred Schütz, but they were the only two interesting people still there. In saying this, he directed a jab at Morgenstern and Karl Menger, who still worked at the institute but were doing "horrible scientific things." The emigration of "our economic school" pained Hayek enormously, especially since emigration was beginning to splinter the school's collective project.[60]

The exodus of Austrian economists developed in waves. After Hayek's and Rosenstein-Rodan's departures to the United Kingdom in the early 1930s, the next crest came in 1934 in the face of rising fascism. Mises leapt at a visiting professorship offered by William Rappard and the Geneva Institut Universitaire des Hautes Études Internationale, the RF-funded center designed to furnish the League of Nations with policy experts. Although he continued to work part-time for the Vienna Chamber of Commerce, Mises returned for only a few days at a time over holiday breaks. Surrounded by émigrés and exiles, including his Viennese colleagues Hans Kelsen and Karl Pribram and the German Wilhelm Röpke, Mises found Geneva a congenial intellectual environment. Switzerland in the 1930s was an oasis of liberal internationalism in a time of crisis. In addition to the Rappard Institute, the League of Nations and the International Labor Office also had their headquarters in the Swiss city. Geneva became the makeshift hub for European economics: Haberler, Jan Tinbergen, Tjalling Koopmans, Ragnar Nurkse, and many others made their home there. This contributed to Mises's reluctance to immigrate to the United States. An Austrian homecoming was out of the question, however.[61]

Mises's departure from Vienna was destabilizing for the Austrian School. As members sang in "Farewell to Professor Mises," one of the drinking songs from their seminar, "What is to become of the Mises-Kreis / In the year that's coming? Geneva can't for all suffice / . . . / The question will not leave me be / The seminar means ev'rything to me." While Vienna was still the base of operations for many Austrians, it was losing its spirit, its *Geist*. In 1934, Haberler took a position with the League of Nations Economic Section in Geneva. With the support of Joseph Schumpeter, Haberler secured a professorship at Harvard in 1936. This act of generosity was characteristic of Schumpeter. From Cambridge, he helped German intellectuals escape National Socialism. He regularly enlisted the RF in efforts to obtain fellowships for displaced scholars.[62]

Schumpeter's successful intervention for Haberler stymied Machlup's own prospects at the Cambridge institution, where he was an instructor, yet he also found a US landing spot. Machlup arrived in the United States on an RF fellowship in 1934 and spent time at Harvard, the University of Chicago, the University of Wisconsin, and Stanford. Rumors of his desire to remain in the United States circulated widely. Machlup filled in at

Harvard in 1935 when Haberler deferred his arrival. Machlup subsequently received an appointment at the University of Buffalo, with most of his salary covered by the RF.

Even as the situation worsened and the members of the Austrian School began to emigrate, the school in Vienna was not yet moribund. Mayer continued to teach at the university. Morgenstern directed the institute and edited the *Zeitschrift*. Under his leadership, the institute took advantage of the remaining interwar Viennese circles to enrich its approach, drawing into its discussions world-class philosophers and mathematicians. Morgenstern won commissions from the League of Nations, the ICC, and the Bank for International Settlements. Spending more time with Karl Menger and his Mathematical Colloquium—where one could hear presentations not only from Menger but also from Abraham Wald, Kurt Gödel, Werner Heisenberg, Alfred Tarski, and Rudolf Carnap—Morgenstern took an interest in modern mathematics and its potential for improving economic theory. After Mises's departure in 1934, Morgenstern reshaped the school's seminar, inviting more contributions from mathematicians. He also turned away from the "Austroliberal" approach of Mises, Hayek, and Machlup, which had incorporated liberal ideology more readily into seminar discussions.[63]

Austrian economics under Morgenstern's guidance enjoyed great international recognition. The RF esteemed Morgenstern highly, providing monies for his institute's comparative studies of economic conditions in the Habsburg successor states and programs in mathematical economics. Morgenstern built the institute into an internationally acclaimed center. Although it never had a staff of more than eleven, the institute became the envy of other European institutes, eliciting complaints from other directors about Morgenstern's ambition. Despite this resentment, John Van Sickle, the RF program director, maintained "a warm place in [his] heart for the little group down in Vienna which . . . is justified by their performance." These successes coincided with Austria's new regional economic orientation. Leading bankers—including Austrian School friend Rudolf Sieghart—helped to establish a Danube Basin economic network designed to shore up Austrian financial hegemony in central Europe. Morgenstern and the Austrians continued their fight for regional and international economic cooperation even as cries for economic nationalism and protectionism reached a crescendo in the late 1930s.[64]

With the arrival of the Nazis in March 1938, emigration became the only option short of collaboration or death. Even Morgenstern, who had adapted to Austrofascist rule, chose to leave. In winter 1937–38, he accepted a Carnegie visiting professorship to teach in the United States, with the intention of returning to central Europe in the summer. By that time, Austria had vanished from the world map: the German Reich annexed Austria in March 1938. Deciding not to return, Morgenstern wrote feverishly to US colleagues in search of a job. Put in touch with Abraham Flexner, a longtime adviser to the Carnegie and Rockefeller Foundations, founder of the Princeton Institute for Advanced Studies, and driving force behind the Emergency Committee in Aid of Displaced Foreign Scholars, Morgenstern received and accepted a professorship offer from Princeton. The RF paid half his salary for several years.[65]

Morgenstern was lucky. So were the most famous of his cohort. But the Austrian School was much more than the half dozen theorists of worldwide acclaim. Many friends and colleagues—including Martha Steffy Browne, Herbert Furth, Walter Fröhlich, Alexander Gerschenkron, Felix Kaufmann, Erich Schiff, and Alfred Schütz—were stranded in Austria. We will return to their harrowing escapes. The strenuous efforts exerted by the Austrians on behalf of their friends demonstrated the familial loyalty that defined the school. After that shared trauma, it should come as no surprise that they continued to fight for the school's values after escape.

The circumstances of emigration allowed the school to survive, but not in a fashion entirely of its own choosing. In the next fifteen years, the Austrians became intellectuals whose renown extended beyond economics. They cultivated networks that appealed to liberal social theorists and antisocialist scholars, politicians, and businesspeople. To say the earlier school disappeared would be premature, yet it did take new directions. The Austrian School that was remade in America shared a resemblance to its earlier incarnations, yet it possessed crucial differences too. Shorn of its geographic home, the school produced several competing strains and legacies. This reconfigured, "metaphorical" Austrian School would exercise a vital role in postwar transatlantic political, economic, and intellectual life and in the popular imagination of the Anglophone world.

5

"HE WHO IS ONLY AN ECONOMIST CANNOT BE A GOOD ECONOMIST": THE AUSTRIAN TURN FROM ECONOMICS

In the spring of 1945, Friedrich Hayek became an American celebrity. On April 3, Hayek arrived in the United States from the United Kingdom to give a series of academic lectures. En route, a condensed version of his 1944 book *The Road to Serfdom* appeared and made him a household name and best-selling author. Featured on the front page of *Reader's Digest*, which boasted a circulation of almost nine million readers, the treatise was hailed as "one of the most important books of our generation." Individuals and organizations bought one million offprints, and one and a half million copies went to US military personnel. As part of the media blitz, *Look* magazine produced a cartoon version, and Hayek offered a synopsis on NBC's popular radio program *Words at War*. Hayek had to move his scheduled talks to larger venues, hiring a publicity agent to book auditoriums across the country. He spoke to packed houses everywhere he went. He also made connections to anti–New Deal businesspeople and free trade foundations, who paid for Hayek's nationwide tour and later bankrolled many of his late career activities, including the Mont Pèlerin Society (MPS), his professorship at the University of Chicago, the publication of *The Constitution of Liberty* and *Law, Legislation, and Liberty*, and his affiliations with the libertarian and conservative Institute for Humane Studies, Heritage Foundation, and Cato Institute.[1]

That a European scholar who spoke with a thick Viennese accent and wrote about German and British politics would command such a massive US audience was surprising enough. What made Hayek's triumph nearly incredible was that three years earlier, he had stood at a professional cross-roads. His 1941 economics summa, *The Pure Theory of Capital*, met neither his nor his peers' expectations. In many ways, *Pure Theory* was the end of the road for Hayek's professional economics career. Meant as a theoretical "explanation of industrial fluctuations," Hayek hoped to bring clarity to the underlying concepts of capital, production, and interest. His major insight consisted of taking time factors in the business cycle more seriously than his predecessors had. If scholars expected a forceful rejoinder to John Maynard Keynes's *General Theory*, however, Hayek struggled to formulate an alternative. After seven years of work and a five-hundred-page manu-script, major lacunae still existed. Moreover his work seemed disconnected from empirical reality. By the time he penned the preface in June 1940, he conceded that the book had not achieved its aims: "the present book with all its shortcomings is the outcome of work over a period so prolonged that I doubt whether further effort on my part would be repaid by the results." World War II provided Hayek an excuse to abbreviate the inter-minable project and shift attention elsewhere.[2]

Fellow economists, too, regarded *Pure Theory* as an unsatisfactory prod-uct. No fewer than six reviews appeared within a year, a remarkable num-ber considering that the war curtailed mail service, reduced paper supplies, and drew academics away from their scholarly activities. Redoubtable economists Arthur Pigou, Kenneth Boulding, R. G. Hawtrey, Friedrich Lutz, and Arthur Smithies wrote commentaries. Each of them recognized the importance of Hayek's work, yet they found his usage of concepts inconsistent, if not untenable. Even the most generous evaluation— Boulding's—felt the reasoning too abstract for use within the economics profession: "It is not yet the 'Pure Theory of Capital.' For it is required of abstractions that they be fruitful—that they provide a ladder by which we can climb from the more to the less abstract. One has the impression that many of Dr. Hayek's abstractions are foundations without a super-structure." Hayek's roadmap for economics was really a labyrinth that offered little clarity.[3]

It was not just Hayek's Anglo-American peers who took issue with *Pure Theory*; even his Austrian compatriots were unimpressed. Although the mild-mannered, conciliatory Fritz Machlup defended it, Gottfried Haber-ler and Oskar Morgenstern rejected its hollow abstractions. Haberler damned the book's empty deductions: "He [Hayek] has entered into highly unfruitful and unrealistic considerations. He very much gives the impression of a completely unworldly, ivory tower [*weltfremd*] person who merely plays around with deductions from entirely unrealistic premises." Haberler failed to see how Hayek's meditations could advance economics or resolve contemporary problems. Morgenstern concurred: "Hayek's book displeases me greatly. . . . I find that one cannot go any further with this kind of science." For economics to advance, scholars had to demand higher scientific standards than the current "state of stupid palaver." In his final judgment, Morgenstern declared, "[*Pure Theory*] is higher nonsense. . . . This type of 'economic theory' *must* vanish."[4]

The year 1942 was therefore a nadir on Hayek's journey, 1945 an unexpected revival. His experience was not unique, and his case serves as a microcosm for the fortunes of the Austrian School during the war years. The destruction of Europe loomed over its members, as they worried about friends and loved ones, not to mention their professional prospects. After emigration, they confronted barriers to acceptance of their scholarly work in the new intellectual environment. US economics appeared to be moving in a more mathematical and formal direction that felt constraining for Europeans who had long seen the discipline as a grand, humanistic science, a *Geisteswissenschaft*. Faced with a disciplinary and existential crisis, they wrestled with their place in the US academy and the emerging neoclassical mainstream. They also grappled with how to make their work matter. Feelings of marginalization loomed large in contemporary self-descriptions. The Austrians did not fade from view, however. They mostly succeeded in becoming well-regarded intellectuals and advisers like their predecessors Menger, Böhm, and Wieser. We will track how exactly Hayek and the Austrians achieved the transition from struggling émigré economists to leading intellectuals pivotally involved in midcentury US policy discussions and ideological debates.

The process of translation and assimilation that the Austrian School underwent after emigration was a complex and often ironic one. Some of their ideas entered the economic mainstream; much disappeared. Hayek, Mises, Morgenstern, and Schumpeter wrestled with charges of esotericism and backwardness, and they feared for the intellectual exhaustion and extinction of their tradition. The Austrians bickered with one another and endured a period of intellectual waywardness, as they ceased to be at the forefront of economic thinking. The Austrians adapted to disciplinary marginalization by drawing on a wellspring of Viennese talents: networking with academic, business, and government insiders; forming autonomous institutions; and stimulating one another's work. Even as the appeal of their economic ideas waned, their political views waxed, finding new support in conservative circles. The Austrian School of economics, always known for its liberalism, became better known for its politics in its Anglophone translation than for its marginalism. Slowly but surely, the urbane, cosmopolitan Austrians attracted new sources of support. They projected an image of status and authority that resonated with US elites and conservative intellectuals. "Austria" as a symbol carried with it an Old World charm, and it lent a patina of sophistication to anti–New Deal and anticollectivist ideas that had seemed obsolete a few years prior. Austrian political theory seemed an appropriate starting place for a program that hoped to revive liberalism in the face of socialism and totalitarianism. With a new basis of support in new lands, the Austrian School ceased to be the coffeehouse school of earlier vintage. Its members became standard-bearers for a program to restore the values of another age, the Austrian world of yesterday. This metaphorical Austrian School, inspired by Vienna but made in the USA, assured a second life for the tradition.

Saving a School

Understandably, Austrian School theory was not the foremost concern for the Viennese in 1938. Anxiety about friends and loved ones and concern for their country weighed on those abroad. After the Anschluss of Austria by Nazi Germany in March 1938, it was no longer safe for Jews to remain in the country. The orgy of violence initiated by the Nazi invasion also impacted political "undesirables": Catholics associated with the Austrofascist state and liberal opponents of National Socialism. Nearly every institution associated with the school felt the Nazis' wrath. Most notably the Institute for Business Cycle Research, the quintessential Austrian School project, was taken over by the economist and Nazi Party member Ernst Wagemann, the head of a similar center in Berlin. The Austrians lamented the "coordination" of their beloved institute and wryly noted that its monthly journal was now published by Goebbels's Ministry of Propaganda. Sensing that their school was no longer viable in its home-land, its representatives abroad mobilized all means at their disposal to save their friends.[5]

There was one notorious exception to the collective persecution expe-rienced by the school's members. Hans Mayer, Mises's former rival and the leading exemplar of the school at the University of Vienna, quickly "adapted" to the Nazi order. Mayer joined the Party and purged the *Zeitschrift* of "Jewish" editors and contributions. After the Anschluss, he offered an editorial greeting to the new Nazi authorities in the Ostmark. He introduced an Aryan paragraph into the bylaws of the Economic So-ciety and expelled Jewish members. According to rumors, he also de-nounced his rival Othmar Spann to the Nazi authorities. To the end of their lives, Hayek, Machlup, and the others regarded Mayer as a "scoun-drel" and a traitor.[6]

While Mayer reached an accommodation with the Nazis, Austrian School émigrés corresponded feverishly with their stranded compatriots and scrambled to account for their loved ones. Ominous tidings filled their letters, as friends begged for positions, fled with their families, or faced imprisonment. In these trying times, we see the full scope of the Austrian School family, as well as the intensity of feeling it inspired. To the Viennese already in the United Kingdom and the United States, the situation was dire. Haberler, Hayek, and Morgenstern shared whatever news they had: "[Max] Mintz is en route with nine family members to the USA, without an affidavit. . . . As a result, Herbert Fürth was taken into custody for 48 [hours] because it was alleged that he knew about the Mintzes flight. Mintz's Vienna assets have been confiscated and his citizenship revoked." Max Mintz and Herbert Furth, founding members of the Geist-Kreis and participants in Mises's seminar, operated a law practice together. In 1926, Mintz married Ilse Schüller, the daughter of one of Carl Menger's students, Richard. Schüller-Mintz was an outstanding economist and scholar in her own right. She worked for the institute with Hayek and Morgenstern and attended the Mises-Kreis. Because of the families' Jewish ancestry, the Mintzes and Furths experienced the Nazis' wrath.[7]

Austrian émigrés sprang into action to save their peers. With Hayek's aid and the backing of the Society for the Protection of Science and

Learning (SPSL), Richard Schüller followed his daughter, making his escape to England via Italy in July. The Mintzes, including their six-year-old daughter, Gabriele (later the renowned literary scholar Marjorie Perloff), found their way to New York City via Switzerland in the spring of 1938. Furth, Haberler's brother-in-law, did not enjoy the same financial advantages as the Mintzes, nor did he possess the academic reputation of his cohort. Haberler, Morgenstern, and Schumpeter worked for over a year to land him a permanent position in the United States. Drawing on their Rockefeller Foundation (RF) connections, they found him an economics professorship at the historically black university Lincoln University, in Pennsylvania.[8]

Morgenstern, Haberler, Machlup, and Schumpeter wrote countless letters endorsing their Viennese friends to aid societies and immigration groups, and they tracked progress closely. In addition to working with the RF, they assisted their peers with the Emergency Committee in Aid of Displaced Foreign Scholars, headed by Stephen Duggan, and the University in Exile at the New School for Social Research, led by Alvin Johnson. After facilitating Morgenstern's permanent appointment to Princeton, Haberler kept his friend apprised of other news. Haberler and Morgenstern rejoiced when the phenomenologist Felix Kaufmann and the economist Erich Hula received permanent offers from the New School. The former Böhm seminar participant Emil Lederer was vital in the recruitment. They also followed the ordeal of Erich Schiff, a Mises seminar regular, with alarm. Schiff, who was the editor of the institute's monthly report, fled Austria in March, believing he had a position lined up at the University of Michigan. Although he possessed an affidavit for entry to the United States, his visa was delayed. Hayek used his contacts at the SPSL and the Oxford Refugee Committee to land him a temporary position at Balliol College. Schiff only arrived at Michigan a year later and in 1940 received a research fellowship at the Brookings Institution, with recommendations from Haberler and Morgenstern.[9]

The case of the mathematician Abraham Wald best reveals the extensiveness of the efforts of Austrian economists. Born in 1902 in Cluj in the Hungarian half of the Austro-Hungarian Empire (present-day Romania), Wald was raised in an Orthodox Jewish household. In 1927, he began his studies at the University of Vienna with Karl Menger, completing his doctorate in 1931. He became Menger's favorite student and distinguished himself as a precocious talent in the fields of axiomatics and topology. He also showed a nuanced understanding of general equilibrium problems and seasonal variations in economics. His eastern European and Jewish backgrounds precluded a permanent position at the University of Vienna, however. Despite personal misgivings about Wald and his Jewishness, Morgenstern helped him acquire RF funds and employed him at the institute.[10]

As conditions in Austria worsened, Wald became increasingly anxious. Behind the scenes, Rockefeller officials and Viennese scholars conducted numerous conversations about the fate of Viennese institutions and the plight of scholars, especially Jews. Few were ready to help Wald, since he was, according to an RF officer, "a man without a country" and a "homeless Jew." Nevertheless, Wald's colleagues continued to press his case. Menger, Morgenstern, Haberler, and Gerhard Tintner all rated Wald as the finest scholar under consideration for an RF grant. However, the foundation instead awarded the travel money to Reinhard Kamitz, a scholar with a "convincing and businesslike" appearance, that is, not Jewish. Kamitz rejected the fellowship, since he assumed leadership of the Vienna institute after the Anschluss. Still, the RF did not act on Wald's behalf. Only through the strident activities of the younger Austrians did Wald land a poorly paid position on the Cowles Commission in the United States. Morgenstern in particular helped to rustle up travel funds for the penurious Wald to make it to Colorado. The laconic prose of the RF officer John Van Sickle captured Wald's predicament: "I see no possibility of a fellowship for A. Wald. Morgenstern admits that Wald ought to come to this country as there is no permanent future for him in central Europe. . . . We are not planning on offering any encouragement at this point." This summary understated the dangers Wald faced. With the exception of one brother, the rest of Wald's family vanished into the concentration camp system, perishing at the hands of either the murderous, antisemitic Romanian regime or the genocidal Nazis. Wald narrowly escaped Europe, making it to the United States via Cuba in 1938. He eventually found a permanent position at Columbia in the Statistical Research Group, and his work played an instrumental role in the development of game theory and operations theory.[11]

Austrian scholars exhausted all avenues in seeking the placement of their endangered friends. In addition to cultivating connections with Anglo-American foundations, they drew on their academic network. Howard Ellis and Charles Gulick, both economists at the University of California, visited Vienna in the early 1930s and established relations with Morgenstern and the institute. When Alexander Gerschenkron, a close associate of Morgenstern's who was working on a comparative economic study of the Habsburg successor states, decided to flee Austria in April 1938, he turned to the Berkeley scholars. Ellis landed him a three-month appointment as a research assistant; Gulick then employed him on his massive history of interwar Austria. Morgenstern also procured for the multitalented young Austrian a $1,200 honorarium to finish his research. All three scholars worked to get Gerschenkron over from Austria (via Switzerland, the United Kingdom, and Cuba) and provided support letters for his visa application with the Mexican consulate, which enabled his US residency. Gerschenkron became an indispensable member of the Berkeley community, as Gulick related to Morgenstern: "Gerschenkron has been working like hell—we can hardly drag him out to a movie! I always liked him, but I am learning much more what a really fine and lovable character he has. Somehow or other he must be kept in the U.S. and I am going to do everything in my power to aid in that."[12]

Looking back on Vienna in 1938, one can multiply the number of these noble rescue endeavors, since the rescue of Austrian intellectuals was the number-one priority for Austrian intellectuals, be they Austrian School economists or Freudian psychoanalysts, logical positivists or Austro-Marxists, twelve-tone composers or legal positivists. The war had a galvanizing effect on members of the Austrian School in particular, since they were directly involved in all aspects of the rescue effort. And even though many of them were out of harm's way by 1940, the war years continued to interrupt their academic work and challenge their resolve. They relied on one another for jobs and advice, information and solace.[13]

If escape to the United States was torturous, conditions were little better in Europe. As the Battle of Britain raged in the skies over London, European-based Austrians like Hayek began to explore all options, including ones across the Atlantic. Paul Rosenstein-Rodan, a professor at

University College London, followed his department from its English home to its wartime base of operations in Aberystwyth, Wales. He looked for new sources of income from think tanks like the London-based Chatham House and ended up in Washington, DC, after the war's end.[14]

Friedrich Hayek's employer, the London School of Economics (LSE), evacuated its premises and relocated to Peterhouse College, Cambridge. In an interesting turn, John Maynard Keynes helped Hayek find rooms near his own office, and according to an apocryphal account, they served on the same nighttime patrols on the roof of King's Chapel. Increasingly despondent, Hayek wrote to Haberler and Machlup about opportunities in the United States. Machlup cautioned that it was unlikely a position could be found without a firm commitment from Hayek to accept. Haberler appealed to Alvin Johnson, who offered Hayek a position at the New School, albeit at a substantial salary reduction. Hayek, a proud, status-conscious man, took the offer as an insult: "The offer from the New School which I owe to Haberler has really caused me some indignation. . . . I could not help regarding its nature as a personal slight. I wonder what a Professor at Harvard or Chicago would say if in similar circumstances he were offered without asking for anything a nondescript job at about a fourth of his present salary." Hayek declined the offer; the ordeal soured relations with Haberler for a time.[15]

The rapid military advances of German forces in western Europe imperiled the existence of Austrian School members and sympathizers even in neutral Switzerland. Based in Switzerland since 1934, Ludwig von Mises made periodic trips back to Vienna. He happened to be in Austria in March 1938, getting out days before the Anschluss. The Gestapo ransacked his Vienna home and confiscated many of his books and valuables. His future wife, Margit, and her daughter, the journalist Gitta Sereny, departed a few months later. Mises found the Swiss experience favorable until the war. In Geneva, he was surrounded by sympathetic scholars like Wilhelm Röpke, William Rappard, and Paul Mantoux. The presence of Haberler (until 1936), Helene Lieser, Louise Sommer, and other Austrians provided the city a Viennese inflection. Nevertheless, as the Nazi war machine swallowed up Scandinavia, the Low Countries, and France in 1940, Ludwig and Margit worried for their future. Ludwig reached out to Machlup and

Hayek. Machlup secured an offer at the University of California–Los Angeles (UCLA) for a reasonable salary, which the haughty Mises rejected as inadequate. After signaling his disapproval, however, Mises reversed course, placing Machlup in the unenviable position of reopening negotiations. UCLA demurred. Eventually, the Mises family escaped Switzerland with the help of a French transit visa obtained by Hayek and Machlup. They arrived in New York City in August 1940.[16]

While Machlup welcomed the opportunity for a "grand reunion" in California in the summer of 1940, with Haberler (who was at Berkeley), Machlup (at Stanford), and Mises, he expressed consternation at Mises's aristocratic, elitist bearing. The Austrian's excessive salary demands doomed any prospect of tenured employment, whether at UCLA or elsewhere. Machlup lamented to Hayek, "Mises is still my problem child. My efforts to reopen negotiations with Los Angeles—whose call Mises turned down in March—were without success. Mises had some possibilities at New York University, but nothing came out of this." In a confidential letter of recommendation to NYU, Machlup recounted the strengths and the flaws of his mentor. He observed that "the neo-Austrian school is to a large extent the Mises School." However, he also noted that Mises's unyielding style repelled as often as it attracted. "It is the conviction with which he expounds his ideas which arouses the students' interest, partly by convincing them, partly by provoking their criticism." Mises did not receive a full-time offer from NYU, not for Machlup's lack of trying.[17]

Because of the tireless activity of the Austrian School members, by late 1940 virtually everyone who would escape from the European maelstrom had made it out. They had expended significant psychological, physical, and financial means to ensure one another's safety. For the school, the consequences of emigration were far-reaching. Emigration spelled the end of its European phase and threw the tradition into turmoil. It also left members' intellectual projects in suspended animation, and they remained in abeyance until the Austrians were fully established in safer climes. While the Austrians remained connected to one another through their shared traditions and continued interactions, their interests increasingly diverged "in the wilderness." They all drew on their Austrian backgrounds in facing obstacles, yet they also devised new solutions that transformed the school and its collective project.

An Economic Dead End?

If Hayek reached an intellectual crossroads with his *Pure Theory*, he was not the only Austrian to face a crisis in the early war years. The economic program that had reestablished the Austrians as a recognizable school in the early 1930s—a combination of marginal utility, monetary theory, and business cycle theory—yielded little new insight by the late 1930s. Their criticisms of equilibrium theory increasingly fell on deaf ears, especially in the United States. The experiences of Mises and Schumpeter in particular revealed the troubled state of Austrian economics. The Austrians had to adapt if they wished to remain relevant in the social scientific and intellectual worlds.

As Mises prepared for the arduous journey from war-torn Europe to America, he was also putting the finishing touches on what he believed to be his intellectual masterwork. Titled *Nationalökonomie*, it encapsulated all of Mises's ideas from the past four decades. Stretching to eight hundred pages, it contained a lengthy theoretical discussion of the fundamental principles of the science of human action, or praxeology. It also offered an extended defense of marginal utility theory and the Austrian ideas of exchange, price, and capital. It reiterated his critiques of socialist calculation, his advocacy of market economics, and his views on credit and business cycles. The final section also presented concrete policy applications. He responded to ongoing debates about "the end of laissez-faire" and "the crisis of capitalism" with a full-throated reassertion of the superiority of unrestrained "Manchester-style" liberalism. In the lead-up to the book's publication, Mises expressed optimism about the book and its expected reception. In a letter to Machlup, Mises offered a bittersweet assessment: "It is anyway probably the final economics book in the German language." Mises believed he would get the last word on German economics, something he and his Austrian predecessors, going back to Menger, had always wanted. Of course the rise of the Nazis and World War II also signaled the likely end of German-language economics, which Mises decried.[18]

Unfortunately for Mises, almost no one noticed the book's appearance. Mises's "last word" was more eulogy than valedictory. It was either ignored or rejected as a tome using obsolete concepts in a discredited language published in a dying world. *Nationalökonomie* appeared in May 1940 in

Switzerland, briefly before its publisher closed its doors. While Mises's Austrian friends Haberler, Hayek, Machlup, and Morgenstern received copies, it is unclear which journals did. Only one major review appeared, and Hayek wrote it. The younger Austrian, whose methodological and economic positions diverged from Mises's by the mid-1930s, tempered his criticisms. A reader familiar with Mises's ideas would find "much that is familiar if not accepted doctrine." Hayek found the "main interest" in the opening and concluding parts, which presented Mises's methodology and policy applications, respectively. On the latter, Hayek applauded Mises's "really imposing unified system of a liberal social philosophy." Hayek enthused that the book was "much more like that of an eighteenth-century philosopher than that of a modern specialist" and "feels throughout much nearer reality, and is constantly recalled from the discussion of technicalities to the consideration of the great problems of our time." Coming from Hayek, whose own work had been criticized for its abstractness, it is fair to question just how good a judge of "reality" Hayek was.[19]

Hayek could not refrain from interjecting his concerns, however. Many of these issues had come out in the course of conversations between the younger Austrians, none of whom found much to admire in *Nationalökonomie*. Hayek conceded that the book showed a glaring ignorance of recent developments: "it must be admitted that he seems to have been little affected by the general evolution of our subject during the period over which his work extends." In fact, Mises displayed "a certain contempt for contemporary economics." Hayek's critique followed the lead of Haberler, who had argued for years that Mises was no longer a significant economist and that his work offered no insights for anyone who had learned economics since the Great War: "If one had studied the classics and Marshall in 1912, then one would have learned nothing more from Mises." Hayek also noted that the major innovations in the Austrian subjective approach introduced in *Nationalökonomie* were "less convincing." Hayek criticized Mises's a priori methodological approach, which everyone from Morgenstern to Felix Kaufmann to Fritz Machlup questioned. Hayek's review exuded a profound sense of ambivalence. The reviewer was sympathetic to Mises's political and theoretical goals and to Mises himself, yet he recognized that Mises's work did not contribute much that was new. As with Hayek's *Pure Theory*, Mises's *Nationalökonomie* suggested that perhaps the Austrian economic approach had run aground. Perhaps "liberal social philosophy" was all that Mises had left to offer.[20]

If Mises and Hayek found modern economics constraining for their broader social and political projects, Oskar Morgenstern and Joseph Schumpeter grew exasperated by the discipline's inability to incorporate new trends in mathematics and the social sciences. They, too, found their work underappreciated. Between the 1937 translation of *The Limits of Economics* and 1943, Morgenstern did not publish another substantial piece of scholarship. In *Limits*, he attempted to show the shortcomings of modern economics and the work of its leading exemplars, such as Robbins, Keynes, and Mises. He argued that the discipline existed in an inchoate state of development, plagued by value judgments and imprecision. He called out empiricists and theorists alike—the former for their inability to generalize from statistical data and the latter for their distance from reality. He demanded that economics restrict itself to the realm of policy. A corrosive, critical treatise that captured Morgenstern's skepticism, *Limits* dismayed even his closest friends. Eve Burns, a Columbia economist and the wife of the future Federal Reserve chair Arthur Burns, welcomed the book, yet she told him, "[I got] a little mad at the predominately negative turn to all your writings. . . . It is time you turned your fine mind to building up and showing possibilities of development rather than to explorations of limitations." The Chicago economist Frank Knight felt that *Limits* fell short of a significant contribution: "frankly it did not seem to me, or to some colleagues whom I have heard comment, that the book represented a terribly serious effort on your part to penetrate the more fundamental issues." Mises and Hayek rejected the work outright, the latter finding it incoherent at best and rude at worst.[21]

Joseph Schumpeter also fought unsuccessfully against prevailing trends in economics in the name of a more precise science. His 1939 attempt, *Business Cycles*, met with shrugs. He intended to integrate economic theory, statistical analysis, and historical investigation into a comprehensive study of economic fluctuations during the age of capitalism, from 1789 to 1938. Business events could not be explained solely by economic laws, he argued. Statistical methods also could not yield a better understanding of business cycles without theory. To answer economic questions, Schumpeter turned to history and analysis. While this may sound like a far cry from the deductive approach of his fellow Austrians, it was not. For Schumpeter, economic analysis was always theory laden. Accordingly, he started with an elaboration of equilibrium theory. He introduced the concepts of general and partial equilibrium and perfect competition first to provide a baseline for understanding the economy. Like the other Austrians, he also found the phenomenon of disequilibrium more significant than equilibrium: "Every event impinges on an economic world that is already disturbed and in disequilibrium, our understanding of the way in which the economic organism reacts to any given new event is unavoidably based upon our understanding of those equilibrium relations." Sounding a bit like Hayek in "Economics and Knowledge," Schumpeter argued that the dynamism of the economic world required better explanations than static equilibrium models could ever hope to provide.[22]

Instead of focusing on the length of the cycles, as his predecessors Joseph Kitchin, Clément Juglar, and Nikolai Kondratieff had done, Schumpeter developed a theory to account for the constant disruptions of economic activity. His biggest innovation was a theory of economic evolution and entrepreneurship. For Schumpeter, "New Men" and "New Firms" drove innovation, and innovation propelled the economy. He elaborated these insights with historical evidence from Britain, Germany, and the United States. More than a history, it was a love letter to capitalism. Schumpeter told a swashbuckling tale of capitalist booms and busts, transporting the reader from textile owners in Lancashire to railroad and steel barons in Essen to assembly lines in Detroit. Schumpeter wove a tapestry of capitalist evolution, valorizing efficiency, economies of scale, and disruption. In the end, Schumpeter defended the capitalist process, even in the face of the Great Depression and the "end of laissez-faire": "Capitalism and its civilization may be decaying, shading off into something else, or tottering toward a violent death. . . . But the world crisis does not prove it and has, in fact, nothing to do with it. It was not a symptom of a weakening or a failure of the system." Schumpeter railed against efforts to dampen the creative destruction of capitalism, especially New Deal programs and Keynesian economics: "Without that change or, more precisely, that kind of change which we have called evolution, capitalist society cannot exist; . . . without innovations, no entrepreneurs; without entrepreneurial achievement, no capitalist returns and no capitalist propulsion. The atmosphere of industrial revolutions—of 'progress'—is the only one in which capitalism can survive."[23]

Despite the book's sweeping scope, vast erudition, and hortatory rhetoric, *Business Cycles* misfired. The academic community lavished praise on its ambition—Oskar Lange grouping it in "intention and horizon" with Marx's *Kapital*—yet few read the work and fewer still deemed it an important contribution. Schumpeter, Simon Kuznets argued, had not produced the "exact economics" to which he aspired, nor had he reconciled economic, statistical, and historical approaches successfully. At a 1939 workshop at Harvard, it became clear that nobody had studied the book, which exasperated the vain Schumpeter. He viewed *Business Cycles* as his magnum opus, which would confirm his status as the era's greatest economist. It had taken him seven years to complete, during which Germany succumbed to National Socialism, Keynes wrote his *General Theory*, and the world descended into war. The book's lack of focus or policy applications undermined its success. Schumpeter grudgingly recognized the need to reformulate his ideas.[24]

In summary, several Austrian economists faced intellectual crossroads by 1941. Their work within the economics profession seemed out of step with the discipline's development toward formalized models based on utility-maximizing individuals. The features that distinguished the Austrian approach—theoretical rigor, interdisciplinarity, skepticism about "scientistic" models and forecasting, attention to subjective factors and the time preference, emphasis on the roles of institutions in economic development—had either entered the economics mainstream or had faded from consideration. In particular, the emerging "Neoclassical-Keynesian synthesis"—which applied neoclassical ideas of supply and demand to Keynesian macroeconomic concepts—left little room for Austrian research questions. The Austrians grew frustrated by the narrow-mindedness and parochialism of mainstream economics, yet they struggled to find a new idiom for their more expansive and exacting understandings of the social sciences. The Austrians risked getting lost in translation. In seeking a new research direction and intellectual audience, they turned increasingly to social and political theory. The Austrians embarked on a second act in the Anglophone world, reinventing themselves as intellectual entrepreneurs who transplanted their ideas into related disciplines while simultaneously drawing inspiration from novel sources.[25]

Schumpeter's "Literary" Turn

If the early 1940s represented a low point for the popularity of the Austrian economists, then the mid- and late-1940s resurgence was a vindication of Austrian and central European thought styles. The list of impactful titles produced by the Austrians between 1942 and 1945 is staggering: Schumpeter, *Capitalism, Socialism, and Democracy* (1942); Hayek, *Road to Serfdom* (1944); Mises, *Bureaucracy* (1944); John von Neumann and Morgenstern, *The Theory of Games and Economic Behavior* (1944). If you include the works of Karl Polanyi and Karl Popper—*The Great Transformation* (1944) and *The Open Society and Its Enemies* (1945)— the Austrians may have produced more important texts in social and political theory than any other midcentury group. In light of this dramatic change of fortune, we must explore the factors that helped transform the intellectual fate of this émigré group. In addition to a successful assimilation into Anglophone society, the Austrians' willingness to escape the bounds of traditional economics opened their work to new audiences. The Austrians showed that they were not only economists. Their wide-ranging philosophical investigations espoused the sanctity and power of "Western" liberal values, anticipating similar trends in the Anglophone world. Several of the Austrians, namely, Mises, Hayek, and Machlup, re-created themselves as the torchbearers of a new ideological movement. Meanwhile Schumpeter and Morgenstern also found new audiences forging paths that led them even further afield from their Austrian origins.[26]

Schumpeter's *Capitalism, Socialism, and Democracy* initiated a change of fortunes for the fifty-nine-year-old Austrian. After *Business Cycles*, Schumpeter turned his attention to contemporary affairs. He identified socialism as the key concern for this synoptic work: "This volume is the result of . . . almost forty years' thought, observation and research on the subject of socialism." Fin-de-siècle Vienna had inculcated in him a deep mistrust for socialism. Like Menger, Böhm, Wieser, and Mises, he objected to it on both scientific and ideological grounds. While he avoided calling *Capitalism* a "political" text, he admitted it would not offer a "well-balanced treatise." He examined the possibility that a socialist order of society, supported by a democratic method of government, could emerge out of bourgeois, capitalist society. He concluded that the singularity of purpose demanded by a socialist economic system made it incompatible with democracy and freedom. Written in a lively, ironic tone, *Capitalism* became one of the most influential social philosophical texts of the post–World War II era.[27]

Schumpeter built his argument around answering two questions: (1) Can capitalism survive? (2) Can socialism work? A third, related question about the compatibility of socialism and democracy emerged from the first two. His answers were, all things equal, no and yes; however, a huge "but" loomed. Although he stated, "Can capitalism survive? No. I do not think that it can," this was a bit of legerdemain. Schumpeter believed that yes was possible if people changed their ways: "What counts in any attempt at social prognosis is not the Yes or No that sums up the facts and arguments which lead up to it. . . . Analysis, whether economic or other, never yields more than a statement about the tendencies present in an observable pattern. And these never tell us what *will* happen to the pattern but only what *would* happen if they continued to act as they have been acting."[28] Like Hayek's critique of socialist planners in "Economics and Knowledge," Schumpeter argued that scientists can analyze present conditions and extrapolate from that information, but they cannot anticipate the effects of all actions chosen by individual agents. While capitalism in its current, desiccated form seemed destined for collapse, this need not transpire. Deploying a satirist's wit and an ironist's pen, *Capitalism* revealed that Schumpeter believed just the opposite. Capitalism may sow seeds of its own destruction, but it still constituted the surest guarantee of prosperity and democracy. Socialism was technically feasible and seemed a logical consequence of industrial capitalism, yet the restrictions required to maintain it made repression a virtual certainty and democracy unattainable.[29]

At the heart of Schumpeter's capitalist defense was creative destruction. "The opening up of new markets, foreign or domestic, and the organizational development from the craft shop to the factory . . . incessantly revolutionizes the economic structure *from within*, incessantly destroying the old one, incessantly creating a new own. This process of Creative Destruction is the essential fact of capitalism." Creative destruction has become Schumpeter's most lasting contribution. For many people, it captures capitalism's relentless energy and revolutionary power that boosters applaud and detractors deplore. In extolling this vitality, Schumpeter also leveled a hearty criticism against his economist colleagues, whose static models of perfect competition and complete information, of partial and general equilibria, possessed little explanatory power for a dynamic world.[30]

In making a normative argument for capitalism, Schumpeter went beyond the more staid tone of *Business Cycles*. Like a latter-day Isaiah, Schumpeter argued ominously that innovations were becoming routine and that progress seemed to stall. Businesses stagnated and entrepreneurial energy dissipated. Moreover, capitalism produced a treasonous class of intellectuals that undermined the system from within. Socialism appeared the answer for these critics, since it promised to remove the uncertainties of competition, improve organizational efficiency, smooth the business cycle, and reduce friction between state and economy. Schumpeter identified clear costs that accompanied these socialist "gains": a loss of middle-class motivation, an increase in authoritarian discipline, the disappearance of economic and political freedom. Socialism *could* work, but it would not be benevolent or democratic. It required a degree of control that undermined the very freedoms it set out to instill. Capitalism was thus the only model for freedom lovers.[31]

In *Capitalism*, Schumpeter also offered an interpretation of democracy that became enormously influential among midcentury thinkers, especially those associated with modernization theory. Schumpeter advanced one of the first procedural definitions of democracy: "Democracy is a political method, that is to say, a certain type of institutional arrangement for arriving at political—legislative and administrative—decisions and hence incapable of being an end in itself, irrespective of what decisions it will produce under given historical conditions." Democracy is a means, not an end in itself. It works through competitions among elites for support rather than through mass participation. The minimal act of voting is therefore the proper form of popular involvement, meaning democracy should be representative and not direct. Schumpeter inspired countless scholars from Gabriel Almond to Raymond Aron in their elite theories of democracy, which verged on theories of aristocracy. It also gibed with the instrumental, means-ends justifications for democracy that Mises and Hayek articulated in their later works.[32]

Capitalism, Socialism, and Democracy is one of the greatest and subtlest apologia for capitalism and elitist liberalism ever written. Despite this, many readers misread it as a defeatist text. They homed in on what they under-stood as Schumpeter's inference that capitalism sowed the seeds of its own destruction. They failed to pick up on the abundant sarcasm and irony. These literary features led the Marxist historian and Viennese émigré Eric Hobsbawm—no fan of Schumpeter's—to call *Capitalism* a "very central European work." Those who grasped its nuance appreciated it, especially his fellow Austrians. Haberler and Morgenstern excitedly discussed *Capitalism* in their letters. Machlup wrote a glowing review. "Professor Schum-peter's respect and sympathy for bourgeois achievements can be sensed . . . in every part of his book." He lauded its "humorous-ironic rococo" style and withering cynicism about socialism. Machlup expressed "sheer pleasure and intellectual satisfaction" with Schumpeter's social philosophy. He likened the work to a novel or mystery book. Even if you disliked the characters or the plot, you could admire the style. Machlup concluded his paean in a haughty European tone: "Schumpeter's literary style is grandi-ose: it is almost too good for a book with scientific ambitions and achieve-ments; for it distracts the readers, slows him down and makes him pause—for applause, so to speak." Bravo, Machlup intoned, Schumpeter had created a Viennese work of art!³³

Even if few people appreciated *Capitalism* as fully as the Austrians did, it was Schumpeter's greatest intellectual success. Published in late 1942, it received positive reviews from scholars across the political spectrum. By the time of its second edition in 1947, it had already been translated into seven languages. It saw a third edition before Schumpeter's death in 1950 and two more thereafter. It became a hit in intellectual circles: the historian Arthur Schlesinger even reviewed it in the *Nation*. It was Schumpeter's most accessible work and also his most impactful, receiving a retrospective treatment in 1978 from the neoconservative journal *Commentary* and a 1981 tribute from scholars and friends. It has earned a place on several lists of the century's most significant works of social theory. *Capitalism* launched the final act of Schumpeter's career, which included influence over the postwar Japanese economic recovery through the appointment of former students to advisory roles, the presidency of the American Economic As-sociation, and the publication of a seminal work on the history of economic thought. The book turned Schumpeter into an intellectual lodestar for the entrepreneurial age in which we still live.³⁴

The Road to Stardom

Friedrich Hayek, too, began a transition from economic to political theory in the late 1930s with his "Abuse and Decline of Reason" project. In 1938, he wrote an essay titled "Freedom and the Economic System," his initial foray into social and political theory and a precursor to *The Road to Serfdom*. He became acting editor of the journal *Economica*, the leading British economics journal, and he published several articles between 1941 and 1944. In these publications, Hayek challenged the idea that National Socialism and fascism were capitalist reactions against socialism. He crafted a history of European thought centered on competing notions of individualism. He distinguished between "true" individualism predicated on the English and Scottish Enlightenment and "false" Cartesian rationalism. The former stressed the importance of society and its spontaneous forces for the growth of knowledge, ethics, and prosperity. The latter supposed that individual minds could know better than the collectivity and could devise plans based on ratiocination. Hayek showed how modern socialism derived from false individualism and was inherently antidemocratic and authoritarian. Turning socialist arguments on their head, he intimated that National Socialism was not a consequence of capitalism but of socialism, since its leaders claimed to have better plans for the *Volk* than individuals themselves had. Nazism was therefore grounded in false individualist and socialist misconceptions. Hayek was so excited about his Abuse and Decline project that he shared his outlines with Machlup, Haberler, and Walter Lippmann with the hope that it would serve "as a basis of future application to one of the foundations for funds." Haberler and Machlup eagerly assisted in this endeavor.[35]

This new project took Hayek far afield of his earlier work. Though he distanced himself from the economics that animated his Austrian scholarship, a Viennese influence remained strong, albeit from an unlikely source. His primary interlocutor for Abuse and Decline was not Haberler, Machlup, or Mises but Karl Popper. The two had not known each other in Vienna and were seemingly unaware of each other's work before 1935, when they met for the first time. Their mutual admiration intensified after 1937. Popper, safely at Canterbury College in New Zealand, was working on "A Social Philosophy for Everyman," later *The Open Society*. Hayek, who read

Popper's work with great satisfaction, proposed to a British publisher that it translate and publish Popper's first book, *Die Logik der Forschung*. In the course of revision, Popper decided that Hayek's work on knowledge and the social sciences required critical engagement, leading the two into a fruitful correspondence. Popper published three long articles in Hayek's *Economica*, titled "The Poverty of Historicism." Meanwhile Hayek's and Popper's political ideas fell into harmony, which was somewhat surprising given Popper's social democratic tendencies and Hayek's liberal ones. They sensed, however, that they had found kindred spirits. Their views became so alike that Popper added dates of completion to sections of the *Open Society* manuscript to avoid accusations of plagiarism.[36]

From April 1943 until November 1945, the two men dissected each other's works, writing pages-long letters from halfway around the world. They debated planning, notions of freedom, the fate of capitalism, and the methodological differences between the natural and social sciences. They did not agree on everything, but their disagreements remained minor. Popper believed that piecemeal engineering was possible and that there was a methodological unity for all sciences. He also felt Hayek's attacks on "scientism" and rationalism in the social sciences showed a deficient understanding of the nature of scientific inquiry. Nonetheless, Popper looked up to Hayek, three years Popper's senior. Moreover, Hayek's political project was nearer completion, so their repartee mostly contributed to reworking Popper's, not Hayek's, manuscript. Finally, Popper needed Hayek's assistance more: he struggled to find a publisher in the United Kingdom. Hayek and the Viennese émigré art historian Ernst Gombrich acted on Popper's behalf. Hayek played an instrumental role in Routledge's acceptance of *The Open Society* in 1944. Popper felt indebted to Hayek, saying that Hayek had "saved his life" by finding an outlet for the work that jump-started Popper's later career.

Even with the productive stimulation provided by Popper, *Road to Serfdom* languished without a publisher for almost a year. Machlup had been working as Hayek's de facto literary agent in the United States since 1942 with little profit. Walter Lippmann, whom Hayek also approached, had no luck with his publisher and displayed little enthusiasm for the project. The intercession of Aaron Director, Frank Knight, and Jacob Marschak at the University of Chicago proved decisive. Director proposed that their university press publish the book. Knight deemed the book "an able piece of work, but limited in scope and somewhat one-sided in treatment." He judged it "hardly a 'popular' book" yet worthy of publication. Jacob Marschak believed it would start "a more scholarly kind of debate." Chicago accepted it after receiving these reports. *Road* appeared in March 1944. Even though Chicago (and Marschak) expected some response, no one could have expected the éclat that *Road* engendered. Within a year of its appearance, Hayek was a celebrity and *Road* a sensation.[37]

What happened? As Marschak and Popper had recognized, Hayek wrote with verve and passion. The book's dedication—"To the socialists of all parties"—signaled his polemical intent. He acknowledged that the book was political and would alienate many of his socialist friends. He also understood that *Road* might undermine his future scholarly endeavors. Nevertheless, he felt duty bound to complete his task, because he felt that economic policy was increasingly dictated by "amateurs and cranks, by people who have an ax to grind or a pet panacea to sell." Drawing on his acquaintance with socialism in Germany and central Europe, Hayek believed he discerned a "very similar evolution of ideas." Hayek was not suggesting that either the United Kingdom or the United States was on the road to Nazism; rather, they were headed to the failures of Weimar and the destruction of liberal democracy. If British and American socialists proposed the same solutions as their German brethren, they would open the door to future fascisms. Hayek offered a narrative for the rise of Nazism that identified socialism as its producer and liberalism as the bulwark against totalitarianism: "Few are ready to recognize that the rise of fascism and naziism was not a reaction against socialist trends of the preceding period but a necessary outcome of those tendencies." In fact, World War II revealed that "the National Socialist 'Right' and the 'Left' in Germany is the kind of conflict that will always arise between rival socialist factions." With these lines, Hayek announced his assault on socialism and collectivism and his defense of liberal, capitalist society.[38]

Hayek waged his war in the theater of ideas, since he discerned a worldwide retreat from nineteenth-century, individualist values. For at least twenty-five years, Europeans "progressively abandoned that freedom in economic affairs without which personal and political freedom has never existed in the past." Hayek advocated a return to liberalism grounded in the defense of private property and "laissez-faire" economics, one that relegated civil liberties and political rights to secondary status. He hailed Alexis de Tocqueville and Lord Acton, Adam Smith and David Hume as his inspirations. In telling the story of Europe's recent past, he painted a Whiggish picture: the history of Western civilization was one of overcoming hierarchic systems and of "freeing the individual from the ties which had bound him." Through the "spontaneous and uncontrolled efforts of individuals," a complex economic order emerged that promised prosperity for the many. Economic freedom unchained intellectual capabilities via scientific progress and lifted the standard of living for all. The retreat into socialism jeopardized "Western civilization" by stifling spontaneous impulses through coercive government action. These illiberal ideas derived from German thinkers and their rationalistic, collectivist impulses: "Whether it was Hegel or Marx, List or Schmoller, Sombart or Mannheim, whether it was socialism in its more radical form or merely 'reorganization' or 'planning' of a less radical kind, German ideas were everywhere." In rejecting "liberalism and democracy, capitalism and individualism, free trade and any form of internationalism or love of peace," German thinkers, including Carl Menger's bête noire, Schmoller, embarked on a special path of development that imperiled true individualism and freedom.[39]

Much of *Road* is dedicated to refuting the assumptions of socialist thinkers and to demonstrating that the socialists' "Road to Freedom was in fact the High Road to Servitude." The planned economy erected by socialists did not consist of "rational permanent frameworks . . . according to . . . individual plans" but the central direction of all economic activities according to a single plan. For Hayek, "frameworks" were liberal forms of planning established through the rule of law. On the contrary, he defined socialists as "total planners," incapable of designing rules-based models. He argued that total plans necessarily led to totalitarian outcomes. For him, like Mises and Schumpeter, it was impossible that a socialist system could produce equal or better results than a capitalist system. The socialists would inevitably produce oppression and misery, as the central planners took greater control of the economy in the pursuit of "freedom" or "equality."[40]

Although the book is often read as an antistatist or even libertarian treatise, Hayek actually distanced himself from Mises on the role of the state. After all, Hayek hoped to win converts from the socialist camp. He reiterated that he was not advocating for laissez-faire or libertarianism: "It is important not to confuse opposition against this kind of planning with a dogmatic laissez faire attitude." He conceded the need for a "carefully thought-out legal framework" and for protections against imperfect competition (even though free competition was better than regulation). He permitted restrictions on production if they applied equally to all, opening the door for environmental and health regulations, safety and labor standards, and even welfare provisions. Sounding a lot like Popper, he stressed that a competitive market economy was compatible with a democratic state and a robust welfare apparatus: "Nor is the preservation of competition incompatible with an extensive system of social services." In seeking accommodation with progressives and social democrats, Hayek conceded that social welfare and private calculation were sometimes at odds, and competition may not always provide the best solution to social problems. He also seemed to acknowledge that Keynes's focus on macroeconomic policy and unemployment in defense of capitalism was warranted: "There is, finally, the supremely important problem of combating general fluctuations of economic activity and recurrent waves of large-scale unemployment which accompany them. This is, of course, one of the gravest and most pressing problems of our time." In almost all instances, competition and individual initiative guaranteed the fullest development of society, however. As he put it, "planning and competition can be combined only by planning for competition but not by planning against competition."[41]

With the book's broad, interdisciplinary scope and polemical tone, *Road* marked a turning point in Hayek's career. It wedded some of his earlier economic concerns with his burgeoning interests in social philosophy and political advocacy. He showed how Austrian ideas about subjectivism, individualism, planning, and knowledge could serve as the basis of a critique of socialism and a defense of capitalism. He conceived a theory of totalitarianism that linked Nazism and Communism into a single threat to Western values, an enormously influential view during the Cold War. He also articulated a chilling vision of the totalitarian state, ranging from economic domination to ideological indoctrination to annihilation of truth and morality. That said, the book was a departure from his earlier Austrianism too. If the historical examples came from his central European experiences, his intellectual arguments came from British and French traditions. In his first extended articulation of the rule of law and of legal frameworks, he resorted to the works of Lord Acton, Adam Smith, John Locke, and Alexis de Tocqueville. Most importantly, however, the admonitory tone of *Road* set it apart. Hayek sounded a war cry for those who felt that Western civilization was succumbing. His stridency inspired readers, especially younger ones: "The young are right if they have little confidence in the ideas which rule most of their elders. . . . If in the first attempt to create a world of free men we have failed, we must try again. The guiding principle that a policy of freedom for the individual is the only truly progressive policy remains as true today as it was in the nineteenth century." Hayek identified the group most open to his seductive message of individualism, freedom, and capitalism: young men of European origin, who viewed themselves as civilization's defenders.[42]

Road's overheated rhetoric was destined to inspire debate. After its publication, the book initially elicited responses only from economists and social scientists: Frank Knight and Jacob Marschak reviewed the work; Alvin Hansen critiqued it in the *New Republic*; Evan Durbin attacked it in the *Economic Journal*; John Maynard Keynes wrote letters to Hayek. Two scholars, Barbara Wootton and Herman Finer, offered book-length critical responses—*Freedom under Planning* and *Road to Reaction*, respectively. Reviews were mixed. The oversimplification of German history bothered Knight. An inattention to contemporary economic theory and the mischaracterization of socialism irked Durbin. The lack of clear demarcating lines between acceptable and unacceptable planning rankled Hansen and Keynes, as did the absence of positive reforms. Finer's response was the most incendiary. He accused Hayek of antidemocratic, authoritarian views because of Hayek's defenses of monopolies, wealth, and privilege.[43]

While Hayek responded to these criticisms in subsequent editions, the academic response paled in comparison to the popular one. *Road* became a sensation in the United States in early 1945. Henry Hazlitt, a prominent business journalist, offered a glowing, front-page review in the *New York Times Book Review*. Hazlitt, who had reviewed other Austrian works favorably, had a long-standing relationship with Hayek, having introduced the latter to businessmen like Leonard Read, the head of the Western Division of the United States Chamber of Commerce and a founder of the libertarian Foundation for Economic Education (FEE). The condensed version of *Road* that appeared in *Reader's Digest* exposed Hayek to millions of other potential readers. Max Eastman, one of the United States' most famous lapsed socialists and a dogged anti-Communist, edited the abridgment. On the heels of this massive exposure, Hayek transformed his academic lecture series into a grandstanding book tour, professionally managed by a promotional agency. He had interviews with national magazines and New York and Chicago newspapers. Despite the acclaim, Hayek was disappointed that approval came almost exclusively from businesspeople, while his intended audience—"socialists of all parties"—spurned the work: "I was at first a bit puzzled and even alarmed when I found that a book written in no party spirit and not meant to support any popular philosophy should have been so exclusively welcomed by one party and so thoroughly excoriated by the other." Characteristic of his central European background, Hayek did not see *Road* as "political," in the sense that it endorsed a particular party program. The same was true of the "pro-business" accusations against him—he did not feel he was defending particular business interests. That the book was touted by anti–New Deal, Republican businesspeople chagrined him, but it also revealed a degree of either naïveté or disingenuousness. *Road*'s tone and arguments should not have left any doubts about the potential reading audience. The book espoused viewpoints popular with individuals of a particular ideological persuasion. It did not offer much to actual socialists or to people skeptical of contemporary capitalism.[44]

The reservations Hayek harbored "at first" dissipated as businesspeople sought him out and agreed to finance his work. In Detroit, he met Harold Luhnow, who became one of Hayek's primary benefactors. Luhnow, a Kansas City businessman, worked for William Volker & Company, managing its philanthropic trust, the Volker Fund. The foundation was devoted to the dissemination of free-market ideas. Luhnow saw Hayek as the ideal scholar to further his own ideological machinations, and he offered Hayek research support for a "market study" of the United States—a *Road to Serfdom* for America. He hoped Hayek would bring together like-minded scholars to mount a popular defense of free enterprise. Luhnow offered to establish a center at a US university built around Hayek or to pay his salary at a US institution. In 1946, Luhnow orchestrated Hayek's introduction to Jasper Crane, a former vice president of Du Pont, an active participant in anti–New Deal, pro-business organizations, and a trustee of the FEE. Crane and Hayek discussed the possibility of an international society devoted to free-market ideas. The positive conservative reaction to *Road* therefore made Hayek's next act a possibility: it turned him into a public figure in the Atlantic world, especially the United States, and introduced him to the people who could further his ambitions. The networks they financed laid the groundwork for the conservative resurgence of the latter half of the twentieth century.[45]

"In the Hands of an Evil Collective": Morgenstern's Alternate Path to Influence

Road to Serfdom opened up opportunities for Friedrich Hayek and increased the exposure of the Austrian School more generally, but not everyone was pleased with the added notoriety. Oskar Morgenstern, another reader of the early manuscript, damned it with faint praise: "There is nothing profound in it. Naturally I don't like planning either, but the intellectual situation is much more complicated." When the Friedrich Hayek celebrity tour breezed through Princeton in April 1945, the jealous and competitive Morgenstern had even more complaints: "Hayek was here ten days ago. I threw a party. He is seemingly unchanged; unfortunately, in the hands of an evil collective. In Col. [colloquium] I heard him after a dinner. I simply cannot make common cause with him anymore. Neither with him nor his opponents; none of it is Science." His disappointment stemmed from Hayek's abandonment of economics for seemingly partisan politics and the bad name that *Road* gave to the Austrian tradition. Like the other Austrians, Morgenstern suffered through a serious crisis of faith, finding himself at a crossroads during the war years, which forced him to reconsider his prospects. He selected an alternate path to recognition: first, by elaborating his economic work with new mathematical techniques; second, by seeking influence not in popular forums or ideological conclaves but in the world of public policy. Morgenstern thereby created an alternate road forward for the Austrian School, one that he and (to a lesser extent) Machlup and Haberler would follow.[46]

As chapter 4 showed, Morgenstern's path began to diverge from his Austrian peers in the early 1930s. Morgenstern pivoted away from his earliest work on time and economic methodology under the influence of Karl Menger and through collaboration with Abraham Wald. He became convinced that advanced mathematics provided the way forward for economics. Upon arrival at Princeton, he struck up a fast friendship with the Hungarian émigré mathematician John von Neumann, who had been at the Institute for Advanced Studies since fleeing Germany in 1932. This friendship became the most meaningful of Morgenstern's life. Its culmination was the 1944 book *The Theory of Games and Economic Behavior*, the foundational work of game theory. Morgenstern believed that the work continued the revolution that the marginalists had initiated.

Von Neumann's mathematical genius bewitched Morgenstern, drawing the Viennese into the former's intellectual world. In 1937, von Neumann began to lecture and write on the analysis of games. Examining two-person games like dice and poker, von Neumann used the "modernist" mathematical tools of his mentor, David Hilbert, and the Göttingen School—axiomatization, mathematical logic, set and group theory—to examine the kinds of strategies and behaviors available to players to achieve optimal results. With conditions deteriorating for his family and friends in Hungary and the threat of European war looming ever larger, von Neumann began to apply his game theoretical concepts to questions of more immediate significance, like economics, diplomacy, and warfare. Morgenstern's expertise in economics and interest in formal mathematics dovetailed with von Neumann's strengths. Shortly after meeting in 1940, they set to work on "a treatise . . . about games, minimax, bilateral monopoly, and duopoly. What fun." If von Neumann delighted in the formalization of game theory, Morgenstern reveled in the possibilities that the theory opened for marginal utility theory: "the treatise will surely be of far reaching significance, especially because it touches upon the foundation of the subjective theory of value." By laying out the actions available to an individual in a given scenario, game theory could analyze player choices as strategies and thereby assess the values of subjective decisions. In other words, game theory offered a way to evaluate subjective choices.[47]

Theory of Games derived its novelty and power from von Neumann's mathematical prowess, yet its broader success owed to Morgenstern's successful translation of arcane concepts into comprehensible prose. Morgenstern was the primary author of only one section, the introduction. The rest of the book is a mathematician's dream—and a layperson's nightmare. Reading the table of contents alone can induce headaches. Topics include the set-theoretical description of a game, linearity and convexity, zero-sum *n*-person games, a family of solutions for a neighborhood of the center, composition and decomposition of games, and the characteristic function. As a further example, take one of von Neumann's more straightforward explanations from early in the book, the elements of a game:

> 6.2.1. Let us now consider a game Γ of *n* players who, for the sake of brevity, will be denoted by 1, . . ., n. The conventional picture provides that this game is a sequence of moves, and we assume that both the number and the arrangement of these moves is given *ab initio*. . . . For the present let us denote the (fixed) number of moves in Γ by *v* this is an integer v = 1, 2, . . . The moves themselves we denote by M_1, . . ., Mv, and we assume that this is the chronological order in which they are prescribed to take place.
>
> Every move M_k, k = 1, . . ., v, actually consists of a number of alternatives, among which the choice—which constitutes the move M_k—takes place. Denote the number of these alternatives by α_k and the alternatives themselves by α_k (1), . . ., α_k (α_k).[48]

Chess has never sounded so fun! Virtually no economists at the time were familiar with set notation or group theory, rendering this passage incomprehensible even to its intended audience. Morgenstern had a tall order to explicate these ideas. His explanation became a standard articulation not only of game theory but of mathematical economics in general.[49]

Morgenstern proposed that the "theory of 'games of strategy'" could provide a new way of tackling fundamental questions in economics. True to his Austrian roots, he situated the economic behavior of individuals and the maximization of utility at the core of economic inquiry. He suggested that economic theory remained underdeveloped and required greater formalization to rise to the level of the physical sciences. *Theory of Games*, Morgenstern argued, offered the beginning of a partial theory in economics, not a "universal system." Only by starting small and building out into larger areas could economics progress.[50]

To make the argument for game theory, Morgenstern challenged a variety of methodological positions—from the antitheoretical stances of the German historicists to the antimathematical and antiquantification rejoinders from the Austrians. He made short work of the historicists, ceding to them the empirical work that would improve economists' abilities to measure phenomena and theorize economic behavior. He devoted most of his attentions to those who doubted the possibility of measuring utility, including his compatriots. He agreed with his fellow Viennese that the tools in use had not succeeded. Instead of deploying differential calculus and a large system of equations, as Walras, Pareto and the Lausanne School had done, Morgenstern indicated that economic theory had to retreat to "a limited field": "the behavior of the individual and . . . the simplest forms of exchange." He believed that this starting point squared with the views of the Austrians. Formalizing individual behavior would unlock the understanding of individual preferences and choices. Like Menger and Böhm, he returned to the examples of the isolated individual (Robinson Crusoe) and the idea of barter exchange to ground his economic theory. It was at this fundamental level that von Neumann's game theoretical model could provide an opening for quantification.[51]

Previous attempts to comprehend individual behavior focused primarily on an individual's subjective assessments of value and utility to explain human action. In the Crusoe example, the individual controls all the variables and decisions. As the number of participants in the market increases, earlier models had aggregated the individuals' attempts to maximize satisfaction. For Morgenstern and von Neumann, this was flawed: "Each participant attempts to maximize a function (his above-mentioned "result") of which he does not control all variables. This is certainly no maximum problem, but a peculiar and disconcerting mixture of several conflicting maximum problems. Every participant is guided by another principle and neither determines all variables which affect his interest." This discussion bore similarities to the way that Austrians like Hans Mayer, Leo Schönfeld, and Paul Rosenstein-Rodan spoke about complementarity of values in the 1920s and 1930s. Individuals are not necessarily in the position to maximize their utility in a straightforward way, since they are constrained by the actions of others. Exchange within society is not a "maximum problem" but a "minimax" one, in which the expectations and calculations of participants may coincide, but they may also conflict. Economic actors could act individually or form alliances with others. Individuals therefore have to devise plans, "strategies," to account for the full range of potential actions by their fellow participants and adjust their actions to maximize their return. To make such complex calculations—which grow more complex the more actors and choices involved—a theorist needed a new method. If this description sounds like a game, Morgenstern argued, you're right. Game theory could provide insight into how to measure utility and how to understand exchange. Measurement would not consist of the calculation of marginal units using infinitesimal calculus but computation of the expected, maximum result in an n-person (generally zero-sum) game. *Theory of Games* was the monograph that would guide the way forward.[52]

Morgenstern had traveled a great distance in his own intellectual development in arriving at game theory. His generally pessimistic attitude toward economics as a science had softened. He possessed a positive program for the first time, and he was less concerned with "limits" than possibilities. He introduced new assumptions into his theoretical apparatus—rationality, perfect knowledge, free competition—that ran counter to his earlier views and those of his mentors. He had broken from the Austrian and Walrasian traditions methodologically, yet he remained a proud marginalist, believing that his work stood in the tradition of the "intellectual eminence" of Böhm and Menger. For him, *Theory of Games* was a "catharsis" that restored his faith in his profession and his heritage. By becoming mathematical, economics could complete its journey to rigorous science.[53]

Despite the fertility of the von Neumann partnership and the power of *Theory of Games*, the social scientific community reacted tepidly to the book. There were few reviews, and they questioned the usefulness of such recondite mathematical approaches. Even if von Neumann's proofs were correct, game theory did not seem capable of offering much in the way of testable predictions or useful applications. Given the complexity of the calculations involved, real-world strategies seemed unattainable. While more mathematically astute economists like Jacob Marschak applauded the introduction of new techniques into the ossifying world of equilibrium economics, most scholars looked askance. With the book's lack of "practical" applications, *Theory of Games* seemed an untimely contribution. Morgenstern, after a presentation to Princeton's economics department, was so dismayed that he declared he was "living outside the world of most economists."[54]

If academe shrugged its shoulders, the US government did not. It immediately grasped the revolutionary power of game theory, which launched von Neumann's and Morgenstern's subsequent careers. For war planners, defense experts, and policy advisers, *Theory of Games* pointed to potential solutions to issues of operations, logistics, military strategy, and diplomacy. Both men received requests from the state, even if von Neumann was the hotter commodity. In the coming years, he worked for the following governmental agencies: the Ballistic Research Laboratory, the National Defense Research Committee, the Navy's Section for Mine Warfare, the Atomic Energy Commission, and, most famously, the Manhattan Project. He was also hired on by the RAND Corporation, the think tank of "defense intellectuals" at the heart of Cold War social scientific thought.[55] Morgenstern too landed at the hub of US policy work. By the late 1940s, he conducted work for RAND, the US Strategic Bombing Survey, and the Office of Naval Research. He produced studies on logistics and operations research for the Navy. He wrote a number of studies for the National Bureau of Economics Research (NBER). He also established an Economic Research Project at Princeton in 1948 (later the Econometric Research Program), which received commissions from the Lawrence Livermore Laboratory and the Sandia Corporation. The latter owned Sandia National Laboratories, which spearheaded research on the nonnuclear components of nuclear arms. In the 1960s, he worked on Operation Plowshare, which sought peaceful uses of for nuclear explosives. He testified to Congress and advised government agencies, becoming a well-regarded defense intellectual.[56]

By the 1960s, Morgenstern tired of government advising and shifted in the direction of management and strategic consulting. He served on the board of the Market Research Corporation of America and founded Mathematica, Incorporated, which advised corporations and government agencies on investment strategies. His list of clients included General Motors, General Dynamics, DuPont, Raytheon, and Scudder Investments. Even as he grew disillusioned with US foreign policy decisions and US party politics, he made a substantial portion of his living by catering to the military-industrial complex and power elite.

Despite these new opportunities, the opinions of Austrians still mattered to Morgenstern. "I was at Harvard 1–4 [June 1944], staying with the Haberlers. It was really great. Every night saw people. . . . The best was

Schumpeter, especially when one could talk about the history of doctrines with him. We amused ourselves brilliantly many times. . . . However, no-body had read *Theory of Games.*"⁵⁷ This diary entry captures the complex-ity of the interactions within the Austrian School nicely. Morgenstern traveled up to Harvard to see his boyhood friend Haberler and his peers in the Harvard Economics Department, especially Schumpeter. He also expected to lead a discussion on *Theory of Games*. The Austrians had sev-eral soirees together, engaging in the refined art of conversation that they had honed in Viennese seminars and coffeehouses. As much as they reveled in economic discussions, they preferred debates about ideas and ideologies, philosophy and culture. Expansive, "brilliant" repartee fueled the Austri-ans' exchanges on those spring nights. In spite of the joy of nocturnal hours well spent with peers and friends, rivalries and resentments still loomed. Schumpeter, doubtless in an ebullient mood, expounded on his successful *Capitalism, Socialism, and Democracy* and took too little notice of *Theory of Games* for Morgenstern's ego to bear. Haberler also failed to show proper respect. Even though the first edition of *Theory of Games* was selling well, this did not matter. Morgenstern left the party and Cambridge disgruntled. As we can see, the Austrians measured themselves against one another, and they maintained a core identity through the trials and tribu-lations of the mid-twentieth century. They supported one another through their trials, and they maintained their interaction rituals as best they could. They pressed each other in new directions, even as they sought new ways to gain influence. They also feuded with one another over status and reputation. In spite of emigration, in spite of new homes and new languages, some things never change.

Theory of Games, like *Road to Serfdom*, represented a reformulation of the Austrian project and pointed a way forward for the Austrian School in emigration. The Austrians pursued distinctive paths to influence, which these two works neatly encapsulate: a Hayekian one involving liberal social philosophy, free-market advocacy, and ideological work; a Morgensternian one dedicated to social scientific research, policy expertise, and behind-the-scenes governmental influence. Both of these tendencies had their origins in their Viennese experience working at the institute and arguing in the Geist-Kreis and Mises seminar. In fact, they trace back further to the days of Menger, Böhm, and Wieser, who served as bureaucrats and policy advisers, as well as antisocialist, liberal polemicists. The older Austrians cultivated elite support, political influence, *and* academic hegemony. As the prospect for the latter waned in emigration and their feelings of marginalization grew, the former gained in significance. Scholarly production mattered, but prominence in the transatlantic discussions surrounding economics, politics, and worldviews rated higher.

While Morgenstern was the most prominent Austrian School member who followed a policy and institutional track to success, he was not alone. Austrians, with their theoretical sophistication, linguistic capabilities, and intellectual broadmindedness, were coveted by government agencies and the burgeoning policy sector. Fritz Machlup joined the Office of Alien Property Custodian, which managed the property and assets of enemy aliens. With a specialization in intellectual property and business enterprises, Machlup dealt with seized German assets. Herbert Furth joined the Federal Reserve Board. Alexander Gerschenkron worked at the Fed in the Research and Statistics department, becoming the bank's foremost scholar on the Soviet economy and the head of its International Section. Karl Pribram worked for the Brookings Institution on labor economics, unemployment policy, and social insurance. These members of the Austrian School found success as "quiet invaders" of US society. Even as they became US citizens and staunch patriots, they remained engaged with their fellow émigrés. Their attempts to rebuild the lost world of Austria and Europe accelerated as the war drew to a close. In these efforts, members of the Austrian School saw another road to success: as institution builders.[58]

6

AUSTRIAN SCHOOLS: POSTWAR ATTEMPTS AT INSTITUTION AND INFLUENCE BUILDING

War in Europe ended on May 8, 1945, with the unconditional surrender of Germany and the Axis Powers. The Allies, led by the United Kingdom, the Soviet Union, and the United States, had repulsed the Nazi and fascist threats at great human cost. Tens of millions of soldiers and civilians had perished, and millions more were homeless, stateless, or displaced. Millions of buildings were in ruins, and damages ran to billions of dollars. The economies and societies of European nations were at a nadir in spite of Hitler's defeat.

The demise of Nazism and its murderous ideology of racism, militarism, and nationalism betokened a restored hope for many people, yet a small group of scholars, journalists, and businesspeople was less sanguine. At the posh Hotel du Parc in the Swiss Alpine resort town of Mont Pèlerin, thirty-nine men assembled in April 1947 to discuss threats to freedom and the prospects for a restoration of liberty. Rather than focus on the defeat of fascism and Nazism or the validation of democracy and capitalism, they stressed unresolved threats to civilization:

> The central values of civilization are in danger. Over large stretches of the Earth's surface the essential conditions of human dignity and freedom have already disappeared. In others they are under constant menace from the development of current tendencies of policy. The position of the individual and the voluntary group are progressively undermined by extensions of arbitrary power. Even

that most precious possession of Western Man, freedom of thought and expression, is threatened by the spread of creeds which, claiming the privilege of tolerance when in the position of a minority, seek only to establish a position of power in which they can suppress and obliterate all views but their own.

The members of the fledgling Mont Pèlerin Society (MPS) claimed that they did not "aspire to conduct propaganda" and represented "no particular party." They asserted a commitment to the rule of law, private property, competitive markets, international economic relations, and liberty. "Totalitarianism" was their enemy, since it was antithetical to "free society." Soviet-style Communism was the primary adversary, yet the MPS criticized all groups deemed "nonvoluntary," like trade unions and socialist organizations, which it deemed coercive and oppressive. For them, World War II had not resolved the Manichean struggle for the soul of Western civilization between individualism and collectivism. It was up to the freedom fighters of the MPS to wage the war of ideas.[1]

The inspiration behind the MPS was Friedrich Hayek. For the better part of a decade, he had hoped to organize liberal intellectuals into a fighting organization. After localized initiatives between 1938 and 1944, he became convinced of the desirability of a closed circle of thinkers committed to the long-term promotion of liberal goals. The spectacular success of *Road to Serfdom* in 1945 steeled him in these convictions. Relying on his growing circle of contacts, he cultivated an ideological network. Hayek first turned to European social scientists, primary among them the Austrians Ludwig von Mises, Fritz Machlup, Gottfried Haberler, and Karl Popper. They were joined by Hayek's English friend (and fellow "Austrian") Lionel Robbins, the German economists Wilhelm Röpke and Alexander Rüstow, the Swiss Albert Hunold and William Rappard, and the Chicago economists Aaron Director, Milton Friedman, Frank Knight, and George Stigler. In the small Swiss town one thousand meters above Lake Geneva, these men extended their earlier untimely meditations, cultivated in small meetings in the 1930s, hoping to find greater resonance in the postwar era.

Although the MPS started small and struggled to remain solvent in its first decade, by the 1950s, it crossed the one-hundred-member mark, and it has not looked back. The MPS has over five hundred members today.

Past members have included a president of the US Federal Reserve, presidents of Italy and the Czech Republic, a chancellor of the German Federal Republic, a prime minister of Sri Lanka, and eight Nobel Prize winners. The MPS remains a significant forum for the dissemination of liberalism and for discussions on the contemporary importance of concepts like the rule of law, defense of property rights, free markets, and globalization. Alongside the Davos World Economic Forum, the MPS is perhaps the best-known and best-articulated elite network connecting economic liberals around the globe.[2]

Despite Hayek's stated preference for an apolitical society of intellectuals and his advocacy of the "open society," the MPS was a closed collective. It intentionally excluded social democrats and progressives, who Hayek believed harbored collectivist beliefs. Consequently moderate liberals like Jacob Viner declined participation; Karl Popper pushed for a broader, politically pluralist society. After the initial meetings, Popper restricted his involvement. Intellectual professions notwithstanding, the MPS also was not just an intellectuals' conclave. Publicists and businesspeople made the gathering possible. Journalists from liberal magazines and newspapers attended and promoted the meeting. These included Hunold, John Davenport of *Fortune*, Henry Hazlitt of *Newsweek*, Felix Morley of the libertarian *Human Events*, and George Revay of *Reader's Digest*. Equally important were the moneymen that financed the endeavor. Floyd "Baldy" Harper and Leonard Read, the founders of the free-market, anti–New Deal Foundation for Economic Education (FEE), attended at the insistence of Harold Luhnow, the head of the Volker Fund, a pro-business philanthropic foundation. Luhnow also requested that the former DuPont executive Jasper Crane be present, since he provided financial support for FEE and other pro-business, anti–New Deal organizations. Crane declined to attend, but Loren Miller, another businessman and a gadfly in early libertarian politics, did make the trip. Crane and Miller worked to get the oilman H. B. Earhart to support the MPS. The Earhart Foundation became a primary sponsor of the MPS and several other Hayek projects. Gone was Hayek's appeal to "socialists of all parties," to whom he had dedicated *Road to Serfdom*. In its place was elite outreach.[3]

Hayek's MPS is significant for its role in the rise of neoliberalism and the emergence of contemporary conservatism and libertarianism. It is also fundamental for understanding the transformation of the Austrian School after emigration. The Austrians faced more than an intellectual crossroads; they lacked institutional backing for their diverse projects. In the postwar era, the Austrians sought to re-create the vitality of their prewar institutions and interpersonal exchanges to address intellectual and ideological needs. They did not set out to create something "Austrian" per se; however, their projects bore the clear stamp of that collective identity. The MPS was the most successful of those constructive endeavors. Yet it was but one of many examples of institution building.

In fact, the Austrians made several attempts in the early postwar years to meld ideas and institutions, often with a dash of ideology. These efforts met with varying degrees of success. The constitutive elements of the earlier tradition—subjectivism or marginal utility theory, advocacy for liberalism and capitalism, elite networking—resurfaced in the school's postwar iterations, yet it was the latter two that found the greatest resonance in the transatlantic world. These neo-Austrian variations did not replicate earlier institutions perfectly. Unmoored from a fixed locality and incapable of reestablishing a school of Viennese stamp, the Austrians struggled to establish intimate, local networks. They turned instead to global networks to establish influence. While the Austrians continued to produce scholarly works, the creation of advocacy groups, centers for social scientific research, and policy advisory councils took on increased importance. In this way, the Austrians, alongside Chicago School contemporaries and German ordoliberals, promoted a resurgence of capitalist internationalism buttressed by self-confident economics, conservative politics, and liberal social theory.[4]

The Austrians were trendsetters in this kind of intellectual entrepreneurship. Their vision of an open society, composed of autonomous individuals interacting across disciplinary lines in collegial settings, jibed with postwar US concerns. They served on the front lines of the cultural Cold War, helping to restore the social sciences in Europe as a bulwark against the threats of Communism and totalitarianism. Like their Austrian School forebearers and US contemporaries, the Austrians brought an elitist sensibility to this activism. They felt obligated to defend the order that had produced the wealth and prosperity from which they had benefited so richly. This elitism informed their defense of so-called universal civilizational values. As the preamble of the MPS evinces, their interventions, despite professed objectivity and scientific neutrality, had ideological impacts that reinforced conservative values.[5]

To understand this institutional and ideological work, we will look at how the Austrians rooted their Viennese traditions on new soil. From resort hotels in the Alps to luxurious Italian lakeside villas, from Manhattan apartments to Hudson River mansions, from the war-ravaged University of Vienna to the University of Chicago, the Austrians built intellectual and ideological empires. First we explore Hayek's endeavors to create a postwar neoliberal order. We then join the Austrians on their first trips back to Austria, as they sought to reestablish Austrian and European social science. The limitations of these efforts showed the unlikelihood of restoring an Old World "Austrian School." Hayek's time at the University of Chicago demonstrated possibilities for collaboration with conservatives, but it also pointed to the difficulties of re-creating Viennese culture in the United States. Meanwhile in New York City, Mises faced similar challenges. He had to wait nearly a decade to establish a stable circle. When he did, the Mises-Kreis little resembled its predecessor, producing a different, more dogmatic "Austrian economics." Haberler and Machlup took on leadership roles in incipient debates on globalization and trade liberalization by spearheading new policy initiatives. Haberler's recasting of international trade signaled the beginning of a new "liberal international economic order." Machlup starred in "reforming the world monetary system," propelling the international monetary debates that overturned the Bretton Woods order. In the first decades after World War II, the Austrians shifted their attention to developing new thought collectives and epistemic communities, modifying and adapting earlier Austrian School traditions along the way.[6]

The Creation of the MPS

The MPS was the most enduring postwar Austrian institution, drawing much of its appeal from the earlier ideas, interaction rituals, and ideological views of the school. In it, the Austrians formalized the vigorous defense of liberalism and capitalism initiated in prewar forums like the Colloque Walter Lippmann. Even before the first MPS meeting, the future participants returned to these earlier efforts, recognizing the need for a sounder basis for their worldview. To their dismay, the first forays foundered. Röpke and Hunold discussed forming a new journal, *Occident*, to revitalize humanistic discourse in Europe. Röpke attracted the support of Hayek and the Italian éminence grise social scientist Benedetto Croce, yet Röpke's demand for complete editorial control ran afoul of the project's financial backers. *Occident* never got off the ground.[7]

Röpke intended *Occident* as an ecumenical journal, unifying antifascist scholars under a common banner. This reinforced the German's preference for partnership over conflict in a changed postwar Europe. Hayek preferred greater ideological purity. When he began developing the idea of a neoliberal organization, he avoided the eclecticism of Röpke's vision. The early MPS restricted the range of acceptable views to ones that fell within the liberal spectrum. This proscription ruled out European social democrats, UK Labour supporters, and US New Dealers. Hayek also permitted nonintellectuals to participate in the conference's proceedings, including journalists and the society's financial backers. This gave the MPS a more clearly partisan profile than earlier endeavors had.[8]

With a broader base and a clearer mission than Röpke's project, the first MPS received with a positive response. The founding members agreed on a statement of aims, penned by Robbins. Within a year of establishment, the society's membership expanded from 40 to 115, and its European members arranged a second meeting, again in idyllic Swiss surroundings. Despite concerns about financing, Hayek and the founders remained optimistic. The fund-raising efforts of Hunold and Luhnow ensured continued viability by providing the cash to make all-expenses-paid meetings possible.[9]

In recent years, the MPS has become associated with a neoliberalism that advocates "market fundamentalism" predicated on neoclassical economics, limited government, international trade liberalization, and globalization. In its formative years, it looked less single-minded and dogmatic. Within the society, there were staunch antistatists like Mises. There were also German ordoliberals like Röpke and Rüstow, who saw the state serving a central role in the creation of markets and the maintenance of law, order, and prosperity. The early Chicago School economists constituted a third major tributary. They concentrated on the limits to laissez-faire rather than unleashing the market. Hayek himself stressed reeducation for liberalism. The neoliberal project required a small collective devoted to instilling proper moral values: "The latter [general political ideals] need probably be no more than a common belief in the value of individual freedom, an affirmative attitude towards democracy . . . and, finally, an equal opposition to all forms of totalitarianism." Hayek singled out historians and political thinkers for this work. These thinkers were the true "students of society" who could initiate moral change. Of course, these intrepid individuals were all of European origin, white, and male, which fit the idea of "universal" civilization espoused by most midcentury transatlantic social scientists.[10]

The early MPS attested to this broadly conceived civilizational project. The 1947 meeting consisted of nine panel discussions. Hayek chaired the first panel with Aaron Director and Walter Eucken, and they debated the merits of free enterprise and competitive order. The future Nobel laureates George Stigler and Milton Friedman offered specific talks on monetary reform, taxation, and income distribution, but others tackled broader social concerns. The British-Hungarian scientist Michael Polanyi explored the emerging political tensions of the Cold War, and Röpke speculated on the future of Germany. Frank Knight sought the origins of Western liberalism in Christian thought. Subsequent meetings considered a similarly broad array of subjects, including European integration, academic freedom, comparisons of socialism and capitalism, underdevelopment theory, and colonialism.[11]

Hayek envisaged the MPS as a broad-based association dedicated to reanimating liberalism through scholarly articles, intellectual exchange, and collegial discourse. The programs were cosmopolitan in conception, drawing on the best traditions of central Europe. Even if it was not expressly an "Austrian" project, one would be hard-pressed to miss the MPS's *mittelëuropäisch* and *bürgerlich* stamp. The society met eight times in Europe between 1947 and 1957. The early meetings all occurred in opulent surroundings: Mont Pèlerin (1947); the Swiss town of Seelisberg near Lake Lucerne (1949, 1953); Bloemendaal, the wealthiest region in the Netherlands (1950); the French Rhone town Beauvallon (1951); Venice (1954); Berlin (1956); and St. Moritz (1957). The first US meeting took place in 1958 in Princeton. The selection of resort towns set in the natural splendor of Europe's mountain and lake regions recalled the summer trips of the Habsburg *Bildungsbürgertum*. The seclusion and lavishness recalled the cultural and socioeconomic values that these men associated with culture and civilization. The stress on extracurricular activities—walks, tours, and meals—evoked the spontaneity of Alpine hikes and late-night *Kaffeeklatsch* of Viennese cafés.[12]

The early MPS programs reveal the significance of sociability to the thought collective. One can almost picture the first MPS meetings as scenes out of Thomas Mann's *Magic Mountain*, whose iconic sanatorium was set in Davos, Switzerland. The 1947 meeting scattered its nine panel discussions across ten days. Several hours separated panels at 9:30 a.m., 2:30 p.m., and 8:30 p.m., permitting long repasts and relaxing intermezzi. Like Viennese seminars, there was the expectation that conversation would continue into the night. The conference organizers built in time for excursions in the mountains, trips to chateaux, and visits to surrounding areas. When the MPS visited the United States in 1958, organizers planned trips to corporate headquarters and historical sites. Machlup, tasked with organizing the event, worried that the schedule had become too overcrowded, and he forced Jasper Crane to reduce the number of trips from five to three. One cannot force genteel acculturation.[13]

Unsurprisingly, central Europeans took to the MPS like fish to water. Mises, Machlup, and Popper were members of the first hour; Haberler joined after the first meeting. The Austrians attended all the meetings in the 1940s and 1950s and appeared on every program. Mises, often portrayed as an outcast, played a vital if underappreciated role in the society's success by bridging the gap to anti–New Deal US businesspeople. For these American crusaders, Mises's participation signaled an unwavering commitment to freedom and free enterprise. Two of the MPS's primary backers, Crane and Pierre Goodrich, who founded the Liberty Fund in 1960, scoured the list of invitees for undesirables. They personally collected over $40,000 for travel and operational expenses for the Princeton meeting. Most of the money came from Crane, Goodrich, J. Howard Pew of Sun Oil, Sterling Morton of Morton Salt, Irene Du Pont, and the Volker and Relm Foundations. Crane and Goodrich stressed to Hayek the indispensability of Mises, since he embodied uncompromising dedication to principle: "This is Hayek's society, of course . . . but there is also in this *First American Meeting* a top place for Von Mises. I would not be suggesting this if I did not also think that Von Mises had a great deal to contribute.

It is no argument against Von Mises that he may seem to some people to be more clear and adamant in his theories than some others are." Because of these interventions, Mises received top billing, delivering the opening keynote at the 1958 meeting.[14]

Behind the scenes, it was not just Hayek and Mises who played outsized roles; Fritz Machlup did too. Austrians were so prominent that Machlup was concerned. When Hayek proposed that his friend run for the position of US treasurer of the MPS, Machlup demurred: "People may wonder why it should be necessary to turn to an ex-Viennese, why no native American can be found to work for the American section of this international society. They may wonder why the Council should be so heavily weighted in favor of Austrians. They may frown on a distribution of offices that gives two old pals from Vienna these key positions." Nevertheless, Machlup did not deny his friend's request. The MPS was truly a Vienna circle reborn.[15]

The society did an impressive job of creating Hayek's network of like-minded activists. It drew from the upper echelons of the academy and European governments. Contrary to MPS members' self-professions of marginalization, they emerged as leaders in postwar European politics and in international associations, which were experiencing a conservative up-turn. The election of Luigi Einaudi as president of Italy in 1948 and the appointment of Ludwig Erhard as the minister of finance in West Germany in 1949 signaled the ascendancy of a more conservative European liberal-ism. Both men were MPS members. Walter Eucken, another member, helped design the postwar West German "social market economy." Mean-while the final chapter of Hayek's *Road to Serfdom*—"The Prospects of International Order"—inspired British free-market Tories like Winston Churchill and Maxwell Fyfe as they created international institutions like the Council of Europe and the European Convention on Human Rights. Individuals at the European Economic Commission also turned to Hayek's globalist visions in designing regulations on capital and investment rights.[16]

Hayek celebrated these developments, yet he despaired over the fate of the MPS and liberalism. US members felt disconnected, since most meet-ings took place in Europe, and Hunold, the European secretary, was dismissive of the British and Americans. MPS members disputed in more and more heated terms about the relative importance of economics and politics, liberalism and democracy, and neoliberalism and laissez-faire. A series of nasty exchanges between Anglophone members and Hunold and Röpke erupted in the late 1950s, sparking the Hunold Affair. Hayek, who opposed Hunold's propagandistic style, sided with the Anglophones. The Chicago and Austrian clans rallied to him, whereas Continental Europeans supported Hunold. The Europeans saw the affair as not over tactics but over vision. To them, the Mises-Hayek-Friedman faction seemed too laissez-faire. They elevated economics to a worldview, reducing social and political problems to economic ones. The German cadre preferred to balance philosophical and cultural ideas with economic concerns. Hunold's worries were somewhat justified; the MPS shifted toward more "economistic" concerns in the years to come. At the affair's climax, Hayek resigned the presidency, and Hunold and Röpke left the MPS. The Hayek faction carried the day. Though scarred, Hayek remained an active member for the rest of his life.[17]

The MPS was the institution that did the most to preserve the Austrian School's values and ideological commitments. Highlighting cosmopolitanism and Viennese interaction rituals, the Austrians projected "Austrianness" onto the MPS. "Austria" became a seductive symbolic utopia—and has remained so. Nevertheless, we must be careful not to reduce the school's tradition and legacy to the MPS, or neoliberalism to Austrian economics. The Viennese also sought to reestablish circles, seminars, and institutes in central Europe and to create new ones in their adoptive homes. This was especially true of Hayek and Mises, who struggled to replicate the Geist-Kreis and Privatseminar, respectively, in their US homes of Chicago and New York.

Hayek and Chicago

The connections between Austria and Chicago, established before the war, enjoyed an efflorescence after 1945—and not just because of the MPS. The Austrians had enjoyed positive relations with the Chicagoans since the early 1930s, when the Viennese traveled to the United States as Rockefeller fellows, and Frank Knight and Jacob Viner reciprocated with visits to the Mises seminar in Vienna. Even during the capital debates between Knight and the Austrians, interactions remained good. Members of both schools were used to the rough-and-tumble of intellectual disputation—the Austrians from their seminars and public debates and the Chicagoans from their workshops—and they reveled in such repartee. When Hayek created the MPS, the Chicagoans were natural allies. Hayek's interlude at the University of Chicago from 1950 to 1962 further enhanced the Austrian-Chicago nexus. His departure for Germany, while not a result of a break, indicated a growing distance between their visions of neoliberalism.[18]

Hayek's recruitment to Chicago began before the war's end and owed equally to Hayek's financial backers and the Chicagoans. Harold Luhnow and the Volker Fund played a pivotal role in these incipient plans: Luhnow wanted an American *Road to Serfdom* and was prepared to bankroll its creation. The Volker Fund supported Hayek during a sabbatical year in Chicago in 1946. Henry Simons seemed enthusiastic about developing a project around Hayek with Volker money. He proposed an institute with Aaron Director as head and involving Friedman, Machlup, and Herbert Stein. Among insiders, it was affectionately called "The Hayek Project." This proposal evolved into the Free Market Study (FMS), a three-year pilot program dedicated to the production of a popular work on free markets and economic freedom. Although Simons died in 1946 and Hayek returned to London, the FMS brought Director and Friedman back to Chicago. The Volker Fund paid Director's salary at the Law School for five years until he could go up for tenure. One can justifiably say that Hayek laid the foundations for the Chicago School's postwar success, since Director was the driving force behind Chicago's economics imperialism.[19]

The difficulties Hayek faced in securing permanent employment in the United States were nevertheless discouraging. The Volker Fund tried to find a position for Hayek at the Institute for Advanced Studies in Princeton and the Department of Economics at Chicago in 1948, yet both declined, raising concerns about appointments funded by private donors. Eventually, Chicago's Committee on Social Thought agreed to terms with Hayek in 1949. The Volker Fund, not the university, paid his full salary throughout his US academic career. Hayek's arrival was delayed by his collapsing marriage, however. For years, he had wanted to divorce his first wife, Hella, to marry his childhood sweetheart, Helene. The generous Chicago salary facilitated the separation and covered child support, yet he also needed to find a location that would permit the divorce over Hella's opposition. To this end, Hayek arranged a one-term stay at the University of Arkansas; the state of Arkansas had the laxest divorce laws in the United

States. He kept his Austrian friends apprised via letter—Mises, Haberler, Furth, Morgenstern, Machlup, and Alfred Schütz. As Hayek related, the process was far from smooth. The acrimony of the estrangement turned friends like Lionel Robbins against him. Moreover, his new wife, a Viennese through and through, found adjustment to Chicago's lack of refinement difficult.[20]

The Chicago years proved stimulating and productive. Hayek was academically active and well liked. His seminars became the stuff of legend. As described by Shirley Letwin, "Every Wednesday he conducted a seminar of staggering catholicity. On Wednesdays after dinner, a large assortment of the wise and the callow, coming from all disciplines and all nations, assembled around a massive oval oak table in a mock Gothic chamber to talk about topics proposed by Hayek." Among the luminaries were Knight and Friedman, the physicists Enrico Fermi and Leo Szilard, and the sociologist David Riesman. Letwin enthused that "[Hayek] presided over this remarkable company with a gentle rectitude." The seminar channeled the Austrian tradition, with its ecumenism, philosophical gravitas, and lively interaction rituals.[21]

Hayek's seminars—for example, "The Liberal Tradition," "Justice and Equality," "Social and Political Thought," and "Scientific Method and the Study of Society"—helped him refine earlier arguments and elaborate his own philosophy. In 1952, he completed *Counter-Revolution of Science*, a revised compilation of 1940's essays. In the work, he attacked rationalistic, or "false," models of individualism inspired by French Enlightenment theorists. Articulating his version of methodological individualism, Hayek stressed the importance of subjective valuations in human action and the impossibility of applying the models of the natural sciences in the social realm. He disparaged the orientation of rationalistic social scientists toward the natural sciences as "scientism." Instead he advanced a "constitutive" approach, which offered a nuanced portrayal of the interaction of individual autonomy and social change.[22]

The seminars' themes animated much of Hayek's later work, culminating in *The Constitution of Liberty*, his most sustained defense of liberal society and capitalism. The work represented the apogee of his Chicago experience. Hayek believed *Constitution* would increase his popular reputation and restore his academic status. Dedicating the book "to the unknown civilization that is growing in America," Hayek positioned it as a sequel to *Road to Serfdom*, which he had addressed to "socialists of all parties." In *Constitution*, he fused decades of economic, philosophical, and political work. He stressed the limitations and dispersion of knowledge in society and chastised scientistic experts for their overconfidence in rational planning. He criticized technical economics for its narrow methodological focus and its inability to offer positive solutions for improving institutions to maximize liberty. The disregard of broader social, political, and ethical concerns also galled him. He advocated for a new broader, interdisciplinary program for liberalism's defense.[23]

In the book's three sections, Hayek laid out a definition of freedom, freedom's connection to the law, and the possibility of freedom in the modern welfare state. If the opening two parts were abstract and philosophical, grounded in his economic and epistemological ideas, the third offered a program for liberal society: it "picture[s] an ideal, to show how it can be achieved, and to explain what its realization would mean in practice."[24] Looming over the project was the decline of the civilized world. The "West" was in an existential struggle: "if we are to succeed in the great struggle of ideas, . . . we must first of all know what we believe." For Hayek, this meant understanding freedom, or "the state in which a man is not subject to coercion by the arbitrary will of another or others." A policy of freedom must minimize coercion and maximize the transmission of dispersed knowledge among individuals for positive social effects. It also required adherence to and protection of established institutions and the rule of law. According to Hayek, these institutions spontaneously emerged from voluntary interactions between autonomous individuals historically. Undesigned and unplanned, these bodies took on lives of their own, producing consequences that eluded the foresight of their creators. These entities, combining with the actions of millions of free individuals, constituted the beating heart of a liberal society.[25]

To ensure the rule of law, Hayek insisted, states require constitutions that put limitations on the powers of the government, especially the democratically elected legislature: "It [the rule of law] is a doctrine concerning what the law ought to be, concerning the general attributes that particular laws should possess." It must transcend mere lawmaking or constitution building, since there are different *types* of law, operating at different levels of generality—those passed by legislatures to deal with concrete issues and higher-order ones that ensure legislation does not encroach on certain shared values. General, abstract rules, with long-term applicability to unknown cases, are substantive and prospective rather than retrospective. The rule of law is therefore "a meta-legal doctrine or a political ideal." Judicial review and the separation of powers are the necessary instruments to thwart the threats of unchecked legislators or unlimited democracy. Equality before the law and the just application of the law's precepts undergird liberal society.[26]

In Hayek's defense of liberalism, he took an increasingly wary attitude toward democracy. While limited democracy makes peaceful government transitions possible, protects individual liberties, and raises the level of civic engagement, the tyranny of the majority always looms as a threat to individuals and minorities. He thus made an extended argument for the restriction of democracy in the name of the rule of law, economic freedom, and liberalism: "Those who profess that democracy is all-competent and support all that the majority wants at any given moment are working for its fall. The old liberal is in fact a much better friend of democracy than the dogmatic democratic. . . . It is not 'anti-democratic' to try to persuade the majority that there are limits beyond which its action ceases to be beneficial." Offering a caricature of democracy's supporters, Hayek tendentiously asserted that his more realistic and restrictive attitudes were closer to democracy's spirit. Over the years, Hayek had become more concerned about unlimited democracy's tendencies toward totalitarianism: better a restrictive liberalism, shading into authoritarianism, than unlimited democracy. Hayek's evaluations in *Constitution* echoed the theories of the emerging Virginia school of public choice theory, spearheaded by James Buchanan and Gordon Tullock, which invited Hayek for a semester-long stay at their Thomas Jefferson Center at the University of Virginia in 1961, just after *Constitution* appeared. A shared skepticism about democracy and political freedom informed much of their theoretical work and political advocacy in future years.[27]

Hayek's positive proposals sought to limit coercion to unavoidable and predictable circumstances. In these schemas, we see the anti-interventionist, antistatist strain of earlier Austrian thinking, which emerged from their subjectivism and economic theories. Taxation and compulsory services, such as the armed forces, were permitted, as were certain "non-coercive services" like systems of currency, weights and measures, and public education. Otherwise the private sphere should be left alone. With the exception of rules and regulations that ensured the operation of the market, government interference in the economy must be rejected. Hayek directed his ire at organizations and policies that tried to impose top-down structures on dynamic exchanges. He rejected unions, calling them a grave threat to freedom, an unsanctioned coercive power, and a drain on economic growth. As opposed to *Road*, in *Constitution* he begrudgingly accepted basic provisions of Social Security to prevent coercion of the socially vulnerable, yet he alleged that Social Security had become nothing more than a monopolistic state program for the redistribution of income. He proposed rolling back health, unemployment, and disability insurance to a "uniform minimum" and leaving the rest to free competition. He also sought the elimination of progressive taxation. These "social justice" measures produced an alarming reliance on experts and precipitated special pleading on behalf of interest groups, according to Hayek. These ad hominem attacks relied more on assertion than evidence, leaving these sections of *Constitution* less compelling than earlier ones.[28]

Constitution brought together Hayek's experiences in Chicago with social and political theory, his Austrian and LSE economics, and his ideological work with the MPS. The acknowledgments demonstrate this confluence: "If I had regarded it as my task to acknowledge all indebtedness and to notice all agreement, these notes would have been studded with references to Ludwig von Mises, Frank H. Knight, and Edwin Canaan; of Walter Eucken and Henry C. Simons; of Wilhelm Röpke and Lionel Robbins; of Karl R. Popper, Michael Polanyi, and Betrand de Jouvenel." He singled out the MPS and its "two intellectual leaders," Mises and Knight. He mentioned a number of Viennese friends (Machlup, Mises, Walter Fröhlich, and Gerald Stourzh), Chicago contacts (Knight, Friedman, Viner, David Grene), financial backers (Pierre Goodrich, Floyd Harper, Richard Ware), and foundations (Volker, Guggenheim, Earhart, and Relm). Hayek saw *Constitution* as the culmination of a lifetime's work.[29]

The book was not the success Hayek envisaged, however. The clearest articulation of Hayek's social vision, it was intended as a philosophical meditation, political statement, and ideological polemic. Even if grounded in his science and meant as a serious philosophical work, for many readers its polemics undercut its intellectual intentions. The book received few reviews outside Hayek's neoliberal network. The book was criticized on the left by Sidney Hook as a "road to disaster" and Jacob Viner on the right as too doctrinaire about free-market liberalism. Its lack of impact coincided with the end of his American phase, since he left Chicago in 1962 when the Volker Fund disbanded and the money for his salary dried up. Although *Constitution* would have a significant and controversial afterlife in the 1970s because of its connections to Margaret Thatcher and Augusto Pinochet, the book's initial reception was limited.[30]

One of the biggest blows for Hayek had to be Mises's ambivalent response. Mises lauded the first two parts for "brilliant exposition" on the meaning of liberty and civilization, but he panned the last part. Mises called it "disappointing" because of its misjudgment of the compatibility of the welfare state and liberty. Even though Hayek had become less tolerant of state intervention and the welfare state since *Road*, it was still not enough for Mises. Mises's criticism is hardly surprising, yet it highlighted the separate path to preserving the Austrian tradition that Mises traveled.[31]

Mises's New School

In an oft-repeated anecdote, Milton Friedman recounted Mises's dissatisfaction with the MPS and its "soft" version of liberalism: "I particularly recall a discussion of this issue, in the middle of which Ludwig von Mises stood up, announced to the assembly 'You're all a bunch of socialists,' and stomped out of the room, an assembly that contained not a single person who, by even the lowest standards, could be called a socialist." Mises considered any but the most limited concessions to the state a capitulation, and he could not condone the willingness with which Hayek and the German ordoliberals accommodated the prevailing, interventionist order. Although he continued to take part in the MPS, Mises felt he was liberalism's only defender.[32]

Mises's perceived isolation in the United States exacerbated his anger and despondency. As much as he wanted to return to academe and establish a new circle of followers, he struggled to make scholarly connections or find gainful employment. Despite ample savings and an affordable rent-controlled apartment, his first years in Manhattan were trying. Unlike his younger Austrian colleagues or his contemporary Joseph Schumpeter, Mises did not receive a permanent academic appointment, nor did he garner academic attention for his polemical writing. Eventually he received a series of one-year fellowships from the RF to work for the National Bureau of Economic Research (NBER). He made an initial essay at a renewed *Privatseminar* in 1941, which the émigrés Machlup and Helene Lieser visited. Mises relayed to Hayek the seminar's disappointing achievements: "My seminar is going on. Last week M. and L. took part. I think that their impression was that it is still far below the Stubenring standard." At a nadir, Mises referred to his ongoing research as his "posthumous works."[33]

Mises's fortunes began to turn with the aid of new friends and a few sympathetic pro-business associations. The National Association of Manufacturers (NAM) offered Mises a yearly honorarium to serve as a consultant for its antistatist agenda. These payments more than doubled his income. NAM was founded in 1895 as an advocacy group supporting free trade. By the 1930s, it had become one of the leading organizations opposing Franklin Delano Roosevelt and the New Deal. After World War II, it saw the defense of free enterprise as the central bulwark against Communism. Its vice president, Robert Welch, spun off the radical John Birch Society in 1958 to counter the Communist threat. The two organizations made common cause on many issues. With NAM's support, Mises wrote position papers excoriating the Bretton Woods international monetary system and advocating a return to the gold standard. In the wake of the 1944 publications *Bureaucracy* and *Omnipotent Government*, Mises traveled the country lecturing to local NAM chapters as "the most eminent and uncompromising defender of English liberty and the system of free enterprise which has reached its highest development in the United States." Those two books, which focused on history and politics more than economics, barely made a ripple outside this ideological community, however.[34]

While in California, the emerging epicenter of US libertarianism, Mises encountered Leonard Read, who became one of Mises's patron saints. Read disseminated Mises's works and provided him a regular stipend. Read, Henry Hazlitt, and Lawrence Fertig, a New York University trustee, orchestrated Mises's appointment to a visiting professorship at the NYU

Graduate School of Business Administration in 1945. Like Hayek at Chicago, NYU did not pay Mises's salary; private contributions did. After the appointment, Mises began holding lectures and seminars, first in Manhattan and later in Irvington-on-Hudson, where FEE purchased an opulent estate in one of New York City's wealthiest suburbs. Harold Luhnow and the Volker Fund also provided support for Mises's endeavors from 1947 onward. Thanks to his benefactors, Mises found stability, yet his reputation and profile remained lower than he expected, especially in comparison to his Austrian compatriots.[35]

Mises's unexpected breakthrough came in 1949 with the appearance of *Human Action*, the nine-hundred-page English revision of the stillborn 1940 *Nationalökonomie*. Hazlitt reviewed the book in *Newsweek*, calling it the "most rigorously reasoned statement of the case for capitalism that has yet appeared." John Kenneth Galbraith critiqued it in the *New York Times Book Review*. It went through three reprints in 1949, selling four thousand copies. One of Mises's earliest New York followers, George Koether, distributed one hundred thousand excerpts through the Christian Freedom Foundation (CFF). Percy Greaves, a CFF employee, and his future wife, Bettina, joined Mises's small New York seminar, which restarted in the wake of *Human Action*'s success. The Greaveses would be the key popularizers of Misesian economics in the 1960s and 1970s. *Human Action* also inspired the conservative Sun Oil magnate J. Howard Pew to establish a libertarian journal, the *Freeman*, in 1950. *Human Action* attracted a couple of important libertarian converts to Mises's economics, Murray Rothbard and Ayn Rand. Finally, it increased Mises's profile at NYU and the reputation of his flagging seminar. This drew the most important figure of the subsequent academic revival of Austrian economics into Mises's orbit, Israel Kirzner.[36]

Whereas Mises's fellow Austrians increasingly looked beyond the confines of economics for inspiration and developed social theories incorporating noneconomic considerations, Mises based his approach on a single, a priori principle: the action axiom. For him, all human action is rational, meaning that it is a purposeful consideration of means and ends. We make choices to achieve preferred ends. "Praxeology" was his name for the science of human action. It explained not just economics but all human interaction:

Choosing determines all human decisions. In making his choice
man chooses not only between various material things and
services. All human values are offered for option. All ends and
all means, both material and ideal issues, the sublime and the
base, the noble and the ignoble, are ranged in a single row and
subjected to a decision which picks out one thing and sets aside
another. . . . Out of the political economy of the classical school
emerges the general theory of human action, *praxeology*. The
economic or catallactic problems are embedded in a more general
science, and can no longer be severed from this connection.[37]

We can see a number of traditional Austrian tropes in this description. The
subjectivist theory of value and the ranking of preferences traced back to
Menger. The centrality of the individual for economic analysis recalled the
earlier Viennese. Focus on exchange (catallactics) also highlighted the role
of markets as the site for the interaction of consumers and producers.

Mises's most controversial assertion was his insistence on the a priori
quality of the praxeological axiom: "Its statements and propositions are
not derived from experience. They are, like those of logic and mathematics, a priori. They are not subject to verification or falsification on the
ground of experience and facts." This unremitting stance, which denied
explanatory power to inductive reasoning or empirical observations, left
many scholars cold. There seemed little room for scientific development
if the entire economics edifice derived from a single rule that permitted
no deviation across time and space. Moreover, it did not seem that praxeology was supple enough to address contemporary problems. Since the
1930s, when Mises first discussed these ideas at length, various Austrians—
Karl Menger on logical grounds, Felix Kaufmann and Alfred Schütz on
phenomenological ones, Mises's brother Richard on empiricist terms—had
challenged this train of Mises's thought. Hayek's "Economics and Knowledge" can also be read as a rejoinder. Haberler and Morgenstern elaborated
criticisms in the early 1940s, while Machlup offered evasions, reinterpreta-
tions, and tepid defenses. In spite of this resistance, Mises remained
unmoved.[38]

Mises's elevation of economics to the status of logic had great seductive
power. If all of Mises's economic assertions could be deduced from his

core tenet—"Human action is purposeful behavior"[39]—then decisions that impeded the smooth functioning of human action violated scientific law and human will. Following this insight, *Human Action* outlined Mises's general economic theory. It deduced the factors that impact decision-making, and it articulated marginal utility theory, presenting Austrian ideas about valuation, economic calculation, exchange, and market processes. He recapitulated his business cycle and monetary theories. The most influential parts of *Human Action* were the latter sections devoted to practical policy. He decried taxation, interventionism, socialism, trade unions, and the welfare state. He also demanded an immediate return to the gold standard.[40]

Even if some of Mises's prescriptions enjoyed popularity among economists, his justifications seemed from a different time—charitably, pre–World War I Vienna (when he published his *Theory of Money and Credit*); or, otherwise, 1840s Manchester of Richard Cobden and the Anti-Corn Law League. If unpopular academically, his positions found growing support in business and libertarian circles, since his theory seemed to provide irrefutable proof for their assumptions. These groups felt they had found their bible. As the convert Murray Rothbard gushed, "From you [Mises] I have learned for the first time that economics is a coherent structure, and I am sure that this has been impressed on the other members of the seminar as well."[41]

With a raised profile and financial backing from pro-business organizations, Mises had a second chance to create what he had in Vienna: a Kreis. It was still not the Mises-Kreis 2.0, however. From the outset, it was a dogmatic project, with strong ideological undertones. To sustain Mises's circle, the Earhart Foundation provided travel funds and scholarships for his acolytes, and NAM financed lectures and tours. The Volker Fund paid him for talks and seminars and provided a yearly fellowship for deserving students to attend NYU. Mises himself nominated the candidates. Richard Cornuelle, an officer of NAM and Volker, started attending the seminar in the late 1940s and described it thusly:

> Mises arrived last, always on the stroke of the appointed hour, impeccably dressed. He took a single page of notes in German from a small envelope . . . and spoke without interruption for an

hour and a half, in a kind of accented chant as if he were reciting scripture from memory. Then there were questions, which he usually answered by repeating, almost word for word, the part of his recitation the question suggested. His method seemed entirely appropriate. We sensed we were in the presence of a towering and uncommonly disciplined intelligence, martyred and misunderstood. We knew Mises had paid dearly for his beliefs.[42]

A new breed of students flocked to Mises's NYU seminar and his FEE talks in the 1950s, from which he selected for a *Privatseminar* held in his apartment. As opposed to the earlier seminar—in which Mises was *primus inter pares* in a group that ostensibly cultivated "neither school, nor community, nor sect"—the new circle relied on idol worship and adherence to dogma. Primary among the nascent Misesian "Austrians" were Hans Sennholz and Israel Kirzner. Libertarians affiliated with FEE, especially Rothbard, George Reisman, Ralph Raico, and Leonard Liggio, also participated. Mises himself enjoyed cordial relations with Ayn Rand and her emerging circle. The two groups cross-pollinated in the late 1950s before an acrimonious falling out. While Mises attracted an imposing group of followers, without the richness of the Viennese cultural world, much of the school's earlier diversity was lost.[43]

This is not to say that none of the seminar participants produced original work or that some of them did not achieve new insights in economic thought. Kirzner selected Mises as a mentor at NYU, since the Austrian was the most prestigious economist on staff. He completed his dissertation in 1957, and his first book, *The Economic Point of View* (1960), connected praxeology with ideas of rationality and valuation prevalent in economics. In the 1960s, Kirzner published two monographs, which tried to reconcile Austrian skepticism about the concepts of general equilibrium and perfect competition with mainstream economics. His work hinged on subjectivism, particularly how the actions of individuals in the marketplace shape prices and exchange. Kirzner would spend much of his career elaborating specific Austrian themes and attempting to build bridges back to academic economics from a remote Misesian outpost.[44]

The climax of the new Mises-Kreis arrived in 1956 at a party connected to the publication of a Mises Festschrift. While old friends Machlup and

Hayek contributed, the Sennholzes limited the contributions of his earlier circle. For them, American "Austrians" represented the true inheritors of the Viennese tradition. As Mises's biographer Jörg Guido Hülsmann noted, "The *Festschrift* became a faithful reflection of the change of Mises's intellectual environment. It was to be a celebration of the intellectual case for human liberty and the free market, and of the man who had done so much to develop this case." Mises had managed to reconstitute a social group with the outward trappings of earlier Viennese institutions, yet it lacked most of the characteristics that had made the Böhm or earlier Mises seminars dynamic. This strain of the Austrian School would survive on the margins until the 1970s. Ironically, though Mises's seminar was one of the least impactful of postwar Austrian ventures, it was to have the greatest influence on the "rebirth" of Austrian economics in the 1970s and on contemporary understandings of Austrianism.[45]

Haberler, Hayek, Machlup, and Morgenstern kept their distance from Mises's sect, yet they also tried to revive earlier traditions. If Mises focused on reestablishing his seminar and a narrow set of ideas, the younger Viennese desired a restoration of their diverse heritage in the social sciences. They therefore worked to create new institutions in their *Heimat*.

Exiles' Return: Alpbach, Vienna, and the Institute for Advanced Studies

"Will you go to Alpbach this summer?" Machlup inquired of Hayek in spring 1954, as he prepared for his own European travels. Machlup knew that Hayek spent his summer vacations in the picturesque mountain town of Obergurgl in the Austrian Tyrol, around one hundred miles from Alpbach, "the most beautiful village in Austria," but Machlup's query was more intellectual than personal. "I should very much like to know something about this year's plans of the Austrian college." Since 1947, Hayek and his compatriots made a habit of returning to their homeland to participate in the Alpbach International Summer School of the Austrian College. Hayek and Popper were regulars, while Haberler, Machlup, and Morgenstern participated during the 1950s. The Summer School, renamed the European Forum in 1949, rekindled the spirit of interwar Austrian intellectual life and pointed the way to economic, political, and cultural recovery. It also offered a vision of future European integration. Spearheaded by Austrian resistance fighters, financed by the Austrian state and US philanthropic foundations, and patronized by young European scholars and elites, the forum was an important early postwar cultural outreach program, with the Austrian School at the center of its success.[46]

Like in much of decimated Europe, reconstruction and cultural rebirth were desperately needed in Austria after 1945. Anyone who has seen Carol Reed's 1949 film *The Third Man*, adapted from Graham Greene's novel and starring Orson Welles, is familiar with the grim conditions in the war-ravaged Austrian capital. The prewar population of Vienna had decreased from roughly two million to seven hundred thousand in October 1945. Thousands of buildings lay in rubble; a fifth of the capital was destroyed. Food and fuel remained in short supply for years. People subsisted on fewer than 1,750 calories per day. The city had no coal as late as December 1945. Infant mortality increased fourfold between 1938 and 1945. Few people had hard currency, rationing was strict, and the black market barely sustained the population. Meanwhile politically and administratively the country was divided into four occupied zones, as was Vienna. Travel was severely restricted: prior to 1947, it was nearly impossible to reach the country from outside Europe. Hope was as fleeting as material resources.[47]

To begin the process of reconstruction, a handful of Austrian resistance figures conceived the idea of a "community of free European intellectuals" and a "collection of an intellectual and political elite" that would create a unified Europe freed from the nationalism and chauvinism that had plagued the continent. The brothers Otto and Fritz Molden, the University of Innsbruck professor Simon Moser, and the Tyrolean resistance leader Karl Gruber initiated conversations about a "college meeting" in early 1945. The Moldens, whose father was an editor of the Viennese liberal newspaper *Neue Freie Presse* and whose mother was the author of the Austrian national anthem, were members of the Viennese intellectual elite, as was Moser. All had identified with the Austrofascist government and had been involved with anti-Nazi organizations prior to 1938. After the Anschluss, Otto Molden was arrested, Fritz went underground, and Moser had his teaching position suspended. While Moser and Otto Molden reached accommodations with the Nazis, Fritz Molden and Gruber reached out to the Allies. By war's end, all four committed to the new project, which included a summer seminar, an intellectual club, and a journal.[48]

The early Alpbach Seminar enjoyed modest success. The inaugural meeting consisted of eighty participants, mostly from Austria and Switzerland. Gruber, now governor of Allied-occupied Tyrol, established ties with Western authorities on the basis of his resistance bona fides. He helped find the seminar a home in Alpbach, near the world-famous Kitzbühel ski resort. Most sessions took place *en plein air* or in pubs and inns. In 1946, there were 200 participants; by 1948, there were 350 from across Europe.[49]

The Alpbach founders recognized the importance of transatlantic cooperation and US financial support for their plans. Fritz Molden took advantage of his ties to the US political and business elite. He had married Joan Dulles, daughter of OSS (and future CIA) head Allen Dulles, in 1948. Fritz urged his brother to reach out to John Dulles, Allen's brother, who was chairman of the Board of Trustees at the RF. In application materials, Fritz cited the commitment of the Austrian College to "break[ing] down the barriers of nationalistic resentments" by "study[ing] and discuss[ing] the problems, spiritual and scientific." In a supplemental report, Otto emphasized the commitment of the college's founders to Austrian patriotism, anti-Nazism, resistance to totalitarianism, and the principles of Western freedom. Molden wanted to help Austria "play a full part in Western Civilization as a whole." Speaking in the idiom of the emerging Cold War discourse, the Moldens' entreaties succeeded: starting in 1949, the European Forum received $2,000 yearly from the RF. With the US dollar exchanging for between twenty-one and thirty-seven Austrian schillings in 1948–49, this represented 40,000–70,000 schillings. Total expenditures for the 1947 meeting had been 80,000 schillings, meaning that the RF immediately became the forum's biggest donor, surpassing Austrian federal and provincial outlays. The RF renewed the grant the following year. The funds came out of Marshall Fund grants that the RF received from the US government. The RF expanded its participation in 1950 with a $7,000 grant to establish an Institute for Current European Cultural Research, a group committed to "European unity, especially on the cultural side." The RF provided another $52,000 through 1955 to support these endeavors. In this way, the RF and Alpbach contributed to the "Coca-Colonization" of Austrian culture after the war.[50]

The émigré Austrian School scholars quickly enlisted in the Alpbach cause. The same year as the initial MPS meeting, Hayek attended the forum and, convinced of its merits, began touting it. Over the next twenty years, he developed his work on spontaneous orders, systems theory, and cybernetics in these conferences. He contacted the RF about the forum's successes and its need for financial support. He also gushed to Morgenstern about the quality of the students: "the group of Austrian students, with whom I spent three weeks in Alpbach, were as keen, intelligent and open-minded as one could wish to find anywhere." This initial exposure to postwar Europe and younger Austrians inspired the men to attempt a restoration of Austrian economics. Simultaneously, Hayek recruited Popper for the 1948 meeting. The rest of the Austrian economists soon joined. Haberler led the economics discussions in 1949; Machlup participated before the decade was out. They developed their ideas on international trade and monetary policy in the cozy, *gemütlich* confines of the Austrian Alps.[51] The involvement of prominent Austrian School émigrés attracted other leading intellectuals to the event. Vienna Circle philosophers like Viktor Kraft, Philipp Frank, and Rudolf Carnap returned for Alpbach. Popper recruited political theorists and philosophers, namely, the philosopher of science Paul Feyerabend and the author Arthur Koestler. Hayek and Popper encouraged the art historian Ernst Gombrich to attend. The Nobel laureate physicist Erwin Schrödinger, social scientist Paul Lazarsfeld, and historian Eric Hobsbawm all returned to Austria for these gatherings.[52]

Given the international appeal and pluralist approach of Alpbach, it played a small but significant role in European integration. Some of the earliest discussions about a European Economic Community (EEC) took place in the Austrian mountains. The 1954 meeting included a panel titled "Banking—an Artery of European Life." Nearly 150 theorists explored the future of European financial collaboration. Many of the participants later took part in the 1957 Treaty of Rome negotiations that produced the EEC, including the EEC's first president, Walter Hallstein. These Alpbach intellectuals, featuring Machlup and Haberler, then took part in a 1957 discussion on the coordination of European fiscal and monetary policy, which impacted the thinking on the EEC and its successors, the European Common Market and the European Union. Via Alpbach, Austrian School members connected to the economic and political elites who led European reconstruction and integration.[53]

While Alpbach was important for the economists on its own terms, it proved even more significant as an inspiration for their own institution-building endeavors. After Hayek's first trip to Vienna in 1946, he wrote to the RF, "There is clearly an opportunity to preserve Vienna as an intellectual centre, and the Austrians themselves are trying hard to get the help of those people who during the inter-war period have left Austria. . . . I am naturally most interested in seeing the tradition in Economics preserved." Hayek proposed "to get some of the Austrian economists who are now located in the United States or in England to go to Vienna for a short concentrated course." He mentioned Haberler, Machlup, Morgenstern, Mises, Schumpeter, and Eric Voegelin. This list represented a diverse group of Austrian thinkers and suggested Hayek's catholic interpretation of the Austrian School. By March 1947, Hayek and Morgenstern began to outline a "Seminar in Vienna with Haberler, Schumpeter, [Hayek], etc." Morgenstern sounded out Machlup and Haberler and confirmed their interest. He also began to work on the RF to fund the venture. He secured travel funding for himself, Hayek, Haberler, Machlup, and Voegelin, though the latter two eventually withdrew.[54]

For the émigrés, the four-week Vienna trip was encouraging, yet it also highlighted the unlikelihood of reestablishing something resembling their former school in their homeland. After the sojourn, they redoubled their efforts at Austrian and European intellectual rejuvenation. They furnished the RF with reports on the state of Austrian science and Vienna's future prospects. The reports limned humble yet promising conditions. In Vienna, Morgenstern taught on economic theory, specifically marginal utility theory and game theory; Haberler presented on international trade; and Hayek lectured on monetary theory. The émigrés met with a receptive audience. Their lectures attracted hundreds of people, and their seminars drew fifty to eighty. Students appeared "eager" and "intelligent" yet "inadequately prepared." Morgenstern identified a "considerable interest in economics" that "may perhaps produce very lasting effects." He feared that Austrian economics teaching was "very poor" with ill-trained faculty. The only way to rectify the situation at the University of Vienna was to bring in foreign scholars as visiting professors. Only then could one "resurrect what might still remain an important center of economic studies."[55]

Hayek's observations mirrored Morgenstern's. He expressed disappointment about the absences of Mises and Schumpeter, since they would have broadened the economic offerings. Still, the lectures went well. His pent-up resentment toward Austrian higher education boiled over in these pages, however. He blamed poor conditions on the low quality of the professors and the lack of adequate institutions. He argued that the University of Vienna had "deteriorated," with the social sciences and humanities suffering the greatest setbacks. "Mediocrities" and "second and third raters" abounded. The scholars who had avoided the political purges of the 1930s and 1940s because of callowness and lack of convictions managed to hold onto their positions. They stifled the recovery of the Austrian School, which appeared moribund: "The death of Richard Strigl, the one outstanding teacher in the field of economic theory, has definitely broken the great tradition of the Vienna school." Although Hans Mayer survived the war, Hayek and his peers treated him as persona non grata, beginning a process of erasure that removed Mayer from the tradition.[56]

The situation in Vienna was not beyond hope, according to Hayek. He had encountered young academics whose "natural talent" scintillated. Strategic cultivation of those individuals and selective hiring of eminent senior scholars could produce a sea change. Hayek, along with Morgenstern and Haberler, pressed the RF and the Ford Foundation (FF) to renew their commitment to central European social sciences. They pointed to the Institute for Economic Research (WiFo), the successor organization to their own interwar institute, as a ray of hope. All that was needed was a long-term plan: "a few endowed professorships which would give the holder not only security independent of political developments in Austria but also a material position which would enable them to act as a social centre for the community of scholars . . . [and] the creation of three or four such 'Rockefeller Professorships' for a limited period of 15–20 years . . . would seem . . . the most profitable way." Hayek had been arguing for a large-scale, college-style private institution in various settings since the early 1940s. Now was the time to realize it, and Vienna was the natural site.[57]

The initial Austrian economics seminar did not produce a commitment from the foundations, yet Hayek and Morgenstern saw their efforts bear fruit in the 1950s. The Institute for Advanced Studies (Institut für Höhere Studien; IAS) that emerged was not quite the restoration of the tradition they envisioned, yet it followed their guidance. Between 1955 and 1960, Hayek devised a program for an "Institute for Advanced Human Sciences at Vienna" that he proposed to Henry Ford II, then the FF, and finally the Austrian government. Conceived as a private, autonomous institution like the Institute for Advanced Studies at Princeton, it would concentrate on political and moral thought and the social sciences and humanities. Hayek foresaw a grand undertaking: a center with twenty senior fellows with permanent positions, forty junior fellows (five- to seven-year appointments), and a guaranteed yearly budget of about $1 million ($8.5 million in 2019 dollars). He also sought either an endowment of $25 million ($212.9 million) or a $15 million ($127.3 million) commitment over twenty years. He provided a list of "ex-Austrian" scholars who might be lured back. In economics, he identified Haberler, Machlup, and Morgenstern. In making his case, he marveled at the caliber of scholars that tiny Austria had produced through the years and expressed optimism that the best of the émigré generation could be enticed back. For him, the Austrian tradition was something sui generis: "Although the first aim would be to bring back so far as possible the men who can revive and continue the interrupted tradition, the efforts should not be confined to this. Much as Vienna has always owed to native talent, the fact that it has been the center of a multi-national empire has contributed not a little to its eminence. And there are probably few other intellectual communities in Europe of which a foreigner can become as rapidly a full member."[58] Historically Vienna had been a melting pot of diverse individuals and competing ideas, and it could again. Hayek met with representatives of the FF, the Austrian education minister and secretary of state, the head of the Austrian National Bank, and others to get the project off the ground.[59]

Ultimately, a less expensive proposal from Paul Lazarsfeld won favor. Central to the negotiations was Morgenstern, a favorite of the FF and the ruling conservative party in Austria, the ÖVP. Hayek was left somewhat out in the cold. He served as an inaugural fellow in 1962–63, but he only played a minor role thereafter. The IAS became the site of administrative dysfunction and political infighting, which soured him on it. Hayek also felt betrayed by its members and the Austrian government after an abortive attempt to return to Vienna from Chicago in 1961. When neither the University of Vienna nor the IAS agreed to pay the shipping costs for his six-thousand-volume library, he instead accepted a professorship in Freiburg, Germany, the home of German ordoliberalism.[60]

Morgenstern, not Hayek, became the driving force behind the IAS in the 1960s: he cofounded the institute with Lazarsfeld and became director in 1965. The IAS became one of the leading European centers of social scientific research. A large number of émigrés made their way back to Vienna to teach summer courses and serve as visiting professors. Morgenstern, Hayek, Haberler, and Gerhard Tintner accepted fellowships or professorships. Even with this success, only Tintner permanently returned, suggesting that there was no real going back for the others.[61]

As these early postwar initiatives show, the Austrian economists committed to their homeland and its postwar revitalization with enthusiasm. Their dedication to the Austrian tradition was about more than institutions, however; it was also about ideas and influence. Many of the Austrians' activities built on expectations of elite influence and institutional leadership. This accounts for their disappointment with the IAS, which did not resuscitate these aspects of the prewar school. Fortunately for the émigrés, efforts at global networking proved more propitious than Austrian ones. The Austrians discovered their continued relevance on the international, not Viennese, stage.

Gottfried Haberler, Globalization, and the 1958 GATT Report

Hayek, Mises, and Morgenstern focused their attempts at institution building in Chicago, New York, and Vienna. Haberler and Machlup, while also creating small working groups, turned their attentions to the realm of international economics. As we saw earlier, by the mid-1930s Gottfried Haberler was a leading expert on international trade. Since 1933, he had advocated for the reduction of tariffs, an end to protectionism, and curtailment of government intervention in foreign trade. Using a marginal utility framework and the idea of opportunity costs, he argued that tariffs increased comparative costs of exchange, reducing trade. Nations should therefore stick to what they produced at greatest comparative advantage.

For him, the economy must always be thought of in global, not national, terms. This work led Arthur Loveday to recruit Haberler to Geneva to join the League of Nations Economic Section. His work *Prosperity and Depression* became the model for all subsequent League publications on economic conditions. His approach became known as the "Haberler method." While in Switzerland, he participated in the discussions of the "Geneva School" of neoliberalism, which featured William Rappard, Wilhelm Röpke, and Mises. By the time Haberler applied for jobs in the United States, no less an authority than Joseph Schumpeter called him "the best horse in the Viennese stables." The elder Austrian attracted Haberler to Cambridge, Massachusetts, where he worked for the remainder of his academic career. Haberler fit well at Harvard, where interdisciplinary workshops similar to the Viennese seminars served as the foundation of the social sciences. In 1943, he joined the Board of Governors of the Federal Reserve; he recruited his brother-in-law Herbert Furth there. In time, Haberler was appointed to the board of directors of NBER and acted as president of the International Economic Association and American Economic Association (AEA). He consistently connected his scholarship back to the Austrian tradition, citing his antecedents and soliciting the opinions of his fellow Viennese.[62]

In the postwar world, experts like Haberler were in high demand. In response to the economic hardships produced by the Great Depression and World War II, diplomats and policy makers dedicated themselves to stabilizing the postwar economic order. In 1944 and 1945, officials established several institutions to address these concerns: the United Nations, which would replace the League of Nations; the International Bank for Reconstruction and Development (IBRD; later, the World Bank), which would facilitate the flow of private capital into war-ravaged areas; and the International Monetary Fund (IMF), which would simplify international payments and stabilize national currencies and financial exchanges. In 1947, diplomats gathered in Geneva to hammer out a multilateral agreement to reduce restrictions on trade and lay the groundwork for an International Trade Organization (ITO). While the ITO never came into existence, the framework—the General Agreement on Tariffs and Trade (GATT)—became the basis of future trade treaties. Signed by 23 countries in 1948, 128 nations joined by 1994, when the World Trade Organization (WTO) replaced GATT.[63]

From the outset, tensions beset GATT and its signatories, especially between developed and developing countries. During the early 1950s, the terms of international trade shifted in favor of the producers of finished goods (developed countries) and away from exporters of primary goods and raw materials (developing countries). These conditions called into question earlier models of development and precipitated worldwide discussions about growth and trade. Hans Singer and Raul Prebisch, two prominent development economists, hypothesized that these trends signified a structural, secular decline in the terms of trade and required active intervention from GATT and the United Nations. Garnering support from the countries of the Non-Aligned Movement, the Prebisch-Singer thesis called for industrialization based on import substitution and preferential tariffs on exports from developing countries. The United Nations Conference on Trade and Development (UNCTAD) and the G-77, the caucus of Third World countries, both formed in 1964, adopted these principles. The latter organization launched the New International Economic Order (NIEO) based on these tenets. Meanwhile liberal economists such as Mises and Jacob Viner excoriated Prebisch-Singer, arguing that it hindered international trade and global economic growth. Still, the model reflected the reconstruction and development ideas that undergirded Bretton Woods and the IBRD.[64]

It was in this context that Haberler applied his ideas. He used his organizational abilities and intellectual connections to produce an alternative to Singer-Prebisch. Haberler made a lasting contribution as an economic adviser for GATT and a proponent of the anti-NIEO program, the Liberal International Economic Order (LIEO). The GATT Report of 1958, nicknamed the "Haberler Report," marked the reorientation of liberal internationalism away from developmentalism toward trade liberalization and globalization.

After GATT's postpartum struggles, GATT officials chose to investigate the international terms of trade discussed by Prebisch-Singer, commissioning a report in 1957 with Haberler as the lead economist. Two future Nobel laureates, Jan Tinbergen (Haberler's former colleague at the League of Nations) and James Meade, served under him. In the final report, Haberler argued for the liberalization of trade policies, especially in developed countries. He recommended that developing countries specialize in the production of primary goods, insisting that "the old fashioned argument (which is not false simply because it is old) that a country gains by developing the export of the things which it is relatively best fitted to produce and by importing the things which it is least fitted to produce still contains truth."[65]

The Haberler Report, characterized as one of the opening salvos in the "counter-revolution in development economics," was an unlikely revolutionary tract. Haberler drew on his interwar work and employed the Haberler method to produce a comprehensive report that could appeal to, or repel, most observers, depending on which critical elements were highlighted. It advocated a classical model of international trade consistent with Adam Smith's and Ricardo's thought. However, the report did not fully refute Prebisch-Singer, nor did it endorse popular modernization theory, exemplified by Walt Rostow's *Stages of Economic Growth*. It had bracing words for developed and developing countries alike. Haberler conceded that the prices of primary goods had declined and those of industrial goods had risen since 1955. He therefore took developed countries to task for their tariff regimes. In particular, he called out the newly created EEC for its restrictionist actions. The authors admitted that some level of protection against price fluctuations was justified for developing countries in this climate. In all of this, the Haberler Report resembled the Prebisch-Singer view. Haberler made it clear, however, that he rejected the secular decline thesis. The only answer to current problems was trade liberalization, not development economics. While short-term trends may confirm Prebisch-Singer, Haberler said, there was no empirical basis for its structural argument. In the final analysis, distortions of free trade had a greater impact on the terms of trade than protective tariffs, import substitutions, or forced industrialization did. Developing countries could not force growth through an inefficient rush to industrialization. In other words, industrialized countries should produce industrial goods, and primary producers should produce primary goods—why fight economic law? Ultimately, Haberler reaffirmed liberal principles by arguing that both developed and developing countries had strayed from free trade, even if the former used the language of liberalism for its purposes.[66]

In rejecting the development theories of the South and the modernization theories of the North, Haberler took a first step toward a neoliberal reorientation of international trade. Instead of relying on top-down plan-

ning, state-run industrialization schemes, or international arbitration entities like the ITO, worldwide growth required free markets on a global or
transnational level. Haberler would amplify these arguments in his work
as the first fellow of the conservative think tank the American Enterprise
Institute (AEI). His ideas found resonance with the MPS members Karl
Brandt, Peter Bauer, and Deepak Lal. AEI, the London-based Institute
for Economic Affairs (IEA), and the Heritage Foundation touted these
ideas in the late 1970s and early 1980s, providing a new model for development, neoliberalism's LIEO.[67]

As Haberler developed his insights on international trade, he found an
ally in his old friend Machlup. After receiving one of Machlup's essays, he
gushed about their shared vision of international economics: "I just read
your paper on econ. development and find it excellent. It should be required
reading for all 'developing' economists." In a series of methodological
articles on "economic semantics," Machlup elucidated the meaning of
concepts such as the balance of payments, partial and general equilibrium,
and the dollar shortage. Machlup took economists to task for the laziness
of their conceptual definitions and for their overconfidence in static models and inadequate quantitative tools. Haberler used Machlup's insights
to differentiate his approach to trade—with its Austrian epistemological
grounding.[68] Machlup found inspiration from Haberler's work in turn. In
"The Theory of Foreign Exchange," Machlup argued that opportunity
cost curves should be applied in the theory of foreign exchange as in foreign trade. This insight was not his but Haberler's: "much of the subject
matter present here is based on Professor Haberler's *International Trade*."
Haberler approvingly noted this intellectual convergence, stating that he
and Machlup were "moving in the same direction."[69]

The two men's affinity only increased in the late 1940s and early 1950s.
Machlup published on the international patent system, and he recruited
impressive students to Johns Hopkins, especially Edith Penrose and Randall Hinshaw. Like Haberler, Machlup expressed concerns that governments
would use patent policy to inhibit trade and restrict innovation. What was
needed was greater liberalization—if not at the national level, then internationally. The significance of this ongoing Haberler-Machlup collaboration
climaxed in the 1960s with the Bellagio Group, also known as the "Machlup Group," which revolutionized the international monetary order.[70]

The Machlup Group

Writing to Haberler and the economists Willy Fellner and Robert Triffin in 1982, Machlup reminisced about their decades-long collaboration on elite advisory boards: "The four of us were once called 'the Quartet.' . . . I can assure you I miss the presence of you [at the Group of Thirty, or G-30]."[71] The G-30, a powerful consulting group formed in 1978 to address problems in the global economy, evolved out of a series of conferences on the international monetary system that "the Quartet" had orchestrated in the early 1960s. Over twenty-seven meetings, Machlup and his colleagues reshaped the Bretton Woods landscape, providing the intellectual foundation for the shift from the postwar gold exchange standard to floating exchange rates and financial liberalization. In coordinating elite networks of academics, government officials, and financial leaders, the Machlup Group proved as significant to the neoliberal order as Hayek and the MPS or Haberler and GATT.[72]

By the time Machlup convened the first conference of scholars at the RF-owned Villa Serbelloni on Lake Como in Bellagio, Italy, in 1963, the Bretton Woods monetary system faced mounting problems. Established in the waning days of World War II, the Bretton Woods participants hoped to avoid the problems that plagued interwar European economic stability: uncoordinated exchange rates, balance of payments discrepancies, and punitive national economic policies. The US delegation, led by Harry Dexter White, and the UK delegation, headed by John Maynard Keynes, negotiated a regulated system of fixed exchange rates, pegged to a gold-convertible US dollar. This arrangement was meant to reduce currency speculation and encourage foreign direct investment. The planners designed instruments to prevent currencies from drifting from their pegged value, which were enforced by the IMF and IBRD. Tensions arose between the United Kingdom and the United States during negotiations, however. The British favored a system more oriented toward growth and international liquidity; the Americans preferred price stability. The United States ended up dictating most terms, especially with respect to the IMF.[73]

The Bretton Woods agreement worked reasonably well into the early 1960s, when new concerns surfaced. The United States ran increasing balance of payments deficits, meaning that foreign states and investors held ballooning sums of US debt. If confidence in the US economy or the dollar waned, foreign actors would draw down US gold reserves. This would not only undermine the US economy but also put a brake on international trade, as the United States would probably move to shore up the dollar's value by hiking interest rates, reducing foreign investments, and reducing imports. The IMF did not possess adequate resources to counteract these issues. An economic crisis loomed if leaders could not find a way to address concerns about balance of payments, liquidity, and confidence. In 1962, ten industrialized countries established the Group of Ten (G10) to shore up the IMF and its reserve system. Thereafter, finance ministers, governmental officials, and banking professionals held regular meetings to evaluate conditions.

Academic economists, Machlup foremost among them, trained their attention on these concerns, producing a litany of works on monetary theory. Machlup had worked in this field for decades and was the first economist to link monetary adjustments and liquidity to the idea of confidence. Observing the meetings of the G10, he saw a clear opportunity to shape policy. If academics held a regular conference that just preceded the G10 meeting, their ideas could have a direct impact. In *Plans for Reform of the International Monetary System*, Machlup began to frame policy discussions. He reached out to Haberler, the fellow central European émigré and MPS member William Fellner, and the Yale economist Robert Triffin for assistance. They then approached the RF and FF. Both foundations came through with funding, permitting thirty-two academics to gather four times between December 1963 and June 1964.[74]

Calling the gatherings "an experiment which may have significant results," Machlup dictated the proceedings. He acknowledged that scholars may advocate different policies because of their different assumptions and priorities of values, but he insisted that economists must "identify and formulate these assumptions" if they wished to make substantive contributions to "the present conflict of ideas." His leadership reflected his Austrianism. He started conversation on the level of theory and highlighted logical fallacies, semantic confusion, incomplete information, and the uncertainty of prediction. Only after clearing the ground methodologically could scholars proceed to policy debates. Ultimately, the conferences did not produce a consensus, yet Machlup got the panel to agree on his framing of the issues. His core terms—adjustment, liquidity, and confidence— provided the parameters for future discussions and recommendations.[75]

Machlup realized that if academic economists wanted to gain a hearing from financial institutions and governments, they needed direct access to officials. After the first four conferences, Machlup published *International Monetary Arrangements*, which he shared with the IMF and G10. Machlup caught the attention of the G10's chairman of deputies, Otmar Emminger, with whom he forged a working relationship. This collaboration produced Bellagio 2.0: the Joint Meeting of Officials and Academics. Over the next thirteen years, the Machlup Group met eighteen times. Although officials attended the conferences as private individuals, not as state representatives, the Bellagio meetings reconciled policy directives with the latest academic research. After the final official Bellagio meeting in 1977, its leaders introduced the G-30, which exists to this day. Machlup served on the Group of Thirty as its intellectual lodestar until his retirement.[76]

Economic experts acknowledged the significance of the Bellagio Group at the time, yet they disagreed about its aims and underestimated its lasting effects. In 1965, Machlup's friend Herbert Furth criticized it for its lack of clear prescriptions. Milton Friedman, an early advocate of floating exchange rates, also disapproved of the lack of policy direction. However, the Bellagio Group was the main site of international monetary discussions in the 1960s and 1970s, and its members transformed the terms of debate. They helped bring about the end of the Bretton Woods system by proposing viable alternative monetary regimes, including a floating currency system, which replaced the gold exchange standard after the United States went off gold in 1971. The shift from gold-backed to floating currencies has been called "probably the most significant market reform of the last 25 years," and Machlup spearheaded its inception. The Machlup Group, MPS, AEI, and other free-market institutions turned a fringe idea into a dominant one. Supporters for liberalized capital exchange and floating currencies were a tiny minority in the early 1950s (about 5 percent of economists), but by the late 1960s they were hegemonic (about 90 percent). According to Matthias Schmelzer, no two individuals were more instrumental than Machlup and Haberler. The monetary changes they wrought developed hand in hand with liberalized international trade, globalization, the rise of multinational corporations, and a growing confidence in the power and logic of market thinking. Behind these developments were ideas about value and the economy, commitment to elitist policy intervention, and a knack for institution building, several of the Austrian School's calling cards. The Machlup Group, while hardly a school in the Viennese sense, was a significant legacy of the Austrian tradition as one of the most significant epistemic communities of the mid-twentieth century.[77]

As the myriad examples of institution building show, the Austrian School did not dissolve entirely "in the wilderness." After some setbacks in the late 1930s and early 1940s, the Austrians launched themselves into the social, political, and economic concerns of the midcentury transatlantic world. As they tried to reanimate their tradition, different characteristics came to the fore. None of the seminars, societies, or groupings quite recaptured the heady Viennese mélange of the prewar years, yet the institutions the Austrians made demonstrated the continued relevance of their work. They were active participants in postwar political and economic discussions, as their strident ideological views found resonances among intellectuals, government officials, businesspeople, and policy makers. Austrianism lived on—not as a school of economics, per se, but as a thought style of immense appeal in the Cold War world. Austrian tentacles extended further than we typically acknowledge.

Ironically, the successes of the postwar Austrian project precipitated further splits within the school. We have already seen how Mises, Hayek, and Morgenstern developed in distinctive directions as early as the 1930s. Those strains developed apace at midcentury, but new fissures also emerged. In 1965, Machlup argued against a return to the gold standard in several venues—at Bellagio, before the US Congress, and at the AEA and MPS. Mises was in attendance at the latter discussion, and he was not happy. For him, the abandonment of gold was a betrayal of Austrian principles and an unforgivable offense committed by his most loyal student. The Austrian tradition had stood against inflationary credit expansion and for the stability of gold as a medium of exchange since Menger. The gold standard had become a litmus test for Mises. After the MPS talk, Machlup "tried to talk to Professor Mises, but he abruptly turned around and marched away. The break in friendly relations lasted for several years." This overreaction was profoundly hurtful for Machlup, who solicited his mentor's opinions on a regular basis and was his staunchest defender among the younger Viennese.[78]

The school would continue to undergo reinterpretation as its Austrian-born members thought about its legacy in their declining years. The Machlup-Mises tiff points to an inflection point. It was not enough for Mises that Machlup had studied under him or had organized a grand celebration of his eightieth birthday in 1961. Nor was it relevant that Machlup was having an outsized impact on international finance. Intellectual purity mattered to Mises. The final years of the Austrian economists' lives thus involved repeated attempts at conceptualization and definition, commemoration and canonization. Complicating matters was the emergence of "neo-Austrians" or "non-Austrian Austrians," individuals who felt they carried the school's true mantle. Their "Austria" had nothing to do with coffeehouses, drinking songs, or the Ringstrasse; instead, it centered on received wisdom about marginalism and subjectivism, unfettered capitalism and freedom. How to preserve and understand the true Austrian tradition preoccupied all of these actors; ironically it produced competing legacies and visions of the school instead.

7

AUSTRIANS, "UN-AUSTRIAN AUSTRIANS," AND "NON-AUSTRIAN AUSTRIANS": THE COMPETING LEGACIES OF THE AUSTRIAN SCHOOL

As Ludwig von Mises approached his eightieth birthday in 1961, not one but two separate groups of well-wishers prepared fetes to celebrate the éminence grise of the Austrian School. Fritz Machlup and Oskar Morgenstern, recently reunited at Princeton University, set in motion plans for an intimate gathering of the Vienna Mises-Kreis, at which members could swap anecdotes and sing drinking songs from half a lifetime ago and half a world away. As Machlup explained to Lawrence Fertig, "I am sure you will understand the desire of the 'old guard' to have the old master as much to themselves as one can decently arrange." Machlup did not deny the significance of Mises's new students; he acknowledged their role in Mises's current popularity. Mises's "new friends" had made a 1956 Mises celebration a success, and they could easily organize a "second big celebration in New York" if they wished. Fertig, the advertising executive, libertarian journalist, and NYU trustee who had arranged Mises's appointment as a visiting professor, was preparing a New York tribute, so Machlup meant to create separation between the two festivities.[1]

Over the next several weeks, the discussions between the organizers hit a snag. Fertig pushed for a merger of the soirees, since it made more logistical sense to hold one event that everyone could attend. Fertig wanted to include Mises's "two star students, Machlup and Morgenstern," and he believed a New York gathering would be more appropriate. Machlup felt that Fertig misunderstood the purpose of the Princeton event: it was a celebration not only of Mises but also of a bygone time and place. Machlup wrote, "There is a lack of understanding about the basic sentiments behind the 'family reunion' plan for Professor Mises on September 29. How many 'friends of the family' can one invite before it becomes just a party? The 'family' we had in mind was the group of people who gathered around Mises every other Friday during practically all of the 1920's and the early 1930's." Between Machlup, Morgenstern, Gottfried Haberler, Martha Steffy Browne, Ilse Mintz, the widows of Felix Kaufmann and Alfred Schütz, and several others, a large contingent of former Austrians lived near enough to make the Princeton event an opportunity for celebration and reminiscence. While the new Misesians were valuable as students, Machlup maintained that they were not part of the Austrian family. After some additional back-and-forth, the men reached a compromise. Machlup and Morgenstern's Princeton family reunion included twenty-six attendees with ties to the Vienna circle. Fertig's October date comprised Mises's American disciples and a couple Austrians, including Machlup. To cap the festivities, the *Mont Pèlerin Quarterly* published a tribute to its tireless defender of free markets.[2]

Mises's eightieth-birthday celebrations illuminate the competing legacies of the Austrian School of economics with which the Austrians concerned themselves in their final years. By 1961, there were already several "Austrian" varieties in the United States, and they had starkly different characteristics. For Machlup, it was about more than Mises himself or a dogmatic school of thought; it was a family. For Fertig, it was the Mises tradition. For the Viennese, the "Austrian" descriptor was not just about subjectivism, marginal utility theory, market processes, or liberalism; it was about halcyon fin-de-siècle Austria. For the American "Austrians," it was the theory and ideology that defined it. By the late 1960s, Mises's US followers had produced their share of innovative work, especially Israel Kirzner and Murray Rothbard. A growing cadre of scholars, journalists, conservative and libertarian activists, and business elites esteemed the new Mises School, yet original Austrian School members felt somewhat estranged and perturbed by the identification of their tradition solely with libertarianism and political individualism. The European scholars Emil Kauder and Erich

Streissler further complicated the picture of the school by drawing attention to its founders and the ecumenism of the earlier tradition. Strong centrifugal forces seemed to be pulling the school apart.

Ironically, just as the school's enduring legacy seemed most obscure and least clear-cut, "Austrian economics" was becoming a recognized, if marginal, economic tradition in the United States in the early 1970s. To clear up this confounding picture, we will trace the final decades of the original, Austrian-born members of the school in their last activities and writings. In addition to their intellectual and political work, the different "Austrians" produced a number of memory projects in the 1970s and 1980s. The legacy of the Austrian School loomed large for the Viennese. The Austrian School, which had gone through several discrete stages and iterations, had always defied easy categorization. It was equally true in the 1960s and 1970s. How the Austrians told their own story and what was lost in the telling concerns us here, since the school's meaning and its legacies still bedevil us today.

Conventional narratives of the school's postwar marginalization, neglect, and rebirth leave a little something to be desired. A "revival"—as the post-1974 moment is often characterized—was hardly necessary given the heights the Austrians had scaled. If Hayek and the others had wandered "in the wilderness," as has been claimed, they found myriad oases. Mont Pèlerin, Alpbach, Bellagio, Irvington-on-Hudson, Palo Alto, and Santa Monica offered respite for the beleaguered Viennese when they needed to escape their isolation at Harvard, Johns Hopkins, Princeton, the University of Chicago, and NYU. When they were not presiding over the American Economic Association (AEA), the Econometric Society, the International Economics Association (IEA), or National Bureau of Economic Research (NBER), the US government called on their expertise, candidates from conservative parties in the United States and United Kingdom sought their advice, and the International Monetary Fund (IMF), the General Agreement on Tariffs and Trade (GATT), and the World Bank solicited their opinions on trade and monetary matters. Finally, a growing number of think tanks—the American Enterprise Institute (AEI), the Foundation for Economic Education (FEE), the Hoover Institution, the Institute for Economic Affairs (IEA), and the Institute for Humane Studies (IHS)—sustained their research and promoted their ideas through fellowships, grants, and conferences. Even if the Austrians found themselves outside the mainstream of US economics, one would be hard-pressed to argue that the Austrians and their ideas had failed to penetrate economics or that they were marginal intellectual figures. In other words, the revival myth serves other purposes than explicating the historical development of the Austrian tradition. It seeks to justify a particular interpretation of that history.

After a brief look at 1974, the revival year, we explore the continued evolution of the Austrians and the postwar institutions they created. The émigrés continued to work on themes close to their Austrian training: economic methodology, the role of knowledge in the economy, economic and political liberalism, and international economics. Meanwhile they used their international profiles to engage in numerous public debates. Finally, they produced interviews, articles, tributes, diaries, memoirs, and even a songbook that chronicled their heritage. The very variety of output associated with the Austrian School memory project attests to the expansive understanding of the school that the Viennese hoped to preserve. Untangling these skeins allows us to glimpse the many significant Austrian legacies, even if they do not provide a single, conclusive answer about the true nature of the Austrian School.

1974: Annus Mirabilis

If any year deserves the title "year of Austrian economics," it is 1974. The previous decade had been building to a climax—and this was it. In the late 1960s and early 1970s, Austrian thinkers like Hayek, Machlup, and Haberler enjoyed greater attention in political and economic discussions, whether on topics of inflation, monetary policy, trade liberalization, or political liberalism. The collapse of the Bretton Woods regime represented a major victory for defenders of floating exchange rates and free trade. The shocks of the Vietnam War and the oil crisis of 1973 undermined confidence in Western economies. The demand-side macroeconomic policies associated with Keynesianism seemed to offer no answers to slowing growth, rising inflation, and persistent unemployment. The postwar welfare state seemed to face a crisis. Governments in the United States, the United Kingdom, France, and West Germany struggled to contain growing discontent. Even if the road to serfdom was nowhere in sight in the developed world, for the Austrians, who had long anticipated the failure of interventionist governmental policies, these troubles were seen as validation of their warnings.

In this context, advocates of free markets and open societies redoubled their efforts to contest ideological battles. In 1974, the libertarian IHS sponsored a small conference on Austrian economics to showcase the enduring impacts of the tradition. Founded in 1961 by F. A. "Baldy" Harper, a former Cornell professor and early MPS member, the IHS dedicated itself to "scholarly research and advanced study for the strengthening of a free society." Harper, an early champion of Mises's, was a hero to free-market thinkers and activists like the public choice theorist James Buchanan and the billionaire Charles Koch. The Volker Fund provided seed money for the IHS; by the mid-1970s, Koch served as president and financial patron. While the IHS cast itself as an educational society, it operated with the belief that it was engaged in a life-or-death struggle of ideas: "The two great powers in conflict are really not certain nations and races. . . . The conflict is between adversaries armed with conflicting ideas about the nature of man and his relations with others." As Koch drew up his battle plan, he reached out to Hayek in 1973 to undertake leadership of the institute after Harper's death. Hayek declined, yet Koch followed up with an Austrian economics conference proposal. A group of nearly fifty individuals gathered in South Royalton, Vermont, in June 1974. The program focused on select "Austrian" themes: methodology and praxeology, market processes, capital theory, and business cycle theory. Israel Kirzner, Murray Rothbard, and Ludwig Lachmann were the keynote participants. Unfortunately for the assembled, Hayek withdrew at the last minute. Thus, at the first official "Austrian economics" conference, no one from Austria attended![3]

Even though Koch reached out to Hayek first, the real inspiration for the conference was Mises, who had passed away in 1973. More than an Austrian year, 1974 was about Mises. In addition to the South Royalton conference, a panel at the Southern Economic Association (SEA) conference offered a reappraisal of Mises's legacy, involving Machlup, Kirzner, Rothbard, and others. These two conferences led to the first edited volumes expressly referring to something called "Austrian economics." They were the first synthetic and avowedly "Austrian" works to appear since Wieser's *Social Economics* in 1914. Nearly two hundred economists attended the

SEA panel; one hundred participated in a postconference luncheon. These two events precipitated a series of conferences and meetings throughout the 1970s that helped develop a new network of scholars sympathetic to Austrian ideas. The conservative publisher Sheed and Ward published the proceedings as books, exposing a still-larger audience to these discussions.

From a disciplinary standpoint, these events launched Austrian economics as a heterodox economic approach. And it was fundamentally a Misesian interpretation of Austrianism that came out of these discussions. As Edward Dolan, the editor of the South Royalton volume, defined it, Austrian economics was about praxeology: "The Austrian method, simply put, is to spin out by verbal deductive reasoning the logical implications of a few fundamental axioms. First among the axioms is the fact of purposeful human action." Although most members of the original tradition would have objected to this interpretation, it met with general consensus from the US Misesians and emerging "Austrian economists."[4]

Even though the 1974 confabulations attested to Mises's primacy in a reconceived "Austrian economics," the most important symbolic event for the school's legitimacy was the conferral of the Nobel Memorial Prize in Economic Science on Friedrich Hayek. As a contemporary pamphlet claimed, the Nobel Prize "helped spark the tremendous revival of interest in the Austrian School." The Nobel committee recognized Hayek's landmark contributions to business cycle theory and capital and monetary theory in the 1920s and 1930s. The committee said that his "analysis of the functional efficiency of different economic systems is one of his most significant contributions to economic research." By highlighting "decentralization in the market system," Hayek provided a powerful defense of the importance of dispersed knowledge for efficient economic systems. Hayek's Nobel Prize indicated the end of a period when Hayek "was all but ignored by other economists for 30 years."[5]

According to a recent history of the Nobel Prize, the Hayek selection "may well have been the most significant of all [selections]. Hayek's claim to the prize was not obvious." In fact, the award was a shock to many people in the economics profession, since Hayek's work was rarely cited and he had not worked primarily in economics since 1941. The Nobel rescued his reputation from desuetude. For Hayek, the prize money freed him from a dependence on the welfare state for costly medical treatment and lifted his spirits in a time of despair. Given the surprising conferral, reactions were intense. His fellow recipient, the Swedish theorist Gunnar Myrdal, believed the Hayek award demeaned the prize. It pointed to the partisan tendencies of the key figure on the selection committee, Assar Lindbeck, a staunch opponent of social democracy and an advocate of Hayek's philosophy. Lindbeck's intervention on the Nobel committee ushered in a more ideological phase in the prize's history, during which neoliberal economists, many associated with the MPS, received a large number of the prizes. These included Hayek, Milton Friedman (1976), George Stigler (1982), James Buchanan (1986), Maurice Allais (1988), Ronald Coase (1991), and Gary Becker (1992).[6]

Even if 1974 was a remarkable year, we should not overstate its singularity. Hayek's reputation in economics may have stood at low ebb with professional economists, but his general intellectual reputation was sound. The Nobel press release belied the narrative of neglect and rediscovery: "Hayek's ideas and his analysis of the competence of economic systems were published in a number of works during the forties and fifties and have, without doubt, provided significant impulses to this extensive and growing field of research in comparative economic systems. For him it is not a matter of a simple defence of a liberal system of society as may sometimes appear from the popularized versions of his thinking." The Nobel committee distanced itself from "popularized versions," yet it acknowledged Hayek's insights and impacts.[7]

Meanwhile Hayek remained productive into the 1970s, and his works enjoyed broad circulation. In 1973, the first volume of *Law, Legislation, and Liberty* appeared; in it, he presented his most sustained defense of the rule of law and liberal society and elaborated his distinctions between liberal "spontaneous orders" (*cosmos*) and rationalistic, planned social orders (*taxis*). Meant as a further clarification of the ideas articulated in *Constitution of Liberty*, Hayek enriched his ideas with recent work on systems theory and cybernetics. Even if the book did not achieve the success of *Road to Serfdom*, it, like *Constitution*, precipitated discussion within the growing neoliberal network of intellectual activists. The book enjoyed especial significance within the "Geneva School" of neoliberalism, whose members deployed his concepts at the European Economic Community (EEC) and GATT (not to mention its successor, the World Trade

Organization). The 1974 Nobel Prize was merely the most notable of many examples of recognition for Hayek.[8]

The Austrian "revival" was therefore primarily a tribute to Ludwig von Mises and a rebranding of praxeology into "Austrian economics." Hayek's Nobel was used to burnish the reputation and legitimacy of this reimagined tradition, but his ideas were much less relevant for most US Austrian economists. Some skeptics resisted this newfound attempt to define a distinctive Austrianism. Milton Friedman, showing up unannounced at South Royalton, archly commented on the Austrian revival. He challenged the assemblage with the provocative assertion that "there is no such thing as Austrian economics—only good economics, and bad economics." Despite methodological and intellectual differences, Friedman possessed great respect for Austrian contributions to economic science and political theory, yet he bridled at the idea of a distinct approach defined by geographic boundaries or theoretical dogma.[9]

Although this was not Friedman's point, his statement can also be used to ask why Mises and Hayek represented true Austrian School economics. There were still many Austrian-born members of the school alive who had made distinctive contributions to economics in general and the school in particular. For example, neither Gottfried Haberler nor Oskar Morgenstern attended the early revival events. Machlup participated at the SEA retrospective panel, but he only reflected on Mises's oeuvre. The new, US-based Austrians rarely mentioned anyone besides Mises and Hayek in early articulations of their Austrian economics. Friedman, in his acerbic way, demonstrated the sectarianism and dogmatism of the Austrian revival.

Rewriting the Austrian School: Kauder and Machlup

With the renewed interest in the Austrian School of the late 1960s and 1970s, older presentations of the tradition seemed hopelessly out of date. The first attempts at reinterpretation came from an earlier German convert to Austrianism, Emil Kauder. Kauder was born in Berlin to a Jewish family of Bohemian ancestry in 1901—two years after Hayek, a year after Haberler, and two years before Machlup and Morgenstern. Shortly after the Great War, he matriculated at the University of Berlin, where he studied with Werner Sombart, famous at the time for his massive history of economic thought, *Der moderne Kapitalismus*, and his speculations about the emergence of capitalism. Kauder's turn toward modern economics and marginal utility probably began around 1930. In later years, he reported meeting Mises in 1930, and he probably attended the Stubenring seminar around then. This was not a solitary trip to Vienna either, since he struck up a correspondence with Oskar Morgenstern, beginning in 1932. It was at this time that Kauder began tutoring Ludwig Lachmann, one of the key figures in the Austrian economics revival.[10]

Unlike Kauder's Viennese contemporaries, his emigration tale was neither quick nor seamless. Coming from a "racially Jewish" family and living in Germany, Kauder faced immediate persecution from the National Socialist regime after it gained power in 1933. Kauder did not yet speak about emigration, possibly because his sixty-year-old Jewish mother resided in the Reich. His earliest documented overtures to aid organizations date from 1937. Over the next four years, he made four unsuccessful appeals to the Emergency Committee in Aid of Displaced Foreign Scholars. Unlike his better-known Viennese allies, who all benefited from the patronage network associated with the Rockefeller Foundation to help them find academic positions in Europe and the United States, Kauder had no such connections to facilitate his transition. When he departed Europe in 1938, it was not for an academic position; he worked as a farmhand and a schoolteacher. Unfortunately, his mother, Ernestine, did not make the journey with him; she perished in the Holocaust. Eventually he was hired on the periphery of the US university system: first at the University of Wyoming, then Illinois Wesleyan University and Florida Presbyterian College, and lastly the University of South Florida.[11]

Beginning in the 1950s, Kauder, with the assistance of Mises, Morgenstern, and Rothbard, began writing articles on the history of marginal utility theory and the unsurpassed contributions of the Austrians Menger, Böhm, and Wieser to its formulation. This work culminated in his 1965 *History of Marginal Utility Theory*. Kauder offered an idiosyncratic telling of the marginalist story, tracing it all the way back to Aristotle. He argued, "Several times the history of the marginal utility theory had to be rewritten. The triumvirate Jevons, Menger, Walras knew only Gossen as their forerunner. To-day we recognise that the analysis of subjective elements in economic valuation starts with Aristotle. He begins a trend of thought whose traces abound in the writings of the Middle Ages, the Renaissance and the enlightenment." Thomas Aquinas, Hugo Grotius, Robert Turgot, and Daniel Bernouilli all featured in this controversial history of an idea. Because of the hegemony of British classical economists, this tradition languished for centuries. Kauder perhaps channeled his own feelings of marginalization when he lamented that these scholars "wrote in vain, they were soon forgotten. . . . Instead, the father of our economic science wrote that water has a great utility and a small value. With these words Adam Smith had made waste and rubbish out of the thinking of 2,000 years. The chance to start in 1776 instead of 1870 with a more correct knowledge of value principles had been missed."[12]

If many people disputed Kauder's interpretations of Aristotle or the un-disputed priority he assigned the Austrians in the marginalist tradition as the true heirs of Aristotle, one group did not: self-identifying Austrians. The circle forming around Ludwig von Mises, especially Rothbard, took an interest in his justificatory tale. Kauder had reestablished contact with Mises in 1956; their correspondence intensified in the next decade. Kauder viewed Mises as the true lineal descendant of Aristotle, Menger, Böhm, and Wieser: "Today only von Mises, the most faithful student of the three pio-neers, maintains the ontological character of economic laws. His theory of human action (in his words praxeology) is a 'reflection about the essence of action.' Economic laws provide 'ontological facts.' The ontological structure will be materialized if the rational individual acts in a free market. Also Mises' teachers had a strong predilection for the free market mechanism, at least in theory." Kauder proceeded to excommunicate Austrians who did not fit his understanding of the school. Viennese who did not conform—Rudolf Auspitz, Richard Lieben, and, most crucially, Joseph Schumpeter—were treated as apostates. Gone, too, was the figure who informed much of Kauder's early knowledge of the Austrian movement: Hans Mayer. The Austrian School was also now a school of free markets, an assertion belied by many of the actions and writings of Böhm and Wieser at the turn of the twentieth century. One can see why the vain Mises would have appreciated this reading, as did Rothbard. Rothbard referred Kauder's works to the Volker Fund for financial support, and he used Kauder's interpretation in every subsequent history he wrote. In time, Kauder was invited to partici-pate in the earliest Austrian revival events.[13]

After cataloguing Carl Menger's personal library (which was now located in Tokyo) and conducting interviews with many living members from the Austrian tradition, Kauder published his *History*. His definition of marginal utility followed Mises's, and he cited members of the Mises-Kreis throughout to buttress his arguments—he even quoted from the original seminar songs! It is no wonder that the Austrians loved the book, but outsiders—including Hayek's friend Lionel Robbins—found the book polemical and biased.[14]

The Viennese drew on Kauder when they began producing their own retrospective accounts of the tradition, yet they also had to negotiate where to place themselves *and* the new US converts. In 1968, Hayek wrote an encyclopedia article that followed the general contours of Kauder's history. His picture kept the number of original contributors small and omitted all postemigration work. He limited the total number of members from the first three generations, emphasizing the work of Menger, Böhm, and Mises. He also restricted the school to work done in Austria by Austrians. His cohort represented the end of the tradition, since "most of these men, however, did the greater part of their work outside Austria." This meant that Mises's New York network represented something distinct and new—and hardly Austrian. Hayek tried to sidestep questions about "Austrianness"—whether it was a geographical, sociological, or theoretical distinction. He did not succeed. When the editor asked Hayek to review Rothbard's article on Mises, Hayek spoke out against Rothbard's hagiographic portrait. Confidentially Hayek criticized Rothbard for overemphasizing Mises's centrality to the movement.[15]

European-born scholars directed their attentions to the early years of the school and left open the question of continuity to the post–World War II US variety. Hayek's account terminated in the 1930s and excluded his own generation from consideration. So did Mises's memoirs, which were written around 1940 but appeared in 1978. They cut off with World War II. The "fifth-generation" Austrian Erich Streissler focused on the theoretical work of the pre–World War I school in his 1960s and 1970s articles.[16]

Eventually it fell to Fritz Machlup to write a new account that explained the continuities and divergences between the older and newer Austrian approaches. In drafting his narrative, he exposed the fissures that traversed the school's foundation. He constructed his article around three groups: "Austrians," "un-Austrian Austrians," and "non-Austrian Austrians."

"Austrians" were Austrian born and raised scholars who contributed to the elaboration of a scholarly approach; "un-Austrian Austrians" were Austrian-born scholars who "absorbed so many other influences" that they could not be subsumed under the Austrian rubric; "non-Austrian Austrians" embraced the teachings of select Austrians and advanced a Misesian project. Elaborating Hayek's work, which drew a straight line from Menger to Böhm to Mises, Machlup excluded seminal figures like Rudolf Auspitz, Richard Lieben, Emil Sax, and Joseph Schumpeter. He also included American Misesians. Machlup's friend Herbert Furth rejected this conceptualization: "You know that I consider Hayek the 'Dean' of the Austrian School; nevertheless, he still is only one of many members, and has no authority to excommunicate those who are not fully in agreement with his views. Moreover, the sentences you quote don't contradict my opinion about Auspitz, Lieben, and Schumpeter: sure, they can be included in the school only 'with qualifications' or 'not wholly'—but that is very different from calling them 'un-Austrian'! Incidentally—would you deny that you, too—like every original thinker—has absorbed 'many other influences' besides Menger, Boehm, and Wieser?"[17]

Furth felt Machlup had written several luminaries (and Machlup himself!) out of the tradition. Machlup seemed to cede Austrianism to the dogmatic Americans, with their teleological interpretation. Furth declaimed the "non-Austrian Austrian" libertarians for distorting Austrianism. He insisted that Machlup "indicate that the equation of Austrian economic theory with radical libertarianism is simply wrong." Furth feared that Machlup's definition of the school elevated an ancillary principle—political liberalism of a laissez-faire variety—to a central tenet. Machlup found himself caught between a rock and a hard place, between a school denoted by geography, theory, and style and one defined by dogma. Machlup ultimately qualified his comments, yet his article still emphasized the US Austrian approach.

In addition to Furth, Machlup also shared his Austrian economics article with Israel Kirzner, the most distinguished of Mises's US students, who expressed complementary concerns to Furth's. The American felt some trepidation about a definition of Austrian economics that emphasized libertarianism—and Murray Rothbard—too heavily. Although proud of his intellectual patrimony, Kirzner struggled with the politics that contemporary Austrians derived from their economics:

1) Your [Machlup] reference to "political individualism" . . .
can surely be questioned. While Mises and Hayek indeed
endorse this view, it can hardly be described as part of Austrian
economics. . . . 2) It is quite true that for many in the U.S. the
term "Austrian economics" is synonymous with laissez-faire.
And I suppose it happens to be true the Austrian economists *are*
generally "in favor of" the free market. But it can, I believe,
be maintained (at least I hope so) that Austrian economics by
itself does *not* embody those judgments of value without which,
I believe, a case for non-intervention cannot be built.

Kirzner believed that Austrian economics qua economics should be kept free
of political or ideological ballast. There was nothing about methodological
individualism and subjectivism, marginal utility and opportunity costs, or
market processes and entrepreneurship that implied laissez-faire, "free markets," or libertarian values. These concerns informed his hesitancy about the
inclusion of non-Austrian Austrians. Machlup's early draft had only mentioned
Kirzner. Kirzner felt that Machlup either had to include Rothbard and Lachmann too or drop them all. These alternatives produced a dilemma. Kirzner
doubted whether "Rothbard's work should or will have lasting value within
the Austrian School," yet without him, Machlup's account of Mises's students
would be "seriously incomplete." Rothbard's inclusion, however, could lead
to the accusation that Austrian economics was a political program. Kirzner
had identified the crux of the problem: Austrian economics had become as
much about ideology as economics for many US practitioners.[18]

Machlup's conciliatory nature led him in search of common ground.
After initially excluding Schumpeter, he added him back. He included a
section on non-Austrian Austrians, which highlighted the work of Kirzner,
Rothbard, and Lachmann. Heeding Furth, he also downplayed the political aspirations of the Mises branch. In defining the school, he identified
eight main tenets, yet he downgraded consumer sovereignty (which implied
"complete avoidance of governmental interference with the markets") and
political individualism (that economic freedom is constitutive of political
and moral freedom) to "controversies within the School." These were the
most Misesian of the tenets and also the least consistent with the tradition
as a whole.[19]

Machlup's interlocutor Furth felt vindicated by these concessions; interestingly, so did Kirzner. Kirzner's views on the school paralleled Machlup's preference for value-free science. Since Kirzner had completed his dissertation in 1957 under Mises, he had always worked to reconcile Austrian precepts with mainstream economics. His work hinged on subjectivism, particularly how the actions of individuals in the marketplace shape prices and exchange. As Kirzner argued, "we look to price theory to help us understand how the decisions of individual participants in the market interact to generate the market forces which compel *changes* in prices, in outputs, and in methods of production and the allocation of resources." In the early 1970s, Kirzner introduced the agent of these equilibrations: the entrepreneur. This concept had a rich genealogy within the Austrian tradition, going back to Menger. Unlike earlier analyses that offered sociological characterizations of the entrepreneur (Schumpeter) or functional ones (Menger), Kirzner built an epistemological definition. Kirzner argued in *Competition and Entrepreneurship* that neoclassical economists had underestimated the entrepreneur in their models of perfect competition and information. Channeling Hayek, Kirzner highlighted the role of information, ignorance, and learning in the market process: "Ignorance of the decisions that others are in fact about to make may cause decision-makers to make unfortunate plans. . . . Exposure to decisions of others communicates some of the information these decision-makers originally lacked." An entrepreneur is not a buyer or seller, per se, but an individual attuned to opportunities for profits that "*exist because of the initial ignorance of the original market participants.*" Entrepreneurship drives the market process by correcting initial ignorance through a process that leverages increased information for greater profits.[20]

Machlup and Kirzner enjoyed cordial relations since the 1960s; the elder Viennese enthused about the American's work. Machlup worked on issues of imperfect competition throughout the 1940s and 1950s. His studies with Edith Penrose and others on the impact of patent protections in the 1950s stressed the distortive effects of intellectual property restrictions on the market and economic growth, since they stifled information flows. Most salient for his affinity with Kirzner was his two-decade research on the role of knowledge in the economy, a monumental task that occupied him until his death in 1983. Beginning with *The Production and Distribution of*

Knowledge in the United States (1962) and culminating with an intended eight-volume project—of which he completed three volumes—Machlup explored the emergence of the "knowledge industry" in the United States. He investigated the diffusion of knowledge within the economy, placing him alongside Jacob Mincer, Theodore Schultz, and Gary Becker in 1960s discussions of the idea of human capital. His venture focused on "the 'promotion' of knowledge from the rank of an exogenous independent variable to that of an endogenous variable." This meant that knowledge production and distribution are not external aspects beyond the purview of economic theory; knowledge factors require theorization. While less mathematical than Becker and more speculative than Kirzner, Machlup felt himself to be in conversation with both of them. In the late 1970s, he and Kirzner exchanged articles on information flows. Like Kirzner, he felt himself to be a bridge between the Austrians and "Anglo-Saxons," yet he bridled at the "Austrian" descriptor: "While you may say that this analysis is essentially Austrian in character, I must point out that this is by no means foreign to Anglo-Saxon equilibrium theory." Machlup was less interested in claiming Austrianness than in advancing good economics.[21]

Creating and maintaining clear definitional boundaries within the Austrian tradition was a challenge. While both Kirzner and Machlup stuck primarily to academic work—Kirzner at NYU and Machlup at Princeton and then NYU—they did not entirely eschew policy and political discussions, particularly Machlup. Elite liberalism informed Machlup's work, yet it was hard to categorize on a left-right political spectrum. He was committed to individual liberty, economic and political, and this led him to speak out on issues rather than to get involved in party political affairs. As president of the American Association of University Professors in the 1950s, Machlup defended academic freedom and civil liberties, rejecting loyalty oaths. He supported his Johns Hopkins colleague Owen Lattimore after Joseph McCarthy accused the Asianist scholar of espionage. Machlup and Milton Friedman engaged in a heated private correspondence about Adlai Stevenson and Dwight Eisenhower and the effects of McCarthyism. The two men disagreed on their preferred presidential candidate—Machlup favored Stevenson, while Friedman backed Eisenhower. Machlup feared an escalation of Cold War tensions, military spending, and government intervention under Eisenhower. He also worried about eroding civil liberties. Friedman stressed Eisenhower's greater commitment to pro-business policy and economic freedom. Machlup's monetary work also cannot be seen as free from liberal ideology, since financial liberalization and freer international trade were taken as undisputed goods. Finally, his preferred method of intervention—behind the scenes with political and financial elites—attested to the lessons he had imbibed from his mentors in the Austrian tradition.

In summary, Machlup best embodies the paradoxes of the Austrian School's competing legacies, since he stood at the confluence of its many streams. In spite of the fight over the gold standard, he remained closest with his mentor, Mises, of all the Austrians. He participated in the activities of the American Misesians, attending panels and conferences. He published adulatory articles on Hayek and Mises and conducted interviews with the *Austrian Economics Newsletter*. Machlup nevertheless struggled to delineate the school and to place himself within it. He even called into question whether a school had *ever* existed. In an oral interview from the late 1970s, he spoke about his Viennese compatriots: "We didn't indulge in parochialism or, let's say, local patriotism." Machlup sought recognition for his economics, not his school affiliation or his ideology. Whether he was an Austrian or liberal should have been immaterial; good science has no nationality. Consequently he found it hard to make common cause with the Austrian revival.[22]

Austrian Economics or Austrian Economists? The Case of Morgenstern

When Machlup and Kirzner conducted much of their exchange, they both taught at NYU, which became the hub of the Austrian tradition in the 1970s. The university had a decades-long affiliation with Mises, even if he was only an untenured instructor. In the 1970s, the Koch Foundation provided a large financial outlay to build an Austrian economics program. Starting with Kirzner, the Kochs provided funds for additional hires, fellowships, and publications. Kirzner recruited Lachmann to NYU from South Africa in 1975. Lachmann, after studying with Kauder in Berlin, became one of Hayek's prize pupils at the London School of Economics in the 1930s. His radical rejection of equilibrium theory meant that there was no hope of reconciliation with mainstream neoclassical economics. Market processes evinced a "kaleidic" quality that had no initial conditions and no final resting point. They were directionless and unceasing, making equilibrium unattainable and general equilibrium theory therefore nonsensical. Economics was about making sense out of this ceaseless flow of interactions and exchanges. This often meant using the interpretive, or *verstehende*, social scientific techniques pioneered by Max Weber, Wilhelm Dilthey, and Werner Sombart and the "causal-genetic" approach to economics associated with the pariah Austrian Hans Mayer. These radical positions put Lachmann at odds with Kirzner, and his Hayekian priors displeased Rothbardians, yet Lachmann enhanced the profile of Austrian economics in New York further. Now the two most influential non-Austrian Austrians were housed at the same institution. One of the first postdoctoral fellows they attracted was Mario Rizzo, a University of Chicago–trained economist sympathetic to Hayekian arguments on knowledge and ignorance. He became an assistant professor in 1978. Several others in the economics department also contributed to the Austrian-inflected environment, including Machlup and Oskar Morgenstern. When the two men retired from Princeton in 1970 and 1969, respectively, they took emeritus positions at NYU.[23]

In NYU's promotion of its Austrian economics program, it highlighted these multifarious connections: "Of course an Austrian flavor in the New York University Economics Department is nothing new. In addition to Mises both Morgenstern and Machlup closed out their distinguished careers here. Although his views diverged sharply from those of Mises on many fronts, Morgenstern was nonetheless a product of the Misesian circle in Vienna, and his writings bear an 'Austrian' stamp far more than many realize. And Machlup, though never formally tied to the Austrian program, was always a resource for and inspiration to it." Again, Mises is the central point of reference for Austrian economics. Morgenstern was a mere "product" of the Mises-Kreis, a dubious assertion at best. Neither he nor Machlup had much, if anything, to do with NYU Austrian economics, so their inclusion was ornamental, with the expectation that their names added luster to the program. Like Machlup, Morgenstern's fraught relationship with not only US Austrian economics but the tradition as a whole requires elaboration.[24]

While Morgenstern had been carving out his own Austrian path since emigration, we can nevertheless see his continued commitment to the tradition by casting him alongside his "old friend" Machlup. For such different men, they traveled similar intellectual trajectories. While they moved in the same Vienna circles, eating lunch together daily in the late 1920s and early 1930s, they were never close friends. Machlup was always closer with Mises and Hayek; Morgenstern identified with Haberler and Karl Menger. Machlup and Morgenstern had little to do with each other in emigration, yet their work bore a family resemblance. Machlup worked on questions of perfect competition, the economics of knowledge, international trade and finance, and economic methodology. He also showed a continued skepticism toward US economics, which he attempted to overcome from within the academy. Meanwhile Morgenstern's work in Austrian areas is overshadowed by his game theory work, yet he too produced works on international trade and the methodology of economics. In particular, he criticized economic observation and forecasting in contemporary macroeconomics. He challenged the positivism of midcentury econometricians and statistical economists. His conclusions placed him in conversation with Machlup. In 1959, Morgenstern also published on international financial transactions and business cycles with Machlup's book series. When Machlup accepted a Princeton professorship in 1960, Morgenstern exulted over the "reunion": "It is, indeed, a rare event that two old friends can join up again after such a long interruption." When Machlup moved to NYU, he took the office next to Morgenstern's, making them neighbors for the first time in fifty years, a point Morgenstern noted with wonder.[25]

Morgenstern passed away in 1977 after a protracted struggle with cancer. In the final decade of his life, he frequently reckoned with his place in his Austrian cohort and the school. Profound ambivalence stamped these relationships. His diaries indicate the extent to which he oriented his career around his Austrian experiences. His closest peers had almost always been German-speaking central Europeans, if not Austrians—Haberler, von Neumann, Kurt Gödel, and Karl Menger. His most intense rivalries involved Austrians, particularly Hayek. He criticized Hayek's turn from real science with *Road to Serfdom* in 1944, even calling him a "propaganda economist" in 1948. Nevertheless, Morgenstern felt many of the same reservations about the economics profession as Hayek did. He complained about the lack of attention his work received, seeking validation from the very individuals he disparaged.

Like Machlup, Hayek, and the others, Morgenstern showed a remarkable knack for institutional organization and intellectual entrepreneurship. He received funding for several projects from the Ford and Rockefeller Foundations after the world war. Morgenstern also had a remarkable ease with political and social elites. Morgenstern got on famously with the erstwhile heir to the Habsburg crown, Otto Habsburg; he enjoyed hobnobbing with the Rockefellers, David and Nelson. Morgenstern also had an uncanny eye for talent, hitching his star to brilliant thinkers. *Theory of Games* represented a successful accommodation by Morgenstern to the US academy, and it was a harbinger of the collaborations that sustained his intellectual path going forward. After John von Neumann's tragic death in 1957, Morgenstern grew close with another Viennese, the mathematician Kurt Gödel. He mentored the Nobel laureate Martin Shubik and produced late-career work on the unpredictability of the stock market with Clive Granger, another Nobelist. The latter work, developed with Burton Malkiel, inspired Malkiel's well-known random walk theory concerning the stock market. Morgenstern believed his work, especially *Theory of Games*, was of the greatest significance for his standing within his Viennese cohort and for economics in general.[26]

Morgenstern was therefore left deeply disappointed when the Nobel Memorial Prize overlooked him year after year. It was an especially bitter blow when Hayek received the nod. Already agonizingly ill, Morgenstern complained about the vagueness of the Nobel's selection criteria and questioned the coherence of their procedures if they could award the same prize in the same year to Hayek and Myrdal. From exchanges with Machlup, Morgenstern sensed that Machlup, too, lusted after the prize. This created even more tension.[27]

Morgenstern measured himself against his fellow Austrians, feeling alternately superior, because of his mathematical rigor and scientific methods, and inferior, for failing to receive adequate recognition. This ambivalence filtered into his attempts to place his work into the Austrian tradition. After decades of near-constant criticism, Morgenstern's appreciation of Mises increased with time. When Mises died, the *New York Times* reached out to Morgenstern. He brought Machlup along for the interview. In his journal, he reminisced about his Viennese days, placing Mises above the other active economists of his generation: "Mises overshadowed Mayer by *a lot*, he was already a personage. He always treated me respectfully, although we did not agree on many things. When I look back I see that I owe him a great deal. The Mises-Kreis was a major factor." These comments stand in stark contrast to his comments in favor of Schumpeter in the 1920s, his disparagement of the Mises seminar in the 1930s, and his dismissal of *Human Action* in the 1940s. Through it all, the Morgenstern and Mises families met regularly after emigration, getting along well.[28]

Methodological divergences did little to sunder the familial affinity, nor did they diminish the intellectual commitment that Morgenstern felt to the Austrian project. He assisted Kauder with his history project at every turn and approved of the inclusion of his game theory within the Austrian, rather than the Walrasian, or mathematical, tradition. Whenever Austrians got together, they spent hours recalling the old days. In the 1970s, Morgenstern and Haberler gossiped about Richard Schüller, then one hundred years old and the last living member of Carl Menger's private seminar. They chattered about the influence of Wieser, Schumpeter, Mayer, and Mises, ranking them against the greatest economists of the day. Morgenstern read with relish the 1972 *Zeitschrift für Nationalökonomie* edition dedicated to Carl Menger. The contributions of Karl Menger, Karl Borch, and Erich Streissler all highlighted the role of uncertainty for the Austrian School, and they recognized the way in which Morgenstern continued a line of thinking that extended from Menger through Böhm and Wieser to Hayek and Morgenstern. Morgenstern wrote to Borch expressing pleasure at his placement within the tradition. He also responded approvingly to Karl Menger's article. The son of the Austrian School founder offered an idiosyncratic reading of the school, arguing that the original Austrians like Menger were not averse to mathematics and that Morgenstern's mathematization of marginal utility theory lent precision to the elder Menger's insights. Morgenstern was therefore a rightful heir to the Austrian tradition, which tickled the proud man's fancy.[29]

"Professional Secondhand Dealers in Ideas": Haberler and Rothbard

Members of the Austrian School had always taken a keen interest in policy advice and influence peddling with political and economic elites. Morgenstern and Machlup were masterful behind-the-scenes operatives like their predecessors Menger and Böhm. After World War II, the "war of ideas" intensified, this time with the focus on publicity and propaganda more than on direct political engagement. Among the Austrians, Mises and Hayek pioneered this strategy. Hayek sensed new opportunities in the postwar transatlantic world: "Over somewhat longer periods they [intellectuals] have probably never exercised so great an influence as they do today in those countries. This power they wield by shaping public opinion." Public opinion and the popular vote were distinct things. The point was not to win democratic battles for votes but ideological debates with opinion makers. "Professional secondhand dealers in ideas" were the people who would win the struggles by popularizing the values and ideas of intellectuals, whose untimely meditations rarely reached a mass public. Hayek's comment has often been misinterpreted to mean that there are two discrete groups of thinkers—those who produce ideas and then those who peddle them. In fact, many of the individuals in Hayek's orbit were academics and advisers, intellectuals and ideologues, policy wonks and propagandists all in one. Members of the Austrian tradition were no exception. Haberler and Rothbard personified the porous boundaries between intellectual and dealer. They both featured in the rise of right-wing think tanks in the 1970s and 1980s, though they represented two distinct strands of political Austrianism: neoliberalism and modern libertarianism, respectively.[30]

As we saw in chapter 6, Haberler made his name in international monetary and trade theory. His views on free trade shaped discussions in the international economics community, especially at GATT, the IMF, the World Bank, and the UN Commission on Trade and Development (UNCTAD). Haberler parlayed his profile as a laissez-faire economist into political relevance. After tentative connections to Barry Goldwater's presidential campaign in 1964, he developed working relationships with Gerald Ford and Ronald Reagan, serving on Reagan's preinauguration economic team and his International Monetary Task Force. He exchanged birthday cards with both men and received an invitation to Reagan's first inauguration. He wrote pro-free-trade and anti-inflation opinion pieces in the *Washington Post*, the *Wall Street Journal*, and the *New York Times*. Most significantly, when he retired from Harvard in 1971, the conservative think tank AEI appointed him its first-ever scholar-in-residence; he remained there until his death in 1995.[31]

The AEI connection defined Haberler's late career, and he arrived at the think tank as its star in the conservative firmament waxed. Established as the American Enterprise Association in 1938 as a pro-business and anti–New Deal outlet, it remained a desultory organization into the 1950s. It enlisted many people in the Austrian orbit for its early propaganda work, such as the former RF officer John van Sickle and the journalist Henry Hazlitt. William Baroody, who took over AEI in 1954, recast the organization as an activist think tank. "Free, competitive enterprise" oriented its policy analysis. AEI barely retained its nonprofit, tax-exempt status in the 1960s when much of its personnel joined the Goldwater campaign and invalidated its "unpolitical" stance. As political debates turned corrosive in the early 1970s, conservative foundations increased their financial support for institutions like AEI. The Coors, Koch, Olin, and Scaife Foundations provided millions of dollars to counter "liberal" outfits like Brookings. With this financial windfall, AEI recruited a stable of prominent conservatives to its ranks, led by Gerald Ford, the former Fed chairman Arthur Burns, the future Supreme Court justice Antonin Scalia, and the neoconservative Irving Kristol. Haberler was the resident guru on business cycles, international trade, and inflation. An inflation and deficit hawk, Haberler assailed the profligate spending habits of the US state, blaming it for the predicament of high inflation and slow growth. He produced dozens of articles, pamphlets, and books disseminated by AEI. He became one of the leading denouncers of "stagflation," a portmanteau word he despised nearly as much as the phenomenon itself.[32]

Despite the turn to political advocacy, Haberler's reputation survived intact. The Nobel laureate Paul Samuelson, a former student and colleague and perhaps the best-known (American-style) liberal economist, extolled Haberler's contributions to the Austrian tradition and the economics profession: "Of the three great Austrian economists who elevated world and American economics—Joseph Schumpeter, Friedrich Hayek and Gottfried Haberler—it was Haberler who was the 'economist's economist,' a creative and eclectic advocate of free trade." Samuelson's verdict evinced clear Harvard chauvinism, yet it also jibed with Schumpeter's assessment of Haberler as the "best horse in the Viennese stables." Even if Haberler trafficked in secondhand ideas at the end of his life, years of sound economics assured his legacy.[33]

Haberler, like his compatriots, grappled with the meaning of the Austrian legacy, and his struggle reflected the competing impulses that constituted the movement. As an active conservative ideologue, he embodied the connection between economics and politics, yet he preferred to elide political discussions in his presentation of the Austrian School. His Austrian School was cultural and intellectual. His reminiscences on the Vienna Mises seminar depicted the Mises-Kreis of the interwar period as the fullest realization of the Austrian project. He wrote tributes to Hayek and Machlup when his friends passed away. He also sustained lengthy correspondence with the young American Austrians Richard Ebeling and Roger Garrison, clarifying his positions on Austrian business cycle theory, Keynesianism, and monetarism. Haberler even edited a collection of songs written by Felix Kaufmann for the Mises circle from the 1930s that highlighted the irreverence and wit of the interwar Austrian School.[34]

Even if Haberler was circumspect about Austrian School politicism, one of the songs in his volume, "A Farewell to Professor Mises," captured the latent ideology of the Mises circle. Addressing Mises's impending departure for Geneva in 1934, it anticipated an Austrian diaspora and a collapse of Austrian liberalism: "The students, who so passionately fought for Mises's lessons, who rode out against every import tax with such clever attacks, they will soon tarry a while in distant lands, because people here so poorly understand."[35] Mises-style militancy on behalf of liberal values was not lost on Haberler, who brought the fight for free enterprise to his policy work. This bellicose lesson was even more consequential for many US Austrians. Murray Rothbard in particular tried to propel Austrian ideas into the public consciousness through "centers of intellectual inquiry and education . . . independent of State power." He made a necessary connection between libertarianism and Austrian School theory. In his work, the school's most radical tendencies congealed in a volatile blend of ideas and ideology, politics and polemics.[36]

Rothbard's conversion experience to Misesian economics came in 1949. Prior to reading *Human Action*, Rothbard possessed inchoate ideas about economics; thereafter, he dedicated his energies to elaborating libertarianism. At that point, the Volker Fund paid him a retainer to compose a primer on *Human Action*. His treatise, *Man, Economy, and State*, was the product of a decade-long patronage. In it, he argued that the logical consequence of Mises's praxeological approach was a form of "anarcho-capitalism," which combined laissez-faire economics with a total rejection of the legitimacy of states to coerce their citizens. Deploying an idiosyncratic reading of natural rights theory, he argued that social organizations formed organically and could regulate their own behavior without state supervision. Without the presence of states, social groupings themselves would protect "the rights of property," the sole protection needed to maintain a well-functioning community. Austrian ideas about the spontaneity of institutions in a free society undergirded this view, as did a subjectivist understanding of value and exchange.[37]

Following the completion of *Man*, Rothbard set to evangelizing. He traveled in the Mises and Ayn Rand circles during the 1950s and early 1960s and then embarked on his own course in the mid-1960s. Calling on intellectuals "to become instruments of transformation by assuming the role of public 'opinion-molders,'" he began to form "open centers" designed to awaken Americans to their libertarian heritage. He formed a Circle Bastiat to discuss ideas. Rothbard also sought sympathizers. He felt that antiwar New Leftists and gay and women's rights advocates were natural allies against the statist policies of mainstream political parties. He and his colleague Leonard Liggio, a fellow Misesian, began publishing *Left and Right* to build bridges. Members of the New Left rejected these overtures—as did Mises and many of Rothbard's fellow-traveling libertarians. The election of Richard Nixon in 1968 and the infamous riot provoked by antiwar libertarians at a Young Americans for Freedom rally in 1969 confirmed for Rothbard that the Republican Party was inhospitable to his ideology. He redoubled the search for fellow travelers.[38]

In 1973, Rothbard published *For a New Liberty* and became involved with the fledgling Libertarian Party (LP) as his political outlet. In his writings and his political activism, he embraced a two-track approach to ideological conversion. He argued for an elite, quasi-Leninist strategy that engaged intellectuals in meetings, conferences, and publications to sharpen the libertarian message. Simultaneously he advanced a popular track that utilized print, radio, and TV to raise public consciousness. In this way, the battle for "Middle America" would be won. Although Rothbard apotheosized average Americans, the elite prong of his strategy mattered more. Rothbard curried support from wealthy backers like Leonard Read at FEE and Dick Cornuelle and Baldy Harper at the Volker Fund and the IHS. Meanwhile he also cultivated an alliance with Edward Crane and Charles Koch. Together they came up with the idea for an open center to rival Brookings and AEI. Conceived in 1974 at the Wichita-based Charles Koch Foundation, the Cato Institute, the first libertarian think tank, opened its doors in 1977, with Rothbard as its *spiritus rector*.[39]

The tempestuous tale of the Rothbard-Koch-Cato relationship has been told and retold because of its floridness. Despite strong ideological affinities, Rothbard diverged from Crane and Koch on tactics for achieving a libertarian society. He preferred educational endeavors aimed at cultivating a vanguard of radical anarcho-capitalists; Crane and Koch, on the other hand, privileged a reformist program directed at political power. If Crane and Koch tolerated some degree of compromise to achieve their aims, Rothbard was unmovable. The dénouement between the men was not long in coming. Rothbard and Koch split irrevocably during the 1980 US presidential campaign, when Crane advised LP candidate Ed Clark to moderate his positions on taxation in order to attract more voters. Rothbard lashed out at this meliorist strategy. This tiff precipitated Rothbard's forcible removal from Cato's board in 1981. Rothbard's hyperbolic recounting lacks impartiality, yet it offers insight into the volatility of libertarian politics: "On Black Friday, March 27, 1981, at 9:00 A.M. in San Francisco, the 'libertarian' power elite of the Cato Institute, consisting of President Edward H. Crane III and Other Shareholder Charles G. Koch, revealed its true nature and its cloven hoof. Crane, aided and abetted by Koch, ordered me to leave Cato's regular quarterly board meeting, even though I am a shareholder and a founding board member of the Cato Institute."[40] Rothbard ascribed diabolical characteristics to Crane and Koch. He asserted that one could not consider oneself libertarian while espousing Koch-style reformism. He accused Crane and Koch of authoritarian tendencies, a damning criticism of any libertarian. The only option for a true libertarian—and true Austrian—was schism. Rothbard found a new patron in Llewellyn Rockwell Jr., a former chief of staff for US Representative Ron Paul. They founded the Ludwig von Mises Institute (LvMI) in 1982, which remains the locus of Rothbardian libertarianism and orthodox Misesian economics. This split was one of the first of many examples of Austrian and libertarian schisms in the United States.

Despite the acrimony of the libertarian divorce, the separation was over tactics rather than strategy. Both sides continued to affirm their commitment to ideas they associated with Austrian economics. The Kochs continued to sustain the IHS and Austrian economics conferences, in addition to Cato. They found publishers for the articles of the Austrian revival. They also financed numerous journals, including the *Journal of Libertarian Studies*, *Libertarian Review*, and *Inquiry*, most of which displayed Austrian predilections. The Kochs continued to play such an outsized role in the libertarian universe that libertarians themselves coined the phrase "Kochtopus" to describe the far-reaching tentacles of the Koch operation.[41]

The Kochs plowed millions of dollars into libertarian institution building, bankrolling the struggle that the Austrians had championed since Mises declared a "battle of ideas" in 1920. The Kochs consciously followed the precepts of their Austrian heroes. IHS, the Center for Libertarian Studies, and the Center for the Study of Market Processes, founded at Rutgers University in 1979, became institutional homes for latter-day Austrian economics. The Rutgers center explicitly invoked Austrian ideas in its name, and its founder, Richard Fink, idolized Hayek and Mises—not only as intellectuals but as ideological impresarios. Fink completed his PhD in the Austrian economics program at NYU in the late 1970s, and he impressed Charles Koch with his ability to "get something done and make it effective." He was instrumental in the move of the Austrian center of gravity from NYU to Rutgers to George Mason University (GMU). The market process center he directed, now known as the Mercatus Center, moved to GMU in 1980. The Kochs have given more than $30 million to GMU, much going to Mercatus and related conservative projects in public choice theory and law and economics. They also moved the IHS from California into the same building in Virginia. Mercatus's primary funding over the years has come from the Koch, Scaife, Bradley, Devos, Earhart, and Goodrich Foundations, a veritable who's-who of conservative donors. While the GMU program and the LvMI have had many disagreements over the years, both have used their profiles in libertarian circles to keep Austrian ideas visible. And through their connections to conservative and libertarian think tanks, Koch-sponsored scholars in particular have been able to moonlight as Hayekian secondhand dealers in ideas for several decades.[42]

"We're All Hayekians Now"

While Machlup, Morgenstern, and Haberler were all vital to the continued relevance of the Austrian School in ways that have often been overlooked, and Mises and Rothbard advanced a significant strain of libertarian economics and politics, Friedrich Hayek was the representative figure. He embodied the strengths—and the shortcomings—of this multifaceted tradition. In examining the final decades of Hayek's career, the multiple legacies of the Austrian School come into clearer relief. He remained an economist, but he was also more than that: a social theorist, a political philosopher, a philosopher of science. He was also an institution builder, a neoliberal policy advocate, and a conservative public intellectual in a growing, global epistemic community in the late 1970s and 1980s. He was simultaneously a scholar, a hero, a seer, and a soothsayer. Hayek the individual and the icon shaped the legacy of the Austrian School more than anyone else.

Hayek's late career arc was perhaps the most idiosyncratic and peripatetic of the Austrians. A British citizen, he spent his later years at three institutions: a dozen years in Chicago (1950–62); six in Freiburg, West Germany (1962–68); eight in Salzburg, Austria (1968–76); and the final seventeen back in Freiburg (1976–93). He resided in London, Los Angeles, and Palo Alto for extended fellowships and visiting professorships. He became a household name for his liberal economics and philosophical defense of freedom. He was also directly involved in epochal events that seemed to belie a dedication to open and progressive liberalism, including the rise of Margaret Thatcher in the United Kingdom, Augusto Pinochet in Chile, and Ronald Reagan in the United States.

Hayek's greatest direct influence came in the political and economic culture of the United Kingdom. The culmination of his intellectual and ideological groundwork came in the form of the IEA. The IEA grew out of Hayek's MPS as the original free-market think tank. It offered educational and policy materials to politicians dissatisfied with the postwar economic order. Antony Fisher founded the organization in 1955. He was a businessman converted to Hayek's positions by the *Reader's Digest* condensation of *Road to Serfdom*. Seeing himself as a secondhand dealer in ideas, he appointed fellow MPS members Ralph Harris and Arthur Seldon to leadership roles. He attracted disaffected Liberal Party members with his mantra of "re-teaching the economics of the free market." The IEA proposed to create a liberal Fabian Society to counteract the pernicious influence of socialist thinkers, Labour Party welfarists, and economic planners. IEA's founders did not see it as a traditional think tank à la Brookings; instead, it was an evangelical association on behalf of traditional liberalism. In this way, Fisher followed the lead of Leonard Read (FEE) and Baldy Harper (IHS), yet he took free enterprise proselytizing one step further. IEA created a template for the activist think tanks that emerged in the 1970s, which was emulated by Heritage, Cato, and AEI in the United States.[43]

In 1959, IEA hosted the annual meeting of MPS in England, and Harris and Seldon presented their tactics and strategies for advancing free enterprise around the world. Over the next decade and a half, they distributed texts defending capitalist principles. By relying on academics for its pamphlets, IEA gained a reputation for intellectual gravitas. IEA published Hayek, Haberler, Milton Friedman, James Buchanan, and Lionel Robbins among its celebrity authors. Hayek served as the ideological polestar. His attacks on inflation and the effects of trade unions became the centerpieces of IEA's arsenal. The popular 1972 publication *A Tiger by Its Tail* collected Hayek's anti-inflation, antiunion essays; it sold widely in the United Kingdom. Hayek argued that trade unions had a monopoly that exerted a baleful impact on the price level. He assigned unions a major share of the blame for deteriorating economic conditions around the world. In contrast to Milton Friedman's monetarism, which argued that inflation could be contained using transparent and consistent monetary policy alone, Hayek maintained that the stranglehold of unions on wage negotiations had to be broken too, to allow market economies to correct. These kinds of pamphlets helped IEA gain the backing of multinational corporations like Barclays and British Petroleum, which, alongside the Kochs, financed IEA's operations.[44]

The rise in visibility of IEA and Hayek's increased popularity mutually reinforced each other. For example, *Constitution of Liberty* provided ballast for IEA's espousal of liberal values. Even though the book did not sell well outside sympathetic circles, IEA propped up its circulation and ensured its continued availability. By the 1960s, IEA attracted young Tories like Keith Joseph and Enoch Powell, who felt the Conservatives needed new ideas and fresh blood. Margaret Thatcher met Seldon and Harris in the early 1960s and joined their ideological ranks thereafter. While the leader of the opposition in the mid-1970s, Thatcher became famous for toting *Constitution of Liberty* in her briefcase, saying, "This is what we believe." When she came to power in 1979, Ralph Harris was one of her first appointees to the House of Lords, and she wrote a letter of thanks to IEA because, she said, "it was primarily your foundation work which enabled us to rebuild the philosophy upon which our Party succeeded in the past." Even if Hayek did not directly shape Thatcher's agenda, he and IEA supported many Tory initiatives.[45]

IEA and its founder, Fisher, were the most proactive empire builders in the broader neoliberal movement of the late twentieth century, extending the movement's reach in several directions at once. IEA cultivated close ties with the *Financial Times*, the *Daily Telegraph*, and the *Times*, building a base of support for free-market thought within the press. They assisted emergent UK organizations like the Adam Smith Institute and the Centre for Policy Studies. By 1981, Fisher and his IEA cadre had so many active projects that Fisher created the Atlas Economic Research Foundation to coordinate the global network of free-market organizations. Fisher and Hayek plotted Atlas's strategy together. Hayek wrote Fisher, "I entirely agree with you that the time has come when it has become desirable and almost a duty to extend the network of institutes. The future of civilization may really depend on whether we can catch the ear of a large enough part of the upcoming generation of intellectuals all over the world fast enough." Today the renamed Atlas Network consists of more than 480 think tanks, including the Michigan-based Acton Institute, which offers religious arguments for libertarian policies; AEI; the American Legislative Exchange Council (ALEC), which produces model legislation for conservative US politicians; Americans for Prosperity; the Ayn Rand Institute; Cato; FEE; Heritage; the Hoover Institution; IHS; the Liberty Fund; the Manhattan Institute; Mercatus; and a half dozen Mises Institutes.[46]

Of course, neither Hayek nor the Austrian School was primarily responsible for IEA's or Atlas's roles in the sharp rightward turn in Western politics after 1973. They did provide intellectual ballast and legitimacy for these ideological efforts. Their ideas continue to do so today. Hayek was of course aware of this. Hayek saw those bodies as a realization of the kind of intellectual activism he had advocated since at least the 1930s. Liberalism required strong defenders—starting with intellectuals, moving to secondhand dealers in ideas, and ending up with politicians. Hayek spread this gospel in his writings, at the MPS and IEA, and to whichever leaders would listen. Hayek's most controversial political intervention took place in Chile. While not as complicit with the Pinochet regime as Milton Friedman and the Chicago School were, Hayek's open advocacy of an authoritarian strongman who espoused a market ideology over a democratically elected socialist leader highlighted the uncomfortable tension between liberalism and democracy embodied in the neoliberal program. In 1977, Pinochet invited Hayek to Chile, four years after Pinochet's violent (and US-backed) coup had overthrown Salvador Allende on September 11, 1973. By the time of Hayek's trip, the international media had reported extensively on the repression and murder initiated by the Pinochet government. These reports inspired worldwide protests, and intellectuals associated with the Pinochet regime, like Milton Friedman, faced public outrage. Famously, the Viennese econometrician Gerhard Tintner attacked Friedman for his support of Chile's "Nazis." A few Austrian-friendly libertarians even warned Hayek about the backlash that a visit would precipitate. He went anyway.[47]

Hayek came away from the visit impressed. He met with politicians, businesspeople, and policy advisers. He called the Chilean officials "educated, reasonable, and insightful men." In a twenty-minute audience with Pinochet, he discussed the evils of unlimited democracy and the need for strong leadership, especially in times of crisis. He promised to send Pinochet an excerpt of *Law, Legislation, and Liberty* to help guide his reconstruction of Chilean society. When he returned to England, he wrote Margaret Thatcher, urging her to introduce similar liberalizing reforms. She demurred, recognizing that the repressive measures Pinochet employed to implement policy were not available to her. In a later interview with the Santiago newspaper *El Mercurio*, Hayek reiterated his support for Pinochet and "temporary" dictatorship in the name of liberal values:

> Well, I would say that, as long-term institutions, I am totally against dictatorships. But a dictatorship may be a necessary system for a transitional period. At times it is necessary for a country to have, for a time, some form or other of dictatorial power. As

> you will understand, it is possible for a dictator to govern in a
> liberal way. And it is also possible for a democracy to govern
> with a total lack of liberalism. Personally I prefer a liberal dictator
> to democratic government lacking liberalism. My personal
> impression—and this is valid for South America—is that in Chile,
> for example, we will witness a transition from a dictatorial
> government to a liberal government. And during this transition
> it may be necessary to maintain certain dictatorial powers, not as
> something permanent, but as a temporary arrangement.

In endorsing this position, he singled out not only Pinochet but also
Portugal's Antonio Salazar, England's Cromwell, and West Germany's
first chancellors, Konrad Adenauer and Ludwig Erhard, as good models
of authoritarian leadership. Rehashing his arguments from *Constitution of
Liberty* and *Law, Legislation, and Liberty*, only strong leaders could introduce rules "as a means of establishing a stable democracy and liberty, clean
of impurities." Without rules, "unlimited" democracies risked devolving
into illiberal, populist regimes and eventually totalitarian states. Why a
dictator did not introduce impurities in the governing system Hayek failed
to explain.[48]

Hayek spent the next year defending Pinochet against the Western media.
He argued that Europeans had a false impression of the regime. Collectivist thought had blinded the international community to the urgent need
for strong liberal states. He also lashed out about comparisons between
Chilean authoritarianism and Communism. Even the liberal *Frankfurter
Allgemeine Zeitung* refused to publish these opinions. His enthusiasm was
rewarded by the Chileans, however. When Pinochet introduced a new,
authoritarian constitution in 1980, he named it after the *Constitution of
Liberty*. Meanwhile Hayek never recanted his support. In fact, he doubled
down, helping to bring the regional meeting of the MPS to the home of
the Pinochet rebellion, the coastal resort town of Viña del Mar, in 1981.[49]

Hayek's ties to US intellectual and political developments, including the
rise of Reagan and his brand of supply-side economics, were less direct
than his British ones and less notorious than his Chilean liaisons. Still, the
impress of his ideas was clearly felt during the Reagan Revolution. Hayek
himself was reluctant to meddle in the party politics of countries where he

was not a citizen. This led him to decline positions on boards of trustees for US think tanks and prevented him from authoring many editorials in the US press. Nevertheless, Reagan acknowledged that he was a "legatee" of Hayek's ideas, greatly admiring *Road to Serfdom*. He employed about twenty MPS members in economic task forces and was known to cite Hayek. The two men exchanged a few letters, and Hayek enjoyed a visit to the White House; yet there is little evidence of Hayek's influence on Reagan's policy choices.[50]

Hayek's network of friends and allies in the United States exercised the kind of impact that the Viennese eminence said he would or could not. His protestations of apoliticism also rang hollow, given his involvement with major conservative institutions. The Hoover Institution and Heritage Foundation served as his primary US benefactors. In 1978, 1983, and 1985, he enjoyed extended stays in Palo Alto, where he was a scholar-in-residence. He also orchestrated the acquisition of the MPS papers for Hoover, which complemented his personal archives. By dint of his efforts, Hoover became the primary location for Austrian School correspondence—Haberler's and Machlup's respective papers also ended up there, as did the archives of the IHS. Meanwhile Heritage invited Hayek to Washington on several occasions for conferences and the conferral of a distinguished fellowship. Hayek was feted at a Heritage Foundation conference on constitutional economics in 1985, which included conservative stalwarts Robert Bork, James Buchanan, William Niskanen, Mancur Olson, Gordon Tullock, and others. In Washington, he shared stages with old friends from Vienna (Haberler and Machlup) and Chicago (Milton Friedman and George Stigler). He participated in several conferences at AEI that Haberler helped organize. Cato paid the salary of his English-language secretary in the late 1970s, and he was its guest of honor at a 1984 conference titled "Planning America: Government vs. the Market." He became a Distinguished Senior Fellow there in 1985.

By the mid-1980s, the reputation of Hayek and the Austrian School achieved its highest level of postwar acclaim. Austrian ideas featured at MPS meetings and in free-market institutes around the globe. Societies expressing fealty to Austrianism existed in Alabama (Ludwig von Mises Institute), London (Carl Menger Society), Brussels (Ludwig von Mises-Instituut), and even Mexico City (El Premio Internacional Ludwig von Mises).

Ironically, one location that did not take to the Austrian School was Austria itself. Hayek's case is again instructive. After retiring from Freiburg, he moved to Salzburg as an emeritus professor. His time there convinced him of the mediocrity of Austrian social sciences, prompting his 1977 departure for Germany. When he emigrated the second time, he fired off an angry editorial to an Austrian newspaper about the shortcomings of Austrian higher education: "When I then discovered that the Salzburg University did not award [PhDs in economics] and for this reason there were no serious economics students, and that current law dictated I could not continue teaching after my 75th year . . . I realized that I had made an error in moving to Salzburg from Freiburg." Although Salzburg had purchased his five-thousand-volume library, it went virtually unused, and the Education Ministry had not even bothered to catalogue it. Hayek continued to summer in the Tyrolean village of Obergurgl, yet his disdain for Austrian intellectual life persisted. This state of affairs was a far cry from his postwar hopes for the restoration of the Austrian School in his *Heimat*.[51]

The ambivalent relationship between the Austrian School and its homeland was one of the legacies of the school. The émigrés attempted to re-establish roots immediately after World War II, but they encountered great resistance from Austrian politicians, bureaucrats, and professors. The arch-conservative leanings of postwar Austrian governments and the country's education ministry under Heinrich Drimmel saw the return of the émigrés as painful reminders of the interwar years. In the 1920s and 1930s, Austrian conservatives persecuted leftist and liberal intellectuals and kept them from securing stable positions. It was these conservatives, not the Nazis, who initiated the interwar brain drain. After the war, Morgenstern (as head of the Institute for Advanced Studies), Machlup (as trustee of the Institute for Business Research and the Institute for International Economic Comparison), and Hayek faced a renewed frosty reception in the Austrian Second Republic.[52]

The biggest symbolic defeat for a restored Austrian School was the failure of the Carl Menger-Institut in the 1980s. Even the backing of the Atlas Network was no match for Austrian apathy. In 1984, a consortium of free-market associations decided to establish a center for "education and research in market economics" named after the founder of the Austrian School. Enlisting Austrian magnates (Julius Meinl and Manfred Swarovski) and international banking institutions (Citibank), executive director Albert Zlabinger envisioned a policy outfit in the mold of IEA. Zlabinger recruited Hayek to the position of honorary president. Haberler, Karl Menger, and Martha Steffy Browne served on the advisory board, which also included younger "Austrians" such as Kirzner, Lachmann, and Erich Streissler and international free-market stalwarts like James Buchanan, Peter Bauer, and the general secretary of the MPS, the Austrian Max Thurn. In publicizing a "think tank for market economics" and its coterie of "militant thinkers," the Menger-Institut relied on endorsements from AEI, Cato, FEE, Heritage, Hoover, and the Liberty Fund. The letters of support stressed the need to restore and develop the liberal tradition in German-speaking central Europe, especially in Menger's home country.[53]

In spite of the best efforts of Austrians and their friends, the Menger Institute collapsed within four years. It hosted lectures and conferences and reconvened Mises's private seminar in his former Chamber of Commerce office. It published seminal Austrian economic texts, many of which had never appeared in German. Nevertheless, the organization's revenues quickly dwindled, dropping by over 50 percent between 1986 and 1987. The institute's board demanded new leadership and a more activist political orientation, which drove away its intellectual adherents. The institute ceased its activities soon thereafter. Its failure seemed to confirm former chancellor Bruno Kreisky's mirthful comment to the economist John Kenneth Galbraith about the lack of interest in Austria for Austrian economics: "'How do you explain, Chancellor,' asked Galbraith, 'Austria's superb postwar economic performance: low inflation, full employment, steadily increasing productivity, a dense and all-encompassing structure of social benefits and public investments?' 'I explain it,' replied Kreisky, 'by our attention to export. We exported all of our economists.'"[54]

To overemphasize the failures of the Menger Institut or Austrian economics in Austria would distort the greater legacy of the Austrian School, however. One of the central ironies of the Austrian School, especially after the Great War, had always been how much more the international community appreciated it than its home country did. It originated in opposition to German economic thought and Habsburg conservatism. It flourished in the interwar years through its connections to US philanthropic organizations. It successfully migrated to the Anglophone world during the war years thanks to these connections. Its members developed trans-national networks of intellectuals and free-market activists using their Rolodexes of like-minded scholars and wealthy elites.

A better testament to the legacy of the original school came from its members themselves in one of the final familial gatherings. Into the 1990s, Herbert Furth convened a Geist-Kreis-style session at his home in the Washington, DC, suburbs for his Viennese friends. Haberler, Machlup, and Martha Steffy Browne joined him. The wide-ranging conversations reaffirmed the most significant features of their movement: its combative discursive style honed in coffeehouses and salons, its intellectual eclecticism and interdisciplinarity, and its skepticism about its own core principles. Furth, as an homage to his high school friend Hayek, devoted a series of discussions to *Law, Legislation, and Liberty*. Despite a half century of disputes and disagreements, Furth commended it for its brilliant for-mulations of liberal theory, ranking it alongside Adam Smith's *Wealth of Nations* and Schumpeter's *Capitalism, Socialism, and Democracy* as one of the three most significant works of political theory. Nevertheless, he rejected Hayek's antistatist policy deductions for their lack of a logical foundation, and he let Hayek know about it. The bond between the two men nevertheless remained ironclad, as it did for the other members of the Austrian School. Talk about hobbies, college remembrances, and old friendships and feuds were the real grist for the Austrian School's mill, and the DC conversations proceeded as the Viennese meetings once had. After a particularly heated back-and-forth with Hayek, Furth felt comfortable stating, "You can complain without worry; if one cannot do that with one's old friends, what sense does the friendship have?" For Furth, the Austrian School was as much a style as it was a coherent body of thought. Most of the original school would have nodded in approval at such a profession of principles.[55]

This chapter has looked at how various Austrians—Austrians, un-Austrian Austrians, and non-Austrian Austrians—attempted to narrate their own story and what was lost in transcription, if not translation. The 1970s and 1980s consisted of a number of novel "Austrian" memory projects. The Austrian School, which had gone through many stages and iterations in its rich history, still defied easy categorization. The chapter also examined the various activities, affiliations, and institutions that advanced the Austrian tradition. The story of the school's legacies in the twilight years of the lives of the Viennese émigrés is replete with ironies. It was the successes of the émigrés in creating postwar, Austrian-inspired institutions that threatened the coherence of the concept of the "Austrian School." Moreover, it was the most marginalized, dogmatic, and perhaps *least* representative grouping, Mises's New York seminar, that played the largest part in propagating "Austrian economics" in the United States.

Had the Austrian legacies remained only the ones just discussed—an ecumenical school of economic theory based on subjectivism and marginal utility theory, a heterodox economic approach in the United States, a network of foundations for neoliberalism, a group of policy entrepreneurs deploying their expertise behind the scenes in advanced societies—this would have been impressive indeed. The fall of the Berlin Wall, the collapse of the Soviet Union, and the end of the Cold War managed to transform the Austrians into seers too—as the prognosticators of socialism's demise. Austrians' predictions about socialism's impossibility had seemed to come true. Their scientific and philosophical pronouncements appeared to bear the mantle of truth.[56]

Vienna itself loomed large in this triumphalist, post-1989 narrative, which would have delighted Austrian School members. As the historian Tony Judt observed, Vienna had long been a synecdoche for Austria, central Europe, and Europe as a whole. Now it had a new power: "In the early years of the twentieth century Vienna *was* Europe: the fertile, edgy, self-deluding hub of a culture and a civilization on the threshold of apocalypse. . . . After Germany was defeated . . . [Vienna's] Nazi allegiance conveniently forgotten, the Austrian capital . . . acquired a new identity as outrider and exemplar of the free world. . . . Vienna in 1989 was thus a good place from which to 'think' Europe. Austria embodied all the slightly self-satisfied attributes of post-war western Europe."[57] Vienna served as the quintessence of twentieth-century European history and the cornerstone of a resurgent European liberalism and worldwide capitalism. The scions of the Viennese *Bildungsbürgertum* would have applauded this judgment. They had been marginalized and expelled, yet they continued to fight for the values of the West and the Enlightenment. Hayek and Mises had been right all along, and the West owed them a debt of gratitude.

In a final irony, though, the post-1989 narrative of "the end of history," which Judt rightly criticized, has further muddied our understanding of the Austrian School. The school has occupied a curious place in the current popular imagination and in the economic and political discourse of the twenty-first century. Its current iterations would probably shock the liberal cosmopolitans of the original school.

CONCLUSION

At a time when most movements that are thought to be progressive
advocate further encroachments on individual liberty, those who cherish
freedom are likely to expend their energies in opposition. In this they find
themselves much of the time on the same side as those who habitually
resist change. In matters of current politics today they generally have
little choice but to support the conservative parties. But, though the
position I have tried to define is also often described as "conservative,"
it is very different from that to which this name has been traditionally
attached.

—*Friedrich Hayek*

In the epochal years 1989–91, a specter was haunting Robert
Heilbroner—the failure of socialism: "Less than seventy-five years after it
officially began, the contest between capitalism and socialism is over;
capitalism has won."[1] In a series of essays in the *New Yorker*, the *Atlantic
Monthly*, *Dissent*, the *Nation*, and academic journals, the eminent historian
of economic thought tried to make sense of Communism's spectacular
failure and the seeming vindication of capitalism. He also wondered at
the direction of global economic developments in the coming decades
and the place of economists in that future order. For a committed democratic socialist, these considerations elicited some pain. In wrestling with
what "Not Socialism" would look like in eastern Europe, he conceded
that market exchange probably underpinned any such system, meaning
that capitalism would serve as the basis for any social order going forward.

From his analysis, he "drew the discomfiting generalization" that the economists Ludwig von Mises, Friedrich Hayek, and Milton Friedman had perhaps been most accurate in their assessments of socialism's shortcomings: "*the further to the right one looks, the more prescient has been the validity of historical foresight; the further to the left, the less so.*"[2]

In these meditations, Heilbroner despaired not only for socialism but also for economics as a science. He wondered why economists across the political spectrum had failed so miserably in their prognostications about actual events. This failure extended to the Austrians. Leveling very Austrian criticisms of economic forecasting and prediction, he speculated that the increasingly positivistic and formalistic tendencies in economic "science" had made economics less rather than more applicable to complex worldly affairs. If economics used to be a "worldly philosophy" in the days of Smith, Mill, and Marx, or even in the times of Keynes, Mises, and Hayek, that phase seemed at an end. He decried the disregard of values, or pre-analytic "vision," in shaping the social analyses of economists. Invoking Joseph Schumpeter, he argued for a broader philosophical perspective that might help social scientists to structure our social reality and imbue it with meaning. Unwittingly Heilbroner evoked Hayek's famous dictum that no good economist is an economist only.[3]

Heilbroner was one of the foremost American leftists to grapple with the collapse of the Soviet Union and the Eastern Bloc in public. Ironically, he did it through an Austrian lens. His example shows how the ideas of the Austrian School remained alive, even in unexpected places. Heilbroner was a student and admirer of Schumpeter, and his seminal 1953 history *The Worldly Philosophers*, already in its sixth edition in 1989, was deeply indebted to the Austrian's *History of Economic Analysis*—Schumpeter was the subject of the book's final chapter. To perform socialism's autopsy, Heilbroner turned to Schumpeter's *Capitalism, Socialism, and Democracy* for answers. He argued that Schumpeter's joint verdicts on capitalism and socialism—"Can capitalism survive? No. I do not think it can," and "Can socialism work? Of course it can"—reflected the pessimism of the late 1930s and 1940s. Fifty years of evidence had shown that capitalism's flaws had not yet sowed the seeds of its own destruction. Moreover, the mechanisms that made socialism seem viable, which Schumpeter adopted from the economist Oskar Lange, had proven unworkable. Setting aside that this interpretation of *Capitalism, Socialism, and Democracy* missed Schumpeter's ironical attitude toward "successful" socialism and "failing" capitalism, Heilbroner built his Schumpeterian argument on Mises's and Hayek's work on socialist calculation. They had pinpointed the fundamental problems that planned economies had not (and could not) overcome. These were not just economic issues with price mechanisms or coordination problems with information either; they were also cultural ones. Channeling his inner Austrian, he wrote, "capitalism is a social order built upon a deeply embedded and widely believed principle expressed in the actions and beliefs of its most important representatives." Or, as he put it succinctly elsewhere, "It turns out, of course, that Mises was right."[4]

Heilbroner's searching essays provoked many people on the left and cheered people on the right. The democratic socialist Irving Howe disputed the death of socialism. Central European liberals like Vaclav Klaus and János Kornai endorsed the triumph of freedom à la Hayek. In the academy, a new generation of scholars affiliated with "Austrian economics" returned to the classics of Menger, Böhm, Mises, and Hayek to explore an array of topics neglected by mainstream economists and social scientists. These discussions briefly placed the Austrian School front and center in the post–Cold War intellectual world. Unfortunately the school's surviving members, all around ninety years old, had little opportunity to bask in their ostensible vindication. Friedrich Hayek suffered a series of debilitating ailments after 1985, bringing an end to his intellectual career. He made no public comments about the end of the Cold War and the collapse of Communism. The story was similar for Hayek's lifelong companions. Gottfried Haberler continued to write on trade and monetary issues for conservative outlets until 1990. He helped collate the collection of Felix Kaufmann's songs from the Mises circle in 1992. He died in 1995. His brother-in-law Herbert Furth passed away the same year.

Simultaneously with the arrival of *Austrian School ideas* in transatlantic intellectual discussions, the *idea of the Austrian School* gained a new political and popular significance. On November 18, 1991, US President George H. W. Bush awarded Friedrich Hayek the Presidential Medal of Freedom "for a lifetime of looking beyond the horizon." As Hayek himself was unable to attend the event, his son accepted the award on his behalf. Nevertheless, Bush took the ceremony as an opportunity to present the popular understanding of Hayek—and that of the Austrian School—which remains largely intact today. He lauded the prescience of *Road to Serfdom* and Hayek's commitment to "freedom's triumph." Bush declared that "Hayek is revered by the free people of Central and Eastern Europe as a true visionary, and recognized worldwide as a revolutionary in intellectual and political thought. How magnificent it must be for him to witness his ideas validated before the eyes of the world." The economics writer Sylvia Nasar, covering the event, likewise enthused that "Mr. von Hayek's views on the economic inadequacies and political ills of central planning are now those of the mainstream." In the popular imagination, the idea of the Austrian School was reduced to a simplified "road to serfdom" argument, hazy pronouncements about freedom, and prophetic defenses of liberty and unfettered capitalism.[5]

In this concluding chapter, we explore these two distinct developments in the quarter century since the last Viennese representatives passed away: the evolution of Austrian School ideas and the appropriation of the idea of the Austrian School for ideological and political purposes. The tensions that have always characterized the movement have only come into sharper relief in these intervening years. If the heterodox school of Austrian economics has carved out a marginal yet vital subcommunity within the economics profession and policy world, it is in the realm of politics and ideology where the school has produced competing legacies, many far removed from anything the original Viennese would have imagined, let alone condoned. After an initial burst of interest in the decade after the Cold War's end, it was the Great Recession of 2008 and the rise of the Tea Party in 2009 that moved the Austrian School—its economics, politics, and ideology—from the margins back into the spotlight. More recently, the fascination of a small faction of Alt-Right extremists, pledging fealty to Mises, Rothbard, and Austrian ideas, has forced the "producers" of contemporary Austrian ideas to confront the unfortunate fact that the "consumers" of Austrianism are not always the well-reasoned, liberal individuals they imagined. Their ideas have had unintended consequences, which demand a greater reckoning from within the tradition.

Austrian Economics at the "End of History"

The "end of history" announced by the political scientist Francis Fukuyama in 1989 seemed to be an Austrian moment. Fukuyama celebrated "the universalization of Western liberal democracy as the final form of human government" and "the total exhaustion of viable systemic alternatives to Western liberalism." For a century, the Austrians had railed against socialists and conservatives in the name of liberalism. Mises and Hayek had declared socialism an "impossible" economic system that paved the way to destructionism and serfdom. When the Berlin Wall fell and the Soviet Union collapsed, the Austrians appeared vindicated. Of course, Hayek's thesis in *Road* had been challenged by the fact that postwar European welfare states, which he disparaged in increasingly shrill terms as the years went by, did not move toward totalitarianism with their "planned" economies. Nor had the collapse of the USSR or the Eastern Bloc necessarily transpired according to the "impossibility" arguments of the Austrians. Nevertheless, the Austrians seemed to have the better part of the argument over socialism's viability, and they were hailed as visionaries and victors.[6]

Although the curtain had fallen on the historical Austrian School by the early 1990s, its intellectual and institutional legacies persevered in this brave new world. Interest in all things Austrian accelerated in the 1990s and early 2000s. Looking at Google Ngrams, we see these trends clearly. The terms "Austrian economics" and "Austrian School of economics" reached all-time highs in 1993, the former term appearing ten times more frequently than it had during the 1970s revival. References to Mises peaked in 1993 at a frequency twice as great as at any point during his lifetime. Hayek crested in 2000, at a rate nearly four times that of 1974, his Nobel Prize year. While Haberler's, Fritz Machlup's, and Oskar Morgenstern's numbers plummeted after the end of their respective careers, Friedrich von Wieser, Eugen von Böhm-Bawerk, and especially Carl Menger saw a spike in their popularity in the early 1990s. Last but not least, Joseph Schumpeter became far and away the most popular Austrian. He reached an all-time high in 1993. JSTOR results on scholarly publications suggest similar trends, though they have emerged more slowly. Articles on the school and its central figures Menger, Mises, and Hayek have increased three- to fourfold each decade since the 1970s. Schumpeter remains in a class of his own in terms of reference numbers. The "other" Austrians have seen no real change in their popularity since their respective heydays—Morgenstern, Machlup, and Haberler all saw their highest citation numbers in the middle decades of the last century.[7]

Quantitative data from the online databases LexisNexis and ProQuest largely confirm the school's rapid upward trajectory. Each decade after the 1970s revival has seen an increase in newspaper and magazine articles, dissertations, books, and scholarly articles on Austrian School themes. Hayek and Mises have been the primary beneficiaries, each seeing more than a tenfold increase in publications from the 1980s to the present. Meanwhile "Austrian economics" has seen a hundredfold upsurge since its revival. Despite this impressive growth, compared to Milton Friedman and the Chicago School of economics, the Austrians lag around an order of magnitude behind in terms of the frequency of their citation. Hayek's citations also register at a rate of one-third to one-half of his onetime rival John Maynard Keynes.[8]

Rather than wading into the weeds with these numbers—which are imprecise at best—a focus on the institutions and individuals that have kept Austrian School ideas alive in the past quarter century will provide greater clarity about contemporary Austrianism. In particular, forums created by American Austrians have promoted the school's legacy. The Mercatus Center at George Mason University (GMU) has trained scholars in Austrian approaches since 1980. Even after the acrimonious Rothbard-Koch split, the Koch-owned Cato Institute has served as a supportive think tank. The Ludwig von Mises Institute (LvMI) has sustained Mises- and Rothbard-inspired scholarship. These two blocs—GMU and LvMI—created intellectual outlets to disseminate their research. The *Review of Austrian Economics* (*RAE*), edited by Rothbard and Walter Block, initially appeared in 1987. After a one-year hiatus in 1998, Peter Boettke and Christopher Coyne, both affiliated with GMU, resumed the *RAE*'s publication in 1999. *Advances in Austrian Economics*, another series published out of GMU, started in 1996 and has linked Austrian developments to the broader economics community. In 1998, Hans-Hermann Hoppe and Joseph Salerno, with the help of the LvMI, established the *Quarterly Journal of Austrian Economics* to ensure a continued outlet for work in the Mises and Rothbard vein. Based on impact factor, none of these journals have high visibility within the economics profession. Even among nonmainstream, or heterodox, economics journals, they do not rate well. According to a recent evaluation of heterodox journals, the *RAE*, *Quarterly Journal of Austrian Economics*, and *Advances in Austrian Economics* rank thirty-seventh, fifty-first, and fifty-sixth, respectively, out of sixty-two heterodox publications in terms of reputation. The most impactful Austrian-inspired publication is again a Schumpeterian one, the *Journal of Evolutionary Economics*. Despite these desultory results, a coterie of devoted scholars keeps these outlets alive and vibrant.[9]

Mainstream evaluations of heterodox economic traditions are likely to be neglectful, disdainful, or dismissive, so we must delve deeper into content to understand current Austrian economic thought. Post–Cold War Austrian developments have been the subject of several books already, and an investigation up to the present would require another. We can therefore only delineate the broadest outlines of these developments here. Many of the themes explored earlier have retained their significance. Topics like praxeology, business cycle theory, and monetary and capital theory all remain integral. Socialist calculation, theories of the entrepreneur and the market process, and ideas about time, knowledge, and ignorance inform much of contemporary Austrian scholarship. Research into the role of institutions has increased, as has attention to the work of Menger and the late Hayek. History of economic thought, too, retains its centrality—the Austrians love their traditions. In recent years, a willingness to reconsider the relevance of "un-Austrian Austrians" like Schumpeter, Alfred Schütz, Machlup, and even Morgenstern has restored some of the ecumenism of the earlier tradition, especially in GMU circles.[10]

Post–Cold War Austrians, like their Austrian-born predecessors, attacked the biggest questions in economics and did not shy from confrontations. As Steven Horwitz has put it, Austrians always "took account of the puzzles that were of interest to the economics profession and aimed their explanations of those puzzles at that audience of their professional peers." The first issue of *RAE* addressed monetarism and Keynesianism. In subsequent years, discussions on public choice, macroeconomics, game theory, and experimental economics filled the pages of *RAE* and *Advances in Austrian Economics*. Austrians sparred with Nobelists like Milton Friedman,

Ronald Coase, James Buchanan, and Douglass North. They reveled in taking apart the arguments of intellectual allies and opponents alike. As the economist Deirdre McCloskey has noted, her conversion to an appreciation of the role of rhetoric in economic thought had a Viennese accent: "I learned from Don [Lavoie] and Karen Vaughn and Jack High as exemplars that Austrian economics was not merely a pointlessly vicious doctrinal war against one's natural allies carried out on the field of German texts. . . . I was drifting towards accepting the force of *words* in the economy." What Lavoie, a follower of Lachmann's and a crucial member of the Austrian revival, understood, and McCloskey gleaned, was the significance of persuasion and interpretation in economics.[11]

Central to the contemporary Austrian project has been an ongoing attempt at defining the school and its core characteristics. Authors have sought—sometimes in vain—intellectual coherence within the movement. Perhaps the two most significant monograph-length studies from the turn of the century are Karen Vaughn's *Austrian Economics in America* and Bruce Caldwell's *Hayek's Challenge*, which both foreground methodological considerations. Vaughn identifies significant points of contention and divergence, that is, between Böhm and Wieser, Mises and Hayek, and Lachmann and Kirzner. For her, the latter schism—between Austrian economists intent on pursuing an independent, heterodox approach to economics that brooked no compromise with neoclassical models (Lachmannians) and those attempting to reintegrate Austrian insights into mainstream economics (Kirznerians)—is the defining debate. The near-total absence of Rothbard from her study perhaps speaks louder than anything else, however. In Caldwell's intellectual-biography-cum-methodological-inquiry, he places the Austrian School and its foremost exemplar, Hayek, into broader debates within economics and social science. For each scholar, the Austrian School continues to offer important correctives to the formalism, empiricism, and "scientism" of mainstream economics.[12]

More recent works on the early school or on individuals like Menger, Mises, Morgenstern, and Hans Mayer have elaborated the rich tradition in important ways. As a result of this growing body of scholarship, the Austrian School remains an inspiration to many scholars, even if its reach within the academy is limited. As the doyen of the GMU program, Pete Boettke, puts it, even though Austrian insights may not always find resonance within contemporary "mainstream" economics, Austrian work occupies a pivotal place within the "mainline" of economic thought, beginning with Adam Smith and David Hume and passing through scholars like Hayek and Buchanan.[13]

A "Libertarian-to-Alt-Right Pipeline"?

This chapter's epigraph, excerpted from Hayek's 1960 "Why I Am Not a Conservative," shows the inherent tensions within the Austrian School project, especially in its efforts to apply liberal values in the real world. Caught between radicalism and conservatism, between democracy and authoritarianism, liberals like Hayek, Mises, Morgenstern, and the others had to make peace with the perverse realization that conservatives were closer to their "progressive" values than social democrats, laborites, or other leftists were. Identifying fully with conservatism was uncomfortable for the original Austrians since they viewed themselves as liberal and democratic, tolerant and cosmopolitan. Supporting Ignaz Seipel and endorsing Mussolini in the 1920s or backing Salazar and Pinochet in the 1960s and 1970s were never optimal solutions for Austrian School members, but they were preferable to socialist-run states or radical democracies. Hayek feared that his readers may think he was a conventional, tradition-bound conservative, and he tried to disabuse them of that notion. This tension within the Austrian School has not attenuated over time, however, and it provokes heated disputes about the tradition to this day, especially given the uncomfortable connection of Austrianism to more radical, rightist movements.

Debates within contemporary Austrian economics typically revolve around two issues: the relationship between Austrian theory and (right-) libertarianism and the openness of the approach to non-Austrian ideas. Schisms are frequent and acrimonious. A major fissure within the school opened in the late 1980s when Koch-financed GMU scholars, inspired by the rediscovery of Schütz and work by Ludwig Lachmann, took a "hermeneutic turn," which downplayed praxeology and even the role of subjectivism, concentrating instead on the "life-world" of human experience to explain complex social phenomena. Deploying the ideas of phenomenology, economic sociology, and Hayekian "spontaneous orders," "cultural

Austrians," represented by Boettke, Horwitz, Lavoie, and Richard Ebeling, proffered new challenges to the "economism" and "scientism" of neoclassical economics. They increased their emphasis on the role of institutions in shaping social and economic orders, offering an alternative economics approach to prevailing models built on a utility-maximizing, rational *homo economicus* living in a world of perfect information, competition, and efficient markets. "Institutions matter" became a rallying cry for this grouping.[14]

The response of Misesian and Rothbardian Austrians to the cultural turn was swift. In some ways, this fight reprised the school's oldest internecine feud: between Böhm's deductive, theoretical approach and Wieser's sociological, institutional method. Rothbard attacked "renegade Austrians" for their skepticism and moral relativism and for their importation of "foreign" ideas into the tradition. Joseph Salerno took the fight one step further in his attempt to distinguish Mises and Hayek. Differentiating the ideas of the two men was crucial for Misesians, since Mises's ideas had been occluded by Hayek's. "True" Austrians had to "undertake a courageous and thoroughgoing doctrinal dehomogenization" if they wished to preserve the tradition against corruption. Only by maintaining a consistent praxeological focus would Austrianism remain distinct. The Misesians laid down a gauntlet, with Rothbard, Salerno, and Hoppe taking the lead. In their often brutal criticisms of deviationist Austrians, they asserted that they spoke for the entire tradition.[15]

At the LvMI's First Annual Austrian Scholars Conference in 1996, tensions within the Austrian camp boiled over. Joseph Salerno rooted Austrianism in the "action axiom" associated with Mises's praxeology. Salerno called non-Misesians "Austro-punks"—individuals "harboring . . . an impious attitude toward the accomplishments of the past and, hence, toward all authority." Austro-punkism "views Austrian economics as a discipline in a state of constant and radical flux, devoid of any fundamental and constant principles but rife with a myriad of endlessly debated questions. Indeed, leading proponents of Austro-punkism proudly trumpet that an Austrian economist is one for whom there should eternally exist more questions than answers. To venture a more meaningful definition of Austrian economics than this represents for Austro-punks an attempt to intolerantly close off the perpetual and open-ended conversation that they uphold as the hallmark of scientific inquiry."[16] Salerno targeted the

Austro-punks for their irreverence toward Mises and Rothbard and their endless carping about hermeneutics. He blamed Austro-punkism on three things: the lack of graduate training in "Austrian economics," the pernicious influence of 1970s left-libertarianism, and the work of Ludwig Lachmann. Contemporary preferences for Hayekian concepts of knowledge and market process over Mises's deductive approach were also poisonous. The Misesians drew clear battle lines against the pernicious influence of Hayek, Lachmann, and "Masonomics."[17]

In this spat, the Austrians of the LvMI renewed their ongoing feud with the Kochs, GMU, and Cato. The Misesians rejected the latter's ecumenical approach and demanded ideological purity. They also rejected the separation of economics and politics; Austrian economics implied libertarianism—of a conservative stripe. The GMU Austrians were consistently anti-interventionist and pro-market not just in their scholarship but in their politics, and many of them identified ideologically with libertarianism. They nevertheless believed that one could keep one's scholarship and politics separate. Rejecting the "value-free" pretensions of the left-leaning libertarians—and the longer *wertfrei* tradition of the Austrian School—the LvMI bloc reached out to other marginal right-wing groups, such as states'-rights organizations, historical revisionists, and neo-Confederates. These overtures retraced Rothbard's own rightward drift since the 1970s. His idealization of "Middle America" and traditional Judeo-Christian values led him to reformulate his libertarianism in a reactionary direction. In his later years, he defended stronger property rights, the right to racial discrimination, and even the right of secession.[18]

The German-born Misesian Hans-Hermann Hoppe has carried this line of "paleolibertarian" thinking furthest. Hoppe studied under the philosopher Jürgen Habermas at the University of Frankfurt but came to reject his teacher's measured critical theory. Reading Rothbard converted him to the New Yorker's political views. Hoppe moved to the United States to work alongside Rothbard. He developed his own a priori theory of argumentation grounded in libertarianism and then elaborated these ideas with the help of historical examples. His most famous book, *Democracy: The God That Failed*, argued that, if one *must* have a state, then "Austrian" predemocratic monarchy was vastly superior to "American" democracy. He hoped to transcend these—and all—state forms by resorting to society's "natural order."[19] To achieve better social orders, communities must protect themselves from corruption through secession and the creation of "covenants" to protect the values of the group from foreign taints. This means that discriminatory practices and restricted freedom of movement are warranted—all in the name of property and individual rights. For him, the most advanced civilizations are all white, Christian, western European societies, meaning that those societies have the most to gain by discriminating to protect liberty. They also have the most to lose, Hoppe argues, if things continue along the same "democratic" path.

In a curious irony, Hoppe reimagined the Austrian legacy as one of authoritarianism, conservatism, antidemocracy, and anti-Enlightenment. He alternately dubbed *Democracy* "An Austrian View of the American Age," in which he celebrated the Habsburg "world of yesterday." For him, the successes of the fin-de-siècle age—and the Austrian School—were not the product of liberal predominance or cosmopolitan values but of the ancien régime and its restrictive social order. He decried the "decivilizational" process that Austria and the world experienced after World War I, identifying ways to supersede the fateful error of democratic governance. To create this revisionist Austrian image, he had to "correct" the soft spot that leading members of the tradition—including Hayek, Mises, and even early Rothbard—had for democracy and the minimal state. He has sustained this vision in the Property and Freedom Society (PFS), founded in 2006 as an alternative to Hayek's "right-wing social democrat" Mont Pèlerin Society. The PFS has become a gathering place for leading thinkers of the European New Right and the US Alt-Right, like the "Alt-Right" coiner Paul Gottfried, the secessionist Thomas DiLorenzo, Richard Spencer, the "race realist" Richard Lynn, and the white supremacist Jared Taylor.[20]

The reactions from the "Masonomics" Austrians to charges of punkism and to the rightist appropriation of Austrianism have been strident. Several scholars renounced their connections to the LvMI. Steven Horwitz dubbed Hoppe and Salerno's approach "a fascist fist in a libertarian glove." Boettke disputed Salerno's argument, calling the latter's philippics a form of "anti-intellectualism" and, quoting the estimable Israel Kirzner, "verbal terrorism."[21] These "Austro-punk" disputes precipitated the establishment of the *Quarterly Journal of Austrian Economics* when the "punks" took over *RAE.*

As we have seen, GMU Austrians have emphasized a broader, "value-free" research program. While they continue to honor Mises and (to a lesser extent) Rothbard, they admit a wider array of figures and ideas into the tradition. In light of the constant controversies involving the Rothbardian branch of the tradition, they have attempted to decouple Austrian theory from any particular political ideology or policy conclusions. As Horwitz has stated, Austrian economics is "*an approach to the study of human action and the social world, not a set of policy conclusions.*" For him, "there is nothing, repeat, nothing, that 'requires' that someone using Austrian ideas take one position or another on those issues. And no position so taken can rightly be described as 'the' Austrian view of the issue." Following his mentor, Kirzner, Horwitz draws a line between a set of economic propositions and ideological, political preferences, disavowing Austrian-associated conspiracy theories and opening up the possibility of Austrian-inspired, progressive policy prescriptions.[22]

What an Austrian progressivism would look like remains unclear, and it reinforces why value-free Austrian economics keeps finding itself in fights with its reactionary bedfellows. The fundamental connection to the Koch machine makes it exceedingly unlikely that these Austrians will be able to build bridges to progressives or the Left. Even Horwitz concedes the antiprogressive bent of classical liberalism, which includes his version of Austrianism:

> Unfortunately, classical liberalism never figured out how to respond to the development of socialism, and especially the state socialism of the Soviets and others in the early 20th century, in a way that maintained our progressive credentials. By default, we moved from the "left" to the "right," thrown in with the conservative opponents of the growing socialist wave. From the Old Right of the 1940s through the Reagan era, libertarianism's opposition to socialism, especially interferences in the market, led us to ally with the forces of reaction. But even with the demise of really-existing socialism, we have been unable to completely break free of that connection to the right, though things are better than they used to be.[23]

Horwitz admits that a full reckoning with a tradition that can be interpreted in a militantly antistatist, antidemocratic, white supremacist, and authoritarian direction is still needed. Many contemporary Austrian scholars confess that the paleolibertarians have gotten the better of the "Austrian" argument. This has led some to back away from the use of a corrupted descriptor. On January 1, 2010, the leading Austrian blog, *Austrian Economists*, changed its name to *Coordination Problem*. In the post announcing the name change, Peter Boettke conceded that they—the GMU crowd—had lost the battle for Austrian economics: "It has become evident to us that our efforts have been futile. Rather than resist the pure ideological identification, we are choosing to devote our efforts elsewhere. The name Austrian economics has been lost as a focal point for a tradition of economic scholarship, and is now a focal point for something else. We have to let it go."[24]

"We Are All Austrians Now"

In recent years, the Austrian School has typically remained just outside the popular imagination, even as it was a fixture in ideological debates among conservatives and libertarians. When it has reached the public's attention, it is in attenuated form: as the champions of liberty and opposers of the "road to serfdom" (as George H. W. Bush suggested) or as radical free marketeers and libertarians. In the latter case, the return of Austrianism occurs when the debates within the marginal libertarian community surface in mainstream political discourse. No one has produced more notoriety for Austrianism than Ron Paul.

The Ron Paul political campaigns in 1996 and 2008 shone light on the larger Austrian School, drawing the tradition out of the shadows. After the early 1990s heyday in the shadow of Communism's collapse, the Austrian School largely receded from view until 2008. Hayek's and Haberler's deaths received mentions in 1992 and 1995, respectively, but few journalists actively cited the school or its ideas in their columns. The fiftieth anniversary of *Road to Serfdom* in 1994 precipitated a handful of popular appreciations, as did reviews of a few Hayek biographies, but most commentary appeared in conservative journals. Only one columnist, Michael Prowse at the *Financial Times*, regularly informed people about the Austrian School. Particular politicians—Massachusetts Governor Bill Weld, Australian Prime Minister John Howard, Ron Paul—were linked at one time or another to the school, but these were mere passing references.

It was the 2012 presidential campaign that announced the Austrian School's return. It started with Ron Paul, but it involved the entire Tea Party phenomenon. On the night of January 3, 2012, US Representative Ron Paul stood before a raucous crowd in Ankeny, Iowa, with his wife at his side and his son Rand behind him. The audience had gathered to celebrate Paul's strong showing in the first contest of the 2012 presidential race, the Iowa caucus. The Texan finished third in the voting, with 21 percent, behind Mitt Romney and Rick Santorum. Because of the arcane rules of the caucus, Paul emerged the winner of the most delegates. In his celebratory speech, Paul made a curious comment. He criticized the "liberal economics" of Democrats and Republicans and their Keynesian prescriptions. The Iowa results left him optimistic that the Keynesian nightmare was over. He exulted, "I am waiting for the day when we can say we are all Austrians now."[25]

For anyone familiar with Paul's brand of libertarian politics, this statement would have been familiar. After reading *Road to Serfdom* as a medical student, Paul turned from Hayek to Mises for a theoretical defense of individual liberty, free markets, and sound money against the scourges of interventionism and socialism. Inspired by the works of Rothbard and Hans Sennholz, Paul developed an ideology fundamentally opposed to government intervention in the economy and committed to a massive reduction in the size of the state. Alongside Rothbard and Lew Rockwell, Paul's former chief of staff, the Texas congressman had been involved with the Auburn, Alabama–based LvMI since its 1982 establishment.[26]

Paul's success briefly shifted attention away from the more troubling elements of his worldview, typified by his connections to the LvMI. In the fortnight leading up to the caucus, Paul faced obloquy for a series of racist, white supremacist, antisemitic, and homophobic articles that appeared in his 1980s and 1990s newsletters, *Ron Paul's Freedom Report, Ron Paul Political Report*, and *Ron Paul Survival Report*. The comments found in those pages fit well with Rothbard, Rockwell, and Hoppe's conservative worldview. Among other salacious claims, the newsletters asserted that black people were lazy, addicted to welfare, and predisposed to criminality; a race war in US cities was imminent; Martin Luther King Jr. seduced underage girls and boys and abused his paramours; Jewish bankers conspired to plot the demise of the US economy; Israel was an "aggressive, national socialist state"; AIDS was a federal-gay cover-up. The newsletters also defended antigovernment militias and the idea of secession. These newsletters first surfaced in 1996 during a congressional run and again during Paul's 2008 presidential campaign, yet Paul never issued a recantation that took responsibility for the hateful comments published under his name (if not necessarily with his express approval). He also failed to renounce his connections to neo-Confederate scholars like Thomas Woods Jr. or Thomas DiLorenzo or his admiration for the Ku Klux Klan's David Duke. He also refused to return a campaign donation he received from the president of Stormfront, a leading neo-Nazi website. He also stood by his 2008 speech to the John Birch Society at the extremist group's fiftieth-anniversary celebration. Instead Paul preferred to lash out at the media. Austrians like Boettke and Horwitz were forced to reiterate their opposition to his brand of libertarianism.[27]

The Paul phenomenon and the rise of the Tea Party reflected the changed conditions wrought by the Great Recession. The economic downturn also produced newfound interest in Austrian economics. The Tea Party movement, with its espousal of free-market ideology and fiscal conservatism, helped avowedly pro-Austrian politicians like Justin Amash, Ted Cruz, Rick Perry, and Paul Ryan in their campaigns. Name checks of Hayek (and occasionally Mises) littered the media coverage on these men. It was in this context that Glenn Beck propelled *Road to Serfdom* to the best-seller list with his hour-long encomium on Fox News. Ron Paul's 2012 presidential run was the culmination of this revival. Even after his departure from the presidential race in June, the selection of Wisconsin representative and self-proclaimed Hayek devotee Paul Ryan as Mitt Romney's running mate suggested it was "prime time" for the Austrians. Articles on Austrian economics appeared in news outlets. Rebuttals from the libertarian community ensued. Many supporters of contemporary Austrianism—Peter Boettke, Bruce Caldwell, Bryan Caplan, Steven Horwitz, George Selgin—fielded interview requests and wrote thought pieces, weighing in on the school's new relevance.[28]

The rise of popular "Austrianism" signaled a rightward political shift in the United States, and it forced liberals, progressives, and radicals to confront them. In the final works of the distinguished career of the European historian Tony Judt, he trained his eye on interwar Austria in an effort to "think the twentieth century." In the works of the Austrians Karl Popper,

Mises, Schumpeter, and Hayek, Judt glimpsed the origins of our age, with its fixations on individual liberty as the supreme human value and free markets as the guarantor of freedom. Judt deplored these ideological developments, arguing that the Austrians learned false lessons from their historical experiences: "Ironically, the Austrian experience . . . has been elevated to the status of economic theory. . . . Relieved of its Austrian historical context and, indeed, even of the very historical reference, this set of assumptions—imported to the U.S. in the suitcases of a handful of disabused Viennese intellectuals—has come to inform not just the Chicago school of economics but all significant public conversation over policy choices in the contemporary United States."[29] The Austrian argument that planning necessarily leads to dictatorship, Judt alleged, paved the way for a reactionary backlash: the destruction of (social) democracy and the rise of neoliberalism; the ascension of Margaret Thatcher and Ronald Reagan; the economic successes of Milton Friedman's libertarian Chicago School; and the "Washington Consensus" at the World Bank, International Monetary Fund, and US Treasury, which advocated deregulation, privatization of state industries, trade liberalization, and other market-fundamentalist positions. Judt called this ideological turn the "revenge of the Austrians."[30]

Similarly, the political theorist Corey Robin saw fin-de-siècle Viennese modernism and Nietzschean cultural criticism in the Austrians' elitist understanding of subjectivity and entrepreneurship. He linked Viennese culture to the reactionary tendencies of the Austrian School and its descendants, the free-market Right. For Robin, this Nietzschean modernism helps explain why Hayek was *the* theoretician of contemporary reaction. Naturally the pushback against these positions has been fierce from scholars sympathetic to the school, especially from those who have struggled to defend Austrianism's progressive bona fides. As problematic as some of Judt's and Robin's respective assertions are, their percipient diagnosis of problems with the Austrian School have yet to be adequately refuted.[31]

What Is Certain Is That I Myself Am Not a Hayekian

The uncomfortable relationship between Austrian economics and reactionary conservatism is not only applicable to US Austrianism.[32] Attempts to return Austrian ideas to European shores have produced disturbing results. The transnational emergence of the "New Right" demonstrates an alarming degree of interaction between rightists and "Austrian" supporters of free markets and economic liberty. In Austria and Germany, self-proclaimed Hayekians have engaged in internecine conflicts about the meaning of the Austrian tradition.

After the Cold War, two new institutions to spread Austrian ideas appeared in Vienna: the Friedrich Hayek Institut and the Austrian Economics Center (AEC). Rather than native projects, they receive much of their initial funding from the Koch Foundation and Atlas Network. These Austrian think tanks advocate market solutions to social problems, publish policy papers, and host conferences, seeking to "bring the ideas and the approach of the Austrian School of Economics back into the discussion." One of their primary vehicles is the Free Market Road Show, a traveling exhibit dedicated to spreading the ideas of liberty across Europe.[33]

Despite liberal protestations, leading members of these think tanks are affiliated with the Freedom Party of Austria (FPÖ), the populist radical Right party, whose program evinces Euro-skeptic, anti-immigrant, and ethnonationalist tendencies. The FPÖ is the former party of Jörg Haider and a seedbed of incipient neo-Nazism. Nevertheless, Barbara Kolm, director of the Hayek Institut, has served as an economic adviser for FPÖ head Hans-Christian Strache, running for the position of president of the Accounting Office in 2016. She has inveighed against the European Union and its banking policies, defended the Tea Party, and attacked Barack Obama for his expansion of social protections, all in the name of Hayek and Austrianism. While scholars of the Austrian School like the University of Vienna emeritus professor Erich Streissler look askance, the alliance persists. Kolm continues to shape the FPÖ's liberal, pro-market economic policies—deregulation, privatization, decreased corporate and income taxes, decreased social services—in an effort to attract wealthy voters to the party's otherwise populist platform. Despite the party's populist reputation, Kolm is not really out of place within the FPÖ. Historically the party has drawn heavily from the traditional *Bildungs-* and *Großbürgertum*—"lawyers, doctors, and also hoteliers of a market liberal persuasion." After the 2017 elections, Kolm spoke positively of the most conservative governing coalition of the post–World War II Austrian state, between a rebranded ethnonationalist People's Party (ÖVP) under the thirty-one-year-old

Chancellor Sebastian Kurz and Strache's FPÖ. Kurz has been described as "Richard Spencer lite," which hardly inspires confidence that the rebirth of Austrianism in Austria will be felicitous.[34]

Similar connections between the Friedrich von Hayek Gesellschaft and the Alternativ für Deutschland (AfD) have haunted liberals in Germany. The AfD emerged as a force in 2013, offering a Euro-skeptic and antistatist critique of the major German political parties. It emulated the success of the Tea Party, the United Kingdom Independence Party (UKIP), France's Front National, and Austria's FPÖ in its radical populism. The refugee "crisis" of 2014–16—which drew five million people to Europe, of whom nearly two million sought asylum in Germany—increased the popularity of the AfD's ethnonationalist, xenophobic, and anti-Muslim message.

As the AfD moved further right in 2015, members of the Hayek Gesellschaft, led by Karen Horn, expressed consternation with liberals who supported the reactionary tendencies of the AfD. Addressing the "right flank of liberals" in the *Frankfurter Allgemeine Zeitung,* Horn admonished, "what was growing on the right fringe does not deserve the name of liberalism." Although she did not name names, Horn alluded to tensions within the "Austrian" society. Founded in 1998, it was conceived as a big-tent convocation of liberals. It awarded Hayek prizes and fellowships, educated young people, and convened small seminars. Horn and her allies witnessed with dismay growing support for "value conservative" and illiberal attitudes, seeing the Hayek Gesellschaft become a "hotbed of the AfD." In her writings, Horn wanted to clarify the meaning of liberalism and to distinguish true and vulgar liberals from one another.[35]

Horn ignited a firestorm. Twenty-six individuals signed an open letter, chastising her and demanding her resignation. Disgruntled members took to the pages of New Right websites and magazines to accuse her of leftist sympathies. Ultimately, Horn and sixty fellow members, including many academics, finance experts, and representatives from the liberal Freie Demokratische Partei (FDP), left the 350-person society. The Hayek Society now has about 250 members. Among them are several prominent AfD figures, including the party's 2017 candidate for chancellor, Alice Weidel. Several of the departing members went on to found a new society, the Netzwerk für Ordnungsökonomik und Sozialphilosophie (NOUS), dedicated to "interdisciplinary research" about "social order and liberty."

Quotations from Hayek, Mises, and Popper litter the pages of NOUS's website, as the network tries to wrest the Austrian mantle from its opponents. Orienting itself more toward German ordoliberalism, NOUS has promised a more cosmopolitan and tolerant version of Western liberalism. Like the GMU Austrians, the German rebrand of Austrian liberalism has given up explicit use of the "Austrian" descriptor. It appears that the dream of Hayek, Morgenstern, and the postwar Austrians of re-creating their intellectual and cultural school in central Europe has been extinguished.[36]

Despite the animosity between the various factions in Europe and the United States, contemporary ideas of the Austrian School operate within the same larger ideological space, reminding us that the far Right did not emerge in opposition to prevailing neoliberal tendencies but from within. This generation of Austrian-inspired scholars is grappling with the same tensions in the tradition that go back to the school's inception. For example, the AEC, Hayek Institut, Hayek Gesellschaft, and NOUS all belong to the Atlas Network of think tanks and organizations. The struggle between these groups remains agonistic, a dialectical one between forces hoping for resolution. The conflict with socialists, progressives, and US-style liberals, however, remains existential. As Horn noted, left liberals are "false friends"; she rejected common cause with the left in toto. The quest for a progressive Austrianism remains unfulfilled.[37]

Marginal Revolutionaries

In the monumental *History of Economic Analysis*, Joseph Schumpeter offered a sociological description of intellectual schools that encapsulates the subject of this book:

> We must never forget that genuine schools are sociological realities—living beings. They have their structures—relations between leaders and followers—their flags, their battle cries, their moods, their all-too-human interests. Their antagonisms come within the general sociology of group antagonisms and of party warfare. Victory and conquest, defeat and loss of ground, are in themselves values for such schools and part of their very existence. They will try to appropriate labels that are considered

> honorific . . . and to affix derogatory labels . . . to the work
> of the enemy. These labels may mean little or nothing in
> themselves, but they acquire a life of their own and in turn
> keep controversy alive. All this gives scope to personal vanities,
> interests, and propensities to fight that may, as they do in
> national and international politics, count for more than any real
> issues—in fact to the point of obliterating the real issues.[38]

Schumpeter knew of what he spoke. Antagonisms, party warfare, and controversy; vanity, interests, and propensities to fight—these elements characterize the "all-too-human" members of the Austrian School. That the school survives today is a testament to the enduring resonance of their answers to "real issues" and the power and seductiveness of the battle cries.

The history of the Austrian School is full of detours and surprises. It is replete with ironies, none greater than the fact that we still talk about it eighty years after the end of the Viennese chapter of the story. In theory and praxis, the school has taught us about the importance of institutions and traditions, which take on lives of their own that even their founders cannot anticipate. In spite of all the accusations and acrimony, divergences and deviations, ruptures and recriminations, Austrian-inspired institutions persist, and they have shaped many of today's economic, political, and ideological realities. This has been their lasting revolution.

The Austrians were revolutionaries in other ways too. From their earliest writings, the members of the Austrian School believed they were taking part in a world-historical endeavor, one that would transform not only economics but also human activity and social policy. Carl Menger proclaimed that a more precise economic science was needed to meet the urgent needs of society: "Never was there an age that placed economic interests higher than does our own. Never was the need of a scientific foundation for economic affairs felt more generally or more acutely." Menger and his students brought this attitude to their scholarship and their social functions as government officials, economic advisers, liberal journalists, and businesspeople. Since the school's inception, the Austrians have been remarkable intellectual entrepreneurs and institution builders. From the Gesellschaft Österreichischer Volkswirte to the Institut für

Konjunkturforschung, Geist-Kreis to Mises-Kreis, Mont Pèlerin to Bellagio, NYU to GMU, Cato to LvMI, Austrians have participated in dozens
of salons, societies, centers, circles, and institutes. Their revolution has
therefore been threefold: institutional, through their circles, schools, and
collectives; intellectual, in the area of subjectivism, individualism, and
marginal utility; and ideological, in their espousal of a reimagined liberalism, whether neoliberal or libertarian.[39]

From the outset, the Austrians faced questions not just about method
but about ideology and values. They were accused by German economists
and socialists of opposing democratic reform and defending free-market
capitalism unapologetically. Böhm rejected the notion that the Austrians
"assume an attitude hostile or even indifferent to social and political reforms." He stated that such attitudes were "foreign and repulsive" to his
brethren, and laissez-faire attitudes to social conditions were "totally
wrong." Despite these protestations, Austrian writings and policy initiatives
have invariably followed liberal prescriptions. This battle over the relationship between values and science, between conservatism and progressivism,
between economic and social theory continues unabated, pitting self-
proclaimed Austrians against those to their left—and against one another.
It plagued Schumpeter and Mises as economic advisers, the "nonconserva-
tive" Hayek as a political theorist and intellectual impresario, and Machlup,
Haberler, and Morgenstern as policy wonks. It haunts the battles between
GMU and LvMI scholars in the United States and members of the various
Hayek societies in Europe.[40]

The Austrian School has had an immense impact on economics and
politics yet has been poorly understood by supporters and detractors alike.
We have examined the school's ideas and activities across a century and a
half and on both sides of the Atlantic in an effort to gain greater clarity
about the tradition. In pursuing the various iterations of the school from
its beginnings, we have espied the key insight of the collective: "nobody
can be a great economist who is only an economist." For Hayek and the
others, this idea meant more than a dedication to intellectual work. It also
meant blending ideological values, scientific work, and political activism
in a heady mélange. As Marxian socialism's doppelgänger, a final irony
appears: the Austrian School has embodied Marx's dictum that philosophers
have only interpreted the world, but the point is to change it.[41]

The Austrian revolution continues today. Whether in university halls or libertarian think tank offices, WTO boardrooms or Silicon Valley confabs, the Austrian School has not only transformed economics and social theory but changed our world. The school's effects are profound and pervasive, and its history permits us to think the present age. The Austrian School story also presses us to reconsider the interrelation of ideas, institutions, and power. By exploring this multifaceted collective, we gain a greater understanding of the issues that face the contemporary world and how we might respond to the problems that the Austrians helped diagnose—and create.

ABBREVIATIONS

AEI	American Enterprise Institute
AEN	*Austrian Economics Newsletter*
AER	*American Economic Review*
AfSuS	*Archiv für Sozialwissenschaft und Sozialpolitik*
AHR	*American History Review*
AJES	*American Journal of Economics and Sociology*
CMP	Carl Menger Papers
EJ	*Economic Journal*
FHP	Friedrich Hayek Papers
FKP	Felix Kaufmann Papers
FMP	Fritz Machlup Papers
GHP	Gottfried Haberler Papers
HOPE	*History of Political Economy*
IfK	*Monatsberichte des österreichischen Institut für Konjunkturforschung*
Jahrbuch	*Jahrbuch der Gesellschaft Österreichischer Volkswirte*
JfNuS	*Jahrbücher für Nationalökonomie und Statistik*
JHET	*Journal of the History of Economic Thought*
JPE	*Journal of Political Economy*
LvMI	Ludwig von Mises Institute
LvMP	Ludwig von Mises Papers
MIH	*Modern Intellectual History*
MPS	Mont Pèlerin Society Papers
NFP	*Neue Freie Presse*
NYT	*New York Times*
OMP	Oskar Morgenstern Papers
QJAE	*Quarterly Journal of Austrian Economics*

QJE	*Quarterly Journal of Economics*
RAC	Rockefeller Archive Center
RAE	*Review of Austrian Economics*
RHETM	*Research in the History of Economic Thought and Methodology*
Schmoller	*Jahrbuch für Gesetzgebung, Verwaltung, und Volkswirtschaft im Deutschen Reich*
TNR	*The New Republic*
ZfN	*Zeitschrift für Nationalökonomie*
Zeitschrift	*Zeitschrift für Volkswirtschaft, Socialpolitik und Verwaltung*

NOTES

Introduction

1. AllThingsBeck, "Road to Serfdom." See also Schuessler, "Hayek."

2. See EconStories, "Fear the Boom"; Wapshott, *Keynes Hayek*; "Ron Paul Newsletters"; Davidson, "Primetime."

3. Among the dozens of pieces, these are the most prominent: Yglesias, "Austrian Economics"; Davidson, "Primetime"; Barro, "Hayek and Mises." For the libertarian response, see Richman, "Austrian Economics"; Bartlett, "Ryan's Guru." See also the *Cato Unbound* issue, "Theory and Practice." On the radicalism of Austrian libertarianism, see Bessner, "Rothbard," 442–44.

4. Hayek, "Dilemma," 463.

5. See Rodgers, *Atlantic Crossings*; Nolan, *Transatlantic Century*. On shifting temporal and spatial frames, see Pomeranz, "Histories for a Less National Age."

6. See Schulak and Unterköfler, *Austrian School*; Vaughn, *Austrian Economics*; Boettke, "History." On the interwar era, see Klausinger, "Academic Anti-Semitism"; Klausinger, "Policy Advice"; Klausinger, "From Mises to Morgenstern"; Leonard, "Collapse"; Dekker, *Viennese Students*. Some of the significant intellectual biographies are Caldwell, *Hayek's Challenge*; Ebenstein, *Hayek's Journey*; Hülsmann, *Mises*; McCraw, *Prophet*; Hacohen, *Popper*. Klausinger and Leonard take the sociological and historical realities of a school seriously.

7. ECAEF, "Generations."

8. See Hayek, "Economic Thought," 461. See also Boettke, "Austrian School"; Schulak and Unterköfler, *Austrian School*.

9. On politics in a new key, see Schorske, *Fin-de-Siècle Vienna*.

10. Judt, *Thinking*, 30; Machlup, "Austrian Economics," 38–43; Boettke, "Austrian School." On Austrianism and laissez-faire, see Wieser, "Austrian School," 120–21; Wile, "Horwitz."

11. Judt, *Ill Fares*, 98. For a sampling of these narratives, see Klein, *Shock Doctrine*; Slobodian, *Globalists*; Burgin, *Great Persuasion*; Stedman Jones, *Masters*; Nash, *Conservative Intellectual*; Doherty, *Radicals*.

12. Voltaire's famous quip goes, "This body which called itself and which still calls itself the Holy Roman Empire was in no way holy, nor Roman, nor an empire."

13. On reflexive sociology of knowledge, see Latour, *Reassembling*, 7; Bourdieu and Wacquant, *Invitation*, 244; Collins, *Sociology*, 13; Bourdieu, "Field." On groupism and identification, see Brubaker, *Ethnicity*.

14. On thought collectives, see L. Fleck, *Genesis*, 9, 22; Mirowski and Plehwe, *Mont Pèlerin*; Mirowski, *Crisis*. On epistemic communities, see *International Organization* 46, no. 1 (1992); Cross, "Rethinking." On schools, see Collins, *Sociology*, 64–69; L. Harvey, "Schools."

15. Streissler, "Intellectual," 197. See also Dekker, *Viennese Students*; Dekker, "Left Luggage," 117. On higher education reform, see Stadler, *650 Jahre*. On the Austrian bureaucracy, see Deak, *Forging*. On Ringstrasse Vienna, see Schorske, *Fin-de-Siècle Vienna*, 24–114.

16. See Hutchison, *Review*; Howey, *Marginal Utility*; Kauder, *Marginal Utility*; Blaug, *Economic Theory*, 277–309.

17. Timms, *Culture*, 7–10; Timms, "Cultural Parameters." See also Kauder, "Austro-Marxism." On interaction rituals, see Collins, *Sociology*, 20–29.

18. C. Fleck, *Transatlantische*. On the Rockefeller Foundation, see Parmar, *Foundations*.

19. Klausinger, "In the Wilderness." See also Craver, "Emigration"; Krohn, "Emigration"; Wasserman, "Beyond Hayek."

20. On neoliberalism, see Foucault, *Birth*, 78–87; Walpen, *Die offenen Feinde*; Denord, *Néo-libéralisme*; D. Harvey, *Neoliberalism*; Burgin, *Great Persuasion*; Stedman Jones, *Masters*; Peck, *Constructions*. On conservative foundations and think tanks, see Mayer, *Dark Money*; Stahl, *Right Moves*. On conservative internationalism, see Duranti, *Conservative Human Rights*; Mazower, *Governing*; Moyn, *Christian Human Rights*.

21. Haas, "Introduction," 3. Haas defines epistemic communities as "network[s] of professionals with recognized expertise and competence in a particular domain and an authoritative claim to policy-relevant knowledge within that domain." Epistemic communities typically have a two-tiered structure, involving academics and specialists at one level and journalists, think tank members, and governmental officials at the other. On the state-neoliberal linkage, see Slobodian, *Globalists*. On trade liberalization and monetary reform, see Bair, "Taking Aim." On game theory and neoliberal thought, see Amadae, *Rationalizing*; Amadae, *Prisoners*.

22. Josef Herbert Furth to Fritz Machlup, June 27, 1979, Box 39, FMP. On invention, see Hobsbawm and Ranger, *Invention*.

23. See Judt, *Thinking*, 30; Judt, *Ill Fares*, 98.

1. The Prehistory and Early Years of the Austrian School

1. "Austrian Economics, George Mason University," Box 26, FHP. Boettke, in "Austrian School," writes, "The Austrian school of economics was founded in 1871 with the publication of Carl Menger's *Principles of Economics*."

2. "Drei neue Handbücher," 343. All translations are mine unless otherwise noted.

3. C. Menger, *Principles*, 45. See also Kauder, "Aus Mengers nachgelassenen Papieren"; Caldwell, *Hayek's Challenge*, 35–38.

4. Zweig, *World*. On early marginal utility theory, see Hutchison, *Economic Doctrines*; Howey, *Marginal Utility*; Kauder, *Marginal Utility*; Blaug, *Economic Theory*.

5. Schumacher and Scheall, "Menger," 1–9.

6. Ibid., 11–13. See also Kauder, "Aus Mengers nachgelassenen Papieren."

7. Zweig, *World*, 21–22. On Jews in late imperial Austria, see Beller, *Vienna*, part 1.

8. On the Ringstrasse, see Schorske, *Vienna*, ch. 2; Schorske, *Thinking*, ch. 10; Nierhaus, *Der Ring*.

9. Schnitzler, *Anatol*, 1102; Kraus, *Literatur*. On Viennese coffeehouse culture, see Segel, *Vienna Coffeehouse Wits*; Ashby, Gronberg, and Shaw-Miller, *Viennese Café*. The most famous works on fin-de-siècle Vienna remain Schorske, *Vienna*; and Janik and Toulmin, *Wittgenstein's Vienna*.

10. See Schorske, *Vienna*. For a response to Schorske's image of the city, see Beller, *Rethinking*.

11. On the university, see Stadler, *650 Jahre*. On Exner, see ibid., 1:77–131, 261–91, 2:183–89; Coen, *Vienna*, 1–31.

12. See Janik and Toulmin, *Wittgenstein's Vienna*; Waugh, *Wittgenstein*. See also Hayek, *Hayek on Hayek*, 51–53.

13. Caldwell, *Hayek's Challenge*, 23–27, 30–32. See also Box 1, CMP.

14. C. Menger, *Principles*, 45–47. Caldwell, in *Hayek's Challenge*, 20–23, calls this approach "compositive."

15. C. Menger, *Principles*, 52.

16. Ibid., 56.

17. Ibid., 67–74.

18. Ibid., 132. Emil Kauder controversially traces Menger's ideas all the way back to Aristotle. See Kauder, *Marginal Utility*.

19. Dingwall and Hoselitz, "Translator's Preface," 38–39. See Kauder, *Marginal Utility*, 76–77; Streissler, "Marginalist."

20. Schumacher and Scheall, "Menger," 18–24; Stadler, *650 Jahre*, 1:77–131, 261–91, 2:183–89.

21. Howey, *Marginal Utility*, 210–14. There is debate on whether the "marginal utility revolution" was a revolution. For opposing interpretations, see Blaug, *Economic Theory*, ch. 8; Mirowski, *Heat*, 195–97.

22. Smith, *Wealth*, bk. 1, ch. 5; Mill, *Principles*, bk. 3, ch. 1, sec. 2.

23. Roscher, *Grundriss*, iv–vi. On the German school, see Caldwell, *Hayek's Challenge*, 42–46; Tribe, *Strategies*, 66–94. On normal science, see Kuhn, *Structure*, chs. 2–4.

24. Howey, *Marginal Utility*, 13, 25–32, 211–12. Again, Kauder and many American Austrians like Murray Rothbard rejected this narrative, arguing that the marginal tradition ran parallel to the "mistaken" views of the classicists and had a lineage dating back to the Greeks. This remains a minority interpretation.

25. This is called the Law of Diminishing Marginal Utility, or Gossen's First Law.

26. Howey, *Marginal Utility*, 76–92, 110–17.

27. On professionalization, see Backhouse, *Ordinary Business*, ch. 8. On the relationship between economics and national institutions, see Fourcade, *Economists*. See also Hobsbawm, *Age of Capital*.

28. Seager, "Berlin and Vienna," 253–54.

29. Quoted in Schumacher and Scheall, "Menger," 18.

30. Menger had difficulties with Stein, too: see ibid., 18–19. On American-German connections, see Schäfer, *Progressives*; Rodgers, *Atlantic Crossings*, 85–89, 103–5; Levine, "Baltimore Teaches."

31. Schumpeter, *History*, 782–83.

32. On the *Methodenstreit*, see ibid., 775–83; Caldwell, *Hayek's Challenge*, 64–82; Louzek, "Battle"; Backhaus, "Methodenstreit."

33. C. Menger, *Principles*, 49.

34. "Drei neue Handbücher," 345; Caldwell, *Hayek's Challenge*, 36–37.

35. C. Menger, *Investigations*, 27.

36. Ibid., 26.

37. Ibid., 35–46.

38. Ibid., 178–92 (quote on 189).

39. Caldwell, *Hayek's Challenge*, 69; Schulak and Unterköfler, *Austrian School*, 22.

40. Feichtinger, "Verletzte Autonomie," 269–76. See also Dekker, *Viennese Students*, ch. 1, on Max Menger.

41. Feichtinger, "Verletzte Autonomie," 276–81. See also Feichtinger, *Projekt*.

42. Schmoller, "Methodologie," 975–76, 987. See also Schulak and Unterköfler, *Austrian School*, 24–25.

43. C. Menger, *Irrthümer*, 86–87.

44. Quoted in Caldwell, *Hayek's Challenge*, 76.

45. Dietzel, "Beitrag." See also Schulak and Unterköfler, *Austrian School*, 25.

46. Three works from the year—Sax, *Wesen*; Mataja, *Unternehmergewinn*; and Gross, *Die Lehre*—reference *Investigations*, yet they were published before the climax of the *Methodenstreit*.

47. Streissler, "Intellectual," 197–99; Dekker, *Viennese Students*, 37. On Pernerstorfer, see McGrath, *Dionysian Art*.

48. Howey, *Marginal Utility*, 111. On Böhm, see Yagi, "First Interest Theory"; Hennings, *Austrian Theory*. On Wieser, see Hayek, "Friedrich von Wieser." Unfortunately, almost none of this work survives. These works probably showed little Mengerian or marginalist influence.

49. See Böhm, *Rechte*.

50. *Katalog*.

51. See Schulak and Unterköfler, *Austrian School*, 49–63.

52. Hayek, "Carl Menger," 419–20. See also Seager, "Berlin and Vienna."

53. Böhm, *Capital*, 421.

54. Böhm, *Kapital*, ii.

55. Ibid., i–vi, 260–63, 428. See also Yagi, "First Interest Theory"; Endres and Harper, "Menger," 359–65. Böhm believed that Menger's work had reached its fullest development, yet it still produced more questions than answers. Menger did not take kindly to this criticism. In their correspondence and Menger's later writings, he disputed Böhm's verdict and then proffered his own capital theory in "Zur Theorie des Kapitals."

56. Wieser, *Über den Ursprung*, 127. See also Hayek, "Freiherr Friedrich von Wieser," 518.

57. R.F., review of *Geschichte*, 77.

58. See Philippovich, *Aufgabe*; Conrad, *Grundriss*; Neumann, *Grundlagen*.

59. Bonar, "Austrian Economists," 24–26.

60. Böhm, *Capital*, 367–91, 422–26.

61. Wieser, *Über den Ursprung*, 211–14. For a different interpretation of Wieser's socialist views, see Bockman, *Markets*, 23–33.

62. A. Menger, *Recht*.

63. Sax, *Grundlegung*, 1–3, 249–55, 509–11.

64. Böhm, "Austrian Economists," 361, 376–78. Italics his.

65. Wieser, "Austrian School."

66. Bonar, "Austrian Economists"; Loria, "Scuola Austriaca"; Böhm, "Austrian Economists"; Wieser, "Austrian School."

67. Schmoller, review of *Wirtschaftsformen*.

68. C. Menger, "Zur Theories," 136, 182–83. See Endres and Harper, "Menger."

69. Baird, "Carey"; A. Cohen, "Mythology"; Hennings, *Austrian Theory*, 12.

70. Hennings, *Austrian Theory*, 20.

71. Böhm, *Positive Theory*, 253–59, 296 (quotes on 296).

72. Ibid., 367. On Austrian School ideas of socialism, see Bockman, *Markets*, 23–33.

73. Wieser, *Natural Value*, 72–73.

74. Ibid., 60–64.

75. See Fuks and Kohlbauer, *Die Liebens*.

76. Auspitz and Lieben, *Untersuchungen*, ix–xiii.

77. Pareto, "La Teoria"; Fisher, "Investigations," 3–4; Schumpeter, *History*, 811, 816. Mises made a similar assessment, yet he excluded Auspitz and Lieven from the Austrian School. See Mises, "Richard Lieben."

78. See Hayek, "Carl Menger," 408–9; Schulak and Unterköfler, *Austrian School*, 53–58.

79. On schools, see Collins, *Sociology*, 64–73. On Freud and Mach, respectively, see Danto, *Free Clinics*; Stadler, *Vom Positivismus*.

80. Böhm, "Unsere Aufgabe," 3, 4.

81. *Jahrbuch*, 162, 166; *Zeitschrift* 1 (1892): 474.

82. Böhm, "Unsere Aufgabe," 10; *Zeitschrift* I (1892): 171–81, 270–87, 472–79. On the social question, see Case, "Social Question."

83. Streissler, "Intellectual," 197.

84. Ibid., 239, 254–60.

85. Böhm, "Austrian Economists," 361.

2. The Golden Age

1. Bukharin, *Economic Theory*, 7, 9.

2. On Bukharin in Vienna, see S. Cohen, *Bukharin*, 13–22. On Vienna before the Great War, see Morton, *Nervous Splendor*; Walker, "1913."

3. On pre–World War I Vienna, see Schorske, *Vienna*; Janik and Toulmin, *Wittgenstein's Vienna*; Johnston, *Austrian Mind*; Anderson, *Utopian Feminism*; Walker, "1913"; Hamann, *Hitler's Vienna*.

4. Hayek, "Economic Thought," 461.

5. Hennings, *Austrian Theory*, 12–15.

6. *Stenographische Protokolle*, iii, 197–223, 267–71. On the Taussig controversy, see Mises, *Theory*, 204. On Austrian currency policy, see Ebeling, *Political Economy*, 65–68. For Menger's verdict, see C. Menger, *Das Goldagio*, 1.

7. *Die direkte Personalsteuern*, 1–7. On the Austrian bureaucracy, see Deak, *Forging*.

8. Fürth, *Die Einkommensteuer*; *Die direkten Personalsteuern*, ii, 11–14.

9. On the housing crisis, see Feldbauer, *Stadtswachstum*; John and Lichtblau, *Schmelztiegel*. On populist politics, see McGrath, *Dionysian Art*; Schorske, *Vienna*; Boyer, *Political Radicalism*.

10. On the Second International, see Braunthal, *International*.

11. Bonnell, "Marx." See Sweezy, introduction to *Karl Marx*, vi–x. The English translation of the title misrepresents Böhm's work, implying that it was an obituary for Marxist socialism rather than an assessment of Marx's complete system.

12. Böhm, *Karl Marx*, 21, 66–68.

13. Ibid., 87.

14. Bernstein, *Evolutionary Socialism*, 50–53.

15. Luxemburg, *Sozialreform*, 39. See also Lenin, "Marxismus."

16. On the Austrian School–Austro-Marxist interactions, see Chaloupek, "Österreichische Schule." See also Kauder, "Austro-Marxism."

17. Adler and Hilferding, "Vorwort," v–vi. On Austro-Marxism, see Leser, *Reformismus*; Glaser, *Austromarxismus*; Bottomore and Goode, *Austro-Marxism*. See also Uebel, *Rediscovering*.

18. Hilferding, "Criticism," 121–23, 132–33, 160–61.

19. Ibid., 196.

20. See Proctor, *Value-Free*, 85–98; Glaeser, *Werturteilsstreit*; Caldwell, *Hayek's Challenge*, 83–99. On the role of values in the Austrian School, see Dekker, *Viennese Students*.

21. Weber, "Objectivity," 50–51.

22. Ibid., 54, 72–85.

23. Philippovich, "Wesen," 329–30, 357–70.

24. *Verhandlungen*, 563, 569–70, 582.

25. Ibid., 615.

26. Ibid.

27. Kauder, "Austro-Marxism," 399.

28. Scott, "Translator's Preface," vi–vii; Böhm, "*Positive*"; Böhm, *Geschichte*.

29. Schulak and Unterköfler, *Austrian School*, 53–62, 127–30.

30. "Appendix"; Plener, "Vierzig Jahre," 123–24; "Appendix II."

31. Schorske, *Fin-de-Siècle Vienna*, xxv–xxvii, 5–10, 116–20.

32. Wieser, "Der Geldwert," 43. This was his introductory lecture at the University of Vienna.

33. Mises, "Zur Frage." See also Hülsmann, *Mises*, 67–74.

34. Weiss, "Moderne Tendenz."

35. Amonn, "Gutsbegriff," 403–63.

36. On Schumpeter's early life, see McCraw, *Prophet*, 10–34.

37. Schumpeter, "Über die mathematische Methode."

38. Schumpeter, *Das Wesen*, vi–viii.

39. Ibid.

40. McCraw, *Prophet*, 62–77.

41. Schumpeter, *Die Theorie*, 1–28.

42. Schumpeter, *Theory*, 65–66.

43. Wieser, "Das Wesen," 396–97.

44. Ibid., 416–17. In *Social Economics*, Wieser made approving references to Schumpeter's insights. Schumpeter was the only younger Austrian to receive such recognition.

45. Böhm, "Eine 'dynamische' Theorie," 2, 61–62.

46. Schumpeter, "Eine 'dynamische' Theorie," 617.

47. Böhm, "Eine 'dynamische' Theorie," 656.

48. Kraus, *Half Truths*, 33. On Kraus, see Canetti, *Memoirs*, vol. 2; Timms, *Culture*; Timms, *Crisis*.

49. On the Böhm/Wieser distinction, see Hayek, "Economic Thought."

50. Böhm, "Macht," 220; Schumpeter, "Die wissenschaftliche Lebenswerk."

51. On the Mises family, see Hülsmann, *Mises*, 3–20.

52. Ibid., 36–44 (quote on 44). See also Winter, *Akademisches Gymnasium*.

53. Hülsmann, *Mises*, 95, 182–86.

54. Ibid., 114.

55. Ibid., 108–23.

56. Ibid.

57. Ibid.

58. Ibid., 365–66.

59. Keynes, review of *Theorie*, 417. For a similar verdict, see Lutz, review of *Theorie*.

60. Wicksell, review of *Theorie*, 144, 149.

61. Hülsmann, *Mises*, 209; Hayek, "Friedrich von Wieser," 549; Mitchell, foreword to *Social Economics*, ix.

62. Schumpeter, "Das Sozialprodukt," 629; Hilferding, review of *Theorie*, 1027.

63. The only retrospective accounts are Mises, *Memoirs*, and Somary, *Raven*. On Pribram, see Tooze, *Statistics*, 72–73.

64. On circles, see Timms, *Culture*, 7–8; Stadler, *Vienna Circle*, 577–88; Dekker, *Viennese Students*, 31–36. See also Hülsmann, *Mises*, 183–84, 272–73.

65. Mises, *Memoirs*, 32.

66. Neurath, "Nationalökonomie," 52. See also Uebel, "Idealist Inheritance."

67. Hilferding, *Finance Capital*, 21–22. See also chapter 25 on imperialism.

68. Schumpeter, "Zur Soziologie," 303. The essay also targeted Emil Lederer for his socialist interpretation.

69. Bottomore and Goode, *Austro-Marxism*, 30–36. On the postwar order, see Tooze, *Deluge*. On liberal internationalism and its critics, see Manela, *Wilsonian Moment*; Mazower, *Governing*; Pedersen, *Guardians*.

70. Somary, *Raven*, 14.

71. Mises, *Memoirs*, 13–16.

72. On the Weber-Wieser connection, see Kolev, "Wieser," 17–18.

3. Austria's End

1. Wieser, *Österreichs Ende*, 9, 316–18.

2. See C. Fleck, *Transatlantische Bereicherungen*.

3. On circles, see Timms, *Culture*, 7–10; Timms, "Cultural Parameters," 21–31; Stadler, *Vienna Circle*.

4. On postwar conditions, see Healy, *Vienna*. See also Boyer, "Silent War."

5. On the end of the empire, see Jászi, *Dissolution*; Sked, *Decline*; Boyer, "Silent War"; Cornwall, *Undermining*.

6. Somary, *Raven*, 120–21.

7. Schumpeter, *Die Krise*, 4–5.

8. Ibid., 22, 41–58. For a detailed analysis, see McCraw, *Prophet*, 87–97.

9. Schumpeter, *Die Krise*, 58.

10. On Schumpeter's career as finance minister, see Haberler, "Schumpeter"; Stolper, *Schumpeter*, 202–93; März, *Schumpeter*, ch. 9.

11. Haberler, "Joseph Alois Schumpeter," 345; McCraw, *Prophet*, 101, 128–34.

12. Mises, *Memoirs*, 60; Hülsmann, *Mises*, 272–75, 290.

13. Mises, *Nation*, 27–29.

14. Ibid., 31–32, 57–65, 71 (quote on 71). See Slobodian, *Globalists*, ch. 2. On Mises's later views, see Kolev, "Leitideen," sec. 4.

15. Mises, *Nation*, 84–102, 120–21. See also Manela, *Wilsonian Moment*.

16. On the limits of radical socialism, see Tooze, *Deluge*, ch. 12.

17. Bauer, *Weg*, 6. On Kautsky's democratic socialism, see Salvatori, *Kautsky*, chs. 7 and 8. On the Marxist socialization discussions, see Steele, *Marx*, 58–65. See also Chaloupek, "Austrian Debate," 659–61.

18. Bauer, *Weg*, 8. On Bauer, see Hanisch, *Illusionist*, 143–99.

19. Mises, *Socialism*, 25. As early as 1798, Malthus had attempted to prove the impossibility of a socialist system. See Steele, *Marx*, 1–2. For a revisionist version of the calculation debate, see Bockman, *Markets*, 17–49.

20. Mises, *Socialism*, 119.

21. Ibid., 511. On the civilizational dimension, see also Dekker, *Viennese Students*, ch. 5. Tooze, in the conclusion to *Deluge*, stresses the inherent conservatism of the postwar liberal order advocated by Woodrow Wilson and others.

22. Van Sickle, review of *Gemeinwirtschaft*; Carl Landauer, review of *Gemeinwirtschaft*.

23. On the calculation debates, see Lavoie, *Rivalry*; Caldwell, *Hayek's Challenge*, 116–18; Becchio, "Early Debate." On Polanyi, see Dale, *Polanyi*, 88–95. Advocates for market socialism emerged in the next wave of debates. See Bockman, *Markets*, 17–49.

24. Mises, *Socialism*, 509.

25. On the Anschluss, see Low, *Anschluss*; Hochman, *Imagining*.

26. Polanyi, *Great Transformation*, 299.

27. See Leonard, "Excluded Middle." On Red Vienna, see Gruber, *Red Vienna*; Hacohen, *Popper*, especially chs. 2, 3, and 7. On Austro-Marxism, see Bottomore and Goode, *Austro-Marxism*; Leser, *Reformismus*.

28. See Taschwer, *Hochburg*; Taschwer, "Nachrichten"; Taschwer, "Bärenhöhle." On antisemitism and the Austrian School, see Klausinger, "Academic Anti-Semitism."

29. Wasserman, *Black Vienna*, chs. 1 and 5. On the CV, see Popp, *CV*; Hartmann, *CV*. These texts downplay the CV's antisemitism. Taschwer, in "Nachrichten," 116–17, highlights this fraught past. For a different interpretation of Catholic antimodernism in the early twentieth century, see Chappel, *Catholic Modern*.

30. On the Vienna Circle, see Stadler, *Vienna Circle*. On the Psychological Institute, see Benetka, *Psychologie*.

31. On the late enlightenment, see Stadler, *Vienna Circle*. On the postwar Freudians, see Danto, *Free Clinics*. On the Psychological Institute, see Benetka, *Psychologie*.

32. On German economics, see Köster, *Wissenschaft*, 77–78.

33. On Furth, see the Josef Herbert Furth Papers, online at http://meg.library.albany.edu:8080/archive/view?docId=ger036.xml.

34. On Hayek, see Ebenstein, *Hayek's Journey*, 7–20; Caldwell, *Hayek's Challenge*, 133–35.

35. Spann, *Wahrer Staat*. On Spann, see Haag, "Spann"; Wasserman, *Black Vienna*, ch. 3.

36. Hayek, *Hayek on Hayek*, 45–46.

37. Ibid., 49–50. *Geist* is notoriously difficult to translate from German to English, meaning "spirit," "mind," or "intellect." It carries Romantic and idealist valences that the English synonyms do not possess.

38. Feichtinger, *Kulturen*, 331.

39. Ibid., 188–90. See also C. Fleck, *Transatlantische*.

40. Mitchell, foreword to *Social Economics*, ix.

41. Wieser, *Social Economics*, xvii–xxii. See Wieser, *Gesetz*. On European social theory, see Hughes, *Consciousness*.

42. Hayek, *Hayek on Hayek*, 48; Rosenstein-Rodan, "Grenznutzen."

43. Weinberger, "Böhm"; Amonn, "Wiesers *Theorie*." On Wieser's sociology, see Kolev, "Reincorporating."

44. Kaufmann, "Logik"; Voegelin, "Zeit." For a more detailed discussion, see Wasserman, "Between Debates."

45. Hayek, *Hayek on Hayek*, 35–36; Caldwell, *Hayek's Challenge*, 151–54.

46. On Austro-liberalism, see Klausinger, "Policy Advice." On the importance of the postimperial context for neoliberalism, see Slobodian, *Globalists*, ch. 2.

47. Klausinger, "Hans Mayer." See also Leonard, *Von Neumann*, 77–92. On Mises's "spurning," see Craver, "Emigration," 5; Caldwell, *Hayek's Challenge*, 145–47.

48. On complementarity, see Rosenstein-Rodan, "Grenznutzen"; Rosenstein-Rodan, "Complementarietà."

49. Morgenstern, Diaries, December 22, 1928, Box 1, OMP, quoted in Leonard, *Von Neumann*, 107. See also Klausinger, "Nationalökonomische Gesellschaft."

50. Mises, *Memoirs*, 81; Browne, "Erinnerungen," 111–13; Haberler, "Mises's Private Seminar," 122–23. On the Viennese singing tradition, see Kaufmann, *Wiener Lieder*.

51. Felix Kaufmann, *Songs of the Mises-Kreis*, trans. by Arlene Oost-Zinner; original music settings by Felix Kaufmann (Auburn, AL: Ludwig von Mises Institute, 2010). Reprinted by permission.

52. Leonard, *Von Neumann*, 83–87.

53. Browne, "Erinnerungen," 114–15.

54. Morgenstern, Diaries, November 30, 1924, Box 1, OMP; Leonard, *Von Neumann*, 100–108. Morgenstern was not Jewish, a fact that he stressed. Morgenstern's early nationalist views contain antisemitic sentiments characteristic of the period.

55. Haberler, *Der Sinn*, v, 97–98, 117; Browne, "Erinnerungen," 112–13. On index numbers, see Tooze, *Statistics*, ch. 2.

56. Mises, *Memoirs*, 81; Browne, "Erinnerungen," 118; Kaufmann, *Wiener Lieder*, 18–27.

57. On the board's composition, see Hülsmann, *Mises*, 575–76.

58. C. Fleck, *Transatlantische*, 58. See also Craver, "Patronage."

59. C. Fleck, *Transatlantische*, 63. On the hegemonic aspirations of the RF, see Parmar, *Foundations*.

60. On Geneva, see Slobodian, *Globalists*; Pedersen, *Guardians*.

61. Van Sickle to Edmund Day, October 13, 1930, Folder 36, Box 4, Series 705, RG 1.1, RAC; Morgenstern to Tracy Kittredge, November 2, 1932, ibid.

4. Depression, Emigration, and Fascism

1. [Hayek], "Österreich," 77, 85, 149.

2. Ibid., 169, 186, 195. On the collapse of the BCA, see Ausch, *Banken*. See also Sieghart, *Großmacht*.

3. Slobodian, *Globalists*, 59–60. Slobodian argues that Morgenstern first used this form of representation.

4. On Austrian policy prescriptions, see Klausinger, "Policy Advice." On reactions to the Depression, see Eichengreen and Temin, "Gold Standard." Whether German Chancellor Heinrich Brüning had alternatives to austerity policies is at the heart of the Borchardt thesis. On the Borchardt debates, see Straumann, "Rule." For Marxian explanations, see Howard and King, "Marxian Economists." The contrast between Austrian and German liberal economists is telling. On the German Institute, see Tooze, *Statistics*, ch. 4. See also Klausinger, "Gustav Stolper"; Strote, *Lions and Lambs*, ch. 2.

5. Klausinger, "Policy Advice."

6. Mises, *Memoirs*, 59–68. On Mises's role, see Hülsmann, *Mises*, 483–517. On Seipel, see Wasserman, *Black Vienna*, 32–43, 127–28; Diamant, *Austrian Catholics*, 91–92. On Mises's chamber of commerce work, see Slobodian, *Globalists*. On Schüller, see Feichtinger, *Kulturen*, 222–25; Nautz, *Unterhändler*.

7. Mises, *Die Kritik*, ix, 3–6, 19–21. Mises made clear what he did *not* consider an "intervention": (1) regulations that protect private property and free competition; (2) the socialization of some means of production; (3) state actions through the market that may influence market processes. He believed anarchism to be erroneous, so a state *must* act to protect property.

8. Slobodian, *Globalists*, 30–42.

9. See Grandner and Traxler, "Sozialpartnerschaft"; Slobodian, *Globalists*, 42–48.

10. On Marienthal, see C. Fleck, *Marienthal*. See also Wasserman, *Black Vienna*, ch. 6.

11. Mises, "Die Krise."

12. Mises, *Liberalismus*, 45, 53.

13. Hayek, *Monetary Theory*.

14. Ibid.

15. Robbins, *Autobiography*, 127. See also Hayek, *Hayek on Hayek*, 77. On Mises and the LSE, see Hülsmann, *Mises*, 631–40.

16. See Klausinger, *Machlup*; Hülsmann, *Mises*, 476–78, 646–49.

17. Machlup, *Stock Market*, x, 3–5 (quote on 5).

18. Ibid., 291–94.

19. Haberler, *Der Sinn*. On Austroliberalism, see Klausinger, "Policy Advice." See also Slobodian, *Globalists*, 49–53.

20. Haberler, *Prosperity*, v, 2, 57–59. On the impacts of *Prosperity*, see Officer, *Prosperity*, 149.

21. Klausinger, "Policy Advice." See also Leonard, *Von Neumann*, 148–49.

22. Machlup, interview with Axel Leijonhufvud, March 16, 1977, Box 49, FMP, copyright Stanford University.

23. On Keynes, see Skidelsky, *Keynes*.

24. Ibid., 395–413. See also Caldwell, introduction to *Contra Keynes*, 21–25.

25. Quoted in Skidelsky, *Keynes*, 397.

26. See Robinson, *Contributions*, 1–3; Wapshott, *Keynes Hayek*, ch. 5; Skidelsky, *Keynes*, 481–84. On Robbins and Hayek, see Howson, *Robbins*, ch. 8.

27. Hayek, "Reflection," 270–71.

28. Ibid., 294–95; Caldwell, introduction to *Contra Keynes*, 27.

29. Keynes, "Reply," 393.

30. Ibid., 395; Hayek, *Prices*, 99.

31. On these debates, see Burgin, *Great Persuasion*, 20–54. See also Caldwell, introduction to *Contra Keynes*, 28–31. For Austrian reactions, see Hayek to Haberler, March 15, 1936, Box 16, GHP; Haberler, "Mr. Keynes' Theory."

32. See Wapshott, *Keynes Hayek*.

33. Kauder to Morgenstern, March 24, 1932, OMP. On Kauder and Lachmann, see Lachmann, *Capital*, 8; Wasserman, "Science Lost." On Keynesianism, see Hall, *Political Power*.

34. Knight to Morgenstern, November 10, 1931, Box 6, OMP.

35. Ibid. See Burgin, *Great Persuasion*, 33. On the capital controversy, see A. Cohen, "Hayek/Knight."

36. Knight to Morgenstern, May 4, 1933, Box 6, OMP; Burgin, *Great Persuasion*, 32–54; Van Horn and Mirowski, "Rise"; Van Horn, Mirowski, and Stapleford, *Building*, especially part 4.

37. Knight to Morgenstern, December 19, 1932, Box 6, OMP. See also Emmett, *Knight*, ch. 6.

38. Knight, "Capitalistic Production," 327–28. See also A. Cohen, "Hayek/Knight," 471; Hayek, "On the Relationship"; Hayek, "Mythology."

39. On the distinctions between the early Chicago School and the Austrians, see Burgin, *Great Persuasion*.

40. Fritz Machlup, "The Older and the Younger Austrian Economists and Their Problems," unpublished lecture, Columbia University, New York, 1935, Box 76, FMP, copyright Stanford University.

41. On *The Good Society* and the Walter Lippmann colloquium, see Audier, *Colloque*; Walpen, *Die offenen Feinde*, 51–61; Denord, *Néo-libéralisme*, 104–25; Denord, "French Neoliberalism"; Burgin, *Great Persuasion*, 55–78.

42. Quoted in Burgin, *Great Persuasion*, 59. See also Walpen, *Die offenen Feinde*, 51–55.

43. Walpen, *Die offenen Feinde*, 60.

44. Slobodian, *Globalists*, 76–79.

45. Wilhelm Röpke and Alexander Rüstow, "A Note on the Urgent Necessity of Re-Orientation of Social Science," n.d., Box 14, MPS. Also cited in Walpen, *Die offenen Feinde*, 58. See also *Comte-Rendu*.

46. Lavoie, *Rivalry*, offers the fullest comparison of Hayek's and Mises's positions. See also Steele, *Marx*, 119–21; Caldwell, *Hayek's Challenge*, 214–20. For a dissenting view on the debate, see Bockman, *Markets*, 19–49.

47. For a summary, see Steele, *Marx*, 151–53.

48. Hayek, "Economics," 35–43.

49. Ibid., 35–43, 49 (quote on 49).

50. See Klausinger, "From Mises to Morgenstern."

51. Morgenstern, Diaries, April 10, 1929, December 28, 1929, Box 13, OMP; Haberler to Morgenstern, March 22, 1932, Box 5, OMP; Machlup to Haberler, January 23, 1934, Box 43, FMP, copyright Stanford University.

52. Haberler to Machlup, October 5, 1934, Box 41, FMP; Machlup to Haberler, November 3, 1934, Box 41, FMP, copyright Stanford University. For Haberler's views on Mises's theories, see Haberler, *Prosperity*, 57–59.

53. Morgenstern, *Limits*, 10, quoted in Leonard, *Von Neumann*, 166–67.

54. Morgenstern, Diaries, January 17, 1934, December 31, 1935, February 26, 1933, Box 13, OMP. See also K. Menger, *Reminiscences*, 10–11. On Menger and Mises, see Leonard, *Von Neumann*, 168.

55. Hayek to Morgenstern, April 2, 1934, Box 5, OMP, quoted in Leonard, *Von Neumann*, 168. On Annecy, see Wasserman, "Un-Austrian." See also Leonard, *Von Neumann*, 156–61; Caldwell, *Hayek's Challenge*, 211–12.

56. Haberler to Morgenstern, August 15, 1934, Box 5, OMP; Haberler to Machlup, March 21, 1935, Box 23, GHP; Machlup to Haberler, April 5, 1935, Box 23, GHP.

57. Morgenstern made concessions to the government to maintain influence. Mises became a member of the Austrofascist Vaterländische Front. Hülsmann argues that membership was probably mandatory (*Mises*, 677), but the scholarship on the *Ständestaat* does not support this claim. See also Klausinger, "From Mises to Morgenstern."

58. Caldwell, *Hayek's Challenge*, 210–14.

59. Hayek to Machlup, January 1935, Box 43, FMP.

60. Hayek to Machlup, May 1, 1936, Box 43, FMP.

61. On 1930s Switzerland, see Slobodian, *Globalists*.

62. Kaufmann, *Songs*, 48–49; McCraw, *Prophet*, 229–32. See also C. Fleck, *Etablierung*, 375–400.

63. Leonard, *Von Neumann*, 123–39; see also Klausinger, "From Mises to Morgenstern."

64. "Program Files, Business Cycle Conference," Folder 29, Box 4, Series 910, RG 3, RAC; Van Sickle to Edmund Day, May 1, 1933, Folder 36, Box 4, Series 705, RG 1.2, RAC. On Morgenstern's rising influence, see Klausinger, "From Mises to Morgenstern," 32–34. See also Weigl, "Beggar-Thy-Neighbour."

65. On Flexner, see Feichtinger, *Kulturen*, 74–84.

5. "He Who Is Only an Economist Cannot Be a Good Economist"

1. On *Road*'s publication history, see Caldwell, introduction to *Road*, 15–23.

2. Hayek, *Pure Theory*, v–viii.

3. Boulding, review of *Pure Theory*, 131. For criticisms of Hayek's concepts of capital and interest, see Hawtrey, "*Pure Theory*." For a critique of Hayek's equilibrium assumptions, see Smithies, "Professor Hayek."

4. Haberler to Morgenstern, April 9, 1941, Box 5, OMP; Morgenstern to Haberler, July 26, 1941, Box 5, OMP; Diary, March 15, 1942, Box 13, OMP.

5. On Wagemann's role in the prewar National Socialist state, see Tooze, *Statistics*, chs. 5 and 6. On Vienna in 1938, see Flügge, *Stadt*.

6. See Klausinger, "Hans Mayer," 292–95.

7. Haberler to Morgenstern, April 11, 1938, Box 5, OMP.

8. Feichtinger, *Kulturen*, 222–24. On the Mintzes' flight, see Perloff, *Vienna*, ch. 1; Furth, interview.

9. On the Emergency Committee and RF, see Feichtinger, *Kulturen*, 74–85, 197–213. On the New School, see Krohn, *Intellectuals*. See also Box 5, OMP; Schiff to Kaufmann, August 31, 1938, FKP.

10. Leonard, *Von Neumann*, 150–55.

11. Van Sickle to Tracy Kittredge, September 16, 1936, Folder 36, Box 4, Series 705, RG 1.2, RAC; Van Sickle to Warren Weaver, June 16, 1937, Folder 37, Box 4, Series 705, RG 1.2, RAC; Howard Ellis to Van Sickle, February 21, 1938, Folder 38, Box 4, Series 705, RG 1.2, RAC; Van Sickle to Kittredge, January 26, 1938, Folder 38, Box 4, Series 705, RG 1.2, RAC. For the Van Sickle quotations, see Leonard, *Von Neumann*, 174–75; on Wald, see also 179–80, 279–80.

12. Gulick to Morgenstern, July 25, 1938, Box 5, OMP. On Gerschenkron, see Dawidoff, *Fly Swatter*, chs. 3 and 4; van der Linden, "Gerschenkron's Secret." Gulick's *Austria: From Habsburg to Hitler* remains a touchstone of Austrian history, owing much to the work of Gerschenkron and his fellow émigré Walther Federn.

13. On Austrian emigration, see Craver, "Emigration"; Stadler, *Vertriebene Vernunft*; Feichtinger, *Kulturen*; Klausinger, "In the Wilderness"; C. Fleck, *Etablierung*.

14. On Rosenstein-Rodan, see Farese, "Culture."

15. Wapshott, *Keynes Hayek*, 192–93; Machlup to Hayek, July 19, 1940, Box 43, FMP, copyright Stanford University; Hayek to Machlup, August 1940, Box 43, FMP. In a conversation on October 9, 2017, Bruce Caldwell told the author that the rooftop story is probably too good to be true; he believes it originated with Hayek's daughter after the war.

16. Hülsmann, *Mises*, 725–34, 748–49. Haberler also found Mises a New School post, which Mises did not entertain.

17. Machlup to Hayek, November 12, 1940, Box 43, FMP, copyright Stanford University; Machlup to Walter Spahr, October 24, 1940, Box 53, FMP, copyright Stanford University.

18. Mises to Machlup, January 30, 1940, Box 53, FMP.

19. Hayek, review of *Nationalökonomie*.

20. Ibid. See also Haberler to Machlup, November 1936 (especially November 11), Box 41, FMP.

21. Eve Burns to Morgenstern, January 26, 1934, Box 4, OMP; Knight to Morgenstern, July 31, 1939, Box 6, OMP; Hayek to Morgenstern, April 2, 1934, Box 5, OMP. See also Leonard, *Von Neumann*, 166–68.

22. Schumpeter, *Business Cycles*, 13, 19, 60.

23. Ibid., 1:72–104, 169–74, 2:908, 1033.

24. Kuznets, "Business Cycles," 270–71. See also McCraw, *Prophet*, 270–78.

25. Nik-Khah and Van Horn call this process "economics imperialism." See Nik-Khah and Van Horn, "Inland Empire." Though typically used to refer to the Chicago School's attempt to use economic methods to solve problems in adjacent social scientific disciplines, the Austrians also granted their economic ideas explanatory power for the realms of sociology and political science.

26. On Cold War thinking, see Cohen-Cole, *Open Mind*; Isaac, *Working Knowledge*; Erickson, *World*; Erickson et al., *Reason*.

27. Schumpeter, *Capitalism*, 409.

28. Ibid., 61.

29. Ibid.

30. Ibid., 83.

31. Ibid., 145–47, 194–202.

32. Ibid., 242. On Schumpeter's influence on democracy theory, see Gilman, *Mandarins*, 47–56. On the state ideas of Mises and Hayek, see Kolev, "Leitideen."

33. Hobsbawm, *Revolutionaries*, 250–51. Quoted in McCraw, *Prophet*, 370–71; Machlup, "Capitalism," 301, 315–16, 320.

34. Schumpeter, *Capitalism*, 411. On the book's reception, see McCraw, *Prophet*, 371–74. On Schumpeter in Japan, see Metzler, *Capitalism*.

35. Hayek to Machlup, June 21, 1940, Box 43, FMP. See Hayek, *Studies*; Ebenstein, *Hayek's Journey*, 103–9; Caldwell, *Hayek's Challenge*, 232–41.

36. Popper to Hayek, April 23, 1943, Box 44, FHP; Popper to Hayek, October 26, 1943, Box 44, FHP. See Shearmur, *Hayek*, 229. On Hayek and Popper, see Hacohen, *Popper*, 364–68, 449–50, 482–86; Nordmann, *Neoliberalismus*.

37. Caldwell, introduction to *Road*, 17; Knight, "Reader's Report," 249; Marschak, "Reader's Report," 251.

38. Hayek, *Road*, 36–38, 58–62.

39. Ibid., 67, 74–75.

40. Ibid., 78, 83–85. See especially ch. 7 on economic activity.

41. Ibid., 86–90. On unemployment, see 148–49. His discussion of "security against privation" defends the ideas of a universal minimum income and minimum provisions of food, shelter, and clothing in developed countries.

42. Ibid., 238.

43. Ibid., 20–23.

44. Phillips-Fein, *Invisible Hands*, 15–19, 41–42. The Hayek quotation appears in *Road*, 20.

45. Phillips-Fein, *Invisible Hands*, 27–34, 42–43; Nik-Khah and Van Horn, "Inland Empire."

46. Morgenstern, Diaries, October 25, 1943, Box 13, OMP; Morgenstern, Diaries, April 19, 1945, Box 14, OMP.

47. Morgenstern, Diaries, July 12, 1941, Box 13, OMP, also quoted in Leonard, *Von Neumann*, 225. On the Morgenstern–von Neumann collaboration, see Leonard, *Von Neumann*, chs. 9–11.

48. Ibid., 49–50.

49. On the introduction, see Leonard, *Von Neumann*, 249.

50. Von Neumann and Morgenstern, *Theory*, 2.

51. Ibid., 1–7.

52. Ibid., 11–15 (quote on 11).

53. Morgenstern, Diaries, June 29, 1943, Box 13, OMP. See also Leonard, *Von Neumann*, 249.

54. Morgenstern, Diaries, November 8, 1942, Box 13, OMP. On the book's reception, see Leonard, *Von Neumann*, 260–64.

55. On defense intellectuals, see Bessner, *Democracy*. On RAND and Cold War rationality, see Erickson, *World*; Amadae, *Rationalizing*, part 1.

56. See Boxes 91–94, OMP. On the rise of defense intellectuals, see Bessner, *Democracy*.

57. Morgenstern, Diaries, June 8, 1944, Box 14, OMP.

58. See Spaulding, *Quiet Invaders*.

6. Austrian Schools

1. Mont Pèlerin Society, "Statement of Aims."

2. On the MPS and the World Economic Forum, see Carroll and Sapinski, "Neoliberalism."

3. On the MPS, see Walpen, *Die offenen Feinde*; Mirowski and Plehwe, *Mont Pèlerin*; Burgin, *Great Persuasion*. The official history of MPS is also helpful: Hartwell, *History*. For a list of the first participants, see Walpen, *Die offenen Feinde*, 391–92. Phillips-Fein, in *Invisible Hands*, 41–51, details the involvement of anti–New Deal businessmen.

4. On economics imperialism, see Lazear, "Economic Imperialism"; Nik-Khah and Van Horn, "Inland Empire."

5. Lionel Robbins drafted the preamble. On US social science, see Cohen-Cole, *Open Mind*. On the transition of the Austrian civilizational project, see Dekker, *Viennese Students*, 141–50, 176–80. For more on conservative internationalism, see Schmelzer, *Freiheit*; Duranti, *Conservative Human Rights*; Mazower, *Governing*.

6. See Connell, *Reforming*. On neoliberal monetary policy and the MPS, see Schmelzer, *Freiheit*.

7. Burgin, *Great Persuasion*, 82–85.

8. See Walpen, *Die offenen Feinde*, 101–17. See also Burgin, *Great Persuasion*. On Röpke, see Strote, *Lions and Lambs*.

9. "Program of the Eight Meetings (1947–1957) of the Mont Pelerin Society," Folder 1, Box 4, MPS.

10. Hayek, "Historians and the Future of Europe," Box 5, MPS. On ordoliberalism, see Ptak, *Ordoliberalismus*; Kolev, "Leitideen." On these inconsistencies in the liberal scientific project, see Cohen-Cole, *Open Mind*, 75–76.

11. "Program of the Eight Meetings." Walpen, in *Die offenen Feinde*, and Slobodian, in *Globalists*, have done the closest analysis of the constituent papers. For a broader assessment of general trends, see Burgin, *Great Persuasion*.

12. On these private interaction rituals, see Coen, *Vienna*.

13. For the 1947 program, see Hartwell, *Mont Pèlerin*, ch. 2. On 1958, see Machlup to Hayek, January 31, 1958, Box 78, FHP.

14. "Excerpts from letter written by Pierre F. Goodrich to Jasper Crane," Box 73, FHP.

15. Machlup to Hayek, May 24, 1954, Box 78, FHP.

16. On the German social market economy, see Ptak, *Ordoliberalismus*. On Hayek's global visions, see Rosenboim, *Emergence*, 157–65. On Fyfe and Churchill, see Duranti, *Conservative*, 219–28. On the rights of capital, see Slobodian, *Globalists*, ch. 4.

17. See Walpen, *Die offenen Feinde*, 118–59. See also Burgin, *Great Persuasion*, 125–37. Burgin stresses the differences between Hayek and Friedman, but their views remained largely consonant, despite methodological and policy differences.

18. On the Chicago workshops, see Emmett, "Sharpening Tools." On the Chicago-Austrian relationship, see Burgin, *Great Persuasion*.

19. See Van Horn and Mirowski, "Rise"; Caldwell, "Chicago School"; Nik-Khah and Van Horn, "Inland Empire."

20. Hayek to Machlup (et al.), April 11, 1950, Box 44, FMP. On Robbins's attitudes, see Folder 13, Box 3.2, Lionel Robbins Papers, LSE. See also Ebenstein, *Hayek's Journey*, 167–76.

21. Quoted in Ebenstein, *Hayek's Journey*, 178–79.

22. Ibid., 183–87. See also Caldwell, *Hayek's Challenge*, 245.

23. Hayek, *Constitution*, 6, 50–52. See also Ebenstein, *Hayek's Journey*, 141–42, 202–5.

24. Hayek, *Constitution*, 39.

25. Ibid., 39, 48, 58–59, 133.

26. Ibid., 309–20.

27. Ibid., 166–83 (quote on 183). On these antidemocratic elements, see Robin, *Reactionary Mind*, 157–64. On the Thomas Jefferson Center, see MacLean, *Democracy*, 45–60.

28. Hayek, *Constitution*, 199–214, 384–450.

29. Ibid., 41–43.

30. Hamowy, introduction to *Constitution*, 17–21.

31. Mises, "Liberty," 174. Mises's acolyte Murray Rothbard described Hayek's tome in even more scathing terms: "*Constitution of Liberty* is, surprisingly and distressingly, an extremely bad, and, I would even say, evil book." See Rothbard, "Confidential," 61. The disagreements between Mises's Austrian and US friends would only increase with time.

32. Friedman and Friedman, *Two Lucky People*, 161.

33. Quoted in Hülsmann, *Mises*, 799, 802. For Mises's financial status, see Bilo, "Mises in NYC."

34. Quoted in Hülsmann, *Mises*, 823. On NAM, see Phillips-Fein, *Invisible Hands*, 56–60.

35. On California conservatism, see Olmsted, *California*; McGirr, *Suburban Warriors*. See also Nash, *Conservative*, especially 13; and Phillips-Fein, *Invisible Hands*, 34–51.

36. Hazlitt, "Capitalism," 70. On *Human Action*, see Hülsmann, *Mises*, 884–87, 893–95. On Rand and Mises, see Burns, *Goddess*, 141–43.

37. Mises, *Human Action*, 3.

38. Ibid., 32. On Hayek-Mises, see Caldwell, *Hayek's Challenge*, 119–26, 193–96. On Machlup, see Scheall, "What Is Extreme"; Zanotti and Cachanosky, "Implications."

39. Mises, *Human Action*, 11.

40. Ibid.

41. Quoted in Hülsmann, *Mises*, 895.

42. Quoted in Vaughn, *Austrian Economics*, 67.

43. Mises, *Memoirs*, 81. On Rand, see Burns, *Goddess*, 141–43. On the new seminar, see Doherty, *Radicals*, 206–12.

44. Vaughn, *Austrian Economics*, 101–3.

45. Hülsmann, *Mises*, 924–35 (quote on 935). On the 1970s rebirth, see Vaughn, *Austrian Economics*.

46. Machlup to Hayek, June 7, 1954, Box 78, FHP.

47. See Judt, *Postwar*, 13–40.

48. Ibid., 4–7. On Austrian resistance, see Neugebauer, *Austrian Resistance*, 216–18.

49. Wirth, *Window*, 7–10.

50. Otto Molden, "The Alpbach Forum," Folder 13, Box 2, Series 700, RG 1.1, RAC; Fritz Molden, "Request for the Support of the Rockefeller Foundation for the 'Österreichische College,'" Folder 13, Box 2, Series 700, RG 1.1, RAC; "Grant in Aid to the Austrian College Society for the establishment of an Institute for Current European Cultural Research," Folder 5, Box 1, Series 705, RG 1.2, RAC; "Austrian College Society," Folder 5, Box 1, Series 705, RG 1.2, RAC. See Wagnleitner, *Coca-Colonization*.

51. Hayek to Morgenstern, October 20, 1947, Box 80, OMP. On Hayek and Alpbach, see P. Lewis, "Emergence"; P. Lewis, "Systems." See also Slobodian, *Globalists*, 224–30.

52. For more participants, see Wirth, *Window*, 7–17.

53. Ibid.

54. Hayek to J. H. Willits, October 31, 1946, Folder 16, Box 2, Series 700, RG 1.1, RAC; Morgenstern to Hayek, March 24 and November 6, 1947, Box 80, OMP.

55. Oskar Morgenstern, "Report on a trip of lecturing and study in some European countries," Folder 16, Box 2, Series 700, RG 1.1, RAC.

56. Friedrich Hayek, "Report on Visits to Austria and Switzerland," Folder 16, Box 2, Series 700, RG 1.1, RAC.

57. Ibid.

58. Friedrich Hayek, "Memorandum on Condition and Needs of the University of Vienna," Box 62, FHP.

59. Friedrich Hayek, "Proposal for the Creation of an Institute of Advanced Human Studies at Vienna, Austria," Box 62, FHP. On the IHS, see C. Fleck, "Wie Neues," 129–32; Pelinka, "Impact."

60. See C. Fleck, "Wie Neues."

61. Ibid. On the difficulty of return, see also C. Fleck, "Rückkehr."

62. Baldwin, "Haberler's Contribution"; Boehm, "Best Horse." On Harvard, see Isaac, *Working Knowledge*. On Geneva, see Slobodian, *Globalists*. See also Wasserman, "Un-Austrian."

63. See Slobodian, *Globalists*, chs. 4 and 6. Geneva School scholars led the effort to scuttle the ITO, which smacked of economic democracy to them.

64. See Helleiner, *Forgotten Foundations*.

65. Leeson, *Ideology*, 42; *Trends*, 125.

66. *Trends*, 3–12, 123–27. On the LIEO, see Bair, "Taking Aim," 357; C. Murphy, *Global Institutions*, 110–11. See also Toye, *Dissent*; Slobodian, *Globalists*; and *Humanity* 6, no. 1 (2015). On Rostow and modernization, see Ortolano, "Typicalities"; Gilman, *Mandarins*.

67. See Bair, "Taking Aim."

68. Haberler to Machlup, August 12, 1958, Box 41, FMP; Haberler, "Foreign Trade." See also Machlup, *Essays*.

69. Machlup, "Theory," 375; Haberler to Machlup, October 26, 1941, Box 41, FMP.

70. On Machlup's significance, see Connell, *Reforming*, 202–9.

71. Machlup to Haberler, July 16, 1982, Box 42, FMP, copyright Stanford University.

72. On the MPS and monetary policy, see Schmelzer, *Freiheit*. On the Bellagio Group, see Connell, *Reforming*.

73. On Bretton Woods, see Helleiner, *Forgotten Foundations*; Helleiner, *States*; Steil, *Battle*. On Villa Serbelloni, see Palacia and Rurali, *Bellagio Center*.

74. Machlup, *Plans*; Connell, *Reforming*, 7–36.

75. Fritz Machlup, "Invitation," Box 43, FMP, copyright Stanford University. See also Connell, *Reforming*, 63–82.

76. On the Joint Meeting, see Connell, *Reforming*, 109–23.

77. Schmelzer, *Freiheit*, introduction (quote on 19). See also Connell, *Reforming*, 115.

78. Machlup, "Ludwig von Mises," 13.

7. Austrians, "Un-Austrian Austrians," and "Non-Austrian Austrians"

1. Machlup to Fertig, June 23, 1961, Box 93, FMP, copyright Stanford University.

2. Fertig to Machlup, June 30, 1961, Box 93, FMP; Machlup to Fertig, July 5, 1961, Box 93, FMP, copyright Stanford University. See *Mont Pèlerin Quarterly* 3, no. 3 (1961).

3. IHS, "Program" and "The Institute's Story," n.d., Box 26, FHP. On Harper, see MacLean, *Democracy*, 133–37.

4. Dolan, *Foundations*, 7; Moss, introduction to *Mises*, vii–ix. I wish to thank Phil Magness for the suggestions on important venues of the Austrian revival. See also Boettke, "History," 219–23.

5. "Austrian Economics, George Mason University," n.d., Box 26, FHP; Nobel Prize, "Sveriges"; Nasar, "Hayek."

6. Offer and Södersberg, *Nobel Factor*, 14, 44–45, 127–31 (quote on 127–28).

7. Nobel Prize, "Sveriges."

8. On the impacts of *Law, Legislation, and Liberty*, see Slobodian, *Globalists*, chs. 6–7.

9. Dolan, *Foundations*, 4; Blundell, "IHS," 97–98. See also *ZfN* 32, no. 1 (1972).

10. Kauder to Mises, July 9, 1956, LvMP. On Kauder, see Wasserman, "Science Lost."

11. See "Emil Kauder," n.d., Folder 42, Box 79, Emergency Committee in Aid of Displaced Foreign Scholars Records, New York Public Library Manuscript and Archives Division, New York, NY. See also Feichtinger, *Kulturen*; C. Fleck, *Transatlantische*.

12. Kauder, "Genesis," 638, 650.

13. Kauder, "Intellectual," 417.

14. See Wasserman, "Science Lost."

15. Hayek, "Economic Thought," 461; Hayek to Elinor Barber, June 4, 1963, Box 62, FHP.

16. See Mises, *Memoirs*; Streissler, "Significance."

17. Furth to Machlup, July 21, 1979, Box 39, FMP.

18. Furth to Machlup, August 6, 1979, Box 39, FMP; Kirzner to Machlup, July 9, 1979, Box 49, FMP. Emphasis in original.

19. Machlup, "Austrian Economics," 39–41.

20. Kirzner, *Competition*, 6, 10, 14. Hayek's later work also dealt with ignorance as a key signaling device.

21. Machlup, *Production*, 5; Machlup to Kirzner, June 14, 1968, Box 49, FMP, copyright Stanford University.

22. Machlup, "Interview." See also Boettke, "History," 217.

23. See Lachmann, *Capital*. On Kirzner and Lachmann's respective approaches, see Vaughn, *Austrian Economics*, 3–6, 101–10, 139–61.

24. C. V. Starr Center for Applied Economics, "'Austrian' School of Economics," pamphlet, New York University, 1983, Box 11, FHP.

25. Morgenstern, *Accuracy*; Machlup, "Three Concepts"; Machlup, *Essays*; Morgenstern to Machlup, April 6, 1960, Box 54, FMP; Morgenstern, Diaries, December 8, 1974, Box 16, OMP.

26. Morgenstern, Diaries, June 29, 1943, Box 13, OMP. See also Leonard, *Von Neumann*, 249; Shubik, *Essays*.

27. Morgenstern, Diaries, November 6 and December 8, 1974, Box 16, OMP.

28. Morgenstern, Diaries, October 11, 1973, Box 16, OMP.

29. See Kauder, *History*; Borch, "Rolle"; K. Menger, "Österreichischer Marginalismus." For the Borch and Menger correspondence, see Boxes 7 and 86, OMP.

30. Hayek, "Intellectuals," 417–18.

31. See Box 28, GHP.

32. On the early AEA/AEI, see Phillips-Fein, *Invisible Hands*, 60–67; Stahl, *Right Moves*, ch. 1. Haberler published a slew of pamphlets and books for AEI on these subjects.

33. Quoted in "Gottfried Haberler"; and Boehm, "Best Horse," 107.

34. See Haberler, "Mises's Private Seminar." Box 10, GHP, contains the Ebeling and Garrison exchanges.

35. Kaufmann, *Wiener Lieder*, 32.

36. Rothbard, "Anatomy," 88, quoted in Bessner, "Rothbard," 445.

37. See Rothbard, *Ethics*, ch. 6; Rothbard, *Man*, 176–85. See also Bessner, "Rothbard."

38. Quoted in Bessner, "Rothbard," 445. See Doherty, *Radicals*, 249–53.

39. Rothbard, *New Liberty*, 302–4.

40. Rothbard, "It Usually Ends," also quoted in Bessner, "Rothbard," 441. For a detailed, if pro-Koch, position, see Doherty, *Radicals*, 413–18.

41. Doherty, *Radicals*, 410. See also Mayer, *Dark Money*, ch. 5.

42. Quoted in Schulman, *Sons*, 261. See also ibid., 99–100, 264–66; Mayer, *Dark Money*, 79–80, 141–56. On GMU public choice, see MacLean, *Democracy*. On GMU's law school, see Teles, *Rise*, 207–19.

43. Quoted in Cockett, *Thinking*, 131. See also ibid., chs. 4–5.

44. Ibid., 147–51.

45. Quoted in ibid., 173–74. See also Ebenstein, *Hayek's Journey*, 284–96.

46. Quoted in Peck, *Constructions*, 171. See also Atlas Network, "Global Directory."

47. On the "Chicago Boys," see Klein, *Shock Doctrine*, 70–106, 144–46; Fischer, "Chile"; Valdés, *Pinochet's Economists*. See also Farrant, McPhail, and Berger, "Preventing the 'Abuses.'" Cato's Ralph Raico warned Hayek about potential backlash if he went ahead with his Chile trip. See Raico to Hayek, June 13, 1977, Box 14, FHP.

48. "Extracts." Writing from opposing positions, Corey Robin and Bruce Caldwell fleshed out the full details of Hayek's Chile time line. See Robin, "Hayek von Pinochet" and subsequent blog posts, summarized in "Hayek-Pinochet"; Caldwell and Montes, "Hayek." See also Farrant, McPhail, and Berger, "Preventing the 'Abuses'"; Fang, "Sphere"; Peck, *Constructions*, 171–81.

49. See Fang, "Sphere"; Peck, *Constructions*, 171–81.

50. Reagan to Eamonn Butler, March 27, 1984, Box 24, FHP. See Ebenstein, *Hayek's Journey*, 208.

51. For the full range of international Mises activities, see "Ludwig von Mises Institute," n.d., Box 4, MPS. On Hayek's unhappy Austrian return, see Hayek, "Warum."

52. See Wasserman, *Black Vienna*, conclusion; C. Fleck, "Rückkehr."

53. See "Carl Menger Institut," n.d., Box 14, FHP.

54. Quoted in Norman Birnbaum, *After Progress*, 157. See also Kreisky, *Erinnerungen*, 118. Kreisky credited Galbraith with the comment in his memoirs. Thank you to Guenter Bischof for referring me to this exchange.

55. Furth to Hayek, March 14, 1977, Box 21, FHP; Furth to Hayek, July 25, 1972, Box 21, FHP.

56. See, for example, Heilbroner and Howe, "World."

57. Judt, *Postwar*, 2.

Conclusion

Epigraph: Hayek, *Constitution*, 517.

1. Heilbroner, "Triumph," 98.

2. Heilbroner and Howe, "World," 430. Italics his.

3. Heilbroner, "Analysis and Vision." For a rebuttal to Heilbroner, see Caldwell, "Hayek."

4. Heilbroner, "Triumph," 102; Heilbroner, "After Communism," 92. On his curious reading of Schumpeter, see Heilbroner, "Was Schumpeter Right?"

5. Bush, "Remarks"; Nasar, "Neglected Economist."

6. Fukuyama, "End"; Heilbroner and Howe, "World."

7. Ngrams Viewer, https://books.google.com/ngrams/. These results refer to English-language sources; German data vary. Several of the Austrians under consideration used several variations on their name; I grouped these together. See also Westley, "Ngrams."

8. I measured these rates of growth by comparing decade-by-decade publication numbers on ProQuest and LexisNexis. This analysis is not meant to be statistically rigorous but impressionistic. It is based on keyword searches on select terms for the years 1970–2018.

9. Scopus, "Review"; Scopus, "Quarterly"; Scopus, "Advances." For the rankings, see Lee and Cronin, "Research Quality."

10. See Boettke, "History." For the best history of the postwar tradition, see Vaughn, *Austrian Economics*, though it is nearly twenty-five years old now.

11. Horwitz, "More on the Austrianness"; McCloskey, "Kirznerian."

12. See Vaughn, *Austrian Economics*; Caldwell, *Hayek's Challenge*.

13. On the American tradition, see Vaughn, *Austrian Economics*. On methodology, see Caldwell, *Hayek's Challenge*, 1–15, 370–405. On the Viennese school, see Schulak and Unterköfler, *Austrian School*; Dekker, *Viennese Students*. On Mises, see Hülsmann, *Mises*. On Morgenstern, see Leonard, *Von Neumann*. On Mayer, see Klausinger, "Hans Mayer." On Menger, see Schumacher and Scheall, "Menger." On contemporary strands, see Boettke, "History." On mainline economics, see Boettke, Haeffele-Balch, and Storr, introduction to *Mainline Economics*.

14. See Lachmann, "Austrian Economics"; Lavoie, *Economics*, especially the introduction; Boettke, "Theory"; Prendergast, "Schutz"; Ebeling, "Hermeneutical Economics." On "cultural Austrians," see Slobodian, "Alt Right."

15. Rothbard, "Hermeneutical Invasion"; Gordon, "Hermeneutics"; Ekelund, review of *Austrian Economics*. See also Salerno, "Mises and Hayek."

16. Salerno, "Sociology," 99.

17. Ibid., 97–108.

18. On Rothbard's rightward turn, see Bessner, "Rothbard." On Austro-punkism, see Boettke, "Setting."

19. On the World War I political landscape, see Hoppe, *Democracy*, ix–xxi.

20. Ibid., xxii–xxiii. See also Slobodian, "Alt-Right"; Slobodian, "Populist Bastards."

21. Horwitz, "How Did We Get Here?"; Boettke, "Setting."

22. Horwitz, "What Austrian Economics IS." Italics his.

23. Horwitz, "How Did We Get Here?"

24. Ibid. Boettke, "New Thinking."

25. TPM TV, "Ron Paul."

26. See Paul, *Mises*.

27. See "Ron Paul Newsletters." For a good summary, see Schwartz and Weigel, "Who Wrote"; Kirchik, "Angry White Man." Regarding the 2011–12 controversy, see Coates, "Shaggy Defense"; Coates, "Old News." For critical libertarian voices, see Friedersdorf, "Grappling"; Horwitz, "How Did We Get Here?"

28. Among the dozens of pieces, these are the most prominent: Davidson, "Primetime"; Yglesias, "Austrian Economics"; Barro, "Hayek and Mises." For the libertarian response, see Richman, "Austrian Economics"; Bartlett, "Ryan's Guru." See also the *Cato Unbound* issue "Theory and Practice." On the radicalism of Austrian libertarianism, see Bessner, "Rothbard," 442–44.

29. Judt, *Thinking*, 29–30 (quote on 30).

30. Judt, *Ill Fares*, 91–106 (quote on 91).

31. See Robin, "Nietzsche's Marginal Children." For a critical rejoinder to Judt and Robin, see Dekker, "Left Luggage."

32. The title of this section is an adaptation of Marx's response to the Marxist French Workers' Party program of 1880.

33. Hayek Institut, "Leitbild."

34. Gasser and Müller, "Freibeuter"; Bonavida, "FPÖ"; John, "FPÖ"; Bonvalot, "Warum." On the 2017 election, see Tomlinson, "Austrian Economics"; Schuman, "Meet Sebastian Kurz."

35. Horn, "Rechte Flanke." See also Riedel and Pittelkow, "Hayek-Gesellschaft."

36. Weede, "Im linken Lager"; "Austritte"; NOUS, "About Us."

37. Horn, "Rechter Auge blind."

38. Schumpeter, *History*, 783.

39. C. Menger, *Principles*, 46–48; C. Menger, *Investigations*, 27–31; Böhm, "Austrian Economists," 380, 383.

40. Böhm, "Historical," 248–49.

41. Hayek, "Dilemma," 463; Marx, "Theses."

BIBLIOGRAPHY

Archives

Allgemeines Verwaltungsarchiv des österreichischen Staatsarchiv. Vienna, Austria.
Archiv der Universität Wien. Vienna, Austria.
Chatham House Archives. London, UK.
Columbia University Rare Book and Manuscript Library. New York, NY.
    Paul Lazarsfeld Papers.
David M. Rubenstein Rare Book and Manuscript Library. Duke University, Durham, NC.
    Carl Menger Papers.
    Karl Menger Papers.
    Oskar Morgenstern Papers.
Harvard University Archives. Cambridge, MA.
    Alexander Gerschenkron Papers.
    Joseph Schumpeter Papers.
Haus-, Hof-, und Staatsarchiv. Vienna, Austria.
    Richard Schüller Papers.
Hoover Institution Archives. Stanford, CA.
    Friedrich Hayek Papers.
    Fritz Machlup Papers.
    Gottfried Haberler Papers.
    Karl Popper Papers.
    Mont Pèlerin Society Papers.
Laurier Archives, Wilfrid Laurier University, Montreal, Canada.
    Felix Kaufmann Papers.
League of Nations Archives. Geneva, Switzerland.
London School of Economics Archives. London, UK.
    Lionel Robbins Papers.
    Paul Rosenstein-Rodan Papers.

Ludwig von Mises Collection. Grove City College, Grove City, PA.
M. E. Grenander Department of Special Collections & Archives. State University of New York Albany, Albany, NY.
  Erich Hula Papers.
  Josef Herbert Furth Papers.
  Karl Pribram Papers.
New York Public Library Manuscript and Archives Division. New York, NY.
  Emergency Committee in Aid of Displaced Foreign Scholars Records.
Rockefeller Archive Center. Sleepy Hollow, NY.
University College London Archives and Special Collections.
  Paul Rosenstein-Rodan Papers.
Wienbibliothek im Rathaus. Vienna, Austria.

Other Materials

Adler, Max, and Rudolf Hilferding. "Vorwort." *Marx-Studien* 1 (1904): v–viii.
AllThingsBeck. "Glenn Beck—6/8/2010—The Road to Serfdom." Aired June 8, 2010. YouTube, March 9, 2012. https://www.youtube.com/watch?v=CMk5_4pBlfM.
Amadae, S. M. *Prisoners of Reason: Game Theory and Neoliberal Political Economy.* Cambridge: Cambridge University Press, 2015.
———. *Rationalizing Capitalist Democracy: The Cold War Origins of Rational Choice.* Chicago: University of Chicago Press, 2003.
Amonn, Alfred. "Der Gutsbegriff in der theoretischen Nationalökonomie." *Zeitschrift* 19 (1910): 403–501.
———. "Wiesers *Theorie der gesellschaftlichen Wirtschaft.*" *AfSuS* 53 (1925): 289–369, 653–701.
Anderson, Harriet. *Utopian Feminism: Women's Movements in Fin-de-Siècle Vienna.* New Haven, CT: Yale University Press, 1992.
"Appendix: Verzeichnis der Mitglieder der Gesellschaft Österreichischer Volkswirte." *Jahrbuch* 1 (1912): 1–11.
"Appendix II: Verzeichnis der Vorträge 1888–1915." *Jahrbuch* 4 (1915): 170–79.
Ashby, Charlotte, Tag Gronberg, and Simon Shaw-Miller, eds. *The Viennese Café and Fin-de-Siècle Culture.* New York: Berghahn, 2013.
Atlas Network. "Global Directory." Accessed January 19, 2019. https://www.atlas-network.org/partners/global-directory/11.
Audier, Serge. *Le Colloque Lippmann: Aux origines du Néo-Libéralisme.* Lormont, France: Le Bord de l'Eau, 2008.
Ausch, Karl. *Als die Banken fielen.* 2nd ed. Vienna: Kramer, 2012.
Auspitz, Rudolf, and Richard Lieben. *Untersuchungen über die Theorie des Preises.* Leipzig: Duncker and Humblot, 1889.
"Austritte aus der Friedrich A. von Hayek Gesellschaft." Erklaerung-Leipzig.de. Accessed January 25, 2019. http://erklaerung-leipzig.de.
Backhaus, Jürgen. "Der Methodenstreit in der Nationalökonomie." *Journal for the General Philosophy of Science* 31, no. 2 (2000): 307–36.

Backhouse, Roger. *The Ordinary Business of Life: A History of Economics*. Princeton, NJ: Princeton University Press, 2002.

Bair, Jennifer. "Taking Aim at the New International Economic Order." In Mirowski and Plehwe, *Mont Pèlerin*, 347–85.

Baird, Henry. "Carey and Two of His Recent Critics: Böhm-Bawerk and Marshall." *Proceedings of the American Philosophical Society* 29 (1891): 166–73.

Baldwin, R. E. "Gottfried Haberler's Contribution to International Trade Theory and Policy." *QJE* 97 (1982): 141–48.

Barro, Josh. "Where I Learned All about Austrian Economics." *Bloomberg*, September 9, 2012. http://www.bloomberg.com/news/2012-09-19/where-i-learned-all-about-about-austrian-economics.html.

———. "Who Needs Posner When You Have Hayek and Mises." *Bloomberg*, July 6, 2012. http://www.bloomberg.com/news/2012-07-06/who-needs-posner-when-you-have-mises-and-hayek-.html.

Bartlett, Bruce. "Why Hayek Isn't Ryan's Guru." *NYT*, August 28, 2012. https://economix.blogs.nytimes.com/2012/08/28/why-hayek-isnt-paul-ryans-guru.

Bauer, Otto. *Der Weg zum Sozialismus*. Berlin: Freiheit, 1919.

———. *Die Nationalitätenfrage und die Sozialdemokratie*. Vienna: Ignaz Brand, 1907.

Becchio, Giandomenica. "The Early Debate on Economic Calculation in Vienna (1919–1925)." *Storia del pensiero economico* 2 (2007): 133–44.

Beller, Steven, ed. *Rethinking Vienna 1900*. New York: Berghahn, 2001.

———. *Vienna and the Jews, 1867–1938: A Cultural History*. New York: Cambridge University Press, 1989.

Benetka, Gerhard. *Psychologie in Wien: Sozial- und Theoriegeschichte des Wiener Psychologischen Instituts, 1922–1938*. Vienna: WUV-Universitätsverlag, 1995.

Bernstein, Eduard. *Evolutionary Socialism*. Translated by Edith C. Harvey. London: Independent Labour Party, 1907.

Bessner, Daniel. *Democracy in Exile: Hans Speier and the Rise of the Defense Intellectual*. Ithaca, NY: Cornell University Press, 2018.

———. "Murray Rothbard, Political Strategy, and the Making of Modern Libertarianism." *Intellectual History Review* 24, no. 4 (2014): 441–56.

Bilo, Simon. "Mises in NYC." Paper presented at the Austrian Economics Workshop, Edmonton, Canada, October 11, 2018.

Birnbaum, Norman. *After Progress: American Social Reform and European Socialism in the Twentieth Century*. New York: Oxford University Press, 2001.

Blaug, Mark. *Economic Theory in Retrospect*. 5th ed. Cambridge: Cambridge University Press, 1996.

Blundell, John. "The IHS and the Rebirth of Austrian Economics." *QJAE* 17, no. 1 (2014): 92–107.

Blyth, Mark. *Great Transformations: Economic Ideas and Institutional Change in the Twentieth Century*. New York: Cambridge University Press, 2002.

Bockman, Johanna. *Markets in the Name of Socialism*. Stanford, CA: Stanford University Press, 2011.

Boehm, Stephan. "The Best Horse in the Viennese Stables: Gottfried Haberler and Joseph Schumpeter." *Journal of Evolutionary Economics* 25, no. 1 (2015): 107–15.

Boettke, Peter. "Austrian School of Economics." In *Concise Encyclopedia of Economics*, 2nd ed. http://www.econlib.org/library/Enc/AustrianSchoolofEconomics.html.

———. "Cosmopolitanism Is the Answer." *FEE.org*, November 15, 2017. https://fee.org/articles/cosmopolitanism-is-the-answer.

———. "The History of a Tradition." *RHETM* 34A (2016): 199–243.

———. "Information and Knowledge: Austrian Economics in Search of Its Uniqueness." *RAE* 15, no. 4 (2002): 263–74.

———. "New Thinking for a New Decade." *Coordination Problem*, January 1, 2010. http://www.coordinationproblem.org/2010/01/new-thinking-for-a-new-decade-1.html.

———. "Setting the Record Straight on Austro-Punkism and the Sociology of the Austrian School of Economics." *Austrian Economists*, August 4, 2009. http://austrianeconomists.typepad.com/weblog/2009/08/setting-the-record-straight-on-austropunkism-and-the-sociology-of-the-austrian-school-of-economics.html.

———. "The Theory of Spontaneous Order and Cultural Evolution in the Social Theory of F. A. Hayek." *Cultural Dynamics* 3, no. 1 (1990): 61–83.

———. "The Use and Abuse of the History of Economic Thought within the Austrian School of Economics." Supplement, *HOPE* 34 (2002): 337–60.

Boettke, Peter J., Stefanie Haeffele-Balch, and Virgil Storr. Introduction to *Mainline Economics: Six Nobel Lectures in the Tradition of Adam Smith*, 1–22. Arlington, VA: Mercatus Center, 2016.

Böhm-Bawerk, Eugen von. "The Austrian Economists." *Annals of the American Academy of Political and Social Sciences* 1 (1891): 361–84.

———. *Capital and Interest: A Critical History of Economic Theory*. Translated by William Smart. London: Macmillan, 1890.

———. "Eine 'dynamische' Theorie des Kapitalzinses." *Zeitschrift* 22 (1913): 1–62, 640–56.

———. *Geschichte und Kritik der Capitalzins-Theorie*. 2nd ed. Innsbruck, Austria: Wagner, 1900.

———. "The Historical versus the Deductive Method in Political Economy." *Annals of the American Academy of Political and Social Sciences* 1 (1891): 244–71.

———. *Kapital und Kapitalzins. Erste Abteilung. Geschichte und Kritik der Kapitalzins-Theorieen*. Innsbruck, Austria: Wagner, 1884.

———. *Karl Marx and the Close of His System*. Edited by Paul Sweezy. New York: Kelly, 1949.

———. "Macht oder Ökonomisches Gesetz?" *Zeitschrift* 23 (1914): 205–71.

———. *The Positive Theory of Capital*. Translated by William Smart. London: Macmillan, 1891.

———. *Recent Literature on Interest (1884–1899)*. Translated by William Smart. London: Macmillan, 1903.

————. *Rechte und Verhältnisse vom Standpunkte der volkswirtschaftlichen Güterlehre.* Innsbruck, Austria: Wagner, 1881.

————. "Unsere Aufgabe." *Zeitschrift* 1 (1892): 1–10.

————. *Zur neuesten Literatur über Kapital und Kapitalzins.* Vienna: Braumüller, 1907.

Boianovsky, Mauro, and Hans-Michael Trautwein. "Haberler, the League of Nations, and the Quest for Consensus in Business Cycle Theory in the 1930s." *HOPE* 38, no. 1 (2006): 45–89.

Bonar, James. "The Austrian Economists and Their Theory of Value." *QJE* 3 (1888): 1–31.

Bonavida, Iris. "FPÖ und Hayek-Institut." *Die Presse*, March 30, 2012. http://diepresse.com/home/innenpolitik/745116/FPOe-und-HayekInstitut_Allianz-mit-Widerspruechen.

Bonnell, Andrew. "Did They Read Marx? Marx Reception and Social Democratic Party Members in Imperial Germany, 1871–1914." *Australian Journal of Politics and History* 48, no. 1 (2002): 4–15.

Bonvalot, Michael. "Warum die FPÖ eine Partei für die Reichen ist." *Vice*, May 30, 2017. https://www.vice.com/de_at/article/kze4qm/warum-die-fpo-eine-partei-fur-die-reichen-ist.

Borch, Karl. "Die Rolle der Unsicherheit in den Theorien der Österreichischen Schule." *ZfN* 32, no. 1 (1972): 29–38.

Bottomore, T. B., and Patrick Goode. *Austro-Marxism.* Oxford, UK: Clarendon, 1978.

Boulding, Kenneth. Review of *The Pure Theory of Capital* by Friedrich Hayek. *JPE* 50, no. 1 (1942): 131–33.

Bourdieu, Pierre. "The Field of Cultural Production; or, The Economic World Reversed." *Poetics* 12 (1983): 311–56.

Bourdieu, Pierre, and Loïc Wacquant. *An Invitation to Reflexive Sociology.* Chicago: University of Chicago Press, 1992.

Boyer, John W. *Culture and Political Crisis in Vienna: Christian Socialism in Power, 1897–1918.* Chicago: University of Chicago Press, 1995.

————. *Political Radicalism in Late Imperial Vienna: Origins of the Christian Social Movement, 1848–1897.* Chicago: University of Chicago Press, 1981.

————. "Silent War and Bitter Peace: The Revolution of 1918 in Austria." *Austrian History Yearbook* 34 (2003): 1–56.

Braunthal, Julius. *History of the International.* 2 vols. New York: Praeger, 1967.

Brentano, Franz. *Psychologie vom empirischen Standpunkt.* Leipzig: Duncker and Humblot, 1874.

Browne, Martha Steffy. "Erinnerungen an das Mises-Privatseminar." *Wirtschaftspolitische Blätter* 28, no. 4 (1981): 110–20.

Brubaker, Rogers. *Ethnicity without Groups.* Cambridge, MA: Harvard University Press, 2006.

Bukharin, Nikolai. *The Economic Theory of the Leisure Class.* New York: International, 1927.

Burgin, Angus. *The Great Persuasion: Reinventing Free Markets since the Great Depression.* Cambridge, MA: Harvard University Press, 2012.

Burns, Jennifer. *The Goddess of the Market: Ayn Rand and the American Right.* New York: Oxford University Press, 2009.

Bush, George H. W. "Remarks on Presenting the Presidential Medal of Freedom Awards." November 18, 1991. American Presidency Project. http://www.presidency.ucsb.edu/ws/?pid=20239.

Caldwell, Bruce. "The Chicago School, Hayek, and Neoliberalism." In Van Horn, Mirowski, and Stapleford, *Building Chicago Economics,* 301–7.

———. "Hayek—Right for the Wrong Reasons?" *JHET* 23, no. 2 (2001): 141–51.

———. *Hayek's Challenge: An Intellectual Biography of F. A. Hayek.* Chicago: University of Chicago Press, 2004.

———. "Hayek's Transformation." *HOPE* 20, no. 3 (1988): 513–41.

———. Introduction to Hayek, *Contra Keynes,* 1–46.

———. Introduction to Hayek, *Road,* 1–33.

Caldwell, Bruce, and Leonidas Montes. "Friedrich Hayek and His Visits to Chile." *RAE* 28, no. 3 (2015): 261–309.

Canetti, Elias. *The Memoirs of Elias Canetti.* New York: Farrar, Straus and Giroux, 1999.

Carroll, William K., and J. P. Sapinski. "Neoliberalism and the Transnational Capitalist Class." In Springer, Birch, and MacLeavy, *Handbook of Neoliberalism,* 39–49.

Case, Holly. "The 'Social Question,' 1820–1920." *MIH* 13, no. 3 (2011): 747–75.

Chaloupek, Günther. "The Austrian Debate on Economic Calculation in a Socialist Economy." *HOPE* 22, no. 4 (1990): 659–75.

———. "Die österreichische Schule und der Austromarxismus." *Wirtschaft und Gesellschaft* 13, no. 4 (1987): 469–86.

Chappel, James. *Catholic Modern: The Challenge of Totalitarianism and the Remaking of the Church.* Cambridge, MA: Harvard University Press, 2018.

Coates, Ta-Nehisi. "'Old News.'" *Atlantic,* December 21, 2011. https://www.theatlantic.com/politics/archive/2011/12/old-news/250331.

———. "Ron Paul's Shaggy Defense." *Atlantic,* December 20, 2011. https://www.theatlantic.com/politics/archive/2011/12/ron-pauls-shaggy-defense/250256.

Cockett, Richard. *Thinking the Unthinkable: Think-Tanks and the Economic Counter-Revolution, 1931–1983.* New York: HarperCollins, 1994.

Coen, Deborah R. *Vienna in the Age of Uncertainty: Science, Liberalism, and Private Life.* Chicago: University of Chicago Press, 2007.

Cohen, Avi. "The Hayek/Knight Capital Controversy: The Irrelevance of Roundaboutness, or Purging Processes in Time?" *HOPE* 35, no. 3 (2003): 469–90.

———. "The Mythology of Capital or of Static Equilibrium? The Böhm-Bawerk/Clark Controversy." *JHET* 30, no. 2 (2008): 151–71.

Cohen, Stephen. *Bukharin and the Bolshevik Revolution: A Political Biography, 1888–1938.* New York: Knopf, 1973.

Cohen-Cole, Jamie. *The Open Mind: Cold War Politics and the Sciences of Human Nature*. Chicago: University of Chicago Press, 2014.

Collins, Randall. *The Sociology of Philosophies: A Global Theory of Intellectual Change*. Cambridge, MA: Harvard University Press, 1998.

Comte-Rendu des Séances du Colloque Walter Lippmann. Paris: Librairie de Médicis, 1938.

Connell, Carol. *Reforming the World Monetary System: Fritz Machlup and the Bellagio Group*. London: Pickering and Chatto, 2012.

Conrad, Johannes. *Grundriss zu den Vorlesungen über Nationalökonomie*. Halle, 1888.

Cornwall, Mark. *The Undermining of Austria-Hungary: The Battle for Hearts and Minds*. London: Macmillan, 2000.

Craver, Earlene. "The Emigration of the Austrian Economists." *HOPE* 18, no. 1 (1986): 1–32.

———. "Patronage and the Directions of Research in Economics." *Minerva* 24 (1986): 205–22.

Cross, Mai'a K. Davis. "Rethinking Epistemic Communities Twenty Years Later." *Review of International Studies* 39 (2013): 137–60.

Dale, Gareth. *Karl Polanyi: A Life on the Left*. New York: Columbia University Press, 2016.

Danto, Elizabeth Ann. *Freud's Free Clinics: Psychoanalysis and Social Justice, 1918–1938*. New York: Columbia University Press, 2005.

Davidson, Adam. "Primetime for Paul Ryan's Guru (the One Who's Not Ayn Rand)." *NYT*, August 26, 2012. http://www.nytimes.com/2012/08/26/magazine/primetime-for-paul-ryans-guru-the-one-thats-not-ayn-rand.html.

Dawidoff, Nicholas. *The Fly Swatter: How My Grandfather Made His Way in the World*. New York: Random House, 2002.

Deak, John. *Forging a Multinational State: State Making in Imperial Austria from the Enlightenment to the First World War*. Stanford, CA: Stanford University Press, 2014.

Dekker, Erwin. "Left Luggage: Finding the Relevant Context of Austrian Economics." *RAE* 29 (2016): 103–19.

———. *The Viennese Students of Civilization: The Meaning and Context of Austrian Economics Reconsidered*. Cambridge: Cambridge University Press, 2016.

Denord, François. "French Neoliberalism and Its Divisions: From the Colloque Walter Lippmann to the Fifth Republic." In Mirowski and Plehwe, *Mont Pèlerin*, 45–67.

———. *Néo-libéralisme version français*. Paris: Demopolis, 2007.

Diamant, Alfred. *Austrian Catholics and the First Republic: Democracy, Capitalism, and the Social Order, 1918–1934*. Princeton, NJ: Princeton University Press, 1960.

Die direkten Personalsteuern. Vienna: Holder, 1907.

Dietzel, Heinrich. "Beitrag zur Methodik der Wirtschaftswissenschaften." *JfNuS* 42 (1884): 107–34, 353–70.

Dingwall, James, and Bert F. Hoselitz. "Translator's Preface." In Menger, *Principles of Economics*, 37–40.

Doherty, Brian. *Radicals for Capitalism: A Free-Wheeling History of the Modern American Libertarian Movement*. New York: Public Affairs, 2007.

Dolan, Edward G., ed. *The Foundations of Modern Austrian Economics*. Kansas City, MO: Sheed and Ward, 1976.

"Drei neue Handbücher der Volkswirtschaftslehre." *JfNuS* 18 (1872): 342–45.

Duranti, Marco. *The Conservative Human Rights Revolution: European Identity, Transnational Politics, and the Origins of the European Convention*. New York: Oxford University Press, 2017.

Ebeling, Richard. *Political Economy, Public Policy, and Monetary Economics: Ludwig von Mises and the Austrian Tradition*. New York: Routledge, 2010.

———. "Toward a Hermeneutical Economics: Expectations, Prices, and the Role of Interpretation in a Theory of the Market Process." In *Individuals, Institutions, Interpretations*, edited by David Prychitko, 138–55. Brookfield, VT: Avebury, 1995.

Ebenstein, Alan. *Hayek's Journey: The Mind of Friedrich Hayek*. New York: Palgrave, 2003.

ECAEF (European Center of Austrian Economics Foundation). "Generations of the Austrian School." Accessed January 19, 2019. http://ecaef.org/austrian-school-of-economics/generations-of-the-austrian-school.

EconStories. "Fear the Boom and Bust: Keynes vs. Hayek Rap Battle." YouTube, January 23, 2010. https://www.youtube.com/watch?v=donERTFo-Sk.

Eichengreen, Barry, and Peter Temin. "The Gold Standard and the Great Depression." *Contemporary European History* 9, no. 2 (2000): 183–207.

Ekelund, Robert. Review of *Austrian Economics in America* by Karen Vaughn. *RAE* 10, no. 2 (1997): 133–38.

Emmett, Ross, ed. *Elgar Companion to the Chicago School of Economics*. Northampton, UK: Elgar, 2010.

———. *Frank Knight and the Chicago School in American Economics*. London: Routledge, 2009.

———. "Sharpening Tools in the Workshop." In Van Horn, Mirowski, and Stapleford, *Building*, 93–115.

Endres, Anthony, and David Harper. "Carl Menger and His Followers in the Austrian Tradition on the Nature of Capital and Its Structure." *JHET* 33, no. 3 (2011): 357–84.

Erickson, Paul. *The World Game Theorists Made*. Chicago: University of Chicago Press, 2015.

Erickson, Paul, Judy L. Klein, Lorraine Daston, Rebecca Lemov, Thomas Sturm, and Michael D. Gordin. *How Reason Almost Lost Its Mind: The Strange Career of Cold War Rationality*. Chicago: University of Chicago Press, 2013.

"Extracts from an Interview with Friedrich von Hayek." Punto de Vista Economico, December 21, 2016. https://puntodevistaeconomico.wordpress.com/2016/12/21/extracts-from-an-interview-with-friedrich-von-hayek-el-mercurio-chile-1981.

Fang, Lee. "Sphere of Influence: How American Libertarians Are Remaking Latin American Politics." *The Intercept*, August 9, 2017. https://theintercept.com/2017/08/09/atlas-network-alejandro-chafuen-libertarian-think-tank-latin-america-brazil/.

Farese, Giovanni. "The Culture of Investment-led International Development: The Chatham House Circle (1939–45) and Lessons for Today." *International Affairs* 92, no. 6 (2016): 1481–98.

Farrant, Andrew, Edward McPhail, and Sebastian Berger. "Preventing the 'Abuses' of Democracy: Hayek, the 'Military Usurper,' and Transitional Dictatorship in Chile?" *AJES* 71, no. 3 (2012): 513–38.

Feichtinger, Johannes. "Die verletzte Autonomie. Wissenschaft und ihre Struktur in Wien 1848 bis 1938." In Stadler, *650 Jahre* 1:259–92.

———. *Wissenschaft als reflexives Projekt*. Bielefeld, Germany: Transcript, 2010.

———. *Wissenschaft zwischen den Kulturen: Österreichische Hochschullehrer in der Emigration 1938 bis 1945*. Frankfurt: Suhrkamp, 2001.

Feldbauer, Peter. *Stadtswachstum und Wohnungsnot*. Oldenburg, Germany: Verlag für Geschichte und Politik, 1977.

Finer, Herman. *Road to Reaction*. Boston: Little, Brown, 1945.

Fischer, Karin. "The Influence of Neoliberals in Chile before, during, and after Pinochet." In Mirowski and Plehwe, *Mont Pèlerin*, 305–46.

Fisher, Irving. "Mathematical Investigations in the Theory of Value and Prices." Ph.D. diss., Yale University, 1892.

Fleck, Christian. *Etablierung in der Fremde: Vertriebene Wissenschaftler in den USA*. Frankfurt: Campus, 2015.

———. *Marienthal: The Sociography of an Unemployed Community*. New Brunswick, NJ: Transaction, 2009.

———. "Rückkehr unerwünscht: Der Weg der österreichischen Sozialforschung ins Exil." In *Vertriebene Vernunft*, vol. 2, edited by Friedrich Stadler, 182–213. Vienna: Jugend und Volk, 1988.

———. *Transatlantische Bereicherungen: Zur Erfindung der empirischen Sozialforschung*. Frankfurt: Suhrkamp, 2007.

———. "Wie Neues nicht entsteht." *Österreichische Zeitschrift für Geschichtswissenschaften* 11 (2000): 129–78.

Fleck, Ludwik. *Genesis and Development of a Scientific Fact*. Chicago: University of Chicago Press, 1979.

Flügge, Manfred. *Stadt ohne Seele: Vienna 1938*. Berlin: Aufbau, 2018.

Foucault, Michel. *The Birth of Biopolitics: Lectures at the Collège de France, 1978–79*. New York: Picador, 2008.

Fourcade, Marion. *Economists and Society: Discipline and Profession in the United States, Britain, and France, 1890s to 1990s*. Princeton, NJ: Princeton University Press, 2009.

Friedersdorf, Conor. "Grappling with Ron Paul's Racist Newsletters." *Atlantic*, December 21, 2012. https://www.theatlantic.com/politics/archive/2011/12/grappling-with-ron-pauls-racist-newsletters/250206.

Friedman, Milton, and Rose Friedman. *Two Lucky People*. Chicago: University of Chicago Press, 1998.

Fuks, Evi, and Gabriele Kohlbauer, eds. *Die Liebens: 150 Jahre Geschichte einer Wiener Familie*. Vienna: Böhlau, 2004.

Fukuyama, Francis. "The End of History?" *National Interest* 16 (1989): 3–18.

Fürth, Emil. *Die Einkommensteuer in Österreich und ihre Reform.* Leipzig, 1892.

Furth, Joseph Herbert. Interview by Gabrielle Simon Edgcomb. German Historical Institute, July 14, 1988. http://collections.ushmm.org/search/catalog/irn513664.

Gasser, Florian, and Stefan Müller. "Freibeuter der Märkte." *Die Zeit,* October 18, 2012. http://www.zeit.de/2012/43/Hayek-Institut-Wien.

Gillespie, Nick. "Is There Really an 'Insidious Libertarian-to-Alt-Right Pipeline.'" *Reason,* August 23, 2017. http://reason.com/blog/2017/08/23/is-there-really-an-insidious-libertarian.

Gilman, Nils. *Mandarins of the Future: Modernization Theory in Cold War America.* Baltimore: Johns Hopkins University Press, 2004.

Glaeser, Johannes. *Der Werturteilsstreit in der deutschen Nationalökonomie.* Marburg, Germany: Metropolis, 2014.

Glaser, Ernst. *Im Umfeld des Austromarxismus: Ein Beitrag zur Geistesgeschichte des österreichischen Sozialismus.* Vienna: Europaverlag, 1981.

Gordon, David. "Hermeneutics versus Austrian Economics (1986)." Mises Institute, April 9, 2015. https://mises.org/library/hermeneutics-versus-austrian-economics.

———. "The Kochtopus vs. Murray N. Rothbard." *LewRockwell.com,* April 18, 2013. https://www.lewrockwell.com/2013/04/david-gordon/explaining-beltway-libertarians.

"Gottfried Haberler, Defender of Free Trade, Dies." *Washington Post,* May 9, 1995.

Grandner, Margarete, and Franz Traxler. "Sozialpartnerschaft als Option der Zwischenkriegszeit?" In *Februar 1934,* edited by Erich Fröschl and Helge Zoitl, 75–117. Vienna: Böhlau, 1984.

Gross, Gustav. *Die Lehre vom Unternehmergewinn.* Leipzig: Duncker and Humblot, 1884.

———. "Steuerreform." In *Österreichisches Staatswörterbuch,* edited by Ernst Michler and Josef Ulbrich, 1–19. Vienna: Holder, 1896.

Gruber, Helmut. *Red Vienna: Experiment in Working-Class Culture, 1919–1934.* New York: Oxford University Press, 1991.

Gulick, Charles. *Austria from Habsburg to Hitler.* 2 vols. Berkeley: University of California Press, 1948.

Haag, John. "Othmar Spann and the Politics of 'Totality.'" Ph.D. diss., Rice University, 1969.

Haas, Peter. "Introduction: Epistemic Communities and International Policy Coordination." *International Organization* 46, no. 1 (1992): 1–35.

Haberler, Gottfried. *Der Sinn der Indexzahlen.* Tübingen, Germany: Mohr, 1927.

———. "The Foreign Trade Multiplier." *AER* 37, no. 5 (1947): 898–906.

———. *International Trade and Economic Development.* Cairo: Bank of Egypt, 1959.

———. "Joseph Alois Schumpeter, 1883–1950." *QJE* 64 (1950): 333–72.

———. "Mises's Private Seminar." *Wirtschaftspolitische Blätter* 28, no. 4 (1981): 121–26.

———. "Mr. Keynes' Theory of the 'Multiplier': A Methodological Criticism." *ZfN* 7, no. 3 (1936): 299–305.

————. *Prosperity and Depression*. Geneva: League of Nations, 1937.

————. "Schumpeter, Ministre des Finances, 15 Mars–17 Octobre 1919." *Economie Appliquée* 3 (1950): 427–39.

Hacohen, Malachi. *Karl Popper, the Formative Years, 1902–1945: Politics and Philosophy in Interwar Vienna*. Cambridge: Cambridge University Press, 2000.

Hall, Peter, ed. *The Political Power of Economic Ideas: Keynesianism across Nations*. Princeton, NJ: Princeton University Press, 1989.

Hamann, Brigitte. *Hitler's Vienna: A Dictator's Apprenticeship*. London: Tauris Parke, 2010.

Hamowy, Ronald. Introduction to Hayek, *Constitution*, 1–22.

Hanisch, Ernst. *Der Große Illusionist. Otto Bauer (1881–1938)*. Vienna: Böhlau, 2011.

Hartmann, Gerhard. *Der CV in Österreich*. 4th ed. Kevelaer, Germany: Lahn-Verlag, 2011.

Hartwell, R. M. *A History of the Mont Pèlerin Society*. Indianapolis: Liberty Fund, 1995.

Harvey, David. *A Brief History of Neoliberalism*. Oxford: Oxford University Press, 2005.

Harvey, Lee. "The Nature of 'Schools' in the Sociology of Knowledge: The Case of the 'Chicago School.'" *Sociological Review* 35, no. 2 (1987): 245–78.

Hawtrey, R. G. "Professor Hayek's *Pure Theory of Capital*." *EJ* 51 (1942): 281–90.

Hayek, F. A. "Carl Menger." *Economica* 1, no. 4 (1934): 393–420.

————, ed. *Collectivist Economic Planning*. London: Routledge, 1935.

————. *The Constitution of Liberty: The Definitive Edition*. Edited by Ronald Hamowy. Chicago: University of Chicago Press, 2011.

————. *Contra Keynes and Cambridge: Essays, Correspondence*. Edited by Bruce Caldwell. Chicago: University of Chicago Press, 1995.

————. *The Counter-Revolution of Science*. Glencoe, IL: Free Press, 1952.

————. "The Dilemma of Specialization." In *The State of the Social Sciences*, edited by Leonard White, 462–73. Chicago: University of Chicago Press, 1956.

————. "Economics and Knowledge." *Economica* 4, no. 13 (1937): 33–54.

————. "Economic Thought: The Austrian School." In *International Encyclopedia of the Social Sciences*, edited by David Sills, 458–62. New York: Macmillan, 1968.

————. "Freiherr Friedrich von Wieser." *JfNuS* 70 (1926): 511–18.

————. "Friedrich von Wieser." In *International Encyclopedia of the Social Sciences*, edited by David Sills, 549–50. New York: Macmillan, 1968.

————. *Hayek on Hayek: An Autobiographical Dialogue*. Chicago: University of Chicago Press, 1994.

————. "Intellectuals and Socialism." *University of Chicago Law Review* 16, no. 3 (1949): 417–33.

————. *Law, Legislation, and Liberty*. 3 vols. Chicago: University of Chicago Press, 1973–79.

————. *Monetary Theory and the Trade Cycle*. New York: Kelley, 1933.

————. "The Mythology of Capital." *QJE* 50 (1936): 199–228.

————. "On the Relationship between Investment and Output." *EJ* 44 (1934): 207–31.

———. "Österreich." *IfK* 3 (1929): 77–86, 149–58.

———. *Prices and Production*. 2nd ed. London: Routledge, 1935.

———. *The Pure Theory of Capital*. London: Macmillan, 1941.

———. "Reflection on the Pure Theory of Money of Mr. J. M. Keynes." *Economica* 33 (1931): 270–95.

———. Review of *Nationalökonomie* by Ludwig von Mises. *EJ* 51 (1941): 124–27.

———. *Road to Serfdom: Text and Documents*. Edited by Bruce Caldwell. Chicago: University of Chicago Press, 2007.

———. *Studies on the Abuse and Decline of Reason: Texts and Documents*. Edited by Bruce Caldwell. Chicago: University of Chicago Press, 2018.

———. "Warum ein Nobelpreisträger Oesterreich so bald verlassen." *Der Kurier*, January 22–23, 1977.

Hayek Institut. "Leitbild." Accessed January 19, 2019. http://www.hayek-institut.at/leitbild/.

Hazlitt, Henry. "The Case for Capitalism." *Newsweek*, September 19, 1949.

Healy, Maureen. *Vienna and the Fall of the Habsburg Empire: Total War and Everyday Life in World War I*. Cambridge: Cambridge University Press, 2004.

Heilbroner, Robert. "After Communism." *New Yorker*, September 10, 1990.

———. "Analysis and Vision in the History of Modern Economic Thought." *Journal of Economic Literature* 28 (September 1990): 1097–1114.

———. "The Triumph of Capitalism." *New Yorker*, January 23, 1989.

———. "Was Schumpeter Right?" *Social Research* 48, no. 3 (1981): 456–71.

———. *The Worldly Philosophers: The Lives, Times, and Ideas of the Great Economic Thinkers*. New York: Simon and Schuster, 1953.

Heilbroner, Robert, and Irving Howe. "The World after Communism." *Dissent*, Fall 1990, 429–35.

Helleiner, Robert. *Forgotten Foundations of Bretton Woods: International Development and the Making of the Postwar Order*. Ithaca, NY: Cornell University Press, 2014.

———. *States and the Reemergence of Global Finance: From Bretton Woods to the 1990s*. Ithaca, NY: Cornell University Press, 1994.

Hennings, Klaus. *The Austrian Theory of Value and Capital*. Cheltenham, UK: Elgar, 1997.

Hilferding, Rudolf. "Böhm-Bawerk's Criticism of Marx." In Böhm, *Karl Marx*, 119–96.

———. *Finance Capital: A Study of the Latest Phase of Capitalist Development*. London: Routledge, 1981.

———. Review of *Theorie des Geldes und der Umlaufsmittel* by Ludwig von Mises. *Neue Zeit* 30 (1913): 1025–27.

Hobsbawm, Eric. *The Age of Capital: 1848–1875*. New York: Vintage, 1975.

———. *Revolutionaries—Contemporary Essays*. New York: Pantheon, 1973.

Hobsbawm, Eric, and Terence Ranger, eds. *The Invention of Tradition*. New York: Cambridge University Press, 2012.

Hochman, Erin. *Imagining a Greater Germany: Nationalism and the Idea of Anschluss.* Ithaca, NY: Cornell University Press, 2016.

Hoppe, Hans-Hermann. *Democracy: The God That Failed.* New Brunswick, NJ: Transaction, 2001.

Horn, Karen. "Auf dem rechten Auge blind." *Schweizer Monat,* July 2015. https://www.schweizermonat.ch/artikel/auf-dem-rechten-auge-blind.

———. "Die rechte Flanke der Liberalen." *Frankfurter Allgemeine Sonntagszeitung,* May 17, 2015. https://www.dropbox.com/s/sgbtg854wx9w8br/Liberalreaktion%C3%A4r-1.docx?d1=0.

Horwitz, Steven. "How Did We Get Here? Or, Why Do 20 Year Old Newsletters Matter So Damn Much?" *Bleeding Heart Libertarians,* December 23, 2011. http://bleedingheartlibertarians.com/2011/12/how-did-we-get-here-or-why-do-20-year-old-newsletters-matter-so-damn-much.

———. "More on the Austrianness of Contemporary Austrian Economics." *Cato Unbound,* September 18, 2012. https://www.cato-unbound.org/2012/09/18/steven-horwitz/more-austrianness-contemporary-austrian-economics.

———. "The Paul Newsletters and the Problem of the Paleos." *Liberty and Power* (blog), History News Network, January 10, 2008. http://historynewsnetwork.org/blog/46313.

———. "The Rhetoric of Libertarians and the Unfortunate Appeal to the Alt-Right." *Bleeding Heart Libertarians,* August 4, 2017. http://bleedingheartlibertarians.com/2017/08/rhetoric-libertarians-unfortunate-appeal-alt-right/.

———. "What Austrian Economics IS and What Austrian Economics Is NOT." *Coordination Problem,* November 29, 2011. http://www.coordinationproblem.org/2010/11/what-austrian-economics-is-and-what-austrian-economics-is-not.html.

Howard, M. C., and J. E. King. "Marxian Economists and the Great Depression." *HOPE* 22, no. 1 (1990): 81–100.

Howey, Richard. *The Rise of the Marginal Utility School.* Lawrence: University Press of Kansas, 1960.

Howson, Barbara. *Lionel Robbins.* Cambridge: Cambridge University Press, 2011.

Hughes, H. Stuart. *Consciousness and Society: The Reorientation of European Social Thought, 1890–1930.* New York: Knopf, 1958.

Hülsmann, Jörg Guido. *Ludwig von Mises: The Last Knight of Liberalism.* Auburn, AL: LvMI, 2007.

Hutchison, T. W. *A Review of Economic Doctrines, 1870–1929.* Oxford: Oxford University Press, 1953.

Isaac, Joel. *Working Knowledge: Making the Human Sciences from Parsons to Kuhn.* Cambridge, MA: Harvard University Press, 2012.

Jackson, Ben. "At the Origins of Neo-Liberalism: The Free Economy and the Strong State, 1930–1947." *Historical Journal* 53, no. 1 (2010): 129–53.

Jahrbuch der GÖV. Vienna: Manzsche, 1915.

Janik, Allan, and Stephen Toulmin. *Wittgenstein's Vienna*. New York: Simon and Schuster, 1973.

Jászi, Oskar. *The Dissolution of the Habsburg Monarchy*. Chicago: University of Chicago Press, 1966.

Jevons, William Stanley. *A General Mathematical Theory of Political Economy*. London, 1862.

———. *The Theory of Political Economy*. London: Macmillan, 1871.

John, Gerald. "FPÖ und Wirtschaftskurs." *Der Standard*, April 11, 2017. http://derstandard.at/2000055690267/FPOe-sucht-Wirtschaftskurs-Schwanken-zwischen-links-und-neoliberal.

John, Michael, and Albert Lichtblau. *Schmelztiegel Wien—einst und jetzt*. 2nd ed. Vienna: Böhlau, 1993.

Johnston, William. *The Austrian Mind: An Intellectual and Social History, 1848–1938*. Berkeley: University of California Press, 1972.

Judt, Tony. *Ill Fares the Land*. New York: Penguin, 2010.

———. *Postwar: A History of Europe since 1945*. New York: Penguin, 2005.

———. *Thinking the Twentieth Century*. New York: Penguin, 2012.

Katalog der Carl Menger-Bibliothek in der Handels-Universität Tokio. New York: Franklin, 1969.

Kauder, Emil. "Aus Mengers nachgelassenen Papieren." *Weltwirtschaftliches Archiv* 89 (1962): 1–28.

———. "Austro-Marxism vs. Austro-Marginalism." *HOPE* 2, no. 2 (1970): 398–418.

———. "Genesis of the Marginal Utility Theory." *Economic Journal* 63 (1953): 638–50.

———. *The History of Marginal Utility Theory*. Princeton, NJ: Princeton University Press, 1965.

———. "The Intellectual and Political Roots of the Older Austrian School." *ZfN* 17, no. 4 (1957): 411–25.

Kaufmann, Felix. "Logik und Wirtschaftswissenschaft." *AfSuS* 54 (1925): 614–57.

———. *Songs of the Mises-Kreis*. Translated by Arlene Oost-Zinner. Auburn, AL: LvMI, 2010.

———. *Wiener Lieder zu Philosophie und Ökonomie*. Stuttgart: Fischer, 1992.

Keynes, John Maynard. *The Economic Consequences of Mr. Churchill*. London: Hogarth, 1925.

———. *The Economic Consequences of the Peace*. 1919. Reprint, New York: Harcourt, Brace, 1920.

———. *The End of Laissez-Faire*. London: Hogarth, 1926.

———. *The General Theory of Employment, Interest and Money*. New York: Harcourt, Brace, 1936.

———. "The Pure Theory of Money: A Reply to Mr. Hayek." *Economica* 34 (1931): 387–403.

———. Review of *Theorie des Geldes und der Umlaufsmittel* by Ludwig von Mises, and *Geld und Kapital* by Friedrich Bendixen. *EJ* 24 (1914): 417–19.

———. *A Treatise on Money*. New York: Harcourt, Brace, 1930.

Kirchik, Jamie. "Angry White Man." *TNR*, January 8, 2008. https://newrepublic
.com/article/61771/angry-white-man.

Kirzner, Israel. *Competition and Entrepreneurship.* Chicago: University of Chicago
Press, 1973.

——. *The Economic Point of View.* Menlo Park, CA: Institute for Humane Studies,
1960.

Klausinger, Hansjörg. "Academic Anti-Semitism and the Austrian School: Vienna,
1918–1945." *Atlantic Economic Journal* 42, no. 2 (2014): 191–204.

——. "From Mises to Morgenstern: Austrian Economics during the Ständestaat."
QJAE 9, no. 3 (2006): 25–43.

——. "Gustav Stolper, *Der deutsche Volkswirt*, and the Controversy on Economic
Policy in the Weimar Republic." *HOPE* 33, no. 2 (2001): 241–67.

——. "Hans Mayer, Last Knight of the Austrian School, Vienna Branch." *HOPE*
47, no. 2 (2015): 271–305.

——. " 'In the Wilderness': Emigration and the Decline of the Austrian School."
HOPE 38, no. 2 (2006): 617–64.

——, ed. *Machlup, Morgenstern, Haberler, Hayek und andere.* Marburg, Germany:
Metropolis, 2005.

——. "The Nationalökonomische Gesellschaft in the Interwar Period and Beyond."
Working Paper, Wirtschaftsüniversitat Wien, 2015.

——. "Policy Advice of Academic Experts: The Case of Austria in the 1930s." *RAE*
11 (2008): 25–53.

Klein, Naomi. *The Shock Doctrine: The Rise of Disaster Capitalism.* Toronto: Random
House, 2007.

Knight, Frank. "Capitalistic Production, Time, and the Rate of Return." In *Essays in
Honour of Gustav Cassel*, 327–42. London: Allen and Unwin, 1933.

——. "Reader's Report." In Hayek, *Road*, 249–50.

——. *Risk, Uncertainty and Profit.* Boston: Houghton Mifflin, 1921.

Kolev, Stefan. "Neoliberale Leitideen zum Staat. Die Rolle des Staates in der Wirtschaft-
spolitik im Werk von Walter Eucken, Friedrich August von Hayek, Ludwig von
Mises und Wilhelm Röpke." Ph.D. dissertation, University of Hamburg, 2011.

——. "Reincorporating Friedrich von Wieser and the Concept of Power into the
Austrian Research Program." HOPE Working Paper, Center for the History of
Political Economy, Duke University, Durham, NC, 2017.

Köster, Roman. *Die Wissenschaft der Außenseiter.* Göttingen, Germany: V and R, 2011.

Kraus, Karl. *Die demolirte Literatur.* Vienna: Bauer, 1899.

——. *Die letzten Tage der Menschheit.* Vienna: Die Fackel, 1919.

——. *Half Truths and One-and-a-Half Truths.* Translated by Harry Zohn. Chicago:
University of Chicago Press, 1990.

Kreisky, Bruno. *Erinnerungen.* Edited by Oliver Rathkolb. Vienna: Styria, 2007.

Krohn, Claus-Dieter. "Die Emigration der Österreichischen Schule der Nationalökonomie in die USA." In *Vertriebene Vernunft*, vol. 2, edited by Friedrich Stadler,
402–15. Vienna: Jugend und Volk, 1988.

————. *Intellectuals in Exile: Refugee Scholars and the New School for Social Research*. Amherst: University of Massachusetts Press, 1993.

Kuhn, Thomas. *The Structure of Scientific Revolutions*. Chicago: University of Chicago Press, 1962.

Kuznets, Simon. "Schumpeter's Business Cycles." *AER* 30, no. 2 (1940): 257–71.

Lachmann, Ludwig. "Austrian Economics: A Hermeneutic Approach." In *Economics and Hermeneutics*, edited by Don Lavoie, 132–44. London: Routledge, 1990.

————. *Capital, Expectations, and the Market Process*. Kansas City, MO: Sheed and Ward, 1977.

Landauer, Carl. Review of *Die Gemeinwirtschaft* by Ludwig von Mises. *JfNuS* 66, no. 2 (1923): 181–82.

Latour, Bruno. *Reassembling the Social: An Introduction to Actor-Network Theory*. Oxford: Oxford University Press, 2005.

Lavoie, Don, ed. *Economics and Hermeneutics*. London: Routledge, 1990.

————. *Rivalry and Central Planning: The Socialist Calculation Debate Reconsidered*. Cambridge: Cambridge University Press, 1985.

Lazear, Edward. "Economic Imperialism." *QJE* 115, no. 1 (2000): 99–146.

Lee, Frederic S., and Bruce C. Cronin. "Research Quality Rankings of Heterodox Economics Journals in a Contested Discipline." *AJES* 69, no. 5 (2010): 1409–52.

Leeson, Robert. *Ideology and the International Economy*. New York: Palgrave, 2003.

Lenin, Vladimir. "Marxismus und Revisionismus." April 1908. Kommunisten.ch. Accessed January 19, 2019. http://www.kommunisten.ch/index.php?article_id=102.

Leonard, Robert J. "The Collapse of Interwar Vienna: Oskar Morgenstern's Community, 1925–1950." *HOPE* 43, no. 1 (2011): 83–130.

————. "Ethics and the Excluded Middle: Karl Menger and Social Science in Interwar Vienna." *Isis* 89, no. 1 (1998): 1–26.

————. *Von Neumann, Morgenstern, and the Creation of Game Theory*. Cambridge: Cambridge University Press, 2010.

Leser, Norbert. *Zwischen Reformismus und Bolschewismus*. Vienna: Europa Verlag, 1975.

Levine, Emily. "Baltimore Teaches, Göttingen Learns: Cooperation, Competition, and the Research University." *AHR* 121, no. 3 (2016): 780–823.

Lewis, Matt. "The Insidious Libertarian-to-Alt-Right Pipeline." *Daily Beast*, August 23, 2017. https://www.thedailybeast.com/the-insidious-libertarian-to-alt-right-pipeline.

Lewis, Paul. "The Emergence of 'Emergence' in the Work of Friedrich A. Hayek: A Historical Analysis." *HOPE* 48, no. 1 (2016): 111–50.

————. "Systems, Structural Properties, and Levels of Organisation: The Influence of Ludwig Von Bertalanffy on the Work of F. A. Hayek." *RHETM* 34A (2016): 125–59.

Lippmann, Walter. *Inquiry into the Principles of the Good Society*. Boston: Little, Brown, 1937.

Loria, Achille. "La scuola Austriaca nell' economia politica." *Nuova Antologia di Scienze, Letteri ed Arti* 1 (1890): 492–509.

Louzek, Marek. "The Battle of Methods in Economics." *AJES* 70, no. 2 (2011): 439–63.

Low, Alfred. *The Anschluss Movement in Austria and Germany, 1918–1919, and the Paris Peace Conference.* Philadelphia: American Philosophical Society, 1974.

Lutz, H. L. Review of *Theorie des Geldes und der Umlaufsmittel* by Ludwig von Mises. *AER* 3 (1913): 144–46.

Luxemburg, Rosa. *Sozialreform oder Revolution.* Leipzig: Heinisch, 1899.

Machlup, Fritz. "Austrian Economics." In *Encyclopedia of Economics*, 38–43. New York: Macmillan, 1982.

———. "Capitalism and Its Future Appraised by Two Liberal Economists." *AER* 33 (June 1943): 301–20.

———. *Essays in Economic Semantics.* New York: Prentice-Hall, 1963.

———, ed. *International Monetary Arrangements: The Problem of Choice.* Princeton, NJ: Princeton University Press, 1964.

———. "An Interview with Professor Fritz Machlup." *AEN* 3, no. 1 (1980): 1, 9–12.

———. *Knowledge: Its Creation, Distribution and Economic Significance.* 3 vols. Princeton, NJ: Princeton University Press, 1981–84.

———. "Ludwig von Mises: The Academic Scholar Who Would Not Compromise." *Wirtschaftspolitische Blätter* 28, no. 4 (1981): 6–14.

———. *Plans for the Reform of the International Monetary System.* 2nd ed. Princeton, NJ: Princeton University Press, 1964.

———. *The Production and Distribution of Knowledge in the United States.* Princeton, NJ: Princeton University Press, 1962.

———. *Stock Market, Credit, and Capital Formation.* London: Hodge, 1940.

———. "The Theory of Foreign Exchange." *Economica* 6 (1939): 375–97.

———. "Three Concepts of the Balance of Payments and the So-Called Dollar Shortage." *EJ* 60 (1950): 46–68.

MacLean, Nancy. *Democracy in Chains: The Deep History of the Radical Right's Stealth Plan for America.* New York: Penguin, 2017.

Manela, Erez. *The Wilsonian Moment: Self-Determination and the International Origins of Anticolonial Nationalism.* New York: Oxford University Press, 2009.

Marschak, Jacob. "Reader's Report." In Hayek, *Road*, 251–52.

Marx, Karl. *Das Kapital.* 3 vols. Hamburg: Otto Meissner, 1867–83.

———. "Theses on Feuerbach." 1845. Translated by Cyril Smith, 2002. *Marxists Internet Archive.* https://www.marxists.org/archive/marx/works/1845/theses.

März, Eduard. *Joseph Schumpeter: Scholar, Teacher, and Politician.* New Haven, CT: Yale University Press, 1991.

Mataja, Victor. *Der Unternehmergewinn.* Vienna: Holder, 1884.

Mayer, Jane. *Dark Money: The Secret History of the Billionaires behind the Rise of the Radical Right.* New York: Doubleday, 2016.

Mazower, Mark. *Governing the World: The History of an Idea, 1815 to the Present.* New York: Penguin, 2012.

McCloskey, Deirdre. "A Kirznerian Economic History of the Modern World." *DeirdreMcCloskey.com*, June 17, 2011. http://www.deirdremccloskey.com/editorials/kirzner.php.

McCraw, Thomas. *Prophet of Innovation: Joseph Schumpeter and Creative Destruction.* Cambridge, MA: Harvard University Press, 2007.

McGirr, Lisa. *Suburban Warriors: The Origins of the New American Right.* Princeton, NJ: Princeton University Press, 2001.

McGrath, William. *Dionysian Art and Populist Politics in Austria.* New Haven, CT: Yale University Press, 1974.

Menger, Anton. *Das Recht auf den vollen Arbeitsertrag in geschichtlicher Darstellung.* Stuttgart: Cotta, 1886.

Menger, Carl. *Das Goldagio und der heutige Stand der Valutareform.* Prague: Haase, 1893.

———. *Investigations into the Method of the Social Sciences.* New York: NYU Press, 1985.

———. *Irrthümer des Historismus in der deutschen Nationalökonomie.* Vienna: Holder, 1884.

———. *Principles of Economics.* Auburn, AL: LvMI, 2007.

———. "Zur Theorie des Kapitals." *JfNuS* 17 (1888): 135–83.

Menger, Karl. "Österreichischer Marginalismus und mathematische Ökonomie." *ZfN* 32, no. 1 (1972): 19–28.

———. *Reminiscences of the Vienna Circle and the Mathematical Colloquium.* Dordrecht: Kluwer, 1994.

"Mercatus Center, George Mason University." *Desmog Blog.* Accessed January 19, 2019. https://www.desmogblog.com/mercatus-center.

Metzler, Mark. *Capitalism as Will and Imagination: Schumpeter's Guide to the Post-War Japanese Miracle.* Ithaca, NY: Cornell University Press, 2013.

Mill, John Stuart. *Principles of Political Economy.* 7th ed. London: Longman, Green, 1909.

Mirowski, Philip. *More Heat than Light: Economics as Social Physics.* New York: Cambridge University Press, 1989.

———. *Never Let a Serious Crisis Go to Waste: How Neoliberalism Survived the Financial Meltdown.* London: Verso, 2013.

Mirowski, Philip, and Dieter Plehwe, eds. *The Road from Mont Pèlerin: The Making of the Neoliberal Thought Collective.* Cambridge, MA: Harvard University Press, 2009.

Mises, Ludwig von. *Bureaucracy.* New Haven, CT: Yale University Press, 1944.

———. "Die Krise und der Kapitalismus." *NFP*, October 17, 1931.

———. *Die Kritik des Interventionismus.* 2nd ed. Stuttgart: Fischer, 1976.

———. *Gemeinwirtschaft.* Jena, Germany: Fischer, 1922.

———. *Human Action.* Scholar's ed. Auburn, AL: LvMI, 1998.

———. *Liberalismus.* Jena, Germany: Fischer, 1927.

———. "Liberty and Its Antithesis." In *Economic Freedom and Interventionism*, edited by Bettina Bien Greaves, 172–77. Indianapolis: Liberty Fund, 1990.

———. *Memoirs*. Auburn, AL: LvMI, 2009.

———. *Nationalökonomie*. Geneva, 1940.

———. *Nation, State, and Economy*. New York: NYU Press, 1983.

———. *Omnipotent Government*. New Haven, CT: Yale University Press, 1944.

———. "Richard Lieben als Ökonom." *NFP*, November 14, 1919.

———. *Socialism*. New Haven, CT: Yale University Press, 1951.

———. *The Theory of Money and Credit*. New Haven, CT: Yale University Press, 1953.

———. "Zur Frage der Altersversorgung der Arbeiter." *Zeitschrift* 13 (1904): 463–65.

Mitchell, Wesley C. Foreword to Wieser, *Social Economics*, ix–xii.

Mohr, Charles. "Three of the Men Who Serve as Goldwater's Advisers." *NYT*, March 31, 1964.

Mont Pèlerin Society. "Statement of Aims." Accessed January 19, 2019. https://www.montpelerin.org/statement-of-aims.

Morgenstern, Oskar. *The Limits of Economics*. London: Hodge, 1937.

———. *On the Accuracy of Economic Observations*. Princeton, NJ: Princeton University Press, 1950.

———. *Wirtschaftsprognose: Eine Untersuchung ihrer Voraussetzungen und Möglichkeiten*. Berlin: Springer, 1928.

Morton, Frederic. *A Nervous Splendor*. Boston: Da Capo, 1989.

Moss, Lawrence. Introduction to *The Economics of Ludwig von Mises*, 1–8. Kansas City, MO: Sheed and Ward, 1976.

Moyn, Samuel. *Christian Human Rights*. Philadelphia: University of Pennsylvania Press, 2015.

Murphy, Craig. *Global Institutions, Marginalization, and Development*. London: Routledge, 2005.

Murphy, Robert. "In Defense of the Mises Institute." *Free Advice* (blog), December 31, 2011. http://consultingbyrpm.com/blog/2011/12/in-defense-of-the-mises-institute.html.

Nasar, Sylvia. "Friedrich von Hayek Dies at 92." *NYT*, March 24, 1992.

———. "Neglected Economist Honored by President." *NYT*, November 19, 1991.

Nash, George. *The Conservative Intellectual Movement in America since 1945*. New York: Basic Books, 1976.

Nautz, Jürgen, ed. *Unterhändler des Vertrauens: Aus den nachgelassenen Schriften von Sektionschef Dr. Richard Schüller*. Vienna: Oldenbourg, 1990.

Neugebauer, Wolfgang. *The Austrian Resistance, 1938–1945*. Vienna: Steinbauer, 2014.

Neumann, Friedrich. *Grundlagen der Volkswirtschaftslehre*. Tübingen, Germany: Laupe, 1889.

Neurath, Otto. "Nationalökonomie und Wertlehre, eine systematische Untersuchung." *Zeitschrift* 20 (1913): 52–114.

Nierhaus, Andreas, ed. *Der Ring: Pionierjahre einer Prachtstrasse*. Vienna: Residenz, 2015.

Nik-Khah, Edward, and Robert Van Horn. "Inland Empire: Economics Imperialism as an Imperative of Chicago Neoliberalism." *Journal of Economic Methodology* 19, no. 3 (2012): 259–82.

Nobel Prize. "The Sveriges Riksbank Prize in Economic Sciences in Memory of Alfred Nobel 1974." Press release. October 9, 1974. http://www.nobelprize.org/nobel_prizes/economic-sciences/laureates/1974/press.html.

Nolan, Mary. *The Transatlantic Century: Europe and America, 1890–2010.* New York: Cambridge University Press, 2012.

Nordmann, Jürgen. *Der lange Marsch zum Neoliberalismus.* Hamburg: VSA, 2005.

NOUS. "About Us." Accessed January 19, 2019. http://nous.network/en/about-us/.

Offer, Avner, and Gabriel Södersberg. *The Nobel Factor: The Prize in Economics, Social Democracy, and the Market Turn.* Princeton, NJ: Princeton University Press, 2016.

Officer, L. H. *"Prosperity and Depression*—and Beyond." *QJE* 97, no. 1 (1982): 149–59.

Olmsted, Kathryn. *Right Out of California: The 1930s and the Big Business Roots of Modern Conservatism.* New York: New Press, 2015.

Ortolano, Guy. "The Typicalities of the English? Walt Rostow, *The Stages of Economic Growth*, and Modern British History." *MIH* 12, no. 3 (2015): 657–84.

Palacia, Pilar, and Elisabetta Rurali. *Bellagio Center—Villa Serbelloni: A Brief History.* New York: Rockefeller Foundation, 2009.

Pareto, Vilfredo. "La Teoria dei Prezzi dei Signori Auspitz e Lieben e le Osservazioni del Professore Walras." *Giornale degli economisti* 4 (1892): 201–39.

Parmar, Inderjeet. *Foundations of the American Century: The Ford, Carnegie, and Rockefeller Foundations in the Rise of American Power.* New York: Columbia University Press, 2012.

Paul, Ron. *Mises and Austrian Economics: A Personal View.* Auburn, AL: LvMI, 2004.

Peck, Jamie. *Constructions of Neoliberal Reason.* New York: Oxford University Press, 2010.

Pedersen, Susan. *The Guardians: The League of Nations and the Crisis of Empire.* New York: Oxford University Press, 2015.

Pelinka, Anton. "The Impact of American Scholarship on Austrian Political Science: The Making of a Discipline." In *The Americanization/Westernization of Austria*, edited by Günter Bischof and Anton Pelinka, 226–34. New York: Routledge, 2003.

Perloff, Marjorie. *Vienna Paradox: A Memoir.* New York: New Directions, 2004.

Philippovich, Eugen von. "Das Wesen der volkswirtschaftlichen Produktivität und die Möglichkeit ihrer Messung." In *Verhandlungen des Vereins für Socialpolitik in Wien, 1909*, 329–70. Leipzig: Duncker and Humblot, 1910.

———. *Grundriß der politischen Ökonomie.* 2 vols. Freiburg, Germany: Mohr, 1893–1907.

———. *Über die Aufgabe und Methode der politischen Ökonomie.* Freiburg, Germany: Mohr, 1886.

Phillips-Fein, Kim. *Invisible Hands: The Businessmen's Crusade against the New Deal.* New York: Norton, 2009.

Plener, Ernst von. "Vierzig Jahre Gesellschaft Österreichischer Volkswirte." *Jahrbuch* 4 (1915): 118–30.

Polanyi, Karl. *The Great Transformation.* Boston: Beacon, 2001.

Pomeranz, Kenneth. "Histories for a Less National Age." *AHR* 119, no. 1 (2014): 1–22.

Popp, Gerhard. *CV in Österreich, 1864–1938*. Vienna: Böhlau, 1984.

Popper, Karl. *Die Logik der Forschung*. Tübingen, Germany: Mohr, 1934.

———. *The Open Society and Its Enemies*. 2 vols. London: Routledge, 1945.

———. "The Poverty of Historicism I." *Economica* 11, no. 42 (1944): 86–103.

———. "The Poverty of Historicism II." *Economica* 11, no. 43 (1944): 119–37.

———. "The Poverty of Historicism III." *Economica* 12, no. 46 (1945): 69–89.

Prendergast, Christopher. "Alfred Schutz and the Austrian School of Economics." *American Journal of Sociology* 92, no. 1 (1986): 1–26.

Proctor, Robert. *Value-Free Science? Purity and Power in Modern Knowledge*. Cambridge, MA: Harvard University Press, 1991.

Ptak, Ralf. *Vom Ordoliberalismus zur sozialen Marktwirtschaft*. Wiesbaden, Germany: Verlag für Sozialwissenschaften, 2013.

Renner, Karl. *Staat und Nation*. Vienna: Dietl, 1899.

R.F. Review of *Geschichte und Kritik der Kapitalzins-Theorien* by Eugen von Böhm-Bawerk. *JfNuS* 46, no. 12 (1886): 77–79.

Richman, Sheldon. "How Liberals Distort Austrian Economics." *Reason*, January 13, 2012. http://reason.com/archives/2012/01/13/how-liberals-distort-austrian-economics.

Riedel, Katja, and Sebastian Pittelkow. "Die Hayek-Gesellschaft—'Mistbeet der AfD'?" *Süddeutsche Zeitung*, July 14, 2017. http://www.sueddeutsche.de/wirtschaft/hayek-gesellschaft-mistbeet-der-afd-1.3589049.

Robbins, Lionel. *Autobiography of an Economist*. London: Macmillan, 1971.

Robin, Corey. "The Hayek-Pinochet Connection: A Second Reply to My Critics." *Crooked Timber*, June 25, 2013. http://crookedtimber.org/2013/06/25/the-hayek-pinochet-connection-a-second-reply-to-my-critics.

———. "Hayek von Pinochet." *CoreyRobin.com*, July 8, 2012. http://coreyrobin.com/2012/07/08/hayek-von-pinochet.

———. "Nietzsche's Marginal Children." *Nation*, May 27, 2013.

———. *The Reactionary Mind: Conservatism from Edmund Burke to Donald Trump*. 2nd ed. New York: Oxford University Press, 2017.

Robinson, Joan. *Contributions to Modern Economics*. London: Academic, 1978.

Rodgers, Daniel. *Atlantic Crossings: Social Politics in a Progressive Age*. Cambridge, MA: Harvard University Press, 1998.

"Ron Paul Newsletters." *TNR*, January 8, 2012. https://newrepublic.com/article/71377/ron-paul-newsletter.

Roscher, Wilhelm. *Grundriss zu Vorlesungen über die Staatswissenschaft nach geschichtlicher Methode*. Göttingen, Germany: Dietrichschen, 1843.

Rosenboim, Or. *The Emergence of Globalism: Visions of World Order in Britain and the United States, 1930–1950*. Princeton, NJ: Princeton University Press, 2017.

Rosenstein-Rodan, Paul. "Grenznutzen." In *Handwörterbuch der Staatswissenschaften*, vol. 4, 1190–1223. Jena, Germany: Fischer, 1927.

———. "La Complementarietà: Prima della tre tappe del progresso della Teoria Economica Pura." *La Riforma Sociale* 44 (1933): 257–308.

Rostow, Walt. *The Stages of Economic Growth: A Non-Communist Manifesto*. Cambridge: Cambridge University Press, 1960.

Roth, Joseph. *Radetzky March*. New York: Overton, 2002.

Rothbard, Murray. "The Anatomy of a State." In *Egalitarianism as a Revolt against Nature and Other Essays*, 2nd ed., 55–88. Auburn, AL: LvMI, 2000.

———. "Confidential Memo to the Volker Fund on F. A. Hayek's *Constitution of Liberty*." In *Rothbard vs. the Philosophers*, edited by Roberta A. Modugno, 61–70. Auburn, AL: LvMI, 2009.

———. *The Ethics of Liberty*. 2nd ed. New York: NYU Press, 1998.

———. *For a New Liberty*. New York: Macmillan, 1973.

———. "Hermeneutical Invasion of Philosophy and Economics." *RAE* 3, no. 1 (1989): 45–60.

———. "It Usually Ends with Ed Crane." *Libertarian Forum* 1–2 (1981): 1.

———. *Man, Economy, and State with Power and Market*. 2nd ed. Auburn, AL: LvMI, 2001.

Salerno, Joseph. "Mises and Hayek Dehomogenized." *RAE* 6, no. 2 (1993): 113–46.

———. "The Sociology of the Development of Austrian Economics." In *Property, Freedom, and Society*, edited by Jörg Guido Hülsmann and Stephan Kinsella, 95–108. Auburn: LvMI, 2009.

Salvatori, Massimo. *Karl Kautsky and the Socialist Revolution, 1880–1938*. Rev. ed. London: Verso, 1990.

Sax, Emil. *Das Wesen und die Aufgabe der Nationalökonomie*. Vienna: Holder, 1884.

———. *Die Grundlegung der theoretischen Staatswirtschaft*. Vienna: Holder, 1887.

Schäfer, Axel. *American Progressives and German Social Reform, 1875–1920*. Stuttgart: Steiner, 2000.

Scheall, Scott. "Hayek the Apriorist?" *JHET* 37, no. 1 (2015): 87–110.

———. "What Is Extreme about Mises's Extreme Apriorism." *Journal of Economic Methodology* 24, no. 3 (2017): 226–49.

Schmelzer, Matthias. *Freiheit für die Wechselkurse und Kapital*. Marburg, Germany: Metropolis, 2010.

Schmoller, Gustav. Review of *Wirtschaftsformen und Wirtschaftsprinzipien* by Gustav Gross. *Schmoller* 12 (1888): 733–34.

———. "Zur Methodologie der Staats- und Sozialwissenschaften." *Schmoller* 7 (1883): 975–94.

Schnitzler, Arthur. *Anatol. Historisch-kritische Ausgabe*. Edited by Evelyne Polt-Heinzl and Isabella Schwentner. 2 vols. Berlin: De Gruyter, 2012.

Schorske, Carl. *Fin-de-Siècle Vienna: Politics and Culture*. New York: Knopf, 1979.

———. *Thinking with History: Explorations in the Passage to Modernism*. Princeton, NJ: Princeton University Press, 1998.

Schuessler, Jennifer. "Hayek: The Back Story." *NYT*, July 11, 2010.

Schulak, Eugen Maria, and Herbert Unterköfler. *The Austrian School of Economics: A History of Its Ideas, Ambassadors, and Institutions*. Auburn, AL: LvMI, 2011.

Schulman, Daniel. *Sons of Wichita: How the Koch Brothers Became the Most Powerful and Private Dynasty.* New York: Grand Central, 2014.

Schumacher, Reinhard, and Scott Scheall. "The Life of Carl Menger: New Insights into the Biography of the Father of Austrian Economics." HOPE Working Paper, Center for the History of Political Economy, Duke University, Durham, NC, 2015.

Schuman, Rebecca. "Meet Sebastian Kurz, the 31-Year Old Opportunist in Charge of Austria Now." *The Awl,* October 19, 2017. https://www.theawl.com/2017/10/meet-sebastian-kurz-the-31-year-old-opportunist-in-charge-of-austria-now.

Schumpeter, Joseph. *Business Cycles: A Theoretical, Historical and Statistical Analysis of the Capitalist Process.* 2 vols. New York: McGraw-Hill, 1939.

———. *Capitalism, Socialism, and Democracy.* New York: Harper, 1942.

———. "Das Sozialprodukt and die Rechenpfennige." *AfSuS* 44 (1917–18): 627–715.

———. *Das Wesen und der Hauptinhalt der theoretischen Nationalökonomie.* Leipzig: Duncker and Humblot, 1908.

———. *Die Krise des Steuerstaates.* Graz, Austria: Leutschner and Lubensky, 1918.

———. *Die Theorie der wirtschaftlichen Entwicklung.* Leipzig: Duncker and Humblot, 1912.

———. "Die wissenschaftliche Lebenswerk Eugen von Böhm-Bawerks." *Zeitschrift* 23 (1914): 454–528.

———. "Eine 'dynamische' Theorie des Kapitalzinses: Eine Entgegnung." *Zeitschrift* 22 (1913): 599–639.

———. *The History of Economic Analysis.* Rev. ed. Oxford: Oxford University Press, 1996.

———. *The Theory of Economic Development.* Cambridge, MA: Harvard University Press, 1934.

———. "Über die mathematische Methode der theoretischen Ökonomie." *Zeitschrift* 15 (1906): 30–49.

———. "Zur Soziologie der Imperialismen." *AfSuS* 46 (1918–19): 1–39, 275–310.

Schwartz, Julian, and David Weigel. "Who Wrote Ron Paul's Newsletters?" *Reason,* January 16, 2008. http://reason.com/archives/2008/01/16/who-wrote-ron-pauls-newsletter.

Scopus. "Advances in Austrian Economics." Accessed January 19, 2019. http://www.scopus.com/sourceid/4100151519.

———. "Quarterly Journal of Austrian Economics." Accessed January 19, 2019. https://www.scopus.com/sourceid/12000154413.

———. "Review of Austrian Economics." Accessed January 19, 2019. https://www.scopus.com/sourceid/29440.

Scott, William. "Translator's Preface." In Böhm, *Recent Literature on Interest,* v–xlii.

Seager, H. R. "Economics in Berlin and Vienna." *JPE* 1, no. 2 (1893): 236–62.

Seal, Andrew. "The Controversy over *Democracy in Chains.*" Society for U.S. Intellectual History, July 17, 2017. https://s-usih.org/2017/07/the-controversy-over-democracy-in-chains.

Segel, Harold B., ed. *The Vienna Coffeehouse Wits, 1890–1938*. West Lafayette, IN: Purdue University Press, 1993.

Shearmur, Jeremy. *Hayek and After*. London: Routledge, 1996.

Shubik, Martin, ed. *Essays in Mathematical Economics in Honor of Oskar Morgenstern*. Princeton, NJ: Princeton University Press, 1967.

Sieghart, Rudolf. *Die letzten Jahrzehnte einer Großmacht*. Berlin: Ullstein, 1932.

Sked, Alan. *The Decline and Fall of the Habsburg Empire, 1815–1918*. 2nd ed. London: Routledge, 2001.

Skidelsky, Robert. *John Maynard Keynes, 1883–1946: Economist, Philosopher, Statesman*. New York: Penguin, 2003.

Slobodian, Quinn. *Globalists: The End of Empire and the Birth of Neoliberalism*. Cambridge, MA: Harvard University Press, 2018.

———. "Neoliberalism's Populist Bastards." *Public Seminar*, February 15, 2018. http://www.publicseminar.org/2018/02/neoliberalisms-populist-bastards/.

———. "The Road to the Alt Right." Working paper, German Studies Association, 2017.

Smith, Adam. *The Wealth of Nations*. Edited by Edwin Canaan. 5th ed. London: Methuen, 1904.

Smithies, Arthur. "Professor Hayek on the Pure Theory of Capital." *AER* 31, no. 4 (1942): 767–79.

Somary, Felix. *The Raven of Zurich: The Memoirs of Felix Somary*. New York: St. Martin's, 1986.

Sombart, Werner. *Der moderne Kapitalismus*. Leipzig: Duncker and Humblot, 1902.

Spann, Othmar. *Der Wahre Staat*. Leipzig: Quelle and Meyer, 1921.

Spaulding, E. Wilder. *The Quiet Invaders*. Vienna: Österreichischer Bundesverlag, 1968.

Springer, Simon, Kean Birch, and Julie MacLeavy, eds. *Handbook of Neoliberalism*. New York: Routledge, 2016.

Stadler, Friedrich, ed. *650 Jahre Universität Wien. Aufbruch ins neue Jahrhundert*. 4 vols. Vienna: Vienna University Press, 2015.

———, ed. *Vertriebene Vernunft. Emigration und Exil österreichischer Wissenschaft 1930–1940*. 2 vols. Vienna: Jugend und Volk, 1987–88.

———. *The Vienna Circle: Studies in the Origins, Development, and Influence of Logical Empiricism*. Translated by Camilla Nielsen. Vienna: Springer, 2001.

———. *Vom Positivismus zur "wissenschaftlichen Weltauffassung": Am Beispiel der Wirkungsgeschichte von Ernst Mach in Österreich von 1895 bis 1934*. Vienna: Löcker, 1982.

Stahl, Jason. *Right Moves: The Conservative Think Tank in American Political Culture since 1945*. Chapel Hill: University of North Carolina Press, 2016.

Stedman Jones, Daniel. *Masters of the Universe: Hayek, Friedman, and the Birth of Neoliberal Politics*. Princeton, NJ: Princeton University Press, 2012.

Steele, David Ramsay. *From Marx to Mises: Post-Capitalist Society and the Challenge of Economic Calculation*. La Salle, IL: Open Court, 1992.

Steil, Benn. *The Battle of Bretton Woods: John Maynard Keynes, Harry Dexter White, and the Making of a New World Order.* Princeton, NJ: Princeton University Press, 2013.

Stenographische Protokolle über die vom 8. März bis 17. März 1892 abgehaltenen Sitzungen der nach Wien einberufene Währungs-Enquete-Commission. Vienna, 1892.

Stolper, Wolfgang. *Joseph Alois Schumpeter.* Princeton, NJ: Princeton University Press, 1994.

Straumann, Tobias. "Rule Rather than Exception: Brüning's Fear of Devaluation in Comparative Perspective." *Journal of Contemporary History* 44, no. 4 (2009): 603–17.

Streissler, Erich. "The Intellectual and Political Impact of the Austrian School of Economics." *History of European Ideas* 9, no. 2 (1988): 191–204.

———. "On the Significance of the Austrian School Today." *ZfN* 29 (1969): 237–66.

———. "To What Extent Was the Austrian School Marginalist?" *HOPE* 4 (1972): 426–41.

Strote, Noah Benezra. *Lions and Lambs: Conflict in Weimar and the Creation of Post-Nazi Germany.* New Haven, CT: Yale University Press, 2017.

Sweezy, Paul. Introduction to Böhm, *Karl Marx,* v–xxx.

Taschwer, Klaus. "Die Bärenhöhle, eine geheime antisemitische Professorenclique der Zwischenkriegszeit." *650 Plus,* March 14, 2017. http://geschichte.univie.ac.at/de/artikel/die-baerenhoehle-eine-geheime-antisemitische-professorenclique-der-zwischenkriegszeit.

———. *Hochburg des Antisemitismus: Der Niedergang der Universität Wien im 20. Jahrhundert.* Vienna: Czernin, 2015.

———. "Nachrichten von der antisemitischen Kampfzone." In Stadler, *650 Jahre,* 3:99–126.

Teles, Steven M. *The Rise of the Conservative Legal Movement: The Battle for Control of the Law.* Princeton, NJ: Princeton University Press, 2008.

"Theory and Practice in the Austrian School." *Cato Unbound,* September 2012. https://www.cato-unbound.org/issues/september-2012/theory-practice-austrian-school.

Timms, Edward. "Cultural Parameters between the Wars: A Reassessment of the Vienna Circles." In *Interwar Vienna: Culture between Tradition and Modernity,* edited by Deborah Holmes and Lisa Silverman, 21–31. Rochester, NY: Camden House, 2009.

———. *Karl Kraus, Apocalyptic Satirist: Culture and Catastrophe in Habsburg Vienna.* New Haven, CT: Yale University Press, 1986.

———. *Karl Kraus, Apocalyptic Satirist: The Post-War Crisis and the Rise of the Swastika.* New Haven, CT: Yale University Press, 2005.

Tomlinson, Chris. "Exclusive: Austrian Economics Think-Tank Backs Populist-Conservative Coalition." *Breitbart,* October 11, 2017. http://www.breitbart.com/london/2017/10/11/exclusive-austrian-economics-think-tank-backs-populist-conservative-coalition.

Tooze, Adam. *The Deluge: The Great War, America, and the Remaking of the Global Order, 1916–1931.* New York: Penguin, 2014.

————. *Statistics and the German State, 1900–1945: The Making of Modern Economic Knowledge*. Cambridge: Cambridge University Press, 2001.

Toye, John. *Dissent of Development*. 2nd ed. London: Blackwell, 1993.

TPM TV. "Ron Paul: We Are All Austrians Now." YouTube, January 3, 2012. https://www.youtube.com/watch?v=467hCNuGvNw.

Trends in International Trade. Geneva: GATT, 1958.

Tribe, Keith. *Strategies of Economic Order: German Economic Discourse 1750–1950*. Cambridge: Cambridge University Press, 1995.

Uebel, Thomas. "Otto Neurath's Idealist Inheritance." *Synthese* 103 (1995): 87–121.

————, ed. *Rediscovering the Forgotten Vienna Circle*. Dordrecht, Germany: Kluwer, 1991.

Valdés, Juan Gabriel. *Pinochet's Economists: The Chicago School of Economics in Chile*. Cambridge: Cambridge University Press, 1995.

van der Linden, Marcel. "Gerschenkron's Secret: A Research Note." *Critique* 40, no. 4 (2012): 553–62.

Van Horn, Robert. "Jacob Viner's Critique of Chicago Neoliberalism." In Van Horn, Mirowski, and Stapleford, *Building Chicago Economics*, 279–300.

Van Horn, Robert, and Philip Mirowski. "The Rise of the Chicago School of Economics and the Birth of Neoliberalism." In Mirowski and Plehwe, *Road from Mont Pèlerin*, 139–79.

Van Horn, Robert, Philip Mirowski, and Thomas Stapleford, eds. *Building Chicago Economics*. New York: Cambridge University Press, 2011.

Van Sickle, John. Review of *Die Gemeinwirtschaft* by Ludwig von Mises. *AER* 13, no. 3 (1923): 533–36.

Vaughn, Karen. *Austrian Economics in America: The Migration of a Tradition*. Cambridge: Cambridge University Press, 1994.

Verhandlungen des Vereins für Socialpolitik in Wien, 1909. Leipzig: Duncker and Humblot, 1910.

Voegelin, Erich. "Die Zeit in der Wirtschaft." *AfSuS* 53 (1925): 186–211.

von Neumann, John, and Oskar Morgenstern. *The Theory of Games and Economic Behavior*. 3rd ed. Princeton, NJ: Princeton University Press, 1953.

Wagnleitner, Reinhold. *Coca-Colonization and the Cold War: The Cultural Mission of the United States in Austria after the Second World War*. Chapel Hill: University of North Carolina Press, 1994.

Walker, Andy. "1913: When Hitler, Trotsky, Tito, Freud, and Stalin Lived in the Same Place." *BBC.com*, April 18, 2013. http://www.bbc.com/news/magazine-21859771.

Walpen, Bernhard. *Die offenen Feinde und ihre Gesellschaft*. Hamburg: VSA-Verlag, 2004.

Walras, Léon. *Éléments d'économie politique pure, ou théorie de la richesse sociale*. Paris: L. Corbaz, 1874.

Wapshott, Nicholas. *Keynes Hayek: The Clash That Defined Modern Economics*. New York: Norton, 2011.

Wasserman, Janek. "Between Debates: The Research Program of Austrian Economics in the 1920s." Paper presented at the annual meeting of the History of Economics Society, Montreal, Canada, June 21, 2014.

———. "Beyond Hayek and Mises: Austrian Economics in America at Midcentury." In *Quiet Invaders Revisited: Biographies of Twentieth-Century Immigrants to the United States*, edited by Günter Bischof, 163–81. Innsbruck, Austria: Studien-Verlag, 2017.

———. *Black Vienna: The Radical Right in the Red City, 1918–1938*. Ithaca, NY: Cornell University Press, 2014.

———. "Science Lost, Science Found in the Post-WWII Austrian Economics Movement: The Case of Emil Kauder." Paper presented at the Austrian Economics Conference, Edmonton, Canada, October 12, 2018.

———. "'Un-Austrian' Austrians? Haberler, Machlup, and Morgenstern, and the Post-Emigration Elaboration of Austrian Economics." *RHETM* 34A (2016): 93–124.

Waugh, Alexander. *The House of Wittgenstein: A Family at War*. New York: Doubleday, 2009.

Weber, Max. *Die Protestantische Ethik und der 'Geist' des Kapitalismus*. Archiv für Sozialwissenschaft und Sozialpolitik 20–21 (1904–5): 1–54; 1–110.

———. "'Objectivity' in Social Science." In *Max Weber on the Methodology of the Social Sciences*, edited by Edward Shils and Henry Finch, 49–112. Glencoe, IL: Free Press, 1949.

Weede, Erich. "Im linken Lager gelandet." *Junge Freiheit*, June 8, 2015. https://jungefreiheit.de/debatte/forum/2015/im-linken-lager-gelandet.

Weigel, David. "Libertarians Wrestle with the Alt-Right." *Washington Post*, August 24, 2017. https://www.washingtonpost.com/news/powerpost/wp/2017/08/24/libertarians-wrestle-with-the-alt-right.

Weigl, Andreas. "Beggar-Thy-Neighbour vs. Danube Basin Strategy: Habsburg Economic Networks in Interwar Europe." *Religions* 7, no. 11 (2016): 1–12.

Weinberger, Otto. "Eugen von Böhm-Bawerk." *AfSuS* 53 (1925): 491–508.

Weintraub, E. Roy. *How Economics Became a Mathematical Science*. Durham, NC: Duke University Press, 2002.

Weiss, Franz. "Die moderne Tendenz in der Lehre vom Geldwert." *Zeitschrift* 19 (1910): 502–60.

Westley, Christopher. "Ngrams and the Austrian School." *QJAE* 17, no. 3 (2014): 365–97.

Wicksell, Knut. Review of *Theorie des Geldes und der Umlaufsmittel* by Ludwig von Mises. *Zeitschrift* 23 (1914): 144–48.

Wieser, Friedrich von. "The Austrian School and the Theory of Value." *EJ* 1 (1891): 108–21.

———. *Das Gesetz der Macht*. Vienna: Springer, 1926.

———. "Das Wesen und der Hauptinhalt der theoretischen Nationalökonomie. Kritische Glossen." *Schmoller* 35 (1911): 395–417.

———. "Der Geldwert und seine geschichtlichen Veränderungen." *Zeitschrift* 13 (1904): 43–64.

———. *Der natürliche Werth*. Vienna: Holder, 1889.

———. *Die Ergebnisse und die Aussichten der Personaleinkommensteuer in Österreich*. Leipzig: Duncker and Humblot, 1901.

————. *Natural Value.* London: Macmillan, 1893.

————. *Österreichs Ende.* Berlin: Ullstein, 1919.

————. *Social Economics.* Binghamton, NY: Greenberg, 1927.

————. *Über den Ursprung und die Hauptgesetze des wirtschaftlichen Werthes.* Vienna: Holder, 1884.

Wile, Anthony. "Steve Horwitz on GMU, the Mises Controversy and the Premise of Austrian Economics in the 21st Century." *Daily Bell,* October 3, 2010. http://www.thedailybell.com/exclusive-interviews/anthony-wile-steve-horwitz-on-gmu-the-mises-controversy-and-the-promise-of-austrian-economics-in-the-21st-century/.

Winter, Robert. *Das Akademische Gymnasium in Wien.* Vienna: Böhlau, 1996.

Wirth, Maria. *A Window to the World.* Abridged ed. Vienna: European Forum Alpbach, 2015.

Wootton, Barbara. *Freedom under Planning.* Chapel Hill: University of North Carolina Press, 1945.

Yagi, Kiichiro. "Böhm-Bawerk's First Interest Theory, with the C. Menger-Böhm-Bawerk Correspondence, 1884–1885." Typescript, Hitotsubashi University, Tokyo, 1983.

Yglesias, Matthew. "What Is Austrian Economics? And Why Is Ron Paul Obsessed with It?" *Slate,* January 6, 2012. http://www.slate.com/articles/business/moneybox/2012/01/what_is_austrian_economics_and_why_is_ron_paul_keep_obsessed_with_it_.html.

Zanotti, Gabriel, and Nicolas Cachanosky. "Implications of Machlup's Interpretation of Mises's Epistemology." *JHET* 37, no. 1 (2015): 111–38.

Zweig, Stefan. *The World of Yesterday.* London: Cassell, 1943.

INDEX

Alpbach Forum, 216–20
Alt-Right, 4, 8, 16, 273, 278, 281
American Enterprise Institute (AEI), 227, 230, 235, 253–54, 264
Atlas Foundation, 261, 265
Auspitz, Rudolf, 48–50, 59, 242, 244
Austria: contemporary, 268, 287–88; fin-de-siècle, 19–22, 53–54, 56, 59–60, 71–72, 81; interwar, 102–4, 107–12, 128, 130–33, 156–57; Second Republic, 265–66; World War One, 93–94, 96–97, 98–100; after World War Two, 216–20
Austrian Economics: 2, 9, 15, 199; definitions, 241–45; first conference, 237; Koch support, 258; George Mason, 275–83; journals, 275–77; LvMI, 275, 279–83; New York University, 248–49; and Ron Paul, 2–3, 285; references to, 274–75; "revival," 212, 235–40
Austrian School: assimilation, 163–64; and Austria, 265–66; and Böhm, 46, 58, 85–87; characteristics, 9–10, 40, 47–48, 90–91, 125–26, 128–29, 163–64, 187, 193–94, 197–199, 230–31, 289–92; and Chicago School, 143–46;

contemporary discussions, 2–3, 283–86; definitions, 6–9, 11–15, 240–43, 243–45; emergence, 41–45; emigration, 156–61, 164–70; and Hayek, 163, 259; institutions, 51–53, 71–73, 116–18, 130, 197–199, 204; internal feuds, 77–80, 152–56, 192–93, 278–83; and Kauder, 240–43; legacies, 233–36, 266–69, 272–73, 276–78, 286–92; and Machlup, 243–45; and Marxism, 55–57, 64–66, 87–90; and Mayer, 116–19; and Carl Menger, 17–18, 45; *Methodenstreit*, 31, 36–37; and Mises, 85, 170; and Morgenstern, 187, 251–52; and neoliberalism, 149; policy work, 58–60, 130–32, 135–39; references to, 274–75; "revival," 236–40; and Schumpeter, 74–80; and socialism, 55–57, 64–66, 87–90, 102; *Werturteilsstreit*, 66–70; and Wieser, 115–16; World War One, 94–95, 112; World War Two, 220–22
Austro-Marxism, 12, 64–66, 89–91, 104, 106

Bauer, Otto, 57, 64, 66, 74, 81, 86–91, 99–100, 102–5

Beck, Glenn, 1–2, 8, 285
Bellagio Group, 227–31
Boettke, Peter, 275, 277, 279, 281, 283, 285
Böhm-Bawerk, Eugen von: Austrian School, 6, 8, 11–12, 39–42, 44–46, 51, 58, 85–87, 291; and Austro-Marxism, 65–66; Böhm tradition, 80, 120–21, 152, 191, 242–44, 272, 277–78; *Capital and Interest*, 40–43; on capital theory, 38, 40–41, 46–47, 145; early life, 37–38; on entrepreneurs, 47; as government official, 57–60, 71; and Hilferding, 65–66, 86–88; institution building of, 51–52, 70–71; *Karl Marx*, 43, 62–66; Marxism, 42–43, 47, 62–65; and Carl Menger, 37–39, 41; as policy adviser, 52–53, 57–60; *Positive Theory*, 43, 46; on roundabout methods of production, 46–47, 83, 145; and Schumpeter, 74, 76–80; seminar, 53, 56, 66, 81, 85–90; on time preference, 46–47; and Wieser, 37–38, 47–48
Böhm seminar, 53, 56, 66, 81, 85–90
Buchanan, James, 208, 237, 239, 260, 264, 266, 277–78
Bukharin, Nikolai, 12, 55–57, 86, 90, 102–3
Bush, George H.W., 272–73
business cycle theory: Haberler on, 137–38; Hayek on 117, 135; Mises on 82–84; Morgenstern on, 155; Schumpeter on, 75–79, 173–75
Business Cycles (Schumpeter), 173–75

Caldwell, Bruce, 277, 285
Capital and Interest (Böhm), 40–43
Capitalism, Socialism, and Democracy (Schumpeter), 176–79, 271–72
Carl Menger-Institut, 265–66
Cato Institute, 4, 15, 161, 257–58, 264, 275, 280

Chicago School, 143–146, 198, 200, 204–5, 262, 286
coffeehouse, 5, 10, 12, 18, 20–21, 49, 56–57, 64, 98
Colloque Walter Lippmann, 146–49. *See also* neoliberalism
conservatism: Austrian, 42, 51, 58, 64, 71, 88, 94–95, 103, 108–114, 121, 123, 131, 222, 265, 281; Catholic, 12–13, 19, 126, 265; European, 106, 139, 203, 287–88; free market, 8, 15, 88, 128–29, 139, 146, 197–98, 212, 227, 258, 280; Hayek on, 270, 278; Horwitz on, 282; postwar, 4–5, 8, 10, 14–15, 164, 187, 197–99, 212, 254–55, 258, 260–61, 264; UK, 260–61; US, 135, 146, 212, 227, 254–55, 258, 264, 284–85
Constitution of Liberty (Hayek), 161, 206–10, 239, 260–61, 263
Crane, Jasper, 186–7, 197, 202–3
creative destruction, 76–77, 177–78

"Economics and Knowledge" (Hayek), 151–52, 157
emigration, 156–61, 164–170

fascism, 134, 156–57
Fertig, Lawrence, 211, 233–34
Fisher, Anthony, 259–61
Foundation for Economic Education (FEE), 185, 197, 212, 215, 256, 260
Friedrich Hayek Gesellschaft, 288–89
Friedrich Hayek Institut, 287, 289
Friedman, Milton, 196, 201, 204–6, 210, 230, 239, 240, 247–8, 260, 262, 264, 271, 276
Furth, Herbert von, 112–15, 165–66, 194, 224, 230, 244–46, 267

Geist-Kreis, 112–16, 121, 137
General Agreement on Tariffs and Trade (GATT), 223–27